THE ONE YEAR®
CHOOSE YOUR OWN ENDING
DEVOTIONS

THE ONE YEAR®

CHOOSE YOUR OWN ENDING

DEVOTIONS

PIONEER CLUBS

TYNDALE HOUSE PUBLISHERS, INC.
CAROL STREAM, ILLINOIS

Visit Tyndale's exciting Web site for kids at www.tyndale.com/kids.

Pioneer Clubs provides church-sponsored, midweek club programs for today's kids, preschool through middle school. For more information, see www.pioneerclubs.org.

TYNDALE and Tyndale's quill logo are registered trademarks of Tyndale House Publishers, Inc.

The One Year is a registered trademark of Tyndale House Publishers, Inc.

The One Year Choose Your Own Ending Devotions

Designed by Mark Anthony Lane II

Stories written by Rebecca M. Allen-Powell, Barbara Collier, Christine Erickson, Louise Ferrebee, Susan Gilliland, Marian Liautaud, Jolene Philo, Hollis Pippin, and Susan N. C. Price.

Unless otherwise indicated, all Scripture quotations are taken from the Holy Bible, New Living Translation, copyright © 1996, 2004, 2007 by Tyndale House Foundation. Used by permission of Tyndale House Publishers, Inc., Carol Stream, Illinois 60188. All rights reserved.

For manufacturing information regarding this product, please call 1-800-323-9400.

ISBN 978-1-4143-3323-6

Printed in the United States of America

16   15   14   13   12   11   10
7   6   5   4   3   2   1

INTRODUCTION

Pioneer Clubs is delighted to partner with Tyndale House Publishers in creating *The One Year Choose Your Own Ending Devotions*. Pioneer Clubs is a Bible-based and Christ-centered church-sponsored midweek ministry that has been helping children learn about God and his Word since 1939. Our slogan, "Christ in every aspect of life," underscores Pioneer Clubs' commitment to teaching children how to study the Bible and apply scriptural principles to everyday life.

Each month of devotions covers a specific topic. These topics match the Pioneer Clubs midweek ministry curriculum and include "Getting Along with Family," "Serving Others," "God's Word," "Creation," "Knowing Jesus," and others. If your child is a Pioneer Clubs member, the devotions will help reinforce the Bible lessons taught at club meetings. However, this book can be used by your children whether or not they are involved in Pioneer Clubs. Pioneer Clubs is privileged to help parents spiritually nurture their children through weekly club meetings, Camp Cherith summer ministry, and this devotional book.

The One Year Choose Your Own Ending Devotions is intentionally designed to get kids into God's Word. For this reason, a Bible will be needed along with this book. Memory verses are quoted from the New Living Translation, which is an easy translation for kids to understand. Kids can read the devotions on their own during a daily quiet time, or families may want to read them together. They make for great family discussions! Parents and kids will enjoy coming up with different endings to each day's story, using the truths found in the Scripture reading. Each daily reading includes:

- A story
- A Scripture reading
- Questions to think about
- An opportunity for children to create an ending to the story
- An optional activity that helps children apply scriptural truths
- A prayer suggestion
- A memory verse
- A suggested story ending
- A takeaway truth for kids to remember

Pioneer Clubs and Tyndale House Publishers hope and pray that God will bless kids and their families as they come to know him better through using *The One Year Choose Your Own Ending Devotions*.

JANUARY 1
The Speech

"Class," said Mrs. Martinez, "it's time to hear the oral reports you've prepared. Be sure to speak slowly and clearly so everyone can hear you. Jason, you can go first."

Sam's heart skipped a beat. His hands became sweaty. His mouth went dry, and he felt his cheeks get hot. The thing Sam dreaded most in life was getting up in front of the class and speaking. "What if I forget what I'm going to say? I'll be so embarrassed!" Sam fretted. Jason finished his report and Jess stood up. Suddenly, Sam had an idea. *Maybe if I told Mrs. Martinez my stomach hurt, she would let me go to the nurse's office.* Sam raised his hand to get Mrs. Martinez's attention.

READ
Psalm 62:5-6. When we are nervous or fearful, God is our source of hope and strength.

THINK

- Are you facing a situation that makes you anxious? What is it?
- What do you know about God's character—and his promises—that makes you feel calm and confident in him?
- Finish the story, showing how Sam could find help from these verses. Then read the possible ending at the back of the book.

DO
- Name some specific Bible stories where God met someone's need.
- Ask family members or club leaders to share ways God has met their needs in past situations.

PRAY
Thank God for being a constant and true source of strength for you. Ask God to help you trust him in every situation.

MEMORIZE
He alone is my rock and my salvation, my fortress where I will not be shaken. Psalm 62:6

WHAT'S THE POINT?
Sam needed help overcoming his nervousness about speaking in front of his classmates. If he prays about that need, God will answer. He can be trusted to meet your needs too. All you have to do is ask. *BA*

JANUARY 2
Missing Gym Class

Haley's gym class started a two-week soccer session. Because she had asthma, Haley would have to go to the library to read. Even though she had an inhaler, running during soccer made her symptoms worse.

"Mom, why did I have to get asthma?" Haley complained after the first day of soccer. "Everyone else is out there having fun, and I'm stuck sitting in the library."

Haley's mom tried to be encouraging, but Haley was still unhappy. Before she stomped off to her room, Haley said, "I've prayed and prayed that God would take the asthma away, but he hasn't. I just want to be normal and play soccer like everyone else!"

READ
2 Corinthians 12:9-10. The apostle Paul is talking about what God said to him. Paul had an ongoing struggle, but that didn't stop God from working through Paul's weakness.

THINK
- When have you felt sorry for yourself because of a weakness or limitation?
- Why do you think God's power works through us best when we are weak?
- Finish the story, showing how these verses could make a difference for Haley. Then read the possible ending at the back of the book.

DO
- With your family, think of how God can work through your weakness or limitation so that you can do good things for him.

PRAY
Ask God to use his power to work through your weakness or limitation. Ask him to do good things through you.

MEMORIZE
"My grace is all you need. My power works best in weakness." So now I am glad to boast about my weaknesses, so that the power of Christ can work through me.
2 Corinthians 12:9

WHAT'S THE POINT?
God used Haley's limitation in soccer as an opportunity for Haley to talk about Jesus with her classmate. God works through our limitations and weaknesses. That way everyone can know it's really God who's at work, not us. *CE*

JANUARY 3
Junk Everywhere

Brooke was in her room getting ready to go to a friend's house. Her little sister, Lindy, was down the hall trying to clean up her room.

"Brooooke," Lindy called. "Will you help me?"

"If I help you, I'll be late," Brooke called back.

"There's too much junk everywhere for me to do it all by myself. Pleeeeeease?"

Brooke shrugged and thought, *Lindy made the mess; she should clean it up.* "No, it's your own fault," she called back.

There was silence for a while. Brooke fixed her hair. A crashing sound came from Lindy's room. Brooke found Lindy standing on a chair with books all over the floor. While trying to put things away on the shelf, Lindy had nearly pulled over the bookcase. Now her room was an even bigger mess. Brooke looked at her watch. It was time for her to leave.

READ
Colossians 1:10. Producing "good fruit" has to do with good attitudes, good things we do for others, and good decisions. These are ways we can please Jesus.

THINK

- How could getting to know Jesus better help us produce good fruit?
- When have you shown kindness this week? When haven't you?
- Finish the story, showing how Brooke could get important help from this verse. Then read the possible ending at the back of the book.

DO
- Choose one of the ways you said you haven't shown kindness this week. Draw a picture or sketch of a way you could change your behavior.
- Discuss with your family ways you could show kindness to a neighbor, friend, or family member. Get ready, and go do it!

PRAY
Pray that God will help you produce "good fruit" and please him this week.

MEMORIZE
The way you live will always honor and please the Lord, and your lives will produce every kind of good fruit. All the while, you will grow as you learn to know God better and better. Colossians 1:10

WHAT'S THE POINT?
Brooke could have made sure Lindy was safe and then left. But God is pleased when we are kind to others and do things for them. The more we get to know God and how he treats us, the more we know how he wants us to treat others. *CE*

JANUARY 4
Will Work for Food

On the way to soccer practice, Emma and her mom noticed a man they had never seen before. He was standing on the corner. "Mom, look!" Emma exclaimed. "His sign says, 'Will work for food.'"

"That means he will take a job where the only pay is food, because he's hungry," Mom said.

Emma looked at his old, torn clothes. Emma was filled with sadness for the man. The next day when they passed, he was on the corner again. This time Emma noticed a woman and a young girl huddled under a blanket on the other side of the road. "They might be his wife and daughter," Emma's mom explained.

Emma thought about the family for the rest of the day. At dinner she wondered if they had anything to eat. As she got in bed, she wondered where the family was sleeping. She just had to figure out a way to help them.

READ
Ephesians 5:1-2. This passage tells us to put our love for others into action. We do this by copying how Jesus loved others when he lived on earth.

THINK
- What are some ways Jesus cared for people when he lived on earth?
- What are ways you could copy the things Jesus did? (You can't heal anyone, but you could bring cookies to someone who is sick, for instance.)
- Make up an ending for the story, showing how Emma could obey God's Word. Then read the possible ending at the back of the book.

DO
- Write down the name of someone with needs you could help this week.
- Make a plan for how to help. Tell your mom or dad your plan. Ask if you should have adult help to carry it out.

PRAY
Ask God to help you carry out your plan.

MEMORIZE
Live a life filled with love, following the example of Christ. He loved us and offered himself as a sacrifice for us, a pleasing aroma to God. Ephesians 5:2

WHAT'S THE POINT?
Emma didn't just hope things got better for this needy family. She wanted to show love by helping. Her idea was a picture of Jesus' love in action. *CE*

JANUARY 5
Driving in the Winning Run

Cole high-fived his teammates. His Little League baseball team had won the championship game by one run in extra innings. And he had driven in the winning run!

The team accepted the trophy and then posed for pictures. Cole's smile was a mile wide. "Way to go, Cole!" said other parents, and he grinned at the praise.

Afterward the team members and their families went out for pizza to celebrate their victory. When the waitress came to take their order, Cole's friends proudly told her about their win. "You should have seen Cole," they said. "He hit the ball right over the shortstop's head."

"Weren't you tired, playing extra innings?" asked the waitress.

"Yeah," said Cole. "But somehow I got the strength to keep hitting."

"We're good!" the boys said, high-fiving again.

READ
Exodus 15:2. The Israelites sang this as a song after God freed them from the Egyptians.

THINK
- Who did the Israelites give credit to for the victory?
- If we work hard, why should we praise God when we have a victory in school or sports or some other area of our lives?
- Finish the story, showing how Cole might give glory to God. Then read the possible ending at the back of the book.

DO
- Sketch a picture showing a situation in which you might be tempted to take all the glory instead of giving it to God.
- Draw a cross over your picture to stand for God. Praise him now for giving you your strength and abilities.

PRAY
Thank God for a victory he has given you.

MEMORIZE
The LORD is my strength and my song; he has given me victory. This is my God, and I will praise him—my father's God, and I will exalt him! Exodus 15:2

WHAT'S THE POINT?
Cole remembered that God is our strength. When good things happen, it's important to thank God. *CE*

JANUARY 6
I Gotta Have It

Audrey loved hanging out with Ella. Ella always wore the newest styles, and she even wore makeup. Audrey wanted to look and dress just like her. "I love the earrings you're wearing, Ella! Are those new?" Audrey asked.

"Yes, I just got them yesterday," Ella replied.

Audrey had to have a pair too. After school Audrey found her mom on the computer. "Mom, you should have seen the new earrings Ella had on today! Can we go shopping Saturday?"

Audrey's mom looked thoughtful. "I think you have enough earrings, Audrey," she said.

"But, Mom, I need a pair like Ella's!" Audrey insisted. When she saw that her mom wouldn't budge, Audrey stormed to her room.

READ
Hebrews 13:5. It can be hard work to learn to be satisfied with what we have. Whether we have a little or a lot, God himself satisfies us most of all.

THINK
- How could knowing God is always with you help you learn to be content with what you have?
- Does always wanting new things help you depend on God more or less?
- Imagine an ending for this story, showing how Audrey could apply the verse. Then read the possible ending at the back of the book.

DO
- Make a list of the new things you really want. Next to each one, write a + if you could learn to be content without it. Put a − if not.
- Make a list of things God has already blessed you with. Thank him for them.

PRAY
Thank God for always being with you. Ask him to help you be satisfied with him.

MEMORIZE
Don't love money; be satisfied with what you have. For God has said, "I will never fail you. I will never abandon you." Hebrews 13:5

WHAT'S THE POINT?
Audrey found herself constantly wanting something. It's okay to get new things sometimes. But God wants us to feel content with him instead of with "things." *CE*

JANUARY 7
Piano or Violin?

Lauren had been taking both piano and violin lessons for three years. She loved to play both instruments and didn't mind practicing. But this year in school, Lauren had more homework. Last semester she struggled to find enough time to get her homework finished and practice two instruments every night. It didn't look like the homework load would lighten up this semester, either.

Yesterday Lauren's dad said, "Lauren, I think it's time for you to choose which instrument you want to continue playing and which instrument to stop." Lauren looked at him in surprise. How could she ever choose? She loved playing both instruments!

READ
James 1:5-6. God willingly gives us wisdom when we ask him and expect him to answer. Wisdom is understanding and the ability to make good decisions.

THINK

- Why do you think God is glad to give us wisdom?
- When would wisdom help you?
- Finish the story, showing how Lauren might apply truth from God's Word. Then read the possible ending at the back of the book.

DO
- Write the names of a few people you could ask for help when you need to make a decision. God often uses other people to help us think through things.
- Write a big question mark on a piece of paper to stand for a decision you're having trouble making. Ask God for wisdom to make the decision. Put the question mark in your Bible to remind you to trust God to answer.

PRAY
Keep praying and trusting God until he helps you know what to do about your "question mark" decision.

MEMORIZE
If you need wisdom, ask our generous God, and he will give it to you. He will not rebuke you for asking. James 1:5

WHAT'S THE POINT?
Lauren knew the best source for understanding is God. When you don't know what to do, God will gladly help you. Just ask and have faith that he will answer. *CE*

JANUARY 8
Missing Baseball Camp

"Carter, I'm sorry to tell you this, but we can't afford to send you to baseball camp this summer," Carter's dad explained.

"What? I've gotta go! My whole team is going. I'll be the only one who isn't going!" Carter cried.

His dad continued, "And if I lose my job, you won't play next season, either."

Carter was crushed. Baseball meant everything to him. Carter called his friend Brad and told him about his problem.

"Maybe you could raise the money," Brad suggested.

"No, I need the money now," Carter said.

"You could borrow the money."

"I don't know how I would pay it back."

"If you want to play, I guess you'll have to steal the money," Brad reasoned.

READ
Jeremiah 29:11. We can live in hope. God knows our wants and our needs. He has good plans for us. Everything may not always turn out just the way we want, but we can trust God to lead us.

THINK
- When something bad happens, does that mean God's plans can't be trusted? Why do you feel this way?
- How does it feel to know that God has good plans for your future?
- Make up an ending for the story, showing how the verse could make a difference for Carter. Then read the possible ending at the back of the book.

DO
- When have you struggled to trust that God has good plans for you? Write down someone you could talk to about it.
- What is something you already know from God's Word that is part of God's plan for your future?

PRAY
Ask God to help you trust him and the plans he has for you and your future.

MEMORIZE
"I know the plans I have for you," says the LORD. "They are plans for good and not for disaster, to give you a future and a hope." Jeremiah 29:11

WHAT'S THE POINT?
Even though hard times come, we can trust God to lead us and give us hope. He has good plans for us. *CE*

JANUARY 9
The New House

Grace and her family piled into the car and followed the moving truck to their new house. Grace bounced up and down with excitement. All she had ever known was a small apartment. Now they would have a house with lots of rooms.

At the new house, she and her brother, Trey, jumped out and ran for the door. Trey yelled, "I get first pick of the bedrooms!"

"No, I do!" yelled Grace. They ran into the house and pounded up the stairs. "This one's mine!" Grace said.

"Good, I like this one better," said Trey. They galloped back downstairs to check out the rest of the house. Grace ran from room to room. "Mom, there are so many rooms!" she exclaimed. "Will we ever use all of them?"

"There certainly are more than in our apartment." Dad laughed.

"It's heaven!" Grace said, flopping down on the carpet.

"It's heavenly," said Mom, "but not quite heaven."

Grace ran her fingers through the soft carpet. "What's heaven like?"

READ

John 14:2-3. Jesus is talking in these verses. If we have invited Jesus into our lives, God will give us life forever and a place in heaven.

THINK

- What do you think it will be like to be with Jesus always?
- If you don't know for sure that you're going to heaven, talk with a Christian adult.
- Finish the story, showing how the verses could affect Grace. Then read the possible ending at the back of the book.

DO

- Sketch a T-shirt design about the home in heaven that Jesus is preparing for you.
- Tell Jesus the first thing you want to do when you see him face-to-face.

PRAY

Thank Jesus for wanting you to be with him forever.

MEMORIZE

There is more than enough room in my Father's home. If this were not so, would I have told you that I am going to prepare a place for you? John 14:2

WHAT'S THE POINT?

As believers, we don't have to worry about our future here on earth or in heaven. God is taking care of it. *CE*

JANUARY 10
The Know-It-All

Jacob thought he knew a lot about the Bible. After all, he had gone to church all his life, attended a Christian school, and memorized fifty verses to win this year's memory verse contest at church. But after memorizing all those verses, he stopped reading his Bible.

I know so many verses—I don't know why I need to keep reading it, he thought.

Gradually Jacob's attitude toward church changed too. Last Sunday morning he argued about going to church. "Mom, do I have to go to Sunday school? I've heard those Bible stories a million times! I know all that stuff!"

READ
Luke 2:41-52. Twelve-year-old Jesus was eager to be in church (the Jewish Temple). Even Jesus had to grow in wisdom—good sense and the ability to make good decisions.

THINK
- Jesus said he had to be in his Father's house. Who is Jesus' Father?
- Why do you think Jesus was so eager to be in church?
- Finish the story, showing how the verses could influence Jacob's feelings about church and God's Word. Then read the possible ending at the back of the book.

DO
- On a piece of paper, list the things you are doing to learn more about God: going to church, going to Sunday school, reading your Bible, listening when others teach you about the Bible, asking questions about God. Put a square around something you want to do more of.
- The next time you hear a familiar Bible story, plan to look for something new in it that you've never thought about before. Discuss it with a family member.

PRAY
Ask God to help you keep learning new things from the Bible.

MEMORIZE
Jesus grew in wisdom and in stature and in favor with God and all the people. Luke 2:52

WHAT'S THE POINT?
Jacob was surprised to find that Jesus grew in wisdom as he changed from a boy to a man. No matter what our age or Bible knowledge, God can always teach us something new. *CE*

JANUARY 11
Stolen!

Connor and his friend Travis raced their bikes up to the apartment building. "I won!" Connor yelled.

"That's because you have a brand-new bike," Travis said. The boys leaned their bikes against the stair railing, said good-bye, and went inside.

The next morning, Connor's new new bike was gone. "Did you remember to lock it to the bike rack like we told you?" Mom asked.

Connor felt miserable. "No," he mumbled. That's when Mom and Dad got mad. After they finished being mad, they called the police. But the police never found the bike.

"If you want another bike, you'll have to earn the money yourself doing chores," Mom and Dad said.

Connor had said, "I'm sorry," about a zillion times, but now he said it again.

"We know you are, and we forgive you," said Mom and Dad. "God promises to forgive you too."

I'm not sure God would forgive anything this big, Connor thought unhappily.

READ
Numbers 23:19. This verse says that God *does* keep his promises.

THINK
- Why does God never lie or change his mind or break a promise?
- When are you glad of God's promise to forgive us?
- Finish the story, showing how the verse could give Connor confidence that he really is forgiven. Then read the possible ending at the back of the book.

DO
- Pray about something you've done that you need God's forgiveness for. Write it down and draw a big check mark over it to stand for God forgiving you. He promises!
- Talk with a Christian adult if you have doubts about being forgiven.

PRAY
Thank God that he keeps his promises and never lies.

MEMORIZE
God is not a man, so he does not lie. He is not human, so he does not change his mind. Has he ever spoken and failed to act? Has he ever promised and not carried it through?
Numbers 23:19

WHAT'S THE POINT?
The Bible is made up of God's words written down for us. The Bible is true because God doesn't lie. *BA*

JANUARY 12
Marco Polo Again

Noah and Kelly were on vacation with their family. Noah made a flying leap into the pool and landed on an inflatable dolphin. Kelly, his sister, laughed and pushed him off.

Just then Bonnie and her family arrived at the pool. She ran over and called out, "Hey, watch me jump!"

Noah grumbled quietly to Kelly, "Oh great, she's back."

"Why won't she leave us alone?" Kelly whispered.

"It's because we let her join our game yesterday. Now she always wants to play with us."

Kelly suggested, "Let's just ignore her. Maybe she'll leave us alone." They swam to the other side, but Bonnie followed them. "Let's play Marco Polo again!" she called. Noah and Kelly hurried out of the pool and found their towels. "Let's play Marco Polo again," Bonnie repeated.

Noah looked around to make sure none of the parents could hear. "We're tired," he lied. Bonnie's smile disappeared.

READ
Proverbs 5:21. God sees and hears us even when others don't.

THINK
- How can God know about everything we do?
- What do you think it means that God examines our paths?
- Finish the story, showing how Noah and Kelly might pay attention to the truth in this verse. Then read the possible ending for this story at the back of the book.

DO
- Write a way you will practice acting differently, knowing God sees everything you do.
- With your family, find more Bible verses that say God is all-knowing and cares about everything you do and say.

PRAY
Ask God to help you examine things you say and do so you can live in ways that please him.

MEMORIZE
The LORD sees clearly what a man does, examining every path he takes. Proverbs 5:21

WHAT'S THE POINT?
God knew about Noah's lie even though no one else did. God sees everything we do, and he wants us to choose what's right. *CE*

JANUARY 13
The Forgotten Science Project

Manuel walked into his classroom in the morning and saw Luis carrying his science project. Manuel's heart started to pound. He'd forgotten his project at home—and they were due today! Mrs. Jimenez had said they would get marked down one grade for each day they were late. *Maybe if I'm really nice all day, she'll change her mind.* Manuel was careful not to talk out of turn. He finished his classwork early so he could collect the others' papers for her. He straightened up the bookshelves while the others were still working.

"What a good helper you are," exclaimed Mrs. Jimenez.

I think God must be pleased too, Manuel thought. Then he remembered why he was really helping and wondered when he should ask about turning in his project late.

READ
Psalm 26:2-3. What's in our hearts is what we're really thinking and feeling. Our motives are the reasons we do things. The psalm writer is confident that he has done things for the right reasons.

THINK

- How do you think God feels when we're helpful or kind for the wrong reasons?
- Think of a time you were helpful or kind for the wrong reasons. Why did you do it?
- Make up an ending for the story, showing how the verses could affect Manuel's behavior. Then read the possible ending at the back of the book.

DO
With your family, role-play a way Manuel could remember God's love and change his motives for helping.

PRAY
Thank God for his love that helps us have right motives.

MEMORIZE
Put me on trial, Lord, and cross-examine me. Test my motives and my heart. Psalm 26:2

WHAT'S THE POINT?
Mrs. Jimenez helped Manuel see that his motives were wrong. Remembering God's love can help us do helpful things for the right reasons. *CE*

JANUARY 14
Is This Worship?

Adam and his family just moved to a new town. Adam's new friend Tyler invited them to visit his church on Sunday. "Every service is different," Tyler explained. "Sometimes there's a group of people singing with a band, and other times there might just be a couple of people singing with a piano." Adam was used to a church that always had the same style of service with a choir, hymns, and an organ. But his parents decided to go.

On Sunday they met up with Tyler's family and found seats. Adam looked at the band instruments on the platform. When the music started and people began clapping and singing praise songs, Adam was surprised. The music was loud!

Between songs, Adam whispered in his dad's ear, "This is different from our old church. Are we still worshiping God?"

READ
Psalm 47:1-6. This passage encourages us to worship God with joyful praise.

THINK
- How do you like to worship God?
- How do you think God likes to be worshiped?
- Finish the story, showing how Adam could answer his questions about worship. Then read the possible ending at the back of the book.

DO
- Write two reasons to praise God joyfully in whatever way your church chooses.
- Sing a song to God that praises him.

PRAY
Ask God to help you focus on him during times of worship in your church.

MEMORIZE
Come, everyone! Clap your hands! Shout to God with joyful praise! Psalm 47:1

WHAT'S THE POINT?
Different churches have different worship styles. What's important is that the music, of whatever style, focuses on *who* we worship. God is an awesome God who deserves all glory and praise. *CE*

JANUARY 15
Star Namer

Sophia blinked as the lights came back on in the classroom. Her teacher had just shown a video about stars and space. The teacher started explaining that nobody knows how many stars there are. Scientists guess that we can see about sextillion stars with the latest equipment. That's ten with twenty-one zeros after it! If the stars were divided up among all the people on earth, each person could have more than one trillion stars of his very own!

"We think there are billions more stars that we can't see yet," said her teacher.

Walking out the door to recess, Paige, Sophia's friend, exclaimed to her, "Didn't you think that was a cool video? Can you believe no one knows how many stars there are?"

Sophia knew Someone who did. Should she say so?

"What's wrong?" Paige asked as Sophia stopped and thought.

READ
Psalm 147:4-5. Our great and powerful God knows how many stars there are because he made them.

THINK
- Since God cares enough to name every one of sextillions of stars, how much do you think he cares about you out of the billions of people on earth?
- How does it make you feel to realize that God knows and understands everything about you?
- Finish the story, showing how the verses could make a difference to Paige and Sophia. Then read the possible ending at the back of the book.

DO
- Go outside and try to count the stars (or look in a book about stars). Remember, God knows each of them by name!
- Sit for a while and take in how very much God loves you—much more than all the stars combined.

PRAY
Ask God to help you remember his great power and his love for you.

MEMORIZE
He counts the stars and calls them all by name. Psalm 147:4

WHAT'S THE POINT?
God is so great and amazing! There are billions of stars, and he calls each star by name. There are billions of people, and God knows about each one—even you! *CE*

JANUARY 16
Stranded on a Country Road

First Taylor heard a clunk, and then she felt the car jolt. Her mom gave her a worried look. "What was that?" asked Taylor.

Before her mom could answer, the car jolted again. Taylor's mom guided it to the side of the country road. Then the engine died. Mom tried to start it again, but nothing happened. Just then Alex, Taylor's baby brother, woke up and began to cry.

Mom pulled her cell phone from her purse. "Oh no, the battery's dead!"

She and Taylor stared at each other. It was evening, and they were stranded on a country road with no people or buildings around. Taylor looked up and down the road for more cars and saw nothing. They had a hungry baby and no way to get help. "Now what are we going to do?" Mom exclaimed.

READ
Psalm 9:9-10. This passage reminds us that we can turn to God in times of trouble. He is a safe shelter. He is always with us.

THINK
- How could God be like a shelter (or refuge) for us?
- Why does God deserve our trust?
- Finish the story, showing how these verses might help Taylor know what to do. Then read the possible ending at the back of the book.

DO
- Remember a time when you needed help. Write down who you asked for help. (Was God one of them?)
- Pray with your family about a family situation that needs God's help.

PRAY
Thank God that he is with you at all times and ready to help when you need it.

MEMORIZE
The LORD is a shelter for the oppressed, a refuge in times of trouble. Psalm 9:9

WHAT'S THE POINT?
Taylor remembered that God is the one to go to when trouble strikes. He will never leave anyone who searches for him. *CE*

JANUARY 17
It's Not Fair!

Cooper opened his eyes and stretched. Today was his big trip to the water park! He'd been praying all week for sunny weather. He jumped out of bed, opened his curtains—and saw storm clouds in the sky. As he stared in disbelief, the rain started pounding on his window.

Feeling as stormy as the dark sky, Cooper stomped down the hall to the family room. "Mom, it's pouring out!"

"I know, hon," said Mrs. Rubenic. "It's supposed to storm all day. We'll have to wait for another day to go to the water park."

Lightning flashed outside. "It's not fair!" Cooper said. "I've been praying all week. You *told* me to pray for good weather. *God's* not fair! He's supposed to listen to our prayers!"

READ
Deuteronomy 32:4. "Just" means reasonable and right.

THINK
- Count the words that describe God in the verse. Say them out loud.
- Think of one more way to say that God is fair.
- Make up an ending for the story, showing how the verse could make a difference for Cooper. Then read the possible ending at the back of the book.

DO
- In a bag, collect a prayer request from everyone in your family. Take turns pulling one out and praying for it.
- Write "God is fair" on the bag. Decorate it. Keep praying for the requests and trusting God's decisions.

PRAY
Thank God for being right and good and fair.

MEMORIZE
He is the Rock; his deeds are perfect. Everything he does is just and fair. Deuteronomy 32:4

WHAT'S THE POINT?
Cooper's dad knew that God is always fair, even when we wish he had answered our prayers a different way. *BA*

JANUARY 18
Facing Divorce

Erika shut the door to her room and lay facedown on her bed. Hot tears came to her eyes as she realized her parents were really getting a divorce. "How could they do this to me?" Erika yelled into her pillow. Questions swirled through her mind. *Why? Why? What will happen now?* As Erika thought about the uncertainty of her future, her worries quickly changed to fear. *Will I have to move? Who will I live with?* Erika felt alone. "I just want to talk to someone," she sighed.

READ
Isaiah 41:10. When times get tough, we can count on God. He will never leave us alone or helpless.

THINK
- How strong is God? How able is he to help you?
- How do you feel when God is giving you strength, helping you, and holding you up?
- Finish the story, showing how the verse might comfort or encourage Erika. Then read the possible ending at the back of the book.

DO
- Discuss with your family how you can be sure of God's help in times of trouble.
- Start a journal, writing how God gives help and peace in hard situations you face.

PRAY
Think of a hard situation you are facing. Ask God to help. Ask him to give you strength and peace.

MEMORIZE
Don't be afraid, for I am with you. Don't be discouraged, for I am your God. I will strengthen you and help you. I will hold you up with my victorious right hand. Isaiah 41:10

WHAT'S THE POINT?
When Erika read her journal, God reminded her that he had provided peace and help for her grandmother in a time of need. We, like Erika, can trust our strong, loving God to help us through difficult situations. *CE*

JANUARY 19
Adopted Twice

"Do you like being adopted?" Peter asked Christopher.

Christopher grinned. "Yeah. I used to feel like no one cared for me. But now I don't. I like having a family."

"You know," Peter said, "you could be adopted twice."

Christopher looked surprised. "What?"

Peter explained, "If you ask Jesus to come into your life, you will be adopted by God and become one of his children, too."

Christopher shrugged. "I think it's enough just to go to church," he replied.

READ

Galatians 4:4-7. Jesus came to earth as a human person, but he never sinned. Even though he didn't deserve to die, he took our punishment when he died and came back to life. So now he can forgive us. When you accept Jesus' payment and forgiveness of your sins, God makes you part of his forever family.

THINK

- Do you think going to church or reading the Bible will make you one of God's children? Why or why not?
- Why do you think God wants you to be his child?
- Finish the story, showing how these verses could help Christopher get interested in another kind of adoption. Then read the possible ending at the back of the book.

DO

- Write "Done!" if you have already asked Jesus to make you God's child. Write "?" if you have questions about doing this. Write down the name of someone you will talk to about your questions. Write "Yes!" if you would like to accept Jesus now. Pray the prayer in the "Pray" section. Write "No" if you are not ready.

PRAY

If you wrote "Done!" thank God for making you his child. If you wrote "?" or "No," talk to Jesus about what is holding you back. If you wrote "Yes!" pray a prayer like this: "Dear God, I know I have sinned (done wrong things). Thank you for sending Jesus to take my punishment. Please forgive me. Please make me your child. Thank you! Amen." If you prayed the prayer, now you are adopted by God!

MEMORIZE

God sent him to buy freedom for us who were slaves to the law, so that he could adopt us as his very own children. Galatians 4:5

WHAT'S THE POINT?

Peter knew we need Jesus' help to be clean of sin. If Christopher asked Jesus to come into his life, he would be adopted by God. *CE*

JANUARY 20
Saving for a Skateboard

Jared took the money from his bank and counted it. He had made thirty dollars pulling weeds, watering flowers, and caring for the neighbor's cat, Tigger. But it was still not enough for the skateboard he wanted. Jared went looking for his big brother, Nate.

"Saving money is too hard," Jared complained. "I really want to buy some game cards now."

"Mom says waiting for good stuff takes discipline," Nate said. "She says it's good to learn discipline."

"You're no help," said Jared as he went back to his room. He stared at the pile of money. *This discipline stuff is too hard,* he thought.

READ
Proverbs 1:7. Fearing God means respecting and obeying him while living in awe of his power. When we respect God, he will help us be wise.

THINK
- Why do you think wise people want to learn discipline?
- Why do you think foolish people don't like wisdom or discipline?
- Make up an ending for the story, showing how Jared could follow the verse. Then read the possible ending at the back of the book.

DO
- What do you need to be wiser or more disciplined about? Being on time? Avoiding bad TV shows or Web sites? Avoiding bad language? Doing chores without complaining? Eating the meals your parents make? Something else?
- Tell a family member how respecting God would help you in the area you want to work on.

PRAY
Ask God to help you respect him more.

MEMORIZE
Fear of the LORD is the foundation of true knowledge, but fools despise wisdom and discipline. Proverbs 1:7

WHAT'S THE POINT?
Jared realized he respected what God said in the Bible. That led him to become wiser and more disciplined. *BA*

JANUARY 21
Let's Talk

Bailey's thoughts swirled in her head as she walked in the door. Her mom wasn't there to greet her, because her new job kept her at work until after dinner. "I wish Mom were here to talk," Bailey sighed. She grabbed a snack and sat down. "I just want to talk to someone!" Bailey said out loud to nobody.

Just then Bailey's older sister, Kate, walked in. Bailey wanted to tell her how hard school was this year. She longed to talk about her disappointment about her best friend moving away. Just then Kate's cell phone rang, and she ran to her room. *She doesn't have time for me either,* thought Bailey. *There's no one I can talk to anymore!*

READ
Psalm 142:1-5. When we are troubled, lonely, or worn out, we can be refreshed and renewed by time with God.

THINK
- What do you do when your thoughts and feelings get all bottled up inside?
- Is there something holding you back from pouring out your thoughts and feelings to God? What is it?
- Finish the story, showing how Bailey could take heart from the example of these verses. Then read the possible ending at the back of the book.

DO
- Doodle some scribbles or swirls or jagged lines to show your feelings and thoughts right now.
- Find or create a special spot where you can go and be alone to talk with God.

PRAY
Pour out some thoughts, feelings, worries, or problems to God right now. He is always listening, and he cares.

MEMORIZE
I pray to you, O LORD. I say, "You are my place of refuge. You are all I really want in life." Psalm 142:5

WHAT'S THE POINT?
Bailey shared her troubles with God. God is a safe person to share our troubles and feelings with. He won't make fun of us. He loves us. He is someone we can always trust to be there for us. Also, don't be afraid to ask others to listen to you too. It may seem like they don't care, but maybe they don't know you need to talk. *CE*

JANUARY 22
New Kid

Yesterday, a new kid named Nia joined Susan's class. Susan's teacher called her aside and asked her to help Nia feel comfortable and welcome. But when Susan tried talking to her, she found Nia's accent made it difficult to understand what she was saying. Plus, Nia dressed differently. She didn't look like Susan's other friends. Secretly, Susan hoped someone else would befriend Nia.

Today at lunch, Susan chose to sit with her friends and ignored Nia sitting by herself. At recess, Susan was playing double Dutch with her friends, but she noticed Nia walking alone along the edge of the playground.

READ
Acts 10:34-35. Favoritism is when a person treats some people better than others. God accepts people from all countries, of all shapes, sizes, and skin colors.

THINK
- How do kids play favorites in your school or neighborhood? Why do you think they do it?
- What do you think God would say to them about it?
- Imagine an ending for this story, showing how the verses might help Susan. Then read the possible ending at the back of the book.

DO
- Write the name of someone you have struggled to treat the same as you treat your friends.
- Plan at least one thing you can do this week to treat that person as you would a friend. For instance, invite the person to sit with you at lunch, play at recess, or join in a conversation.

PRAY
Ask God to help you carry out your plan.

MEMORIZE
I see very clearly that God shows no favoritism. Acts 10:34

WHAT'S THE POINT?
Susan struggled to be friendly to Nia because she was so different. It's easy to play favorites with people we know and leave out people we don't feel comfortable around. But that's not God's way. He wants us to imitate him and not play favorites. Once we get to know people, they may not seem so different after all. *CE*

JANUARY 23
Beads Went Flying

Alejandra got a bead kit for her birthday from Grandma. She excitedly sat down at the kitchen table and opened it up.

"Mom, I'm going to make a bracelet for my friend Lupe," she said.

"Sounds good," said Mom.

Alejandra concentrated hard but couldn't get the bracelet to look like the picture on the box cover. *What's the matter with me?* she said to herself. *I wish I didn't keep goofing up.*

On her third try she started getting mad at herself. On her fourth try, she stuck herself with the needle. *I can't do anything right,* she thought angrily. On the fifth try, she bumped the bead container and beads went flying everywhere.

"Aaaaah!" said Alejandra.

Alejandra was angry with herself the whole time she was cleaning up beads. Then she curled up on the couch in discouragement. "Are you mad at me too, God?" she said.

READ
Exodus 34:6. Since Moses can't really see God, God is telling Moses what he is like.

THINK
- Put God's description of himself in your own words.
- What would you tell Alejandra about God being mad at her?
- Finish the story, showing how Alejandra could learn something from this verse in God's Word. Then read the possible ending at the back of the book.

DO
- Write a reason you get mad at yourself and draw a heart around those words to signify God's love.
- Since God is kind to us, will you be kinder to yourself? Post your drawing where you can see it often as a reminder that God doesn't get angry easily.

PRAY
Thank God for his patience and love for you.

MEMORIZE
The LORD passed in front of Moses, calling out, "Yahweh! The LORD! The God of compassion and mercy! I am slow to anger and filled with unfailing love and faithfulness." Exodus 34:6

WHAT'S THE POINT?
Alejandra learned that God doesn't get angry easily. He loves us very much. She looked for ways to be patient with her mistakes, as God is patient. *BA*

JANUARY 24
The Lie

Lexi sat and stared blankly at her Bible while Mr. Hooper, her Sunday school teacher, spoke. *I know this stuff,* Lexi thought to herself. *Every year we hear about the wise man who built his house on the rock and the foolish man who built his house on the sand.* She sighed and crossed her arms. Mr. Hooper continued talking, "And the house on the sand went splat!" But Lexi didn't care.

Class ended and Abby came up to Lexi. "Ask your mom if you can come over to my house after church," she urged.

Lexi was tired of going to Abby's. Abby didn't have any fun video games like Lexi did. "I have to go see my grandma," Lexi lied.

READ
Matthew 7:24-27. Jesus is talking in these verses. When we listen and obey his teaching (the Bible) we are wise, but if we ignore the Bible we are foolish. We will have trouble in life.

THINK
- What distracts you when you read the Bible or listen to Bible teaching?
- What troubles could happen to us if we ignore Jesus' teaching?
- Finish the story, showing how Lexi could learn from the verses. Then read the possible ending at the back of the book.

DO
- Which of these Bible teachings do you find hard to obey: be kind to others, forgive others, worship God, don't lie, don't be stuck up, something else?
- With your family, brainstorm ways to be wise and obey.

PRAY
Talk to God about being wise instead of foolish. Ask God to help you obey the Bible teaching you thought of.

MEMORIZE
Anyone who listens to my teaching and follows it is wise, like a person who builds a house on solid rock. Matthew 7:24

WHAT'S THE POINT?
Lexi knew she'd disobeyed God by lying. The bad result was that Abby didn't trust her. Lexi wanted to start obeying Jesus' teachings instead so good results would happen. *CE*

JANUARY 25
Cheating

Nathan knew Robert got A's on his science tests. He was glad their teacher had made new seat assignments. From his new position, Nathan had been able to copy answers from many of Robert's tests. But yesterday, Mrs. Chung had unexpectedly called on Nathan twice in science. When he didn't know the answers to her questions, she seemed surprised. Nathan felt embarrassed and slumped in his seat.

Today, when Mrs. Chung gave a pop quiz in science, Nathan's heart had begun to beat fast—Robert was absent! A sinking feeling set in, and his mind became a blur. Walking home after school, Nathan felt he was carrying a weight on his back even though his backpack was empty. He dreaded going to school tomorrow. He just couldn't face Mrs. Chung!

READ

Psalm 32:3-5. The writer is talking to God. When we do wrong (sin), it's like we carry a heavy weight around. God disciplines us with guilt. But there's good news too!

THINK

- Think of a time when you did something wrong. How did you feel inside? What did you do about your sin?
- According to the verses, what happens when you admit your sins to God?
- Finish the story, showing how Nathan could find out from these verses how to get rid of his guilty feelings. Then read the possible ending at the back of the book.

DO

- Write a sin that you need to admit to God.
- Who else do you need to admit this wrong to? Do it today!
- Write Psalm 32:5 on a sheet of paper and put it where you can see it daily to remind yourself to admit your sins to God.

PRAY

Ask God to forgive you of the sin you thought of and remove your guilt and shame.

MEMORIZE

Finally, I confessed all my sins to you and stopped trying to hide my guilt. I said to myself, "I will confess my rebellion to the LORD." And you forgave me! All my guilt is gone. Psalm 32:5

WHAT'S THE POINT?

Nathan's guilt from cheating weighed heavily on him. God tells us that when we admit our sins, he will forgive us and set us free from our guilt and our feelings of guilt. We may still have to pay a price for what we did, but he will give us a new start. *CE*

JANUARY 26
Does He Love Me?

As Kristin's Sunday school teacher spoke about God's love, Kristin thought back to a year ago when she asked Jesus to forgive her of her sins and be her Savior. She had been so full of hope that Jesus would make her relationship with her big brother better. But nothing had changed. Will was still mean and Kristin still yelled and tried to get back at him. "Maybe God doesn't love me because I sometimes get back at Will."

Kristin started listening to the teacher again as he quoted from the Bible, "Nothing can ever separate us from God's love." Kristin's ears perked up. *Did he really say nothing can separate us from God's love? I'm not sure I believe that. I think I've been too mean.*

READ
Romans 8:38-39. Try to name something that could separate you from God's love. Then reread the first part of verse 38. What a promise!

THINK
- When have you felt that God didn't care about you? Why?
- What can you be sure of, based on these verses, if you have accepted Jesus as your Savior?
- Make up an ending for the story, showing how the verses could make a difference for Kristin. Then read the possible ending at the back of the book.

DO
- Draw a face to show how you feel about God's love for you. Are you sure of it or not?
- Make up a song or rap thanking God for his love. His love is there, even if you're not sure of it!

PRAY
Ask God to give you faith and trust in his promise that nothing can separate you from his love.

MEMORIZE
I am convinced that nothing can ever separate us from God's love. Romans 8:38

WHAT'S THE POINT?
No matter what we do or what happens to us, God still loves us. Absolutely nothing can separate us from God's love! *CE*

JANUARY 27
She's Weird

It was the first day of camp. Within five minutes, Madison decided which girls she wanted to be friends with and which ones she wanted to avoid. Erin dressed nicely and had a cool hairstyle. She was definitely someone Madison liked. But Hannah dressed weird and said nerdy things. So Madison stayed away from her.

The day started out great as Madison and Erin sat together to do a craft. But then Madison got paired up with Hannah for the "Getting to Know You" time. Madison went to her leader. "Can I have Erin as my partner instead?"

Her leader responded, "Every day you'll spend time getting to know someone different. Erin can be your partner another day."

Madison groaned. She looked over at Hannah sitting at the lunch table waiting for her.

READ

1 Samuel 16:1, 6-7. When God looks at someone's heart, he sees what the person is like on the inside—the person's attitudes, thoughts, and feelings.

THINK

- Why do you think what's inside people's hearts is more important than how they look?
- What qualities do you think God looks for in a person?
- Finish the story, showing how Madison could follow God's example in these verses. Then read the possible ending at the back of the book.

DO

- Make a "Friends" mini poster. Decorate it with qualities you look for in a friend. Circle the ones that match what God looks for.
- Plan a way to be kind this week to someone you have avoided based on their looks.

PRAY

Ask God to help you look past people's appearances to see who they really are inside.

MEMORIZE

People judge by outward appearance, but the LORD looks at the heart. 1 Samuel 16:7

WHAT'S THE POINT?

Have you heard the saying "Don't judge a book by its cover"? It may be easy to overlook people based on how they appear on the outside. Remember that God looks at what a person is like inside, and he wants us to do the same. *CE*

JANUARY 28
Cool Web Site

Patrick invited Tyrese to come over to his house after school. After shooting hoops for a while, the boys headed inside. "Mom, can we play computer games in the basement?" Patrick asked. He got the okay from his mom, but after playing awhile, the boys got bored.

"What should we do now?" asked Tyrese.

"Hey, let's get on the Internet. I found a cool Web site I can show you," suggested Patrick.

Tyrese stopped. He had been told never to go on the Internet unless his mom or dad was with him. As Patrick described the graphics and games on the site, Tyrese got more and more interested—but more and more uncomfortable. He knew his parents' rule: don't go on the Internet without them. But he really wanted to see the Web site!

READ
Ephesians 6:10. When we need to do what's right, we may not feel very strong or powerful. But we have a power source to "plug into"!

THINK
- Why is it better to rely on God's strength rather than your own?
- How can you rely on God's power when you need to choose to do what's right?
- Finish the story, showing how Tyrese could find wisdom in today's verse. Then read the possible ending at the back of the book.

DO
- Act out a common situation or two where you are tempted to do wrong.
- Then act out stopping and praying that God will give you the strength to choose to do the right thing.

PRAY
Ask God to give you the strength to do what is right the next time you face the situation you thought of.

MEMORIZE
Be strong in the Lord and in his mighty power. Ephesians 6:10

WHAT'S THE POINT?
God gave Tyrese the strength to stand strong and obey his parents. God loves to give us his power to do what's right. *CE*

JANUARY 29
M for Mature

Liam and Joseph were playing video games at Joseph's house. "Yay!" Liam yelled as he completed the last level.

"Let's play another," suggested Joseph.

Liam chose one. "How about this?"

"Nah, I already beat every level. Let's look for my brother's new one." Joseph led the way to his older brother's room. Liam found the new game lying on the bed. "It's rated M for 'mature,'" he said doubtfully.

"That's okay," said Joseph. "David is only fourteen, and Mom got it for him."

As soon as they started playing, Liam realized the game was really violent. But soon he was shouting along with Joseph as the points started piling up. A little voice kept telling him Mom and Dad wouldn't approve, but Liam drowned it out.

READ
Leviticus 19:1-2. Being holy means being pure in our thoughts and actions.

THINK

- Why should we be holy just because God is?
- How could violent video games or TV programs keep us from being pure?
- Finish the story, showing how Liam could follow the teaching of these verses. Then read the possible ending at the back of the book.

DO
- Choose something you're doing that doesn't fit with being holy. Write it on paper. Crumple it up and throw it away to represent getting rid of it from your life.

PRAY
Ask God to help you get rid of the thing you wrote on the paper.

MEMORIZE
You must be holy because I, the LORD your God, am holy. Leviticus 19:2

WHAT'S THE POINT?
Liam believed Dad and wanted to follow God. He understood that God wants us to keep ourselves holy. *BA*

JANUARY 30
Get Your Own Card

Milo and Brandon loved to collect baseball cards. When they got together, they checked out each other's cards and compared sets. Milo had a baseball card that Brandon really wanted. He begged Milo to trade. He nagged. He offered cards and toys and even food to try to get Milo to trade him that card. "No, forget it!" Milo kept saying. "Get your own card!"

One day at Brandon's house, Milo got up to use the bathroom. Brandon stared at the card he wanted so bad. There was no one around. He snatched it and hid it in his pack of cards. *Milo will just think he lost it somewhere*, Brandon thought.

The boys went outside to hit a ball around. Milo kept acting like his favorite baseball players. Every time Milo mentioned another player's name, Brandon remembered the card he'd taken. He felt more and more uncomfortable.

READ
Psalm 25:8-9. God's way is right, and he will show the right way to us when we do wrong.

THINK
- How often does God do what is right?
- Why do you think he wants to teach us to do what is right?
- Make up an ending for the story, showing how the verses could affect Brandon's choices. Then read the possible ending at the back of the book.

DO
- Think of something you've done wrong. Ask God to show you how to make it right.

PRAY
Ask God to help you to do what's right even when it's hard.

MEMORIZE
The LORD is good and does what is right; he shows the proper path to those who go astray.
Psalm 25:8

WHAT'S THE POINT?
Brandon knew God is ready to help us know the right thing to do. He let God teach him when he'd done wrong. *CE*

JANUARY 31
Afraid of the Dark

Olivia crawled into bed and pulled up the covers. She and Mom sang a song. Then Mom kissed her and moved to turn off the light.

"No!" said Olivia. "Please leave the light on."

"Why?" said Mom.

"Well, I'm kind of scared," Olivia admitted.

Mom sat down again on the bed. "There's nothing in your room in the dark that isn't there in the light," she said. "Why don't you pray and ask God to help you not be afraid? He loves you very much, you know."

"It's *nighttime*," said Olivia. "What if he's asleep?"

"God doesn't sleep," Mom said. "Psalm 121:3-4 says so." She kissed Olivia again, turned out the light, and left.

Olivia looked at the dark shapes of her furniture and stuffed animals. They looked scary in the dark. She pulled the covers over her head. *I think Mom is wrong! Everybody sleeps!*

READ
Psalm 121:1-4. It's great to know we can rely on God for help all day long and all night too.

THINK
- Draw a pair of scared eyeballs if you're ever afraid of the dark.
- What do verses 3 and 4 have to do with your fears of the dark? (If you're not afraid of the dark, think of another fear.)
- Imagine an ending for this story, showing how the verses could affect Olivia. Then read the possible ending at the back of the book.

DO
- Talk with your family about ideas for not being afraid of the dark (or any other fears). Don't forget about praying!

PRAY
Ask your family members to pray with you about your fear.

MEMORIZE
He will not let you stumble; the one who watches over you will not slumber. Psalm 121:3

WHAT'S THE POINT?
Olivia trusted the Bible. She discovered God is always awake and ready to help her with her fears. *BA*

FEBRUARY 1
The Cola Question

"Bye, Mom. Thanks for the ride," Malik said as he and John jumped out of the car. Friday was the busiest night at the roller rink. Malik and John liked that their parents didn't stay to watch them anymore. They could horse around and order as much snack food as they wanted.

Malik skated for a while and then got thirsty. John followed him to the snack bar.

The cold soda looked tempting, even though Malik remembered how bad he felt the last time he drank too much of it and couldn't fall asleep. His mom never let him drink soda at home because it made him too jumpy. She always said, "Malik, your body is a temple of the Lord. You need to treat it right."

When it was his turn to order, Malik said, "I'll have a cola."

"I thought you weren't allowed to drink soda," John said. "I'm gonna get a bottled water."

Malik felt kind of guilty, but he had a soda anyway.

READ
1 Corinthians 3:16. The Jewish people called their temple building God's house. Today, if we are believers in Jesus, God's Spirit lives in us, not in a building.

THINK
▸ Where does God send his Spirit to live?
▸ What difference does it make to you that God's Spirit lives in you?
▸ Finish the story, showing how Malik could apply the verse. Then read the possible ending at the back of the book.

DO
▸ Write down some food and drinks adults often tell you to avoid. Then write ideas for food and drinks you're told you should eat. What's the difference?
▸ Cross out one thing you will eat or drink less of, like candy or ice cream. Circle one healthier thing you will replace it with.

PRAY
Ask God what changes he would like you to make in what you eat and drink.

MEMORIZE
Don't you realize that all of you together are the temple of God and that the Spirit of God lives in you? 1 Corinthians 3:16

WHAT'S THE POINT?
Malik knew that treating his body right was a good idea. With God's Spirit living inside of him, he wanted to give God a good home. *ML*

FEBRUARY 2
Couch Potato

"Matthew, it's time to go to basketball," his mom called up the stairs.

"Aw, Mom, can't I just stay home and play video games?"

"I know it's hard to go to practice," Mom said, "but it's not good to sit on the couch every day playing video games. One of the reasons you and your brother are in basketball is that it's good for your body to get some exercise."

"I don't care about being healthy," Matthew lashed out. "It's *my* body."

Matthew's mom appeared in his doorway. "Actually, it's not just your body. It belongs to God. He wants you to take care of it." Matthew groaned. "Get your gym clothes on," Mom said. "It's time to go." She went back downstairs.

Matthew locked the door and flopped down on his bed. It was his body. He wasn't going to practice.

Five minutes later his mom knocked. "Matthew, if you keep us waiting any longer, I'm going to ground you from video games this weekend."

READ
1 Corinthians 6:19-20. If we are God's children, God has "bought" us with the death of his own Son, Jesus. We belong to him. We cost him a lot, but he paid the price because he loves us. Honoring God means respecting him.

THINK
- How are we honoring God with our bodies when we exercise?
- How are we not honoring him when we're too much like couch potatoes?
- Finish the story, showing how Matthew could obey the verses. Then read the possible ending at the back of the book.

DO
- If your mom or dad gives you permission, choose to walk or ride your bike when you're going somewhere whenever you can.
- Choose a way to get more exercise. Draw yourself doing it. Post your drawing somewhere where it will remind you to do it.

PRAY
Ask God to help you take good care of your body, which really belongs to him.

MEMORIZE
God bought you with a high price. So you must honor God with your body.
1 Corinthians 6:20

WHAT'S THE POINT?
Matthew realized that practice helped him stay strong. And staying strong is one way we honor God with our bodies. *ML*

FEBRUARY 3
Crossing Main Street

"Justin, can you come to my house?" Ben asked on the phone.

"Dad, can I ride my bike to Ben's house?" Justin asked.

"You can go to Ben's," Justin's dad said, "but I'll put the bike in the back and drive you over there. I don't want you crossing Main Street on your bike. There's too much traffic."

When Justin arrived, two other boys were there. "Buddy," Justin's dad said, as he lifted his bike out of the trunk, "I'll pick you up at five o'clock. Remember, I don't want you to cross Main Street on your bike."

As soon as he left, Ben said, "Let's ride on the bike path." The four boys jumped on their bikes and set out for the path, which ran behind Ben's house through his neighborhood. The path ended at Main Street. Across the street was a gas station.

"Let's go to the gas station and get something to drink," Ben suggested. Three of the boys got back on their bikes and waited to cross the street.

READ

1 Kings 3:9-10; 4:29; Proverbs 3:13. Solomon was a king. He wanted to make good decisions, so he asked God to give him wisdom. Wisdom is the good sense and understanding that helps us decide between right and wrong.

THINK

◼ Why do you think God was pleased that Solomon asked for wisdom?

◼ How can wisdom help you have joy? How can it help in your everyday decisions?

◼ Make up an ending for the story, showing how the verses could affect Justin. Then read the possible ending at the back of the book.

DO

◼ Tell someone about a time in your life when it was hard to do the right thing. How could asking God for wisdom help?

◼ Ask someone to pray with you about a decision you need to make.

PRAY

Ask God to help you choose wisely between right and wrong.

MEMORIZE

Joyful is the person who finds wisdom, the one who gains understanding. Proverbs 3:13

WHAT'S THE POINT?

Justin didn't want to disobey his dad. God was happy to help him think of a wise solution. Justin felt good that his friends followed his idea. *ML*

FEBRUARY 4
I Forgot!

"Remember, class, tomorrow your book reports are due," Miss Bradley reminded everyone. Steven panicked. He was supposed to have been working on the book report for two weeks, but he had forgotten. *How am I going to get it done in one night?*

Steven worried the rest of the day. After school, his grandma greeted him at the door, asking, "How was school? Do you have any homework?"

"I have a book report due tomorrow," he said in a panicked voice. "I forgot."

"Slow down," Grandma advised. "Panicking will make you think less clearly, and you'll need all your thinking power to get this done."

Grandma helped Steven, but he still didn't get it done. "Let's talk about how you can learn from this. Mistakes are for learning," Grandma said. As they thought of ways to plan ahead next time, Steven couldn't keep his worry down.

READ
1 Peter 5:7. God doesn't want us to make things worse by worrying.

THINK
- Why do you think this verse tells us not to worry?
- How can trusting in God's love take away our worries?
- Finish the story, showing how Steven could apply this verse to his schoolwork situation. Then read the possible ending at the back of the book.

DO
- What kinds of things do you worry about? Imagine placing each of your worries in God's hands so that you don't have to carry them anymore.
- One way to reduce worry is to keep track of schoolwork. Every day after school, check your assignment notebook to see what's due the next day. If you have a longer assignment like Steven, do a little bit every night so you're not rushing.

PRAY
Pray 1 Peter 5:7 for yourself: "I give all my worries and cares to you, for you care about me."

MEMORIZE
Give all your worries and cares to God, for he cares about you. 1 Peter 5:7

WHAT'S THE POINT?
Steven's grandma reminded him how much God cares. We can trust him with our worries. *ML*

FEBRUARY 5
The Deer and the Bushy-Tailed Fox

It was a four-hour car ride from the city to Aunt Yolanda's house. Angel's favorite game while driving was "I Spy." Everyone took turns saying, "I spy with my little eye something beginning with the letter ___." Driving down the country highway with nature on either side, it wasn't hard to work through several letters in the alphabet.

"There's so much in nature to see," Angel said. "How could God have thought of all this stuff?"

Living in the city, Angel didn't get to see all the trees and critters that they saw at Aunt Yolanda's. She jumped out of the car as soon as they got there. "Oh, look," Angel exclaimed. "A deer just ran through the woods!"

"Who gave life to the deer?" asked Aunt Yolanda.

READ
Acts 17:24-25. God's work is everywhere we look. Everything that's alive depends on him.

THINK
- Why do you think God made so many different kinds of trees and animals?
- What is your favorite living thing that God made?
- Finish the story, showing how the verses could make a difference for Angel. Then read the possible ending at the back of the book.

DO
- Play "I Spy," seeing how many living things you can find that God made. Don't forget people!
- Write a thank-you note to God for giving *you* life.

PRAY
Tell God what you love about the world he created.

MEMORIZE
He is the God who made the world and everything in it. Since he is Lord of heaven and earth, he doesn't live in man-made temples. Acts 17:24

WHAT'S THE POINT?
The Bible says God is the one who gives life to every living thing that he made. *ML*

FEBRUARY 6
Bully on the Playground

At recess, Samantha's friends played on the merry-go-round for a while and then jumped off. Samantha started to jump off but someone was in her way. Brittany the Bully.

"Hi, loser," Brittany said. She gave Samantha a push. Samantha sat down with a thud on the merry-go-round. Brittany got into Samantha's face. "You are so clumsy! Do you fall down a lot?" Brittany laughed.

Samantha jumped up and ran for the school doors. "What's wrong?" the teacher asked.

"Nothing," said Samantha, fighting tears. That night Samantha wasn't her usual cheerful self. Her mom asked her if anything was wrong. Samantha told her about Brittany and how the bully was bothering her day after day.

"How can you stand up for yourself?" her mom asked.

Samantha felt hopeless. "Doesn't Jesus just want me to be nice and not cause trouble?"

READ
Acts 22:22-29. Paul stood up for himself when people were going to hurt him. Read Psalm 146:7. God himself stands up for people who are being hurt.

THINK
- Why do you think Paul stood up for himself?
- Do you think it's okay for you to stand up for yourself? Why or why not?
- Finish the story, telling how you think Samantha might handle the bully problem. Then read the possible ending at the back of the book.

DO
- With your family, role-play ways to deal with bullies.
- Tell an adult you trust if a bully is bothering you.

PRAY
Ask God to help you know what to do if a bully is bothering you.

MEMORIZE
He gives justice to the oppressed and food to the hungry. Psalm 146:7

WHAT'S THE POINT?
Samantha's mom knew that the kindest thing to do may be to speak up. Speaking up might help stop the ones disobeying God. God approves of getting help when we're being hurt. *BA*

FEBRUARY 7
Why Can't I Just Watch TV?

Kylie had a beautiful singing voice, and her family loved for her to sing. Usually she liked it too. It was fun to have an audience. "Kylie," her mom asked, "will you sing for Grandma and Grandpa now that we're done eating dinner?"

"I don't really feel like singing right now," Kylie said. "My favorite show is coming on."

Kylie's grandparents looked disappointed. Her grandma loved to hear the sound of Kylie's voice. Kylie sounded like an angel to her.

Her mom tried again. "Kylie, you can watch TV after Grandma and Grandpa go home. You know what a treat it is for them to listen to you."

Kylie sulked. She thought, *Why can't I just watch TV?*

READ
Exodus 35:31; 36:1-2; 1 Corinthians 12:7. Moses recognized that God created people with special abilities. He liked giving jobs to people who wanted to use their gifts. The people were using their gifts for an important job—building God's house, the Tabernacle.

THINK
- Find a word in Exodus 36:2 that tells how the workers felt.
- Why is it important to be eager and willing to use the gifts (special abilities) that God gives us?
- Make up an ending for the story, showing how the verses could make a difference for Kylie. Then read the possible ending at the back of the book.

DO
- God gives everyone special abilities. Write down one that you have. Being kind? Helping people? Playing a sport? Something else?
- Ask a family member to help you use your gifts to serve God or others.

PRAY
Ask God to help you be eager to use your gifts to serve others.

MEMORIZE
A spiritual gift is given to each of us so we can help each other. 1 Corinthians 12:7

WHAT'S THE POINT?
Kylie knew her grandparents loved to hear her sing. She realized that singing for them was a way to use the gift God had given her. *ML*

FEBRUARY 8
The Pitcher

"I choose Emily," Anna said, as she picked her team for kick ball during recess.

"I pick Fatima," said Lillian next. Anna chose, and then Lillian chose, until all the girls except one had been divided between their two teams.

Payton sat alone waiting for someone to pick her. She was used to being last because she used a motorized wheelchair, and everyone thought she was too slow.

"Okay, we've got our teams," said Anna, pretending not to notice Payton. Lillian led her team to the bases, looking down while she walked past Payton.

Payton wheeled onto the sidelines, trying to hold back tears.

READ
Genesis 5:1-2. Being made in God's image means every person is like God in some ways.

THINK
- What are some things you know about God that you see glimpses of in people? For example, God loves and forgives. People can love and forgive too.
- If God made every person in his image, how should we view other people—even those who are different from us?
- Finish the story, showing how the verses could affect Anna and Lillian. Then read the possible ending at the back of the book.

DO
- Write the name of someone who seems really different from you. How do you feel about this person? How do you treat him or her? How do you think God feels about him or her?
- Write a way you will reach out to this person. Remind yourself that everyone is created by God.

PRAY
Thank God for making you unique. Ask him to help you treat all people with respect because they also are created by God.

MEMORIZE
When God created human beings, he made them to be like himself. Genesis 5:1

WHAT'S THE POINT?
Cassidy helped Anna realize that including Payton was a way to be kind and respectful of everyone, no matter what their differences may be. We are all made in God's image, and he says we are his good creation. *ML*

FEBRUARY 9
Pottery Class

Beth loved art, so her foster mom signed her up for a pottery class. For the first project, the teacher had the students roll out clay and shape it into a bowl. Beth started to work with her lump of clay. She liked the feel of it in her hands as she molded it into a round bowl.

Another girl was busy shaping her clay into a square bowl. A boy was carving decorations into his. Beth held her bowl at arm's length and looked it over. She decided hers needed a chunky rim, so she molded one. Then she decided it needed some stripes, so she molded some out of extra clay. *I like my creation,* she thought.

READ
Isaiah 64:8. God molds us like clay. He helps us develop good qualities, like kindness and patience. We are his creation.

THINK
- What qualities do you think God is helping you develop? Gentleness? adventurousness? helpfulness? friendliness? intelligence? peacefulness? something else?
- What do you think God wants us to do while he is at work "molding" us?
- Finish the story, showing how Beth might connect her art project with truth from today's verse. Then read the possible ending at the back of the book.

DO
- Ask family members what qualities they see God developing in you.
- Ask family members to help you choose a way to develop one of these qualities this week.

PRAY
Ask God to mold you throughout your life. Ask him to help you always be willing to learn from him.

MEMORIZE
O LORD, you are our Father. We are the clay, and you are the potter. We all are formed by your hand. Isaiah 64:8

WHAT'S THE POINT?
God forms each one of us like a potter creates something beautiful out of clay. Beth understood more about how God molds us and develops us into the people he wants us to be. God wants us to learn from him as he helps us develop good qualities. *ML*

FEBRUARY 10
Making Shadows

As Logan walked home from the park, he noticed his long shadow in front of him. No matter how he moved, his shadow was always with him. When he got home, his dad was sitting on the front porch. "Dad, how come my shadow won't go away?" Logan asked.

"That's because the sunlight is shining down on you. As you move, it still shines, but the sun never moves. That's how God is too. He keeps shining down on us."

"Some days my shadow is big, and some days it's small," Logan said.

"That's because our shadows are created by where we are in comparison to the sun. The farther the earth is tilted away from the sun, the bigger our shadow appears. Shadows shift and change. But God doesn't change."

"I get it," said Logan. "He's more like the sun."

"I can think of another way God is like the sun," said Dad. "What good things does the sun give us?"

"Heat, light, warm days to go swimming!"

"What good gifts does God give us?"

READ
James 1:17. God is like the sun. He never changes. His truth and love are good gifts for us, like sunlight.

THINK
- According to the verse, how many of the good things that come our way are from God?
- Why is it good that God doesn't change?
- Imagine an ending for this story, showing how the verse might affect Logan. Then read the possible ending at the back of the book.

DO
- Put a piece of paper on the refrigerator. Ask family members to write down good things God gives them each day. See how long a list you can make in a week.

PRAY
Tell God thanks for at least six good things he's given you.

MEMORIZE
Whatever is good and perfect comes down to us from God our Father, who created all the lights in the heavens. He never changes or casts a shifting shadow. James 1:17

WHAT'S THE POINT?
Logan discovered that God is the giver of everything that's good. His best gift to us is himself. He doesn't change, so we can count on him. *ML*

FEBRUARY 11
Lost in the Crowd?

Natalie was at the park with her mom. Since Natalie's dad and mom divorced, she only got to see her dad every other weekend. When Natalie was little, her dad used to bring her to this same park and push her on the swings. Now, though, she was lucky if he made it to one ballet recital during the year. Sometimes Natalie wondered if her dad even loved her.

She pumped her legs to make the swing go high. All the other kids below her looked small. There were too many kids for her to count. *Maybe that's the problem with Dad*, she thought. *There are too many people in his life for me to matter.*

The more she looked at all the kids, the more Natalie worried. *Maybe there are too many kids in the world for me to matter to God, either.*

As Valentine's Day approached, her class created cards to give to their parents. Natalie felt sad. She didn't know if her dad would even remember Valentine's Day.

READ
Jeremiah 31:3. This verse means that God pulls us close to himself with his love.

THINK
- How long does the verse say God's love for you will last?
- What does the verse tell you about how close God wants to be with you?
- Finish the story, showing how the verse could comfort Natalie. Then read the possible ending at the back of the book.

DO
- Make God a valentine.
- People who are close spend time together and tell each other their deep thoughts and feelings. Spend some time telling God about yours.

PRAY
Thank God for loving you and pulling you close to him.

MEMORIZE
Long ago the LORD said to Israel: "I have loved you, my people, with an everlasting love. With unfailing love I have drawn you to myself." Jeremiah 31:3

WHAT'S THE POINT?
Natalie found out she could trust her dad's love. He helped her see that God loved her, too, no matter what. *ML*

FEBRUARY 12
Skin and Bones, Heart and Soul

Sarah dug through her mom's box of family photos. One picture looked kind of like an X ray—a fuzzy image with a black background. Sarah wondered what it was. She found lots of pictures of her older sister and brother. *Why aren't there more pictures of me?* Sarah wondered. Sarah was the youngest. *Maybe Mom and Dad don't love me the way they love Kayla and Michael,* she thought angrily.

Sarah shoved the box onto the floor. Pictures scattered everywhere. Sarah didn't care. She was mad.

READ
Job 10:10-12. God created us. Even before we were born, he formed us.

THINK
- Sarah felt unappreciated. When have you felt this way? What did you do?
- What can you tell from the verses about what you're worth to God?
- Make up an ending for the story, showing how the verses could make a difference for Sarah. Then read the possible ending at the back of the book.

DO
- Ask your mom or dad for a baby picture. Frame it with construction paper and write the words from Job 10:10-12 on it. Keep it to remind yourself how God made you and feels about you.

PRAY
Thank God for all the care he took in creating you—for giving you skin and bones and lots more!

MEMORIZE
You guided my conception and formed me in the womb. Job 10:10

WHAT'S THE POINT?
Sarah realized her parents loved her just as she was. She felt special that she had a picture of herself showing how God was making her before she was even born. *ML*

FEBRUARY 13
The Giant Football Players

Kyle was dreading Saturday's game against the Falcons. The Falcons were the best team in the league, and some of their players were huge compared to Kyle and his teammates.

"Aren't you nervous about playing against the Falcons?" Kyle asked Andrew when he arrived at the field on Saturday.

"Yeah, they're so much bigger than we are," said Andrew. "We'll probably get clobbered."

"I don't think I'm even going to try very hard to block them," said Kyle. "We'll just end up getting hurt."

"I know," replied Andrew. "I think I'm just going to try to get out of their way. I don't even care if we lose. I just don't want to get killed out there."

READ
John 14:1. This verse is an invitation from Jesus to us because he loves us.

THINK
- When are some times Jesus might have felt afraid when he lived on earth? How do you think he faced his fears?
- Why can we trust in God?
- Finish the story, showing how Kyle and Andrew might find courage to face trouble. Then read the possible ending at the back of the book.

DO
- Draw something to stand for a time you've been worried. What did you do to deal with your fear?
- Think of one difficult situation you're facing right now. Draw a T-shirt design that shows some ways you can trust Jesus to help you through it.

PRAY
Let God know what you're afraid of and ask him to help you trust in him. Thank him for loving you so much that he cares about your worries.

MEMORIZE
Don't let your hearts be troubled. Trust in God, and trust also in me. John 14:1

WHAT'S THE POINT?
Instead of focusing on his fear, Kyle trusted God to help him. God reminded Kyle of his good skills for competing against anyone. *ML*

FEBRUARY 14
Valentine from God

Jade was at Madeline's house making valentines. "Who's that one for?" Jade asked as Madeline glued a lacy heart to pink paper.

"Me," Madeline said.

"Why would you make a valentine for yourself?" Jade laughed.

"It's from God," Madeline explained. "It's our family tradition to make ourselves valentines from God. He really loves us." She wrote Romans 5:8 on the card: "God showed his great love for us by sending Christ to die for us while we were still sinners."

"Sinners?" Jade said, looking up. "What's that?"

READ

Romans 5:8. This verse tells us how much Jesus loves us!

THINK
- Why did Jesus have to die for us?
- Since God sent his Son to die for us, how much do you think he loves us?
- Imagine an ending for this story, showing how Madeline could use the verse. Then read the possible ending at the back of the book.

DO
- Make yourself a valentine from God. Have it say that he's glad you're already his child—or that he wants you to decide to be his child.
- If you want to be his child, pray a prayer like this: "Dear God, thank you for sending your Son, Jesus, to die and come back to life for me. I'm sorry for the bad things I've done. Please forgive me and make me your child."

PRAY

Thank God for his great love for you.

MEMORIZE

God showed his great love for us by sending Christ to die for us while we were still sinners. Romans 5:8

WHAT'S THE POINT?

Madeline knew that Jesus' death is good news for us. He came back to life to save us from our sins. This shows God's great love for us. *ML*

FEBRUARY 15
Lemonade: 25 Cents

"Cody, here are cups and lemonade mix." Cody's dad set the supplies down behind the lemonade stand Cody and his friend Jeremy had made. They mixed their first pitcher of lemonade. As cars drove by, they waved signs that said, "Lemonade: 25 cents." Cody and Jeremy sold cup after cup of lemonade.

"Let's count our money," Cody said. So far, they had made four dollars.

"That's pretty good," Jeremy said.

"Not bad," said Cody. "Let's keep going, though. If we get up to ten dollars, we can split it and have enough to get some packs of game cards."

All day the two boys sold lemonade. Finally, at five o'clock, Cody's dad told him it was time to come home. When they counted their money, they only had seven dollars.

Dad said, "Remember that you need to put part of what you earn in the offering at church tomorrow."

"What?! Da-ad!" Cody exclaimed.

"You know the rules," said Dad.

READ
Luke 16:13. In this verse, "serving" something or someone means we put it first and do everything we can to please that thing or person.

THINK
- Why do you think we can't love both God and money the best?
- How much does God love us? What do you think we owe him in return?
- Finish the story, showing how Cody could take this verse to heart. Then read the possible ending at the back of the book.

DO
- With your family, make up a commercial that tells how a kid could love God more than money.
- Ask your family how you can give some money to God or someone in need.

PRAY
Ask God to help you love him above everything else in this world.

MEMORIZE
No one can serve two masters. For you will hate one and love the other; you will be devoted to one and despise the other. You cannot serve both God and money. Luke 16:13

WHAT'S THE POINT?
It's good to work and make money. But God loves us and wants us to love him back by putting him first. *ML*

FEBRUARY 16
My Pants Are Too Short!

Jenna needed new clothes for school. "Mom, can we please go shopping?" she asked.

"Jenna, I'm sorry. Even with my second job, I just don't have money right now for clothes. You'll need to make do with what you have for a little longer."

Jenna stepped over piles of toys and books scattered on her floor and looked through her closet. Nothing seemed to fit quite right, and all of her clothes looked worn out.

"Mom, how am I going to make it through the school year with the old clothes I have? I'm outgrowing everything."

"I know, Jenna. God knows, too, and he cares about what we need. He wants us to concentrate on living lives that are pleasing to him. He wants us to pay more attention to that than to clothes or food or other needs. Let's do that and see how he meets our needs."

READ
Matthew 6:31-33. Living righteously means living in a way that pleases God.

THINK
- Why do you think people who don't believe in God worry so much about what they will eat and drink and wear?
- Why do you think God wants us to concentrate on living in a way that pleases him and not worrying?
- Finish the story, showing how these verses might help Jenna put first things first. Then read the possible ending at the back of the book.

DO
Talk to God about a need you have. Ask him for help. While you wait for his help, choose one way you will pay more attention to living in a way that pleases him. Write it down as a reminder.

PRAY
Tell God how thankful you are for all the ways he takes care of your needs.

MEMORIZE
Seek the Kingdom of God above all else, and live righteously, and he will give you everything you need. Matthew 6:33

WHAT'S THE POINT?
Jenna concentrated on living the way Jesus wants. The Bible says to do that and let God take care of our needs. *ML*

FEBRUARY 17
Mama Bird and Babies

"Dad," Lucy said excitedly, "there's a bird's nest in our tree! Three babies are waiting for food from their mother. Can I bring them something to eat?"

Her dad said, "Let's wait and watch for the mama bird to return. She'll bring food to them—like worms."

"Ick, that doesn't sound very good," Lucy said, scrunching up her face as she imagined eating worms for dinner.

"It's yummy for baby birds." Lucy's dad laughed. "Let's watch how God takes care of them. The Bible says God cares for the birds, and he cares for us even more."

Lucy watched from the kitchen window. After a couple of minutes, she began to worry. "They'll die if their mom doesn't bring them food," Lucy said. "How will she know where to find them?"

READ
Matthew 10:29-31. These verses remind us that God takes care of everything he created—even the birds—and we are more valuable to him than they are.

THINK
- How many creatures can you think of that God made? How do you think God takes care of them all?
- How does it feel to know that God cares so much about you that he even knows how many hairs are on your head?
- Make up an ending for the story, showing how the verses could affect Lucy. Then read the possible ending at the back of the book.

DO
- Learn how an animal mama takes care of her babies. Maybe you could look on the Internet or go to a zoo. What are some ways God takes care of *you*?
- Try to count the hairs on your head. Give up? What else does God know about you if he knows this?

PRAY
Ask God to help you trust that he cares for you a thousand times more than all the creatures he has made.

MEMORIZE
Don't be afraid; you are more valuable to God than a whole flock of sparrows.
Matthew 10:31

WHAT'S THE POINT?
Lucy saw how perfectly God had made the birds, and she began to see how much, much more valuable she was to God. *ML*

FEBRUARY 18
I Want to Be Line Leader

"Everybody needs to line up behind me," Maya said excitedly. Alondra ignored her. Maya was the line leader for the week. She got to lead her classmates to the art and music room. Alondra was jealous. Her job for the week was calendar keeper. When she saw Maya at the front of the line, she wished she could do something that would make the other kids notice her instead.

"Miss Gutierrez, when is it my turn to be line leader?" Alondra had asked her teacher yesterday. "I'm tired of being calendar keeper."

"Alondra, you'll get your turn. But for now, you do a great job highlighting the date for us each day and recording the weather."

Today Alondra still felt jealous. She ignored Maya until Miss Gutierrez said, "Alondra!" Alondra pouted as she took her place at the end of Maya's line.

READ
Proverbs 14:30. This verse says that jealousy is like a bad sickness in our lives.

THINK
- What bad things could come from feeling jealous? If feeling jealous is like a sickness, what is feeling peaceful like?
- Finish the story, showing how the verse could help Alondra overcome her jealousy. Then read the possible ending at the back of the book.

DO
- If jealousy is like a sickness, a peaceful attitude could be like "medicine." Design a magazine ad for this "medicine." Show why it's good for you.
- Think of something you are jealous about and plan a way to be more peaceful about it. If you need ideas, ask someone to help you.

PRAY
Ask God to help you feel more peaceful about the situation you are jealous about.

MEMORIZE
A peaceful heart leads to a healthy body; jealousy is like cancer in the bones. Proverbs 14:30

WHAT'S THE POINT?
Alondra realized that jealousy would hurt her. She found a few ways to help herself feel more peaceful instead of jealous. *ML*

FEBRUARY 19
Beach Slob

Cameron walked barefoot along the shoreline. He and his family were staying at a cabin on a lake for a week. As Cameron walked along, he was amazed at all the strange creatures he saw. When he lifted a rock under the water, a crawfish darted out. Nearby, a turtle was sunning on a log. The sand felt cool on his toes. Suddenly, a burning pain shot through the heel of his right foot.

"Aaaahhh!" Cameron shouted. Blood dripped from a jagged cut, and a piece of glass from a broken bottle stuck out from his heel. Cameron pulled the glass out of his foot. Angry that someone had left a broken bottle in the sand, Cameron yelled, "Slob!" He threw the glass into the woods.

READ
Psalm 8:4-8. These verses remind us how much God trusts us. He made all of creation and then put us in charge of it! Each of us is important to God's world.

THINK
- What words in the verses tell you how God feels about us?
- Why do you think God gave us the job of taking care of the world he made?
- Finish the story, showing how Cameron might put the truth of these verses to work. Then read the possible ending at the back of the book.

DO
- What are some ways you can take care of God's creation? Write down one thing to do today.
- The next time you go out for a walk, bring a trash bag and work gloves with you. You never know when you might find garbage where it doesn't belong.

PRAY
Thank God for trusting you to help take care of the beautiful world he created. Ask him to help you see ways you can take care of it.

MEMORIZE
You gave them charge of everything you made, putting all things under their authority. Psalm 8:6

WHAT'S THE POINT?
Cameron felt good about cleaning up the lake area and keeping it safe for others. He knew he needed to do his part to keep God's world beautiful. *ML*

FEBRUARY 20
Alone and Afraid

Jackson lay in the hospital bed with a tube in his arm. It was dripping medicine into his vein. The doctors called it chemotherapy, and it was supposed to get rid of the cancer cells that were making him sick. For days, Jackson only had enough strength to lie flat.

"When will I start to feel better?" he weakly asked the night nurse who came in to check on him. "I'm so tired of being sick."

"I know, Jackson," the nurse replied. "Cancer's no fun. But this medicine, even though it's making you feel bad now, will actually be the thing that helps you get stronger again. Hang in there."

The nurse closed the door behind her, and Jackson lay there looking at the dark walls. He was afraid.

Tears started to fall down Jackson's face. Why did he have to go through this sickness? Why couldn't he just go back to school and be like everyone else?

READ
Psalm 23:1-5. These verses were written by King David, a man who knew a lot about being alone and afraid.

THINK
- When is God with us? What does he do for us?
- What difference did knowing God was with him make for King David?
- Finish the story, showing how these verses could help Jackson. Then read the possible ending at the back of the book.

DO
- Ask someone in your family to tell you about a time when God helped him or her get through a hard time.
- Tell someone about a fear you have. How would trusting God help you be less afraid?

PRAY
Talk to God about a fear you have and ask for his help and comfort.

MEMORIZE
The LORD is my shepherd; I have all that I need. Psalm 23:1

WHAT'S THE POINT?
Jackson's nurse shared the truth of Psalm 23 with him. Knowing God was with him and that he wasn't alone helped Jackson sleep. *ML*

FEBRUARY 21
No Bears Allowed

Rodney had never been camping before. He boarded the bus that would take his Pioneer Clubs group to a national park an hour away. Everyone had paired up with a friend, but he was new, so he didn't have anyone to sit with.

"Do you want to sit with me?" asked a tall, skinny boy. "I'm Garrett." The two boys talked during the entire ride. They became friends and agreed to share a tent. When the bus arrived, Garrett and Rodney set up their tent. The forest grew dark. After a devotional time, the club leaders said, "Lights out, everyone!"

Quiet descended as Rodney and Garrett burrowed into their sleeping bags. Rodney lay awake listening to the sounds of the night. He wondered about the strange hooting sounds and the scratching noise behind the tent. Rodney felt afraid. His heart pounded so hard, he was sure Garrett would hear it.

READ
Psalm 16:7-9. God is always with us. Day or night, you can relax, because God is in control of every minute of your life.

THINK
- What is God doing while you're playing on the playground? while you're sleeping? when you're afraid?
- When have you been afraid? What difference does it make for you to know God is watching over you?
- Finish the story, showing how these verses could help Rodney feel safe and calm. Then read the possible ending at the back of the book.

DO
- List things that scare you. For each one, write down what you want God to protect you from. Sometimes our fears go away when we identify exactly what they are.

PRAY
Thank God for watching over you. Ask him to protect you from the things you wrote down.

MEMORIZE
I know the LORD is always with me. I will not be shaken, for he is right beside me.
Psalm 16:8

WHAT'S THE POINT?
No matter what kind of fear you're struggling with, God is there to help you and watch over you. *ML*

FEBRUARY 22
Hauling Garbage

In the condo next to Tony lived an older woman whose husband had died. Ever since the neighbor's funeral, Tony noticed that Mrs. Yoshida didn't get out as much as she used to. "Tony, why don't you bring Mrs. Yoshida's garbage bags and recycling bin to the curb for her on Wednesdays before the garbage truck comes," his mom suggested. "Then you can return them to her garage after school."

"That's a lot of work," Tony replied.

"Imagine how much harder it must be for Mrs. Yoshida," Tony's mom said. Tony didn't like the idea, but he felt sorry for Mrs. Yoshida. When Wednesday came, Tony was running behind. *I don't have time to help,* Tony thought. He hurried past Mrs. Yoshida's windows, hoping neither she nor his mom saw him.

READ
Psalm 139:1-4. God knows everything about us—our thoughts, words, and actions—no matter where we are. We can't escape God's attention.

THINK
- What are you glad God knows about what you think or say or do? What aren't you so glad he knows?
- How do you think God can know things about you that no one else can know?
- Finish the story, showing how Tony might act once he understands today's Bible reading. Then read the possible ending at the back of the book.

DO
- If you're embarrassed about something God knows about you, talk to him about it.
- Write the name of one person you will help secretly. The person won't know it was you, but God will!

PRAY
Thank God that he knows everything about you.

MEMORIZE
O Lord, you have examined my heart and know everything about me. Psalm 139:1

WHAT'S THE POINT?
Even though Mrs. Yoshida would never know that Tony was the one bringing the paper to her door, Tony knew that God paid attention to everything he did. Bringing her newspaper to the door was one small step in the right direction. *ML*

FEBRUARY 23
Bad News

"Mom and I have something to talk to you kids about," Dad said in a serious voice after they had finished eating dinner. "Your mom and I love each other," his dad started, "but for a long time we've had trouble getting along. We've decided we need to separate for a while to give ourselves time to work through some problems. This will mean I'll be moving into an apartment on the other side of town."

Jeremiah and his sister, Jamie, were stunned. Jamie began to cry. Jeremiah wanted to scream. He pushed away from the table and stomped up to his room.

READ
Psalm 139:16-17. God knew everything that would happen to us—good and bad—before we were even born. God made plans to help us. No one could ever count how many times a day God thinks of us. We can take comfort in his love.

THINK
- How does it feel to realize that God knows what's going to happen next and he already has a plan to help you?
- What would you like God's plan for you to include?
- Finish the story, showing how the verses could make a difference for Jeremiah and Jamie. Then read the possible ending at the back of the book.

DO
- With your family, take turns remembering how God helped you through hard situations.
- Write down a bad situation you're facing. Write Psalm 139:16 below it. Ask God to help you trust him.

PRAY
Ask God to help you learn and grow from all of the situations that happen in your life.

MEMORIZE
You saw me before I was born. Every day of my life was recorded in your book. Every moment was laid out before a single day had passed. Psalm 139:16

WHAT'S THE POINT?
Jeremiah's dad knew that God knows and cares about everything that will ever happen to us. God will stay with us every step of the way. *ML*

FEBRUARY 24
A Forever Home

James had moved three times by the second grade. At dinner one night, his dad said they would be moving again. "I don't want to move," James shouted, throwing down his fork. "I'm tired of having to make new friends all the time."

"I don't like to move either, Son," Dad said. "But if I turn this job down, I may not be able to find another one."

"How soon will we be moving?" James asked.

"As soon as school is over this year," Mom said.

"You mean I won't even get to stay here for the summer?" James couldn't hold back the tears anymore. "I don't want to go!" he yelled, storming out of the room.

READ
Psalm 23:6. God's goodness and love are with us wherever we go. Someday we will have a forever home in heaven.

THINK
- Think of a place you could go where you wouldn't have God's goodness and love. (Can't think of any now? You're right!)
- What do you look forward to about going to heaven someday?
- Finish the story, showing how the verse could comfort and encourage James. Then read the possible ending at the back of the book.

DO
- Picture a place where you go in your life that is hard for you—maybe it's hard to go to recess because there's a bully on the playground. Maybe it's hard to go to the doctor's office. Think of God there with you, loving you.
- What do you think God's house (heaven) will look like? Draw a picture of it.

PRAY
Thank God for making a place for you in his house forever.

MEMORIZE
Surely your goodness and unfailing love will pursue me all the days of my life, and I will live in the house of the LORD forever. Psalm 23:6

WHAT'S THE POINT?
James's dad knew that we can never get away from God's love. And we will get to live with him forever someday. *ML*

FEBRUARY 25
Red Hair like Dad's

Allison showed her mom the class assignment. "I'm supposed to draw a family tree and put pictures of my relatives on it. Can you help me?"

"I'd love to," her mom replied. "Let's get started after dinner."

Her mom brought a box of photographs to the kitchen table after they finished eating. "This is my grandpa." Allison's mom pointed to one picture. "He died before you were born. I sure loved him."

Allison came across a picture of her own dad when he was about ten years old. "Look how much I look like Dad! My nose is long like his. And I have red hair like his."

"I could tell your mouth looked like mine right when you were born," said Mom.

Allison grinned and made fish lips.

Mom tickled the fish lips. "You were Dad's and my wonderful surprise," she said.

Allison thought that over. "Was I a surprise to God like I was to you and Dad?"

READ
Psalm 139:13-14. "Complex" means complicated. God designed us before we were born. He made all our complicated parts work together.

THINK
- What do you imagine God thought about when he was designing you before you were born?
- Do you look like someone in your family?
- Make up an ending for the story, showing how Allison could apply the verses. Then read the possible ending at the back of the book.

DO
- Draw yourself. Include the color of your skin, eyes, and hair. Show the shape of your nose and mouth. Show how tall you are.
- Make up a rap or rhyme, telling God his workmanship (what he makes) is wonderful.

PRAY
Thank God for the way he designed you. You are his wonderful work!

MEMORIZE
Thank you for making me so wonderfully complex! Your workmanship is marvelous—how well I know it. Psalm 139:14

WHAT'S THE POINT?
Allison saw that God made her before she was born and God's works are great.
ML

FEBRUARY 26
Scrub a Tub

Truman loved Saturdays, except for chores. Every week he was responsible for cleaning the bathroom. "Truman, no television until the bathroom is done," his mom reminded him. "I need to run to the store. I'll be back in a little bit. Please get started on your chores so we can have the rest of the day to do fun stuff." She kissed him lightly on his head.

He pulled the covers over his head as she left. *Why do I always have to clean the bathroom?*

Truman watched his mom walk out the front door. He went downstairs, poured a bowl of cereal, and turned on the TV. *I'll just watch for a few minutes while I eat,* he thought.

READ
John 15:9-11. Jesus is talking in these verses. He says we find joy when we obey God. One of God's commands is to obey our parents.

THINK
- Why do you think Jesus obeyed his Father, God, when he lived on earth?
- Why do you think our joy will overflow when we obey God?
- Finish the story, showing how Truman might act once he understands these verses. Then read the possible ending at the back of the book.

DO
Remember a time when you disobeyed your mom or dad. Draw a face to show how you felt before you got caught. Draw a face to show how you felt after you got caught. If you didn't get caught, how do you feel now?

PRAY
Ask God to help you obey his commandments.

MEMORIZE
When you obey my commandments, you remain in my love, just as I obey my Father's commandments and remain in his love. John 15:10

WHAT'S THE POINT?
Although Truman didn't enjoy doing chores, he knew God would be pleased if he obeyed. *BA*

FEBRUARY 27
But I'm the Best!

Jessica's soccer team looked up to her because she scored goals in every game. Alyssa wasn't as good a player.

"Alyssa, I want you to take Jessica's spot in Friday's game," their coach said at practice. Everyone was surprised, especially Jessica. At the end of practice, Jessica said, "Coach, why aren't you playing me on Friday? No one else scores like I do."

"Jessica, you're right. But I want to give Alyssa a chance to shine."

"But I'm the best," Jessica said.

"I'd like you to take on the job of cheering for the team," he told Jessica.

Jessica walked away feeling angry. When game day came, she sat quietly on the bench. If she couldn't play, she wasn't going to cheer, either.

READ
Romans 12:3. God wants us to see ourselves honestly and not be prideful or stuck up.

THINK
- What's wrong with being stuck up?
- How could remembering that your good points come from God help you not be stuck up?
- Finish the story, showing how Jessica could find wisdom in today's verse. Then read the possible ending at the back of the book.

DO
- Write down something you are good at doing. Do you think you see it honestly or act stuck-up about it?
- Thank God for what you're good at—that gift came from him. Ask him to help you not to be proud.

PRAY
Thank God for the abilities he has given you. Ask him to help you see yourself honestly so that you don't think too highly—or too poorly—of yourself.

MEMORIZE
Don't think you are better than you really are. Be honest in your evaluation of yourselves, measuring yourselves by the faith God has given us. Romans 12:3

WHAT'S THE POINT?
Jessica realized that she wasn't the only one important to her team. She could be pleased with her abilities but not stuck-up about them. *ML*

FEBRUARY 28
Most Improved Player

Diego was unhappy. He had worked hard during his Christian school's baseball season. He wasn't the best player, but he never missed a practice, and he played his heart out—when he got to play. But that wasn't very often.

Tonight was the end-of-season party. Coach Mike had the whole team over for pizza. One by one, he called the boys up and pointed out their accomplishments.

"Xavier gets the 'Hardest Working Player' award," Coach Mike said, smiling at Xavier. "We all owe Xavier a big thanks."

Xavier beamed as Coach Mike handed him a trophy. Diego sunk low in the couch. *I doubt the coach even remembers any plays I made,* he thought. *Xavier earned a trophy for memorizing all the Bible verses this year too.*

READ
Zephaniah 3:17. This verse tells us that God thinks we're pretty cool. God rejoices over us; that means we give him joy.

THINK

- When would it feel good to think of God delighting in you?
- How could God's joy in you make a difference in how you act?
- Finish the story, showing how the verse could affect Diego. Then read the possible ending at the back of the book.

DO
- Make up a line or two of a joyful song that God might be singing over you.

PRAY
Ask God what he likes about you.

MEMORIZE
The LORD your God is living among you. He is a mighty savior. He will take delight in you with gladness. With his love, he will calm all your fears. He will rejoice over you with joyful songs. Zephaniah 3:17

WHAT'S THE POINT?
It feels good when someone delights in us. Diego didn't realize he was an important part of the team until the coach told him how much he mattered to them. The verse reminds us that we give God joy. *ML*

MARCH 1
I Want to Be Alone

Lily's family lived in a tiny city apartment, so she didn't have much time alone. Sometimes she daydreamed about being an only child with her own bedroom and a huge backyard.

One summer evening her mom said, "Uncle Scott and Aunt Stephanie called. They want you to spend a few weeks with them."

Two weeks without my little sister and brother around? Lily thought. She grinned at her mom. "When can they pick me up?"

For a week at her aunt's and uncle's house, Lily watched TV and played video games, hiked with Uncle Scott, and went to the pool with Aunt Stephanie. On Saturday, her mom called. "Lily, I have to go on a business trip. Uncle Scott and Aunt Stephanie invited your brother and sister to stay with them too. What do you think about that?"

READ

Ecclesiastes 4:9-10. It can be good to be alone sometimes, but being together can bring good things too. When people are together, they can get more done and help each other.

THINK

- Why do you think God doesn't want us to be alone all the time?
- How has God used people to help you do something better?
- Finish the story, showing what difference the verses could make for Lily. Then read the possible ending at the back of the book.

DO

- Write down an activity that might be easier to do or be more fun to do with someone else.
- Do the activity with someone. Tell the person you're glad to be able to do it with him or her.

PRAY

Tell God "thanks" for the people he gives you to be with. Ask God to teach you to enjoy both time alone and time with others.

MEMORIZE

Two people are better off than one, for they can help each other succeed. Ecclesiastes 4:9

WHAT'S THE POINT?

Lily realized that some activities are more fun when shared with others. God gives us people to enjoy. Several people can be better than one. *JP*

MARCH 2
Throw, Give, and Keep

"Lamar, I need your help." His dad's voice floated through the open bedroom window.

It was time to clean the garage. Since Lamar's dad learned he had to move for his job, they'd been getting the house ready to sell. It was fun to paint over scuff marks, and running the hedge trimmer while his dad watched was a blast. But cleaning the garage was different. It would take all day, and Lamar wanted to play basketball with his friends.

His dad called again. "Come on, Son. Your job for today is to decide what to do with your old things."

Lamar went to the garage and looked at the jumble of sports equipment and bikes he'd outgrown. Most had been Christmas or birthday gifts. Some of them brought back good memories. How would he sort through the mess?

READ
Genesis 2:8-9, 15. God gave the very first human being, Adam, the job of caring for his home. We have the same job of taking care of what we own.

THINK
- Why do you think God didn't just take care of Adam's home for him?
- What things has God given you to take care of? Think of things you use and own.
- Finish the story, showing how the verses could affect Lamar's feelings about tackling a big project. Then read the possible ending at the back of the book.

DO
- Choose a time to sort through some of your "stuff" with a family member. Decide what to throw away, what to give away, and where to store useful things or things with special memories.

PRAY
Ask God to help you with the organization project you chose.

MEMORIZE
The LORD God placed the man in the Garden of Eden to tend and watch over it.
Genesis 2:15

WHAT'S THE POINT?
Lamar knew it was his job to take care of his things. Beginning with Adam, God knew it would be good for us to learn to be responsible. God expects us to care for our things, even if it means the best thing to do is to give some of them away. *JP*

MARCH 3
Quit Being So Mean!

Francesca waited for her little brother and sister. Why hadn't they come out of school yet? Francesca wondered if they were in trouble with their teachers and that's why they were taking so long.

Just then Carmela and Esteban came out. "Why are you late?" Francesca asked.

"The teacher helped me pack the present I made for Mom." Esteban patted his backpack. "Too bad Carmela didn't make her something."

"What dumb thing did you make today?" Carmela shot back.

Esteban pushed Carmela. "It's not dumb. Mom likes my presents."

"No, she doesn't," Carmela taunted. "She's just pretending."

Francesca grabbed their hands. "Quit being so mean to each other!" She marched them home. "Go to your rooms."

"Can't we have a snack?" they wailed. "We're hungry."

Francesca crossed her arms and glared. What would help them stop picking on each other?

READ
Hebrews 13:1. God wants us to love our family members, who will be our family the rest of our lives.

THINK
- What do you think it means to love someone like a brother or sister?
- Why do you think God wants us to love others and treat each other well?
- Finish the story, showing how the verse can make a difference for Francesca and her family. Then read the possible ending at the back of the book.

DO
- Write down ways your family members still show love to you when you do something wrong.
- Plan to show love to a family member by doing a chore (like clearing the table or making the bed) for him or her this week.

PRAY
Ask God to help you have his kind of love for your family members.

MEMORIZE
Keep on loving each other as brothers and sisters. Hebrews 13:1

WHAT'S THE POINT?
Francesca realized she could help Esteban and Carmela learn how to love each other. God loves his children no matter what, and he wants us to love our family the same way. *JP*

MARCH 4
The Easter Story Again!

When Mom began to talk, Rebecca stifled a yawn. Mom was so serious when she got out the dye kit and hard-boiled eggs. "We celebrate Easter because Jesus loves us so much that he died on the cross and came back to life three days later. Easter eggs are a symbol of new life in Jesus," she began to explain.

Rebecca and her brother, Hunter, knew the speech practically by heart. Mom said the same thing every year before they dyed Easter eggs. Didn't Mom realize how many times they'd heard the story? Why didn't she skip it this year and just let them have fun decorating the eggs? Rebecca rolled her eyes and looked at Hunter.

But he didn't look bored. Instead, he said, "Oh, I get it. The eggs remind us that Jesus 'hatched' new life for us when he died and came back to life."

Rebecca felt crabby. *Why wasn't Hunter going along with her and acting bored about the story?* she wondered.

READ
Deuteronomy 6:5-7. God wants parents to teach their children about him wherever or whenever they can: at home or away from home, morning and evening.

THINK
- Why do you think God wants parents to tell their children about him so often?
- On a piece of paper, write down ways your family helps you learn about God. Here are some ways to choose from: praying, talking about him, sending you to Sunday school or kids club, reading the Bible, reading Bible storybooks.
- Finish the story, showing how the verses could affect Rebecca's attitude about Bible teaching. Then read the possible ending at the back of the book.

DO
- Ask what your family members hope you learn about God from what they teach you.
- Write one way you could pay better attention when they teach you about God.

PRAY
Ask God to teach you about him through your family.

MEMORIZE
Commit yourselves wholeheartedly to these commands that I am giving you today. Repeat them again and again to your children. Deuteronomy 6:6-7

WHAT'S THE POINT?
Rebecca and Hunter understood the Easter story more each time they heard it. God knows we understand ideas we hear over and over. No wonder God wants parents to tell their children about him often. *JP*

MARCH 5
The Shared Birthday

Chase's grandparents always made his birthday special. Grandma baked a cake. Grandpa took a picture of Chase with his parents before the celebration began.

But last year on his birthday, his baby brother, Thad, was born. "You'll have the same birthday!" Grandpa exclaimed.

They celebrated Chase's birthday at the hospital, complete with Grandma's cake and a new baby in the photograph. But to Chase, it all felt strange.

Now, almost one year later, his grandparents were taking him shopping for Thad's present. But Chase didn't want to go. He wanted to celebrate his birthday like they used to, before Thad was born.

READ
Genesis 21:5-8. Abraham and Sarah were excited when their only son, Isaac, was old enough to eat solid food. They celebrated the changes that showed Isaac was growing up. Read Ecclesiastes 3:1. Just as seasons change, we change and grow, and so do our families.

THINK
- How did Abraham and Sarah celebrate Isaac's growth?
- What ideas does this give you about how to celebrate good changes in your family?
- Make up an ending for the story, showing how the verses could make a difference in Chase's feelings. Then read the possible ending at the back of the book.

DO
- Think of a recent change that's been good for your family.
- To celebrate the change, draw a picture or cartoon to post where your family can enjoy it. If the change doesn't feel good to you, write down the name of someone you will talk to about it.

PRAY
Ask God to help you trust him when things change.

MEMORIZE
For everything there is a season, a time for every activity under heaven. Ecclesiastes 3:1

WHAT'S THE POINT?
The pictures showed Chase that even he hadn't stayed the same. God created us to change and grow. We can trust him when things change around us too. *JP*

MARCH 6
Company for Supper

Mariah was grumpy. Tonight Mrs. Jones was coming for supper. Even though Mom had been laid off from the factory and her new job as a waitress didn't pay much, she still invited neighbors over for supper most nights. When Mariah complained, Mom said, "We have enough to eat. God always provides."

Her mom was right. They had enough. But there weren't many leftovers when the company went home, and Mariah was tired of snacking on peanut butter and jelly sandwiches every afternoon.

After school, Mariah walked home and unlocked the apartment. She took the peanut butter from the cupboard. In the refrigerator, she spotted a dish of chocolate pudding. *That would taste really good,* she thought. *But Mom might be saving it for Mrs. Jones.*

She pulled out the pudding, set it on the counter, and stared at it.

READ
1 Kings 17:7-16 and Philippians 4:19. God's prophet Elijah was in a dry land. The crops that were planted were dying, and people were hungry. But Elijah promised that God would provide for a widow (a woman whose husband had died) if she and her son shared their food with him. When the woman trusted God, he provided.

THINK
- How did Elijah's suggestion help the woman learn to trust God?
- How can the story of Elijah and the widow help you trust God too?
- Imagine an ending for Mariah's story, showing how the verses could give her wisdom. Then read the possible ending at the back of the book.

DO
- Plan something that reminds you to trust God more. For example, write out the memory verse and post it in your room.
- Talk to your mom or dad about gathering food or clothing for people who are in need.

PRAY
Ask God to teach you to trust him to provide what you need.

MEMORIZE
This same God who takes care of me will supply all your needs from his glorious riches, which have been given to us in Christ Jesus. Philippians 4:19

WHAT'S THE POINT?
Mariah began to trust God more when she saw him provide through Mrs. Jones. God wants us to trust him to meet our needs so we can share what he gives us with others. *JP*

MARCH 7
Worried Sick

Life was hard when Miguel's dad was in the hospital. They were so happy the day Papá came home. But then Miguel overheard his parents talking.

"After we pay the hospital bills, there's no money left to pay on the house until you can work again," Mamá said.

Papá answered, "Then we'll find a smaller place to live."

How could they do that? Miguel wondered. Miguel and his three brothers were already crammed together in their bedroom. The family barely squeezed around the table at meals. After supper, they tripped over each other in the living room when they watched TV.

Miguel worried all day until his stomach hurt, then he went and told Mamá he didn't feel good. She sent him to bed early and tucked him in. "Is something wrong, Son?"

He started to cry. "Are we going to have to move?"

READ
2 Kings 4:1-7 and Isaiah 58:9. A woman begged Elisha for help so her sons could stay with her. God did more than give her what she needed. Through Elisha, he showed her how she and her sons could earn what they needed to live on.

THINK
▪ What do you think the woman learned about asking for help?
▪ What do you think the woman learned about worrying?
▪ Finish the story, showing how the verses can help Miguel give his troubles to God. Then read the possible ending at the back of the book.

DO
▪ Name a family problem you worry about. Ask family members to help you understand more and worry less.
▪ Talk with family members about who your family can ask for help. Don't forget God!

PRAY
Ask God to help you trust him with the problem you thought of.

MEMORIZE
When you call, the LORD will answer. "Yes, I am here," he will quickly reply. Isaiah 58:9

WHAT'S THE POINT?
Miguel learned that when you ask God for help, just as his parents and the woman in the Bible did, God hears your prayers. God sends people to help people in need. *JP*

MARCH 8
The Trouble with Teasing

Rachel and her cousin Melanie spent the afternoon talking about their favorite pastime—teasing Melanie's little sister, Molly.

Rachel wanted to tell scary stories so Molly would be afraid of the dark. Melanie thought they should hide Molly's blankie and watch her go bonkers looking for it. In the end, they agreed to play princesses and make Molly stand in the corner until she threw a tantrum. Then they would tattle and watch Aunt Heather scold her.

They called Molly to the playroom. "Do you want to play princesses with us?" Melanie's voice was super sweet.

Molly beamed, and her eyes widened. "Can I choose my own name?"

"Uh-huh." Rachel nodded.

Molly took Rachel's hand. "Call me Princess Rachel. I want to be just like you."

READ
Psalm 34:14. God wants what's best for us. He wants us to give up doing wrong. He tells us three things to do instead: do good, look for peace, and keep peace.

THINK
- If someone feels hurt, do you think teasing is harmless and fun? Or is it evil?
- How do *you* feel when you're teased?
- Finish the story, showing how Rachel could make the teaching in this verse practical in her life. Then read the possible ending at the back of the book.

DO
- Draw a speech balloon. Write what you said the last time you were mean or teased someone in your family.
- Design a bumper sticker that shows a way you will follow Psalm 34:14 this week with someone you're tempted to tease.

PRAY
Ask God to show you how your behavior can sometimes hurt others. Ask him to give you a heart that loves your family and seeks peace.

MEMORIZE
Turn away from evil and do good. Search for peace, and work to maintain it. Psalm 34:14

WHAT'S THE POINT?
Rachel remembered how hurtful teasing was. So she decided not to do it and made peace with her younger cousin instead. *JP*

MARCH 9
Grandpa's Hobo

As soon as Dad finished praying for dinner, Shanise begged, "Tell me about Grandpa's hobo."

"That old story again?" Dad chuckled. He told how Grandpa, back when he was a little boy, met a hobo on the way to school. Hobos had nowhere to live. The old hobo's dirty clothes were patched. His face was thin. He hadn't eaten for a long time. "Suddenly Grandpa sensed God reminding him of the yummy cornbread that he, Grandpa, had to eat that morning, and the steaming catfish and hush puppies the night before. Grandpa handed over everything in his lunch pail to the old man.

"'Thank you, my boy,' said the old hobo. 'You're God's answer to my prayers.' And that was plenty for Grandpa to chew on all day."

Shanise loved the story, but something puzzled her. "If Grandpa was a boy, you weren't born yet, right?" Her dad nodded. "Then how do you know the story?"

Dad grinned. "Whenever I complained about meals, my dad—your grandpa—would tell the story and say, 'Maybe we should give your portion to somebody who's really hungry.' Then, instead of complaining, I thanked God for giving me something to eat. Now I'm passing the story on to you."

After supper, Shanise repeated the hobo story to herself, but she couldn't remember all the parts.

READ
Psalm 78:2-4, 7. God wants grown-ups to tell children stories about what God has done. It's one way of passing on God's truth so children will follow God too.

THINK
- Why do you think telling stories is a good way to let kids know what God has done?
- What do your family's stories show about what God has done for your family?
- Finish the story, showing how these verses could help Shanise value her grandpa's stories. Then read the possible ending at the back of the book.

DO
- Ask family members to tell you more family stories. Talk about how they show truth about God.

PRAY
Thank God for your family's stories.

MEMORIZE
We will not hide these truths from our children; we will tell the next generation about the glorious deeds of the LORD, about his power and his mighty wonders. Psalm 78:4

WHAT'S THE POINT?
Grandpa's story taught Shanise and her dad to be thankful for what God provided. Family stories are a way to pass on truths about God. *JP*

MARCH 10
Surprising Gifts

Sophie's coat zipper wouldn't budge. "Mom, could you help me?"

Her mother called back, "Wait a minute. I'm hooking up Brian's feeding tube."

"But if I don't walk Muffy now, she'll mess on the floor." She grabbed Muffy's leash and stomped outside, her jacket flopping open. Mom was never around to help her anymore. Her sick little brother, Brian, took almost all of Mom's time.

When her parents told Sophie a baby was coming, they said children were a gift from God. "You're a gift, Sophie, and so is the new baby." Even after the doctors said Brian would never get well, her parents still called him a gift from God.

Weren't gifts something you *received*? But usually Brian *took* everyone's time and attention away from her. She couldn't understand why her parents thought he was a gift. Mostly, he was a lot of work.

READ
Psalm 127:3. God thinks of children as good prizes for parents! Children are valuable. They are given by God.

THINK
- Do you think God means some or all children are gifts?
- Since all children are gifts, what does God think about you? What does that mean for you?
- Make up an ending for the story, showing how the verse could affect Sophie. Then read the possible ending at the back of the book.

DO
- Ask your family why they think you're a gift.
- When is it hard for you to believe a brother or sister is a gift? Think of one way that your brother or sister is special and tell him or her.

PRAY
Ask God to show you how to treat your family members as gifts.

MEMORIZE
Children are a gift from the LORD; they are a reward from him. Psalm 127:3

WHAT'S THE POINT?
Caring for Muffy showed Sophie how someone who took up a lot of time could also be someone she loved. That helped her be willing to consider how her brother could be a gift from God. It's okay to change your mind a little bit at a time. *JP*

MARCH 11
Lost Glasses

Julian couldn't find his new glasses. He thought he'd left them on the bathroom counter. But when he looked for them later in the afternoon, they weren't there.

Only a month ago, his mom had taken him to the eye doctor to pick out new frames. The extra-tough ones were more expensive, but his mom bought them anyway. "You play hard, Julian. You need glasses that can keep up with you. Just keep track of them, Son."

Now they were gone. Julian prayed a quick prayer, asking God to help him find them. He was throwing cushions off the couch in the living room when his little brother, Barrett, walked in. Barrett stared. "Dude. What are you doing?"

"I lost my glasses."

Barrett grinned. "They're on the nightstand by your bed."

"Thanks, Bro. You're a lifesaver." He headed for the door and then stopped. "You know, I just prayed to God for help right before you walked in."

"So?" Barrett shrugged.

READ
Psalm 143:5. When we stop and think about the great things that God has done, we get to know him better and we trust him more.

THINK
- What is something God has done that you should stop and think about? It can be something from the Bible or from your own life.
- How does what happened tell you more about God?
- Finish the story, showing how Julian and Barrett might apply the example of this verse. Then read the possible ending at the back of the book.

DO
- List or tell someone three ways God has helped you or someone else.
- Choose a time each day to think about what good things God has done in the day.

PRAY
Thank God for what he does in your life each day.

MEMORIZE
I remember the days of old. I ponder all your great works and think about what you have done. Psalm 143:5

WHAT'S THE POINT?
Julian took time to stop and think about how he'd prayed and God had answered. That helped him see God's care for him. When we stop and think about God, we see him at work and can tell others what he's done. *JP*

MARCH 12
Too Many Rules

Learning to cook was supposed to be fun, but ever since Caroline's mother started giving her cooking lessons, Caroline wasn't so sure. There were too many rules.

Last week it was, "Turn the pot handles to the back of the stove so your little brothers can't reach them." This morning when Caroline reached for a pan, her mom said, "Always use a pot holder to pick up pans in case they're hot." And now while her mom sliced potatoes into the frying pan, she added, "Never drop a sharp knife into soapy water, Caroline. You could cut your hand feeling around for it."

Caroline was about to complain when her youngest brother began to cry. Mom put down the knife. "Would you wash dishes until I come back?" She rushed out of the room.

Caroline had just gotten her hands wet when she noticed the frying pan handle hanging over the front of the stove. The pan was full of hot fried potatoes, but it would be a bother to dry her hands, find a pot holder, and push the handle toward the back of the stove. It could wait until the dishes were done.

READ
Proverbs 1:8-9. These verses say two rewards come to kids who learn from their parents. *Grace* has to do with gaining approval and good qualities. *Honor* has to do with gaining respect and credit.

THINK

- Why is it important to follow rules right away?
- Think of something God could help you learn from following a family rule.
- Finish the story, showing how Caroline could find wisdom in the verses. Then read the possible ending at the back of the book.

DO
- Make a list of three important rules your family has. Circle one that is hard for you to follow.
- Talk with someone about how following the rules you wrote could lead to rewards in the future, even when you are grown up.

PRAY
Ask God to help you do better at following one family rule that is hard for you.

MEMORIZE
My child, listen when your father corrects you. Don't neglect your mother's instruction. Proverbs 1:8

WHAT'S THE POINT?
Caroline followed the rule because she cared about her brothers. Their safety was her reward. Her mother can trust her more too, as she sees that Caroline is willing to follow her instruction. God is pleased when our obedience honors other people. *JP*

MARCH 13
Double-Checking the Doors

"Ryan, do you remember what I said about closing the car doors?"

Dad's voice interrupted Ryan's daydream. "Sorry, Dad. I guess I wasn't paying attention."

"I know you think working on the car is boring." Dad tousled Ryan's hair. "But we're almost done. Before we leave, I see a problem with the door you shut."

Ryan looked. "I see a piece of seat belt sticking out."

"Yes, and it's keeping the door from shutting completely. See how the dome light is still on?" Ryan nodded.

"And what's bad about the dome light staying on?"

"I can't remember," Ryan admitted.

"Okay," Dad said. "Are you ready to pay attention?" Ryan nodded. "If the dome light stays on, it runs the battery down. That wastes energy, and sometimes the car won't start. It's always a good idea to double-check the door and make sure it's latched. Give it a try."

Ryan adjusted the seat belt and closed the door. "It's shut," he announced.

"Good job. You can go play."

Ryan went inside for an apple from the fridge and went back outside. Halfway up the ladder to the tree house, he wondered if he'd shut the refrigerator door.

READ
Proverbs 4:1. Learning good judgment has to do with common sense or the ability to make good decisions.

THINK
- Why does God say we should listen to our parents when they correct us?
- Why does your mom or dad correct you? Why should you pay attention?
- Imagine an ending for this story, showing how Ryan could follow the teaching in the verse. Then read the possible ending at the back of the book.

DO
- Write down a few things that help you pay attention when your parents correct you.
- Even grown-ups get corrected—by their bosses, family members, the police, or even God. Ask grown-ups you know what they do to pay attention when they're corrected.

PRAY
Ask God to help you pay attention the next time someone corrects you.

MEMORIZE
My children, listen when your father corrects you. Pay attention and learn good judgment. Proverbs 4:1

WHAT'S THE POINT?
Ryan's dad corrected him to help him learn why double checking is important. Ryan gained good judgment when he paid attention. He was able to apply what he learned to a different situation. *JP*

MARCH 14
A Big Mouth?

Bianca couldn't believe her twin brother had such a big mouth. Last night, Dominic had promised not to tell anyone that she wanted to try out for the school play. First, Bianca wanted to ask her teacher if it was okay for fourth graders to try out. But in the lunch line today, Dominic's friend Chad said, "Bianca, so far you're the only fourth grader trying out!"

Bianca was so angry she couldn't eat a thing. Instead, she imagined what she would say to Dominic on the playground. "You promised you wouldn't tell! You are such a loser." Then she would stomp off and never talk to him again.

Bianca left the lunchroom and hurried outside. She spotted Dominic and started across the playground. His back was toward her. She stopped right behind him and poked him a couple of times in the shoulder.

READ
Proverbs 15:1. This verse tells us that kind words calm people down, while mean words stir up anger.

THINK
- Think of a time when you were so angry you lost your temper. Did your anger make things better or worse? Why?
- What other way of responding is given in Proverbs 15:1? If you had responded this other way, would it have made things better or worse? Why?
- Finish the story, showing how Bianca might get a good idea from this verse. Then read the possible ending at the back of the book.

DO
- Name two situations when it is hard for you to control your temper.
- Talk to someone in your family about things you imagine saying when you are angry. Role-play other responses that follow Proverbs 15:1.

PRAY
Ask God to show you new ways to respond when you get angry.

MEMORIZE
A gentle answer deflects anger, but harsh words make tempers flare. Proverbs 15:1

WHAT'S THE POINT?
To avoid a fight, Bianca asked a question calmly instead of using angry words. The Bible tells us it's better to use gentle words than mean ones. *JP*

MARCH 15
She's My Mom

"Have a good time at Pioneer Club." Shao's mother gave him a hug. "Grandmother and I will see you at the awards ceremony."

Shao's heart sank. He didn't want his mother to come. She had a strong accent, and Grandmother didn't speak English. Besides, they were going to wear their embroidered Chinese jackets. Would the other kids stare at them and point? Would they tease him because of the way they dressed?

When Mother and Grandmother arrived, Shao tried to act as if he didn't know them. But the club leader went right up to them. "We have a few minutes before awards. Would you tell us about the beautiful jackets you're wearing?" he said.

Shao stared at the floor when his mother moved to the front of the room. Everyone was quiet when she explained how she had embroidered the jacket in China.

Shao glanced up when the kid beside him raised his hand and said, "I can't believe you did all that yourself."

"Could you tell us more about China sometime?" someone asked.

Mother looked at Shao. "Do you want me to?" she seemed to say.

READ
Proverbs 17:6. This verse says children can be as proud of their parents as grandparents are of their grandchildren.

THINK
- Why do you think God wants us to be proud of our parents?
- When are you proud of your mom or dad? Why are you proud? How do you let him or her know?
- Make up an ending for the story, showing how the verse could affect Shao. Then read the possible ending at the back of the book.

DO
- Make a card expressing to your dad or mom at least one reason you're proud of him or her.
- Write the name of someone you can talk to if you don't feel proud of your dad or mom.

PRAY
Thank God for the things about your mom or dad that you're proud of.

MEMORIZE
Grandchildren are the crowning glory of the aged; parents are the pride of their children.
Proverbs 17:6

WHAT'S THE POINT?
Shao realized he was proud of his family's culture. God wants us to treat our families with pride and respect. When you show a parent that you're proud of him or her, it will draw you closer together. *JP*

MARCH 16
Sunny's Kittens

Mom and Sabrina were arguing again. They seemed to do that a lot since Dad had to start working extra hours. "You're grounded!" said Mom angrily.

"That's not fair!" yelled Sabrina.

Suddenly the phone rang. "Sabrina, come on over," said Uncle Harlan. "Sunny had her kittens."

Sabrina bolted next door and knelt down beside Sunny's box. The fluffy orange cat was licking one of her kittens. Sabrina watched in amazement as the little creatures tried to stand and walk. They were wobbly!

Uncle Harlan picked up an orange and white one and gently put it in Sabrina's cupped hands. As Sabrina watched it wiggle and mew, she told Uncle Harlan her problems with Mom.

"Sounds like you've both been stressed a lot lately," said Uncle Harlan.

Sabrina thought that over. "Yeah, maybe, but I feel better now."

"Maybe your mom needs to feel better too," Uncle Harlan said.

READ
Proverbs 17:22. Sadness can affect us, and we need times to feel cheerful again.

THINK
- How is feeling cheerful like good medicine? When do people in your family feel sad? What helps them feel cheerful?
- Finish the story, showing how the verse could make a difference for Sabrina and her mom. Then read the possible ending at the back of the book.

DO
- With your family, make a list of good things to say and fun things to do together that can help you feel cheerful.
- Do one of these things this week.

PRAY
Ask God to help you enjoy the time you spend with your family.

MEMORIZE
A cheerful heart is good medicine, but a broken spirit saps a person's strength.
Proverbs 17:22

WHAT'S THE POINT?
Sabrina and her mom discovered that watching the kittens helped them feel better, and that helped their relationship. A cheerful spirit is like good medicine. *BA*

MARCH 17
Fire Escape

"Okay, girls." Dad's voice was serious. "Let's practice our fire escape plan again."

"Dad." Zoe flopped to the floor. "We've done it five times!"

"Prying off the window screen is hard," said Phoebe. "And the escape ladder is scary."

Dad shook his head. "If we have a fire, you'll be glad I trained you so well that you could follow the plan without thinking. Did you know God has given me the job of training you?"

"But, Dad, we won't ever have a fire," Zoe argued. "This practice is a waste of time."

"I hope it is," Dad agreed. "But even if we never need it, I'll have peace of mind."

"What's peace of mind?" Phoebe asked.

"You and Zoe talk it over while I get us something to drink." Dad went to the kitchen.

Phoebe turned to Zoe. "What do you think he means?"

READ
Proverbs 29:17. Discipline has to do with correction, but it also has to do with training.

THINK
- What do you think peace of mind is?
- Why do you think it would give your mom or dad happiness and peace of mind to train you?
- Finish the story, showing how the verse might apply to Zoe and Phoebe. Then read the possible ending at the back of the book.

DO
- Write a code word for something your mom or dad has had you practice often. How does that training help you now?
- Ask a parent how Proverbs 29:17 helps him or her as a parent.

PRAY
Ask God to show your parents how to train you the way he wants them to.

MEMORIZE
Discipline your children, and they will give you peace of mind and will make your heart glad. Proverbs 29:17

WHAT'S THE POINT?
The girls realized the escape plan gave Dad peace of mind because he would know they were prepared. God wants parents to train us to do what is right. Then we will be prepared and our parents will have peace of mind. *JP*

MARCH 18
Worry Stomper

Craig loved his week at Camp Cherith last summer. The guys in his cabin were fun. In Bible Exploration time, their counselor, Chris, called God our worry stomper. "If we give our worries to him," Chris said, "he promises to stomp them out and comfort us."

"Some people talk about 'comfort food,'" Craig said.

"We've got a better way to get comfort, don't we?" Chris said.

By the last day of camp, Craig was tired. His mom had promised to pick him up by one o'clock. At one thirty, the other campers were gone, but he was still waiting.

"If she's not here soon, we'll call." Chris squeezed Craig's shoulder.

"My mom isn't usually late." Craig bit his lip. "Do you think something happened to her? Maybe she had an accident."

Chris knelt down. "You're sounding pretty worried, buddy. In Bible Exploration this week, what did we learn about God and our worries?"

Craig replied, "That he's our worry stomper."

"That's right. So what do you need to do?"

READ
Isaiah 66:13. God is talking in this verse.

THINK
- What would a loving mother do when her child is worried?
- Why do you think God compares himself to a loving mother?
- Finish the story, showing how the verse could remove Craig's worries. Then read the possible ending at the back of the book.

DO
- Picture a time God comforted you. How did he do it?
- Ask family members how they're able to let God stomp out worries and comfort them. Choose a way that you will try next time you're worried.

PRAY
Ask God to comfort you about one worry you have now.

MEMORIZE
I will comfort you there in Jerusalem as a mother comforts her child. Isaiah 66:13

WHAT'S THE POINT?
When Craig prayed, he felt comforted. God wants us to trust him instead of worrying. When we take our worries to God, we focus on him instead of on our situation. God helps us worry less. God is our Comforter. *JP*

MARCH 19
The Arguers

Brodie and Brianna had been arguing all afternoon. First they couldn't agree on what to have for lunch. Then they argued about who had to empty Oreo's litter box. Now they were fighting about which game to play.

"Let's ask Bethany to choose," Brodie suggested.

"Yeah," Brianna agreed. So they found their older sister and asked her to decide.

Bethany closed her book. "Stop. Don't even ask. If I get involved, you'll get mad at me." She shooed them away and found her place in her book again. But Brodie and Brianna's argument got louder and louder. "What should I do, Jesus?" Bethany asked. Then she thought of an idea. She closed her book and went to find her brother and sister.

READ
Matthew 5:9. God thinks working for peace is important. Blessing people who work for peace means giving them favor, approval, and care.

THINK
- How do you think God feels about you arguing with family members? How can you tell?
- Decide which of the following are ways to work for peace: listen to each other, tattle, lie, tell the truth, apologize, tell your side of the story without yelling, get back at each other, blame.
- Finish the story, showing how the verse could give Bethany a solution to her family's problem. Then read the possible ending at the back of the book.

DO
- Think of a disagreement you had with someone in your family. How did you solve it? Write down what you did well or how you could do better next time.
- With your family, create some guidelines for solving disagreements. Pretend to disagree, and then practice the guidelines.

PRAY
Ask God to help you work for peace when you have a disagreement with a family member.

MEMORIZE
God blesses those who work for peace, for they will be called the children of God.
Matthew 5:9

WHAT'S THE POINT?
Bethany gave Brodie and Brianna suggestions about how to solve their argument peacefully. We're not responsible for other people's arguments, but it's okay to make a suggestion—if they want help. But God has put us in charge of looking for peaceful ways to solve *our own* disagreements with family members. *JP*

MARCH 20
Wanted: One Video Game

All Max wanted for his birthday was the latest video game. He hinted to his mom, but since she had married Tom, his new stepdad, she usually chose family activities over video games. "Our family is a gift from God," she said. "We want to spend time together."

His friend Danny helped him make a birthday list. Max wrote down the video game. "But that's the only thing I want."

"What about a new sleeping bag? You're too tall for your old one," Danny reminded him.

"And a waterproof flashlight for campouts." Max finished the list and put it on his mom's pillow.

On his birthday, Max thought about the video game all day. But the present on the table was too big for that. He tore off the paper and found a sleeping bag and a flashlight.

"I know you wanted the video game," Mom explained. "But we're all going camping this summer."

Max was so disappointed, he didn't know what to say.

READ
Matthew 7:9-11. Parents aren't perfect, but they still give good gifts. God is perfect and can be trusted to give perfect gifts.

THINK
- Based on the verses, how willing do you think God is to give you good gifts?
- How much better do you think God's gifts are than a parent's gifts?
- Finish the story, showing how the verses could help Max feel better about his birthday present. Then read the possible ending at the back of the book.

DO
- Thank family members for good gifts they've given you.
- Together, ask God for something you need or want as a family. He may not answer just the way you think he should, but remember he is always ready to give you good gifts.

PRAY
Thank God for being willing to give you good gifts.

MEMORIZE
If you sinful people know how to give good gifts to your children, how much more will your heavenly Father give good gifts to those who ask him. Matthew 7:11

WHAT'S THE POINT?
Max realized that a camping trip was a good gift from his family and that his family was an even better gift from God. God wants us to know that the gifts he gives us are the best. *JP*

MARCH 21
Little Brother

Mason's little brother, Aidan, bugged him all the time. He followed Mason everywhere. He begged Mason to read him a story. And whenever Mason lost his temper and said no, Aidan tattled and got Mason in trouble.

"But, Dad," Mason argued, "he bugs me all the time. I read him a story yesterday. Isn't that enough?"

Dad explained, "To Aidan, yesterday was a long time ago. I know it's tough, Mason, but do you know how much he loves you? He watches everything you do and tells the other day care kids about you. You're his hero."

Mason's voice was angry. "I don't want to be his hero. It's too much work."

Dad looked at him.

"Sorry, Dad," Mason apologized. "But I need a little time alone, without Aidan. Okay?"

"Okay," Dad agreed. "Go outside for a while. Then come back and read to your brother."

READ
John 13:34. Jesus is talking in this verse.

THINK
- How did Jesus show love to people when he lived on earth? How much does he love us?
- How can we show Jesus' kind of love to family members?
- Finish the story, showing how Mason could apply the teaching of this verse. Then read the possible ending at the back of the book.

DO
- Make a list of things you appreciate about each family member.
- With your family, brainstorm ways to show Jesus' kind of love to each other.

PRAY
Ask Jesus to show you how to love others as he loves you.

MEMORIZE
Just as I have loved you, you should love each other. John 13:34

WHAT'S THE POINT?
Mason found a way that would make showing Jesus' kind of love to Aidan easier. *JP*

MARCH 22
Lunch with Gram

"Come on, Ashley," Dad said. "It's time for lunch with Gram."

"Do I have to go?" Ashley pouted.

Dad glanced at his watch. "Yes, and we're running late."

In the car, Ashley fumed. "The nursing home smells funny."

"You're right," Dad said. "Some of the people wear diapers."

Ashley wrinkled her nose. "You're making that up."

"No, honey, it's true," Dad explained. "Sometimes when people get old, their bodies wear out."

"But sometimes the smell is so bad I can hardly swallow."

Dad parked beside the nursing home, and they went inside. "Well, you can wait out here while Gram and I eat lunch." Dad pointed to a chair in the lobby. "What are you going to do, Ash?"

READ
1 Corinthians 13:4, 7. God wants others to show this kind of love to us, and he wants us to show this kind of love to others.

THINK
- Think of a time when you avoided someone in your family. Why did you do it?
- When has someone in your family shown you the kind of love in these verses?
- Finish the story, showing how these verses might change Ashley's attitude. Then read the possible ending at the back of the book.

DO
- Turn 1 Corinthians 13:4 and 7 into a rap or song.
- From these verses, write down two descriptions of love that you will practice.

PRAY
Thank God for loving you no matter how you're acting or what you've done.

MEMORIZE
Love never gives up, never loses faith, is always hopeful, and endures through every circumstance. 1 Corinthians 13:7

WHAT'S THE POINT?
Dad's and Gram's care for Ashley gave her an example of love in action. God wants us to act in loving ways, even when it's hard. *JP*

MARCH 23
Chores on the Farm

Before they moved, Deondre was excited about his parents' dream of owning a vegetable farm. When they finally moved to the farm, life wasn't what Deondre had expected. His chores were hard, and he felt slow and clumsy.

One night he overheard his parents talking after he went to bed. "If it doesn't rain, we're going to lose the corn," his mother said. "That's our big moneymaker. What will we do then?"

"I don't know," his dad replied. "It's too bad Deondre's not old enough to get a job. We could use a paycheck."

Deondre tried to think of a way to help. But what could a kid like him do? Finally, he went to get a drink of water.

His dad was in the hall. "Why are you up so late?"

READ
Galatians 6:2. It says that when we help others through hard times, we are obeying Jesus.

THINK
- Do you think this verse applies to only adults or to kids, too?
- What kinds of problems could family members have that kids could help with?
- Finish the story with your ideas about how Deondre could follow the verse. Then read the possible ending at the back of the book.

DO
- Who in your family is going through a hard time? Write his or her initial on a piece of paper.
- By yourself or with another member of your family, think of a chore to do, a gift to make, or some other way to help him or her. Then do what you thought of.

PRAY
Ask God to help you help the family member you thought of.

MEMORIZE
Share each other's burdens, and in this way obey the law of Christ. Galatians 6:2

WHAT'S THE POINT?
Deondre wanted to help his parents. He learned that doing his chores without complaining helped a lot and that praying was even better. God can show you many ways to share burdens too. *JP*

MARCH 24
The Chalk Line

Daniela stood in the doorway. Yesterday she had cleaned the room she and her sister Mariana shared. Now, thanks to her messy sister, it was trashed again.

"I can't take this." With chalk, she drew a line on the hardwood floor, between the two beds and dressers. She was shoving Mariana's junk on the far side of the line when Mamá called her to supper.

In the kitchen, Daniela sniffed. "Tamales? Yum."

Mariana arranged the silverware and napkins. "That's not where the forks go," Daniela told her sister.

"Daniela, don't order your sister around," Mamá said. "She's the one who suggested tamales for supper because they're your favorite."

"It's okay," Mariana said. "She's bossy sometimes, but I'm messy. She doesn't complain about me, so I won't complain about her, either."

Daniela pictured the chalk line in their bedroom. *Dear God, what should I do?* she prayed.

READ
Ephesians 4:2-3. God wants families to be united—to stand by each other. It's not that we can't ask others to fix mistakes or bad habits, but God wants us to be patient, since we aren't perfect either.

THINK
- How do the people in your family bother you? How do you act when they bother you?
- How closely does the way you act match Ephesians 4:2-3?
- Finish the story, showing how Daniela could offer God's grace to her sister. Then read the possible ending at the back of the book.

DO
- Write a short note thanking someone in your family for being kind and being patient with your faults.

PRAY
Ask God for patience so you can see others' faults and still treat them well.

MEMORIZE
Always be humble and gentle. Be patient with each other, making allowance for each other's faults because of your love. Ephesians 4:2

WHAT'S THE POINT?
When Daniela was bossy and Mariana treated her with love, Daniela wanted to show love too. God is patient even when we do wrong. His love helps us do the same for others. *JP*

MARCH 25
Shrimp and Bigfoot

Kevin dribbled, twisted past his brother Nick, and took his best shot. But the ball bounced off the rim.

Nick whooped. "Why do you try to beat me? You don't have what it takes, Shrimp."

"Don't call me that!" Kevin slammed the ball down. Nick knew how much he hated to be called a shrimp.

Kevin stalked off and found his little brother, Landon. "You wanna get back at Nick for teasing us all the time? You know how his feet are growing so fast?" Landon nodded. "Let's call him Bigfoot when his friends are here this afternoon. It'll be hilarious."

"Do you think it will make Nick stop?" Landon asked.

Kevin thought. Most likely, Nick would tease back or start an argument. "It will make things worse," he admitted.

"Mom says to try giving him a compliment when he teases you," Landon said. "The surprise might make him quit."

"That won't work," Kevin scoffed.

Landon shrugged. "It works with you."

READ
Ephesians 4:29-32. These verses remind us of the power of words. Good words encourage others, while mean words cause hurt.

THINK
- Do you think Nick's teasing was good and encouraging? harsh and hurtful? What makes the difference in how teasing feels?
- How do you feel when you are teased or called names? What do you want to do when it happens?
- Finish the story, showing how these verses could help Kevin convince his brother to stop teasing him. Then read the possible ending at the back of the book.

DO
- Draw some Ts. (Get it? Ts = tease!) By each one, write a reason you might tease people in your family.
- As a family, decide when teasing goes from being fun to being mean. Make guidelines to end hurtful teasing in your home.

PRAY
Ask God to show you how teasing can hurt others.

MEMORIZE
Don't use foul or abusive language. Let everything you say be good and helpful, so that your words will be an encouragement to those who hear them. Ephesians 4:29

WHAT'S THE POINT?
Landon showed Kevin that mean words lead to hurt, but kind words encourage kindness. Our words are powerful, and God wants us to encourage others with them. *JP*

MARCH 26
Under the Bed

Serena looked at the clock. How did her mom and dad expect her to put all her toys away before her favorite TV show began in five minutes? Sometimes her parents were so unreasonable. Then Serena had an idea. If she pushed her toys under her bed and pulled down the spread to hide them, her parents would think she'd obeyed them.

A few minutes later, Serena went to the family room and turned on the TV. As the show began, her mom came in. "Serena, are your toys put away?"

Serena chose her words carefully. "Go take a look. There's not a toy in sight." *That's not really a lie,* she thought, *even if it's hiding the truth.*

"I think I will." When she returned, she hugged Serena. "Thanks for doing what I asked, sweetie. When you obey me, I get a glimpse of the responsible young adult you'll be in a few years. Enjoy your show."

Serena stared at the TV. Her mom would be so disappointed if she knew the truth.

READ
Ephesians 6:1. When we belong to God, we want to do what God wants. God wants us to obey parents or the people who are like parents to us.

THINK
- Why do you think God wants kids to obey their parents? What do you learn by obeying them?
- What would you say to Serena about telling her mother "There's not a toy in sight"?
- Finish the story, showing how this verse could change Serena's outward actions and inside attitude. Then read the possible ending at the back of the book.

DO
- Ask a parent about why he or she wants you to obey.
- If you have times when it's hard to obey, talk to a parent about it and ask for help.

PRAY
Ask God to help you obey right away the next time a parent wants you to do something.

MEMORIZE
Children, obey your parents because you belong to the Lord, for this is the right thing to do. Ephesians 6:1

WHAT'S THE POINT?
Serena realized Mom and Dad gave her guidance and instructions to show her how to become a responsible adult. God wants us to obey our parents so we will learn good ways to live. *JP*

MARCH 27
Fifteen More Minutes

"How can you honor your parents?" When the Pioneer Clubs leader asked that question, Bryce thought he knew the answer—save his dog-walking money and buy them birthday presents.

But other club members had different ideas. "My dad wants me to do my chores without being nagged," Carlos said.

Jim's answer blew Bryce away. "My dad says the best way to honor him and my stepmom is to trust their decisions and obey our family rules."

Bryce thought about his argument with his mom last night when she told him to shut down his video game. "Mom, I just got to the next level. Fifteen more minutes, pleeeeease?"

"The family rule is one hour of video games a night," his mom had reminded him. "And your hour is up."

Mom's face was sad when he'd thrown down the game and stomped away.

READ
Ephesians 6:2-3. Honoring someone means treating that person with respect, as though we think that person is great.

THINK
- What are some ways you could honor your mom or dad?
- Why do you think God wants you to honor your mom or dad?
- Finish the story, showing how Bryce could follow the instruction in today's verses. Then read the possible ending at the back of the book.

DO
- Draw two puffy Hs. In one, write when it is Hard to Honor your mom or dad. In the other, write what could Help.
- Choose one or two ways to honor your mom or dad today: don't talk back; don't complain about the food; do chores without being nagged; ask for advice; or another idea of your own.

PRAY
Talk to God about a time you didn't treat your mom or dad with respect. Ask him to help you do better.

MEMORIZE
Honor your father and mother. Ephesians 6:2

WHAT'S THE POINT?
The way Bryce acts shows his parents how much he respects them. By honoring his parents every day, he also honors God, who gave the commandment. *JP*

MARCH 28
It's Hard Being a Parent

Dad frowned at the broken spokes on Eric's bicycle. "You won't believe what happened," Eric said as he wheeled the bike closer.

"I can guess." Dad's face was red. "You were in a hurry to play catch at the park. How many times have I told you to park it in the bike rack instead of throwing it on the ground?"

"But I didn't—"

"Don't lie to me. I'm not fixing your bike this time!" Dad yanked it away. "Start thinking of ways to earn money to pay the repair shop."

Eric stormed inside. He was sitting on his bedroom floor when Dad came to the door. "Son, I need to talk to you." Eric didn't want to talk to him ever again, but his dad came in and sat down. "A policeman just told me about the teenager who drove his car into the bike rack."

Eric blurted, "See? I wasn't careless, and I wasn't lying!"

READ
Ephesians 6:4. This verse tells parents to teach and discipline their children in ways that please God.

THINK
- Why do you think Eric's dad did what the verse says not to do?
- How could he have followed the verse instead?
- Make up an ending for the story, showing how Eric's dad might apply today's verse. Then read the possible ending at the back of the book.

DO
- Parents are people too. How hard do you think it is for a parent to make good decisions all the time? A little hard? Pretty hard? Really hard?
- Choose what you will do the next time your mom or dad makes a mistake. Does it help to know that parents aren't perfect and have to answer to God?

PRAY
Ask God to give your mom or dad wisdom and patience.

MEMORIZE
Fathers, do not provoke your children to anger by the way you treat them. Rather, bring them up with the discipline and instruction that comes from the Lord. Ephesians 6:4

WHAT'S THE POINT?
Eric could see that his dad wanted to follow God's commands to parents. When Eric remembered how his dad usually responded, he forgave him. We please God when we treat our parents in the same way God wants them to treat us. *JP*

MARCH 29
I Sorry

"Why do we have to babysit Ava while Mom and Aunt Alice visit Grandma?" Trudi sat on the front step beside her dad. "Since Ava's been here, she's crashed the computer and flushed the LEGOs down the toilet."

"That's a toddler for you." Dad glanced at his watch. "She's been napping for a while. Would you check on her?"

Trudi peeked into the bedroom, and her heart skipped a beat. The little girl wasn't there. When she heard a crash from the bathroom, she ran and opened the door. Ava held up pink-streaked hands.

Trudi stared. The fingernail polish she'd bought yesterday lay tipped over at Ava's feet. Bright pink polish puddled on the floor. Trudi burst out, "Ava, you are so naughty!"

Ava burst into tears. "I sorry!"

READ
Colossians 3:13. When we forgive people, it doesn't mean we say what the other person did was okay. It means we choose to let go of our anger and let go of wanting to get back at the person. We can do this because God forgives us for all the sins (wrongs) we do.

THINK
- When is it hard to forgive family members? How can Colossians 3:13 help you forgive?
- Think of a time when you didn't forgive someone. Did it affect your relationship with that person? How?
- Finish the story, showing how Trudi could let the Lord help her forgive Ava. Then read the possible ending at the back of the book.

DO
- What does Jesus do when you ask for forgiveness? Ignore you? Forgive you?
- When you pray to God for forgiveness, write down your requests. Look at the list when you're asked to forgive others.

PRAY
Thank Jesus for forgiving you, and ask him to show you how to forgive others.

MEMORIZE
Remember, the Lord forgave you, so you must forgive others. Colossians 3:13

WHAT'S THE POINT?
Trudi's memory of her mother's forgiveness helped her to forgive Ava. We learn to forgive by being forgiven by people and by God. *JP*

MARCH 30
Washed Clean

Lucas, his sister Kallie, and Grandpa were sitting on the balcony as the sun went down. "What's your memory verse for this week?" Grandpa asked.

"Romans 6:23," Lucas said. "For the wages of sin is death, but the free gift of God is eternal life through Christ Jesus our Lord."

Grandpa said, "I used to be a wild one years ago. Then one day that verse reminded me that Jesus died to save me from my sins—the wrong things I'd done. I asked Jesus to forgive me, and he washed me clean from all my sins."

Kallie took a sip of lemonade. "I've never done anything so bad."

Grandpa fanned himself. "The Bible says that every sin deserves death, no matter how big or small. But if we believe that Jesus is God's Son, and we ask him to forgive us, we get a brand-new life with him."

"You and Mom and Dad have been saying that ever since I can remember," Lucas said.

"Someday we hope you will want to be saved by Jesus too," said Grandpa.

READ
2 Timothy 3:14-15. This passage says children can trust their relatives who teach them about God and how to receive salvation—Jesus' forgiveness and new life.

THINK
- What are some wrong things you've done—big or small?
- What do you think it feels like to be forgiven, washed clean from all your sins?
- Imagine an ending for this story, showing how the verses could make a difference for Lucas. Then read the possible ending at the back of the book.

DO
- Are you ready to ask God's forgiveness the way the grandpa in this story did? If yes, go ahead and talk to God about your need for his salvation. You might use the words Lucas repeats in the possible ending of this story. Then tell someone after you pray it.
- If you have already prayed a prayer like this, thank Jesus for saving you.
- If you're not ready, write some questions you have. Decide who to talk to about them.

PRAY
Thank God for his plan to save you—and the people who teach you about it.

MEMORIZE
You have been taught the holy Scriptures from childhood, and they have given you the wisdom to receive the salvation that comes by trusting in Christ Jesus. 2 Timothy 3:15

WHAT'S THE POINT?
Lucas's family had taught him about Jesus and salvation for many years. Lucas kept growing in his understanding. He decided he wanted Jesus' forgiveness for himself. *BA*

MARCH 31
Pulling Weeds

Cheyenne and Jake flopped down. They'd been pulling weeds at the community garden patch with Gramps, and they were tired. "Don't stop now." Gramps pulled them to their feet. "You're almost done."

"But weeding is hard," Cheyenne complained.

"Gardening isn't easy," Gramps agreed, "but a gardener learns discipline. And once you start tasting the good things that come from the garden, you'll want to stick with it."

Jake brushed dirt from his hands. "But it's so long between planting the seeds and getting something good to eat."

"That teaches you patience. God uses discipline to train us to be better people. God can use the garden to teach you things that will help you later in life. Now you get busy with the last two rows while I get the picnic lunch." Gramps walked toward the car.

"Hey, Cheyenne," Jake nudged her. "Let's break off the tomato plants real low and stick the stems in the dirt. If they died, maybe Gramps would give up, and we could quit coming here."

READ
Hebrews 12:10-11. These verses compare learning from God's discipline to caring for a garden. It's not always fun or easy, but eventually it brings many good things.

THINK
- Why is God's discipline good for us?
- What right ways to live could God be teaching you from working on a project that takes a long time?
- Finish the story, showing how the verses could help Cheyenne and Jake feel good about their work. Then read the possible ending at the back of the book.

DO
- Think of a project you quit partway through. On a calendar, circle the date you want to have the project done.
- Ask someone to hold you accountable to make sure you finish the project.

PRAY
Ask God to show you how to keep working when something takes a long time.

MEMORIZE
No discipline is enjoyable while it is happening—it's painful! But afterward there will be a peaceful harvest of right living for those who are trained in this way. Hebrews 12:11

WHAT'S THE POINT?
The tomato blossom encouraged Cheyenne and Jake to keep up their hard work. God promises good to us when we work hard, even if it's not fun. *JP*

APRIL 1
Worried about Grandma

Keisha couldn't concentrate on her homework. She was worried about her grandma, so she turned on some music to drown out her thoughts, but that didn't help. She put her work aside and picked up a book, but she couldn't concentrate on the words. Nothing seemed to take Keisha's mind off her grandma.

After having a stroke, Grandma had been admitted to the hospital. Keisha wondered what would happen now. Grandma had always been like a second mother to her. When Keisha's mom had returned to work after Keisha was born, Grandma moved in to take care of her during the day. Now tears came to Keisha's eyes. *What if something happens to her and she can't come home?* Keisha worried.

READ
Philippians 4:6-7. This passage tells you what to do if you are worried and anxious.

THINK
- Instead of worrying about something, what two things does God want us to do?
- How do you think God's peace would help you when you have needs?
- Finish the story, showing how Keisha could find comfort and wisdom in today's Bible passage. Then read the possible ending at the back of the book.

DO
- Write a list of things you're worried about.
- Pray about those things and ask God to give you his peace. Tell him at least one thing you are thankful for.

PRAY
Continue to tell God your needs, thank him, and ask him to give you his peace.

MEMORIZE
Don't worry about anything; instead, pray about everything. Tell God what you need, and thank him for all he has done. Philippians 4:6

WHAT'S THE POINT?
When we pray for what we need instead of worrying, and thank God for what he has already done, God hears our prayers. He loves us and wants to help us. He will give us his peace, which is far better than anything. *CE*

APRIL 2
It's like Swimming Practice

Last summer, Rosa made a commitment to read her Bible and pray every day. She did for a while. But when school started, she found herself busy with homework, sports, and everyday life, and she didn't stick to her commitment.

In Pioneer Clubs, Rosa's group had a Bible Exploration time about having a regular "quiet time" with Jesus. Rosa's club leader asked if anyone would commit to starting one.

"I want to read my Bible and pray every day," said Rosa. "I've made that decision before, but I didn't stick to it."

Her club leader asked, "You're on the swim team, right?" Rosa nodded. "You would never enter a race without practicing and still expect to win, would you?" he asked.

READ
1 Corinthians 9:24-27. This passage compares a Christian's life to an athletic race. Paul talks about disciplining himself to practice doing what God wants.

THINK
- What does an athlete need to win a race?
- What do we need to discipline ourselves to do in our Christian life?
- Make up an ending for the story, showing how Rosa could learn from today's Bible verses. Then read the possible ending at the back of the book.

DO
- Before you go to bed each night, take a few minutes to pray. Thank God for all the ways he helped you through the day.
- If you don't have a set time to have your quiet time, choose one now. Draw a clock face with that time on it. This may help you do it more regularly.

PRAY
Ask God to help you develop the discipline and self-control to spend time praying and reading his Word regularly.

MEMORIZE
All athletes are disciplined in their training. They do it to win a prize that will fade away, but we do it for an eternal prize. 1 Corinthians 9:25

WHAT'S THE POINT?
It takes work and discipline to have a godly life and good relationship with Jesus. But it's all worth it when we reach heaven and get to live with Jesus forever. *CE*

APRIL 3
The Challenge

Damon got home from school and headed straight for his book. He had been waiting all day to get back to it. When he finished a few chapters, he decided to play outside with friends. Then after dinner, he played computer games before finishing his homework.

As Damon tumbled into bed, he saw his Bible and devotions book on his bedside table. *I know I'm supposed to spend time with God, but I'm really tired. I'll read my Bible tomorrow morning,* Damon thought to himself.

But the next day he got up late and rushed off to school. After school he saw his Bible and devotions book again. *I'll read before bed,* he thought. But after his bath, his mom said, "It's late. You need to go to bed if you're going to get enough sleep."

READ
Matthew 22:37-39. This passage describes how we should love God with all our hearts.

THINK

- Is there something in your life that you put before God? What is it?
- How can you show God you love him by putting him first?
- Make up an ending for the story, showing how Damon could put the teaching of the verses into practice. Then read the possible ending at the back of the book.

DO
- What's getting in the way of you spending time reading God's Word, the Bible, and praying?
- Organize a daily schedule with time slots to plan your activities. Block out time for sleep, school, playing with friends, spending time on the computer, and other activities. Then decide when to spend time with God. Hint: if you block out time in the morning, be sure to set your alarm a few minutes early.

PRAY
Ask God to show you how to love him with all your heart, mind, and soul.

MEMORIZE
You must love the LORD your God with all your heart, all your soul, and all your mind. Matthew 22:37

WHAT'S THE POINT?
We spend time doing what we love. If we love God, we will spend time reading the Bible and getting to know him better. *CE*

APRIL 4
Growing Strong

Spencer got ready for bed and sat down on his beanbag chair with his new Bible storybook. He liked looking at the pictures, but he wasn't sure how the stories applied to him. As he was scanning the table of contents, his baby sister, Isabelle, started to cry.

"I'm coming, sweetie," Mom called as she hurried to Isabelle's room.

Spencer jumped up and went in too. "She's hungry," Mom said. "Would you like to feed her?"

"Sure," said Spencer. He sat down in the rocking chair beside Isabelle's crib. Mom picked up Isabelle and put her in Spencer's lap. Then Mom gave him Isabelle's bottle.

Spencer pointed the bottle toward Isabelle's little mouth, and she sucked on it eagerly. "Boy, the milk's really going down fast," Spencer commented.

"Yes, she loves her milk," said Mom. "It will help her grow strong. Just like your new Bible storybook can help you grow strong in Jesus."

"I don't get that," said Spencer.

READ
1 Peter 2:2-3. God wants us to want to read the Bible as much as babies want to drink milk. That way we can develop our relationship with him.

THINK
- What are ways milk helps babies grow? What are ways the Bible helps us grow as Christians?
- What "tastes" of God's kindness have you had?
- Finish the story, showing how these verses could make a difference for Spencer. Then read the possible ending at the back of the book.

DO
- How would you rate your desire to read the Bible?
- Choose a topic from the Bible that interests you, such as learning God's promises, discovering what God is like, finding stories of Bible people who can be examples to you, or learning good ways to live. Look for that topic as you read the Bible this week.

PRAY
Ask God to help you want to read the Bible and grow in your knowledge of him.

MEMORIZE
Like newborn babies, you must crave pure spiritual milk so that you will grow into a full experience of salvation. 1 Peter 2:2

WHAT'S THE POINT?
The Bible will help us develop strong Christian lives. God wants us to be eager to read it. *BA*

APRIL 5
Afraid to Go to Camp

Six months ago, when Irena signed up to attend camp, it sounded fun. But as the week of camp grew closer, Irena became more hesitant about being away from home. Her worries spilled out. "What will I do if I get sick?" Irena asked.

"You'll go to the camp nurse," her mom reassured her.

"What if I need something?" she worried.

"Your counselor will help you."

The night before Irena was to leave for camp, she sat on her bed in tears. "I'm not going! I don't want to get homesick!" she cried.

READ

Deuteronomy 31:6. In this verse, Moses is talking to the Israelite people. They were getting ready to go into the land God promised them, but there were enemies in the land.

THINK

- Based on the verse, why can we be strong and courageous in difficult or uncertain situations?
- What do you think it means that God will go ahead of you?
- Finish the story, showing how the truth in today's verse could help Irena right away. Then read the possible ending at the back of the book.

DO

- Draw a three-box cartoon strip. In the first box, draw yourself in a situation where you need courage. In the second box, draw yourself praying for courage. In the third box, show yourself having courage in that situation.

PRAY

Ask God to give you courage in your difficult situation. Thank him for being with you.

MEMORIZE

Be strong and courageous! Do not be afraid and do not panic before them. For the LORD your God will personally go ahead of you. He will neither fail you nor abandon you. Deuteronomy 31:6

WHAT'S THE POINT?

Deep down Irena wanted to go to camp, but her fears were keeping her at home. We can be brave because God is with us. He goes ahead of us in all situations. *CE*

APRIL 6
A Free Gift

As Dawna neared the lunch table in the school cafeteria, she noticed her friends were in a serious discussion. Nyla, the new girl, was sitting among them. Nyla was from a different country, and she dressed differently, but Dawna thought she was nice.

Dawna sat down and took a bite of her sandwich. She heard Nyla explain, "In my religion, we believe people need to do several things in life before they will be able to go to heaven when they die." Suddenly Dawna was all ears. This was different from what she believed.

Should I say something? Should I tell her what the Bible says? Dawna wondered. She didn't want to start an argument, but she felt she should tell Nyla the truth.

READ
Ephesians 2:8-9. Salvation and being saved depend on believing Jesus is God's Son and accepting his forgiveness for our sins (the wrong things we do). When Jesus forgives us, he gives us the gift of going to heaven when we die. We don't get salvation because we do a lot of good things. Salvation is a free gift from God.

THINK
- What are you doing to earn Jesus' acceptance and salvation? (If you said nothing, good! You can't earn them—they're free gifts if you ask!)
- Why do you think God would give salvation and eternal life in heaven to anyone who believes in him?
- Finish the story, showing how the verses could help Dawna find the right words to speak the truth to her friend. Then read the possible ending at the back of the book.

DO
- Design a bumper sticker advertising how good heaven will be.
- Talk to a Christian adult about how to get God's gift of salvation and life in heaven. Have you ever accepted God's free gift for yourself?

PRAY
Thank God for sending Jesus to die for your sins and then come back to life. If you have never accepted God's free gift of forgiveness and heaven, you can do that right now.

MEMORIZE
God saved you by his grace when you believed. And you can't take credit for this; it is a gift from God. Salvation is not a reward for the good things we have done, so none of us can boast about it. Ephesians 2:8-9

WHAT'S THE POINT?
Some people believe they must do good deeds to earn God's salvation. But the Bible says God gives salvation freely to anyone who believes that Jesus is the Son of God and that he died for our sins. All we need to do is confess our wrongs, ask Jesus to forgive us, and ask him to come into our lives and guide us. *CE*

APRIL 7
Using Bad Language

When Dylan was with his church friends, he was careful what he talked about and the words he used. But when he was with his school friends, he found it difficult not to act like them. Sometimes he used bad language and picked on others to fit in.

One evening Dylan went to a church youth activity, and the group played dodgeball. It was fun until Dylan got hit hard. He saw a bigger kid wind up to throw the ball. But before he could move out of the way, the ball hit him so hard it brought tears to his eyes.

Without thinking, Dylan yelled a swear word. Everyone stopped and stared. Dylan got really red in the face and ran to the bathroom. Dylan's friend Homero followed him. After finding out that Dylan was okay, Homero said, "Dylan, I've heard you swear at school, too. That's just not cool."

READ
Joshua 24:15. How we behave shows who we've chosen to follow.

THINK
- If people say they follow God, how do you expect them to behave?
- If people say they follow God, why does it matter how they behave?
- Finish the story, showing how Dylan might make a new commitment based on the teaching in today's verse. Then read the possible ending at the back of the book.

DO
- Write a list of things you've done in the past week that show others that you follow God. Write a list of some things you've done that may not show that you follow God.
- Decide how you will behave differently next time.

PRAY
Ask God to help you act in ways that show that you follow him.

MEMORIZE
As for me and my family, we will serve the LORD. Joshua 24:15

WHAT'S THE POINT?
Instead of acting like he followed God, Dylan was following the crowd. When we commit our lives to God and decide to follow him, our actions will show that commitment. *CE*

APRIL 8
It's My Stuff!

Riley let her brother Chip play with her toy tree house whenever he wanted. She didn't mind when he borrowed her toy people to use in his model castle. But Chip wasn't as eager to let Riley use his things.

One day Riley went to find Chip's bow and arrow set. Chip saw her. "Stop playing with that! You should've asked me before you used it!"

"You're so mean! I let you use my stuff!" Riley griped as she handed it over and marched to her room. *I'm tired of him never letting me use his stuff. He's never using any of my stuff again,* Riley decided.

Pretty soon Chip knocked on her door. "Riley, want to play with me?"

READ
Leviticus 19:18. When we love others as we love ourselves, we don't try to get back at them. God wants us to forgive them when they hurt us.

THINK
- How can you love someone as much as yourself?
- What happens when someone doesn't forgive someone else?
- Finish the story, showing how Riley and Chip could change their lives according to today's verse. Then read the possible ending at the back of the book.

DO
- Is there someone in your life who is difficult for you to love? Why?
- Talk to your family about this situation and think of ways you can respond that would show love for that person.

PRAY
Ask God to help you love that person and forgive him or her.

MEMORIZE
Do not seek revenge or bear a grudge against a fellow Israelite, but love your neighbor as yourself. I am the LORD. Leviticus 19:18

WHAT'S THE POINT?
Chip and Riley often argued because Chip wasn't treating Riley the way he would want to be treated. And Riley was unforgiving. Our relationships will get better if we love others the way we love ourselves and forgive them when they hurt us. *CE*

APRIL 9
The Reading Log

When Niko signed up for the summer reading club at the public library, he was excited to receive prizes for reading. Five hours of reading earned him an ice-cream cone. Ten hours of reading earned him a coupon to go miniature golfing. And fifteen hours of reading earned him a free book. Niko went to the library and picked out interesting books. He carefully kept track of his reading time and earned his prizes.

But as the summer wore on, Niko spent less and less time reading and eventually forgot about the prizes.

"How are you doing on your reading goals?" Dad asked one day. Niko realized he would have to spend a lot more time reading and less time playing in order to earn the last two prizes. *Maybe I should mark off that I've read five more hours,* he thought. *No one at the library will know whether I really read or not.*

READ
Micah 6:8. This passage describes what we need to do to please God.

THINK
- Think of three ways to please God by doing what is right.
- Why is it sometimes hard for you to do what is right?
- Finish the story, showing how this verse might help Niko obey God. Then read the possible ending at the back of the book.

DO
- When have you been tempted to live in a way that was not pleasing to God?
- Act out a situation with your family where you are tempted to do something that would not be pleasing to God. Take turns coming up with good endings.

PRAY
Ask God to help you do what is right.

MEMORIZE
The LORD has told you what is good, and this is what he requires of you: to do what is right, to love mercy, and to walk humbly with your God. Micah 6:8

WHAT'S THE POINT?
Niko could have lied to get the prizes, but he decided to do what was right and earn them. God is pleased when we do right. *HP*

APRIL 10
When I Grow Up

It was career week at Javon's school. Every day someone with a different career came to his class and explained that job and what he or she did. At dinner each night, Javon excitedly told his parents what he had learned. "I think I'm going to be a computer programmer!" he exclaimed the first night. The second night he said, "I want to be a dentist!" Every night Javon wanted to be something different.

At dinner Friday night, Javon's mom asked him what career he had decided on. "I don't know!" Javon moaned and slumped in his chair. "They all sound so fun. How will I ever decide what I'm going to be when I grow up?"

READ
Psalm 32:8. God will watch over us and guide us in the best way to go. It's good to have a God who loves us so much!

THINK
- How does this verse make you feel?
- You may not know what God wants you to be when you grow up, but God has a plan for you. How can you find out God's plan for you?
- Finish the story, showing how the verse could help Javon feel confident about the future. Then read the possible ending at the back of the book.

DO
- Ask family members what talents they see in you. Talk about how you might use them someday in a career.
- Cut out pictures from a magazine of things you might like to do or be someday. Glue them onto construction paper and staple the pages. Add to the book from time to time. Ask God to show you his plan for your life.

PRAY
Thank God for watching over you. Ask him to guide you.

MEMORIZE
The LORD says, "I will guide you along the best pathway for your life. I will advise you and watch over you." Psalm 32:8

WHAT'S THE POINT?
We will face many decisions as we grow up. God promises to guide us in making those decisions. *CE*

APRIL 11
Nightmares

When Shelby's dad nudged her, she awoke feeling sleepy. "I'm so tired!" Shelby exclaimed. "And I had another bad dream last night." It was the third night in a row that Shelby had had a nightmare. When bedtime rolled around again, Shelby was afraid. "Dad, I don't want to go to sleep! I know I'll have another bad dream!"

Her dad sat down on the bed. "Let's pray. Let's ask God to give you good dreams and help you sleep through the night," he suggested.

Shelby looked doubtful. "I don't know. Do you think God really cares about me having bad dreams?"

READ
Psalm 116:1-2. This passage reminds us that God cares about us and is listening carefully to our prayers.

THINK
- When we pray, what is God doing?
- What are two ways the psalm writer responded to God's willingness to listen to him?
- Make up an ending for the story, showing how these verses could make a difference for Shelby. Then read the possible ending at the back of the book.

DO
- What are some requests that you would like to bring to God in prayer?
- Pretend a news reporter is asking you questions about whether God answers prayer and different ways he might answer. Have a family member be the reporter and interview you.

PRAY
Pray about something big or small. No request is too big or too small for God to listen to and care about. Tell him how you feel about his love.

MEMORIZE
I love the LORD because he hears my voice and my prayer for mercy. Psalm 116:1

WHAT'S THE POINT?
God cares about the big and small details of our lives. When we pray, he hears. *CE*

APRIL 12
The Tryout

The baseball tryouts were over. Zack grabbed his baseball glove and slowly walked out of the dugout. David caught up with him and said, "Hey, I wish you would have made the team."

Zack kicked a rock. "Yeah, me too," he mumbled. The two walked on in silence. After a moment, Zack said, "I just don't get it. I thought for sure I would get picked."

Just then they met up with Zack's parents. Mr. Hanson saw the pained look on Zack's face and said, "Zack, you tried your best. That's all you could do." Zack hugged his dad and said, "I just don't understand why God didn't let me make the team."

READ
Romans 8:28. We might not understand everything that happens to us, but God uses all things for good in our lives if we are his children. Maybe he has something better in mind for us. Maybe he will teach us something important.

THINK
- What does it mean to love God?
- How do you think God could make difficult things work for our good?
- Finish the story, showing how this verse could make a difference for Zack. Then read the possible ending at the back of the book.

DO
- What has happened in your life that you don't understand?
- Discuss with a family member how God may be working to bring good out of a situation in your life.

PRAY
Ask God to show you in little and big ways that he is working out his plan for your life.

MEMORIZE
We know that God causes everything to work together for the good of those who love God and are called according to his purpose for them. Romans 8:28

WHAT'S THE POINT?
While we can't see the big picture of our lives, God can. He can bring good out of everything for those who love him, even though they might not understand how. *CE*

APRIL 13
He's Got It All

Christy was cheering on her favorite hockey team on TV. She scanned the players, looking for the big number 3 on the back of a shirt. There he was—her favorite player. She cheered wildly when he bodychecked another player who had the puck. "He's got it all!" she said to her brother. "He's fast, he's a great shot, he's cute . . . what more could you want?"

"Christy's got a boyfriend," Mark said in a singsongy voice. But they both went crazy when "her guy" took a slap shot and scored the winning goal.

The sports reporter interviewed him after the game in the locker room. "You're the complete package," said the reporter. "You're fast, you're accurate, you've got great footwork."

"Just like I said," Christy said excitedly.

"What do you give the credit to? Hours of practice? Your coach?" asked the reporter.

READ
1 Corinthians 10:31. Doing things for God's glory means doing things to give him praise and honor.

THINK
- How could you bring God glory through your schoolwork or when you play with friends?
- When is it easy to give credit to God in what you do? When is it difficult?
- Finish the story, showing how the verse could affect Christy and "her guy." Then read the possible ending at the back of the book.

DO
- Talk with family members about how you are giving God the credit in your life.
- Discuss with family members ways to follow 1 Corinthians 10:31 this week.

PRAY
Ask God to help your everyday actions bring praise to him this week.

MEMORIZE
Whether you eat or drink, or whatever you do, do it all for the glory of God.
1 Corinthians 10:31

WHAT'S THE POINT?
Christy's favorite player was giving God the credit for his abilities. He knew that playing for God was the best way to play. *BA*

APRIL 14
New Toys Wanted

Even though Amy's birthday was still a month away, she could hardly wait to have her party. At the store with her mom, she browsed the toy aisles, making a mental list of all the fun things she hoped to unwrap as gifts at her party. "Mom, I want to invite the whole class *and* the girls from ballet," she said.

"Sounds like fun!" Amy's mom replied. "And Amy, you have plenty of toys as it is. I would like you to think about this: for every two new toys you get, I want you to consider giving one old toy to the homeless shelter."

Amy frowned. Why should she give up any of her toys?

READ
1 Timothy 6:18. God wants his followers to care about people in need.

THINK
- Why do you think God wants his followers to give generously to people in need?
- If you don't have money or "things" to give, what could you give instead?
- Finish the story, showing how today's verse could encourage Amy to follow through on her mom's suggestion. Then read the possible ending at the back of the book.

DO
- Talk with your family about what kind of "richness" comes from doing good.
- Make a plan with your family to give or share something this week.

PRAY
Ask God to give you a heart that loves to give and serve others.

MEMORIZE
Tell them to use their money to do good. They should be rich in good works and generous to those in need, always being ready to share with others. 1 Timothy 6:18

WHAT'S THE POINT?
God wants us to give generously—whether it's our money or our "things" or our time. We get rich inside from doing good. *CE*

APRIL 15
The Most Awesome Person

When Andrea returned home from camp, she felt like a different person. She had learned to canoe, ride a horse, and sing a lot of new songs. But Andrea's most exciting event was when she invited Jesus into her life to be her Savior.

During the drive home, Andrea told her parents all about camp, the fun things she experienced, and her new relationship with Jesus. She couldn't wait to call her friend Jillian.

When she got home, Andrea went straight to the phone and called Jillian.

"Jillian, the horses were awesome," she exclaimed. "Mine was Pinky, and I even got to brush her!" She told Jillian about all the fun things she did during the week. But before Andrea could tell her about Jesus, Jillian had to go.

Disappointed, Andrea put the phone down. She had wanted to tell Jillian about her experience with Jesus!

READ
Acts 1:8. This is Jesus talking to his followers. He will give us the power to tell others about him and his forgiveness and love.

THINK

- Why is it important to share the message of Jesus with others?
- What do you know about Jesus that you could tell others?
- Finish the story, showing how Andrea could still find a way to live by the truth of today's verse. Then read the possible ending at the back of the book.

DO
- Name some people you could tell about Jesus. Maybe they don't know Jesus yet. Maybe they do know Jesus, but your words could encourage them even more.
- With your family, role-play ways to share Jesus with others in your life.

PRAY
Ask God to give you opportunities to talk about Jesus with others.

MEMORIZE
You will receive power when the Holy Spirit comes upon you. And you will be my witnesses, telling people about me everywhere—in Jerusalem, throughout Judea, in Samaria, and to the ends of the earth. Acts 1:8

WHAT'S THE POINT?
Jesus gave us the job of telling others about him, and he will help us. *CE*

APRIL 16
Video Game Crazy

Brett loved to play video games. He would rather do that than anything else. Anytime he wasn't eating, sleeping, or doing homework, Brett was usually playing video games.

When the school year started, Brett took some time in the morning to read his Bible and pray. But as time passed, he spent less time reading and praying so he'd have time to play a game before school. One day after breakfast he went to his room, looked at his Bible, and then saw his games.

I think I'll play first and then do my reading and praying, Brett decided. He sat down to play and before he knew it, his mom was calling. "Brett, you've got three minutes before it's time to leave for school!"

Surprised, Brett realized, *Oh no! I never read my Bible, and I still have to brush my teeth!*

READ
Exodus 20:3. God wants us to love him more than anything else in this world. Nothing should be more important to us than him.

THINK
- What is the most important "thing" in this world to you?
- Do you love it more than you love God? How can you tell?
- Finish the story, showing how this verse might help Brett sort out his schedule and priorities. Then read the possible ending at the back of the book.

DO
- On a piece of paper, write out Exodus 20:3. Below it write something you could do or change to make God most important in your life.
- Post this somewhere where it will remind you to put God first in your life.

PRAY
Ask God to show you ways to make him most important to you.

MEMORIZE
You must not have any other god but me. Exodus 20:3

WHAT'S THE POINT?
Brett realized he had let playing video games take the place of spending time with God. Letting "things" become more important to us than God is easy to do. But God wants to be number one with us. *CE*

APRIL 17
The Mean Brother

When Troy's mom walked out of the room, his older brother, Ethan, grabbed the bag of pretzels and wouldn't let Troy have any more. "Hey!" Troy said. "Mom says to share." But Ethan wouldn't give up the pretzels.

The following day Troy and Aaron, his neighbor, were walking to school. Ethan rode up behind them on his bike and yelled, "Coming through!" He gave Troy a shove as he passed. Troy fell in the mud. "What a jerk!" said Aaron.

READ

Matthew 18:15-16. God knew we would meet people who are hard to get along with. He gave us these ideas for working things out. Pointing out the offense means explaining how the person hurt us or saying what we think is wrong.

THINK

- What kind of attitude do you think we should have when we tell someone what he or she has done to hurt us?
- Why do you think we should try to work things out with the person before telling anyone else?
- Finish the story, showing how Troy might apply the verses to help him in his relationship with his brother. Then read the possible ending at the back of the book.

DO

- On a sheet of paper, write the initials of someone who has been mean to you.
- With your family, role-play how to talk to someone about how he or she has hurt you. Include saying what you want the person to do now.

PRAY

Ask God to help you follow the Bible and talk to the person who hurt you.

MEMORIZE

If another believer sins against you, go privately and point out the offense. If the other person listens and confesses it, you have won that person back. Matthew 18:15

WHAT'S THE POINT?

Troy followed the Bible's advice by first talking to his brother about what his brother was doing wrong. When that didn't work, he followed the Bible's next step of talking to someone else who could help. *CE*

APRIL 18
Overheard at the Drinking Fountain

Allie had been excited for the school year to begin. But as the days went by, she realized her friends from last year had changed over the summer. They now watched TV shows Allie wasn't allowed to watch and read magazines her parents wouldn't let her read. They had started making fun of others at recess. Allie didn't join in because she couldn't bring herself to be mean. As a result, she was beginning to feel left out of their group.

Yesterday in line for the drinking fountain, Wendy whispered something to Kiara and then they both started giggling. Allie could tell they were talking about the girl at the front of the line. "Allie, come here! I have something to tell you," Wendy said. She motioned for Allie to join them.

READ
Genesis 6:5, 9, 22. You may know Noah's story. God told him to build a boat because God was going to send a flood. All the bad people drowned, but Noah and his family were saved. This story shows it is possible to live a life that pleases God even if those around you do not.

THINK
- How do you think Noah felt about living right when everyone else wasn't?
- What clue does verse 9 give about how Noah could do this?
- Imagine an ending for this story, showing how the verses could provide some wisdom for Allie. Then read the possible ending at the back of the book.

DO
- Talk to family members about something kids around you do that you know you shouldn't do.
- Role-play ways to avoid doing this.

PRAY
Ask Jesus to help you stay close to him so you can live in a way that pleases him.

MEMORIZE
Noah was a righteous man, the only blameless person living on earth at the time, and he walked in close fellowship with God. Genesis 6:9

WHAT'S THE POINT?
When Allie's friends began to live in a way that didn't please God, Allie chose to live the way God wanted her to live. Sometimes it's hard to live differently from those around us, but God will honor our decision if we do. *CE*

APRIL 19
A New Baby Sister

Cassandra could hardly wait. She had always wanted a baby sister, and her parents had decided they would adopt a baby girl. Despite warnings from her parents that it would be two years before the adoption process was final, Cassandra was thrilled. Her dream of having a baby sister was going to come true.

"The days are going by really slowly," Cassandra said to her mom.

"Here," said Mom. "I'll circle the adoption date on the calendar, and you can mark off the days."

So Cassandra did. To pass the time, she pretended her doll was her baby sister, and she fed, dressed, and cuddled her every day.

Shortly before the adoption date, a letter arrived. It told Cassandra's parents that there had been a problem and the adoption would be delayed. "The new adoption date is unknown," the letter read.

Cassandra couldn't believe the news.

READ
Hebrews 6:13-15. These verses remind us how Abraham waited patiently for God to give him a son.

THINK
- What does it mean to be patient?
- Abraham waited years for God to keep his promise. Why do you think he waited patiently?
- Finish the story, showing how the verses could help Cassandra handle her disappointment. Then read the possible ending at the back of the book.

DO
- Tell your family about something you are waiting for.
- Have a family member play a reporter, interviewing you on how to wait patiently and why it would be good to do so.

PRAY
Ask God to help you wait patiently for the thing you just talked about.

MEMORIZE
Abraham waited patiently, and he received what God had promised. Hebrews 6:15

WHAT'S THE POINT?
Like Abraham, Cassandra waited patiently over a long period of time. When we're patient, we can learn to trust God more. *CE*

APRIL 20
Too Much Money

José and his buddies scoured the candy aisle before finally making their choices. José chose his favorite candy bar and a pack of gum, paid the cashier, and stuffed his change and the gum in his pocket. After eating the candy bar, he pulled out the gum. Wadded up around the pack were the bills he had received in change. José carefully separated them. "Look at that! The cashier made a mistake and gave me a five-dollar bill instead of a one-dollar bill," he said.

"Lucky you! Let's use it to buy some chips," Dalton suggested.

"Or we could buy some soda," Antonio said.

José frowned. "Don't you think I should take it back?"

"Yes, that's the honest thing to do," answered Daniel.

"Don't listen to him," Romano shot back. "Keep the money. It was her mistake."

READ
Proverbs 11:5. God says honesty is right and dishonesty is sin.

THINK
- What good results could come from honesty?
- What bad results could come from dishonesty?
- Make up an ending for the story, showing how the verse could provide wise advice for José. Then read the possible ending at the back of the book.

DO
- Make up a rap or song about being honest.
- Make a deal with family members to be honest. Shake hands on it.

PRAY
Talk to God about a time you were dishonest. Ask for his forgiveness.

MEMORIZE
The godly are directed by honesty; the wicked fall beneath their load of sin. Proverbs 11:5

WHAT'S THE POINT?
José realized that honesty is God's way. He wanted to obey God. *CE*

APRIL 21
I Don't Know Her

After Marissa's soccer game, she was talking to some of her teammates from another school who she wanted to get to know better. She thought they were cool. Then she saw Elizabeth coming toward them. The two girls went to the same church. Marissa realized that Elizabeth was wearing a T-shirt that said, "With God, all things are possible." Marissa cringed. *Bad timing,* she thought.

Elizabeth stopped by them. "Hi, Marissa," she said. "Will you be at MissionsFest next week?"

One of Marissa's teammates rolled her eyes. "So what's MissionsFest, Marissa?" she asked.

"Nothing," Marissa muttered, embarrassed. She turned her back on Elizabeth and said, "Let's go!" to the other girls. As they ran to the parking lot, Marissa tried to forget the hurt look on Elizabeth's face.

READ
Luke 22:31-34, 54-62. Jesus was being arrested even though he hadn't done anything wrong. Peter, one of Jesus' closest friends, got scared and said he didn't even know Jesus. Now read Romans 1:16. The apostle Paul wrote this.

THINK
- How do you think Jesus felt when Peter said he didn't know him?
- Why wasn't Paul embarrassed about knowing Jesus?
- Finish the story, showing how today's verses might help Marissa not to feel ashamed. Then read the possible ending at the back of the book.

DO
- Have you ever been embarrassed to tell others about Jesus? afraid to invite a friend to a church activity? afraid to admit you go to church?
- Talk to your family about why you might be tempted to not let others know you follow Jesus. Talk about how to stand up for Jesus instead.

PRAY
Ask God to help you stand up for him even when it's tough.

MEMORIZE
I am not ashamed of this Good News about Christ. It is the power of God at work, saving everyone who believes—the Jew first and also the Gentile. Romans 1:16

WHAT'S THE POINT?
Just as Peter said he didn't know his good friend Jesus, Marissa acted as though she didn't know Elizabeth. And just as Elizabeth was hurt, Jesus is hurt when we are afraid to tell others that we know him. Marissa decided to be like Paul in the end. *HP*

APRIL 22
Mom's in the Hospital

She should have been going to bed, but Laura was worried. At the Good Friday church service that night, she had gone to the front to pray at the big cross with her dad and brothers. She'd prayed for her mom. Her mom was in the hospital. Laura didn't know when she would be coming home.

What if the doctors can't find out what's wrong with her? Laura worried. *I've prayed and prayed, and God hasn't made her well. I'm tired of praying.*

Tears came to her eyes. *Why doesn't God answer me? I wonder if God was sad about his Son on the cross like I'm sad about Mom.* Laura crawled under the covers. Even after her older sister, Dana, came to bed in the room they shared, Laura lay awake worrying.

READ
Luke 18:1. Our prayers are important to God. He cares about us very much.

THINK
- Why do you think God would want us to keep praying and not give up?
- God always answers our prayers. Sometimes the answer is no. What could you do then?
- Finish the story, showing how Laura could find encouragement in the verse. Then read the possible ending at the back of the book.

DO
- Describe a situation you are worried about.
- Make a chart. Keep track of how many times you pray about that situation for two weeks. Don't give up!

PRAY
Ask God to help you trust him whether his answer is yes or no or wait.

MEMORIZE
Jesus told his disciples a story to show that they should always pray and never give up.
Luke 18:1

WHAT'S THE POINT?
Jesus taught his helpers to always pray and never give up. He will always answer. Even if he doesn't answer the way we want, we can trust him. *CE*

APRIL 23
A Life Jacket Is like Jesus

During Bible Exploration, Elijah's Pioneer Clubs leader held up a big gift-wrapped box. "Who wants a gift?" he said.

Elijah said, "Me, me!"

Mr. O'Connor tossed Elijah the big box.

"Aaaah!" said Elijah, but he caught it. Jada helped him tear off the wrapping paper. Elijah pulled out a life jacket. Confused, he asked, "Why did you give me a life jacket?"

Mr. O'Connor smiled. "I want to give you a gift that can save your life. Will you take it?"

Elijah nodded.

Mr. O'Connor said, "This life jacket reminds me of Jesus."

"Huh?" Jada said.

READ
John 3:16. God loves us so much that he sent his Son, Jesus, to save us from death and give us life forever.

THINK
- What did God send Jesus to do in this world to help us?
- How is God's love shown through Jesus?
- Finish the story, showing how these verses could make a difference for Elijah and Jada too. Then read the possible ending at the back of the book.

DO
- Draw a cross. In each corner, see if you can write a reason for accepting God's gift of forgiveness.
- Discuss with a family member what it means to have life forever.

PRAY
If you're ready to accept God's gift of forgiveness, ask Jesus to forgive you for the wrong things you do. Tell Jesus you believe in him and trust him to give you life forever. If you have already done this, ask God to help you tell someone else.

MEMORIZE
God loved the world so much that he gave his one and only Son, so that everyone who believes in him will not perish but have eternal life. John 3:16

WHAT'S THE POINT?
When we accept God's wonderful gift of his Son, Jesus, as our Savior, we will be saved from death and have life forever. *BA*

APRIL 24
He's Alive!

Thomas stood offstage in the front of his church. He straightened his costume's head covering and robe. As he waited for his cue, he watched the man playing Jesus carry the big cross across the stage. The soldiers lay "Jesus" on the cross. Thomas jumped as the sharp sounds of a hammer clanking on nails came from the speaker system. The soldiers were nailing "Jesus" to the cross.

Thomas winced. It looked so real. He was getting caught up in the annual Easter morning drama like he never had before. Thomas watched with his mouth open as the soldiers raised the cross. "Alas, and did my Savior bleed?" sang the adult choir quietly.

"It is finished!" shouted "Jesus," and hung his head and died. The lights in the church dimmed. Thomas felt a lump in his throat. He didn't like this part.

READ
Matthew 28:1-8. Jesus died and was buried. On the morning of the third day, an angel announced the news: Jesus was alive again!

THINK
- How do you think the women felt at the beginning of today's story in Matthew? Use facial expressions and body language. How do you think they felt at the end of the story?
- How was Jesus able to come back to life?
- Finish the story, showing how knowing about Christ's suffering and resurrection could affect Thomas. Then read the possible ending at the back of the book.

DO
- With your family, ring bells (or anything that makes noise!) and sing a song you know about Jesus coming back to life. Celebrate!
- Have half of your family announce, "Jesus is risen!" The other half joyfully reply, "He is risen indeed!"

PRAY
Tell God what a difference it makes to you that he brought Jesus back to life.

MEMORIZE
The angel spoke to the women. "Don't be afraid!" he said. "I know you are looking for Jesus, who was crucified. He isn't here! He is risen from the dead, just as he said would happen. Come, see where his body was lying." Matthew 28:5-6

WHAT'S THE POINT?
We can rejoice like the women on that first Easter morning: Jesus is alive! *BA*

APRIL 25
Lost in the Park

Wes and Grady stopped where the path forked and turned to the right. Wes looked at his Global Positioning System and checked their location. "It says that at the end of this path, we should go left."

"It is so cool that Mom and Dad let us try the GPS on our own!" said Grady.

"Yeah, they know we'll never get lost if we have it," Wes added. At the next fork, Wes looked at the GPS. The screen was blank. "Oh no! What's wrong with this thing?" said Wes. After pushing buttons and giving it a shake, he determined the batteries were dead.

"Now what?" Grady asked. "I haven't been keeping track of our location because we have this thing!"

READ
Psalm 25:4-5. Just as the psalm writer looked to God for guidance, so should we.

THINK
- What are ways to find guidance from God?
- How is the Bible like a GPS or map for life?
- Finish the story, showing how these verses could give Wes and Grady some direction. Then read the possible ending at the back of the book.

DO
- Draw an open Bible. Draw a GPS screen on it to remind yourself that the Bible is a guide for you. In the screen, "type" in a decision you need to make that you need guidance about.
- Pray for God's guidance on this decision.

PRAY
Ask God to be your guide in life as you read the Bible and learn about him from other Christians.

MEMORIZE
Show me the right path, O Lord; point out the road for me to follow. Psalm 25:4

WHAT'S THE POINT?
Wes and Grady looked to God for guidance. He is the one who knows everything about us and will guide us and direct us in all we do. *CE*

APRIL 26
In a Tent in the Storm

The lightning flashed and thunder boomed loudly. Startled, Katrina sat up in her sleeping bag. Another flash of lightning split the sky and lit up their tent. The boom of thunder made the ground shake, and Katrina grabbed her dad. "Why did we have to go camping this weekend?" she exclaimed.

"I didn't count on this storm," her dad said as the raindrops began to hit their tent. More lightning and thunder filled the sky, and Katrina cried, "Isn't there somewhere we could go? We might get struck by lightning!"

Her dad tried to reassure her. "Right now we're safest in the tent," he said. With each clap of thunder, Katrina shook with fear. Her dad reached over and put his arm around her. "What we can do right now is pray that God will watch over us and protect us," he said. The thunder was so loud and the lightning so close that Katrina wondered if God would.

READ
Psalm 33:18, 20-22. We can put our hope and trust in God because he is our shield—our protection.

THINK
- What does God say he will do for people who fear (honor and respect) him?
- Describe a time when you were afraid and asked God to protect you.
- Finish the story, showing how Katrina could put her confidence in the truths of the verses. Then read the possible ending at the back of the book.

DO
- Make a bookmark with Psalm 33:20 written on it to use in your Bible. Let it remind you that God is your shield.

PRAY
Think of something you are scared of. Ask God for his protection to cover you like a shield.

MEMORIZE
We put our hope in the LORD. He is our help and our shield. Psalm 33:20

WHAT'S THE POINT?
God knows what is happening to you, and he's watching over you. He will be your shield and give you peace. *CE*

APRIL 27
The Storyteller

Vanessa walked out on the playground and looked around. Some of the girls in her class were swinging on the swings while others were playing on the monkey bars. The boys were playing kick ball.

"Well, where should we go?" Patrice asked her.

"Let's go sit over there," said Vanessa, as she pointed to a nearby bench. They sat down, and Vanessa opened her Bible storybook.

Kimberly ran over. "Hey, what are you doing?" she asked.

"My book has some neat stories. I'm going to read some out loud," replied Vanessa.

"Can I listen?" asked Kimberly, and she sat down.

Asha saw the group and came over. "Vanessa is going to read us a story," Kimberly told her. She joined the group too. "What's the story about?" Asha asked.

READ
Psalm 71:17. The psalm writer thought that God's works were wonderful, and he wanted to tell others about them.

THINK
- Why is it important to tell others about what God has done? What are some things God has done for you that you could tell others?
- Finish the story using your ideas about how Vanessa might use what she knows from the Bible. Then read the possible ending at the back of the book.

DO
- Talk with your family about ways you can share the things God has done with people you know.
- Put together a photo album of things God has done for you. Include photos and captions. Ideas: gave me a loving family, a great pet, a church; forgave my sins and became my Savior.

PRAY
Ask God to show you ways that you can share with others what he has done.

MEMORIZE
O God, you have taught me from my earliest childhood, and I constantly tell others about the wonderful things you do. Psalm 71:17

WHAT'S THE POINT?
Vanessa wanted to share the amazing things God has done with her friends. Reading Bible stories is a great way to share God with others. Give it a try! *CE*

APRIL 28
X-Raying Your Thoughts

Leah grabbed her coat and slammed her locker shut. She was so mad at Calista, she wanted to yell out loud. Leah marched down the hall to the school door. All she could think about was how Calista had told everyone her secret. *How could she do this to me? I thought she was my friend! I hope something really, really bad happens to her,* Leah told herself.

She got on the bus and found an empty seat where no one would bother her. Staring blankly out the window, Leah planned ways to get back at Calista. Maybe she'd tell everyone some of Calista's secrets. *Yeah! That would teach her!* As the bus rolled to a stop, Leah looked at the bumper sticker on a nearby parked car and read, "If we could X-ray your thoughts, what would we see right now?"

READ
Psalm 139:23-24. The psalm writer is asking God to look into his mind and point out what is displeasing to God.

THINK
- Why is it important for God to see our minds and point out what is not pleasing to him?
- What can you do when God points out things in your life that are not pleasing to him?
- Make up an ending for the story, showing how these verses can make a difference for Leah. Then read the possible ending at the back of the book.

DO
- What are some thoughts and feelings that you've had recently that would be displeasing to God?
- Draw several cartoons of yourself thinking and feeling these things. Ask God to forgive you. Ask him to guide you to live in ways that please him.

PRAY
Ask God to help you keep your thoughts pure and pleasing to him.

MEMORIZE
Point out anything in me that offends you, and lead me along the path of everlasting life. Psalm 139:24

WHAT'S THE POINT?
God knows all our thoughts. He often gently points out our wrong thoughts to us so that we will see our sin and ask him for forgiveness. *CE*

APRIL 29
The Broken Airplane

Kwan loved building model airplanes. Several of his airplanes had taken weeks to build. One Saturday Kwan created a whole airport scene, complete with people, runways, and trees on a table in his bedroom. When he finished, it was time to go to soccer practice. Kwan's sister, Min, had invited a friend over to play while he was gone, so he told her, "Don't go in my room. And don't touch my airplane display."

But Min and her friend sneaked into his room anyway to look at the display. As they turned to leave, Min accidentally kicked the table, knocking an airplane onto the floor. It broke into several pieces. When Kwan came home and saw the mess, he was really angry and wanted to yell at Min.

READ
Romans 6:16. This passage reminds us that we are free to choose to sin (do wrong things) or obey God. But our choices will have results—good or bad.

THINK
- What happens if we obey God?
- What happens if we sin?
- Imagine an ending for this story, showing how the verse might change Kwan's life. Then read the possible ending at the back of the book.

DO
- Fold a piece of paper in half. On one side, draw an action that would be wrong, like hitting someone, and what might happen. On the other side, draw a picture of what would happen if you chose to do what is right.
- Put a check mark by one of the pictures to show which choice you will make this week.

PRAY
Ask God to alert you when you are tempted to do something wrong. Pray that he will help you choose to do the right thing.

MEMORIZE
Don't you realize that you become the slave of whatever you choose to obey? You can be a slave to sin, which leads to death, or you can choose to obey God, which leads to righteous living. Romans 6:16

WHAT'S THE POINT?
Kwan chose not to sin in his anger and yell at his sister. We, too, can choose whether we will sin or obey God and his commands. *CE*

APRIL 30
The Service Project

Mei listened as her Sunday school teacher explained the upcoming missions project. The group would be spending Saturday afternoon filling care packages and delivering them to children in need.

Mei was excited about the project, but then began to think of all the things she had to do on Saturday. She had a soccer game in the morning, needed to practice her violin, and had to finish a book report. It was also the day her parents expected her to clean her room and do extra chores around the house. Mei worried she wouldn't be able to get everything done *and* participate in the missions project.

READ
Luke 12:22-32. This passage reminds us that God knows all our needs and he will provide what we need when we put him first in our lives.

THINK
- What is something you or your family needs—money, a job, a house, a friend? How have you tried to meet that need yourself?
- What does Jesus tell us about how God meets our needs in this passage?
- Finish the story, showing how Mei could find wisdom in these verses. Then read the possible ending at the back of the book.

DO
- Has there ever been a time when you wondered if God would provide for you?
- Discuss with your family or a family member what Luke 12:31 can mean for your family. Come up with ideas on how you can "seek the Kingdom of God" as more important than everything else.

PRAY
Ask God to help you turn to him, follow him, and trust him to provide for you.

MEMORIZE
Seek the Kingdom of God above all else, and he will give you everything you need.
Luke 12:31

WHAT'S THE POINT?
Despite her busy schedule, Mei wanted to serve God and others through her class missions project. God honored her desire to put him first and met her needs by providing a way for it to work out. When we seek God first and trust him for our needs, he will provide for us, too. *CE*

MAY I
What Did I Just See?

This is the best vacation we've ever had, Desiree thought. She'd climbed a spiral staircase that went to the top of a lighthouse. She'd fed seagulls by the lake.

"Desiree, it's time to choose a souvenir," Mom reminded her.

"Okay," Desiree said, as she studied the rows of pale gold seashells. Desiree was about to select a shell when a woman came up alongside her, quickly opened her purse, shoved two beautiful shells inside, and snapped her purse shut.

Desiree couldn't believe what she saw. The woman quickly made her way through the crowded store and out the door.

READ
Leviticus 19:11. God tells us not to take what does not belong to us. We need to respect one another's property.

THINK
- How does stealing hurt God? How does it hurt other people?
- Why do you think some people steal?
- Finish the story with ideas about what you would do if you knew this verse and were Desiree. Then read the possible ending at the back of the book.

DO
- Think of a time when you've wanted something very badly but couldn't have it. Picture how this could lead to temptation and then to displeasing God. Then picture how you could resist temptation.
- Discuss with family members how each of you can show respect for each other's property.

PRAY
Ask God to help you please him by following his rules, which include not taking something that doesn't belong to you.

MEMORIZE
Do not steal. Do not deceive or cheat one another. Leviticus 19:11

WHAT'S THE POINT?
God knows that we need to respect each other as his special creations. Part of that respect includes how we treat each other's possessions and property. *LF*

MAY 2
Saving for a Scooter

"Mom, when are we going to the store?" Kirstin asked. "I counted my money. I've got enough to get the scooter."

It was Sunday, and her mom told her they would go the next day. Kirstin hummed as she got dressed for church. She had saved for months for the scooter. Her stepdad had helped her make a plan—how much of her allowance and gifts she should give to church, how much she could spend, and how much to save for the scooter. Tomorrow the scooter would be hers.

In church, the pastor began to talk about a girl in another country who had nothing, not even a pair of shoes. Kirstin thought about all the shoes she had. She heard him say, "The children have one meal a day, and then it is only rice." The church was collecting a special offering to send to the needy children. He said, "You must decide in your heart how much to give."

Kirstin's eyes were wide. She felt bad for the children. She wanted to help. But she had already put her offering in the offering basket.

Then she thought about the money she had saved. The pastor said, "Pray about what God wants you to give."

READ
2 Corinthians 9:7-8. God helps us. Giving money is one way we can help others. We can be glad to give when we see how we can make a difference for others.

THINK
▪ The verses give a reason why we can give generously. What is it?
▪ Why do you think God wants us to give cheerfully and not feel pressured?
▪ Finish the story, showing how Kirstin could take today's verses to heart. Read the possible ending at the back of the book.

DO
▪ Draw a face to show how you feel about giving.
▪ With your family, make a plan to give to someone in need.

PRAY
Ask God to help you be happy about giving to help others in need.

MEMORIZE
You must each decide in your heart how much to give. And don't give reluctantly or in response to pressure. "For God loves a person who gives cheerfully." 2 Corinthians 9:7

WHAT'S THE POINT?
As Kirstin thought about others' needs, she felt happy to give what she had. God had met her needs, and she had extra to give. *LF*

MAY 3
Too Much Mac and Cheese

"I'll do just about anything for mac and cheese," Rudy claimed. His classmates knew how much Rudy liked the hot, gooey dish the school cook made.

"Let's see how much we can get Rudy to eat," agreed Elliott and Cade, two older kids. With the help of a few more kids, the two made sure Rudy had an enormous pile of mac and cheese.

On a dare, Rudy stuffed in forkful after forkful. Sammy said, "You better stop. That's too much!" But it tasted great, so Rudy kept eating. Soon his stomach started to hurt.

"I don't feel so good," he said to Sammy.

Instead of attending the special all-school assembly after lunch, Rudy was explaining to the school nurse why he needed to lie down.

READ
Proverbs 23:19-21. Who we pay attention to is important to God. He knows that some friends can lead us in the wrong direction.

THINK
- Why would God warn us to be careful about who we spend time with?
- When we are wise about friendships, what will happen in our lives?
- Finish the story, showing how Rudy could apply the teaching of the verses. Then read the possible ending at the back of the book.

DO
- Make a chart. Across the top, write, "Does my friend help me make good decisions?" Down the side, write several friends' names. Write yes or no in each blank box to answer the question about each friend. Who will you pay attention to?
- If you realize that you and a certain friend often get into trouble when you're together, ask an adult you trust for advice on what to do.

PRAY
Ask God to help you make good friendship decisions. Thank him for the special friends he has put in your life.

MEMORIZE
My child, listen and be wise: Keep your heart on the right course. Proverbs 23:19

WHAT'S THE POINT?
God cares about us very much. That includes who we pay attention to. He puts friends who want the best for us in our lives for a reason. *LF*

MAY 4
Hot Dogs in the Fire

"Ricky, quit goofing off and help me carry the food," Griffin said to the buddy he'd been assigned to for the Pioneer Clubs cookout. Griffin didn't like Ricky. He talked too much, and he always poked people.

"I'm starving," said Ricky. "I've never cooked out before."

That's obvious, Griffin thought as he watched Ricky stab the tip of a hot dog with a cooking stick. Within seconds of holding the hot dog over the flames, it fell off the stick. Ricky tried again, with the same results.

READ
Proverbs 25:21. God wants us to be kind to people we don't like or people who don't like us.

THINK
- ▪ Why would God want us to show kindness to someone who didn't deserve it?
- ▪ What is the most common way people treat their enemies?
- ▪ Finish the story, showing how Griffin might learn something from the verse. Then read the possible ending at the back of the book.

DO
- ▪ On a piece of paper, draw a circle to make a face. Draw two eyes in the middle of the circle and a half-circle that looks like a frowning mouth under the eyes. Draw another frowning half-circle above the eyes. Next to the frowning face, write the initials of someone who isn't very kind to you or someone you don't like. Now turn the paper upside down. Next to the smiley face that appears, write something kind and unexpected you will do for that person.
- ▪ Sometimes we need to change our beliefs to help us change our actions. Write one thing you believe about this person that God wouldn't agree with, such as "This person is a loser." Now write something you could start believing about the person that would please God.
- ▪ If someone is hurting you, talk to an adult you trust.

PRAY
Ask God to help you be kind to everyone—no matter how you might feel about that person.

MEMORIZE
If your enemies are hungry, give them food to eat. If they are thirsty, give them water to drink. Proverbs 25:21

WHAT'S THE POINT?
God wants us to do good for others, even people we don't like. He didn't say it would always feel easy or natural! If we ask him for help being kind, he will be glad to help us learn. *LF*

MAY 5
What I Don't Like about You

Nina could barely contain her excitement. Tonight was the big sleepover at Kara's. She didn't want to miss a minute of the fun.

After stuffing themselves with pizza, the girls rolled out their sleeping bags. "I have a cool new game we can play," Cynthia said. "But you gotta be brave to play it."

"How brave?" asked Nina, a little worried.

Cynthia rolled her eyes. "It's called, 'What I Don't Like about You.' You say something about the person on your left. For example, 'I don't like Kara's new haircut.'"

READ
Matthew 5:14-16. Our good actions show others what Jesus is like. That's like shining a light for others to see.

THINK
- What kinds of actions would be like hiding your light? What kinds of actions would be like letting your light shine brightly?
- Have you ever wanted to be part of a group of friends so much that you were tempted to do things you normally wouldn't do?
- Finish the story, showing how Nina could live by the instruction of these verses. Then read the possible ending at the back of the book.

DO
- Make yourself a reminder that you are God's light in the world. Draw a lightbulb, cut it out, and place it where you'll see it first thing every morning.
- Talk with your family about what to do when it feels hard to let your light shine.

PRAY
Ask God to help you have the courage to do what is right and tell others why you know it is right.

MEMORIZE
Let your good deeds shine out for all to see, so that everyone will praise your heavenly Father. Matthew 5:16

WHAT'S THE POINT?
Jesus stood up for what was right, even when it wasn't popular. So can we. Jesus wants us to be like a light for the people around us, shining to show them what he is like. *LF*

MAY 6
Chew Toy

"The best thing about collecting action figures is that I can play with them," Caleb explained to his younger brother, Josiah. Carefully, he pulled his oldest and most favorite figure from the shelf above his bed.

"It's time to leave for school, boys," their mother called. "I see the bus."

"We're late, Josiah!" Caleb said as he dropped the figure on his bed.

After school that day, Caleb found his favorite figure missing a hand, and there were familiar chew marks on both legs. He stared and felt his face turn hot with anger.

"Diesel!" he yelled, and went in search of the dog. "I can't believe what you did!"

READ
Matthew 6:19-21. Our lives are full of many "things." But their worth is nothing compared to the riches that God values, such as kindness and doing good for others. Nothing can destroy these riches.

THINK
- Why are the "things" we own so important to us?
- How can we make being kind and doing good for others more important to us?
- Finish the story, showing how Caleb's feelings might be affected by learning from the verses. Then read the possible ending at the back of the book.

DO
- With your family, make up a TV commercial on how and why to store up treasures in heaven.
- Plan something good to do for someone this week to store up treasure in heaven.

PRAY
Thank God that he gives you things like toys to enjoy and collect. Ask him to help you learn more about his treasures that never get teeth marks on them.

MEMORIZE
Store your treasures in heaven, where moths and rust cannot destroy, and thieves do not break in and steal. Matthew 6:20

WHAT'S THE POINT?
Caleb remembered that God values people, and even pets, over things. How he treated his dog or handled his anger was more important to God than a one-handed action figure. *LF*

MAY 7
The House Next Door

Every day before school, Ramón and his sister, María, watched the workers building the house next door. "They aren't doing anything," complained Ramón. After a month, all he saw was a big hole. He wanted to see walls go up.

Finally one morning a cement truck pulled up. Thick, grey concrete poured out of the chute. Carefully the workers smoothed it out over metal rods. Then everyone left.

"Dad, I think they quit working on the house," Ramón said when nothing more happened for a while.

"Give them a few more days," his father said. "You'll be surprised."

READ
Isaiah 33:6. Jesus' teachings give us a firm base for our lives. No matter what happens to us, we can be confident that he'll love and care for us.

THINK
- What does the verse say God will give us as the foundation for our lives?
- Why do some people not listen to God but instead do things their own way?
- Make up an ending for the story, showing how the verse could affect Ramón. Then read the possible ending at the back of the book.

DO
- Build a tepee with toothpicks on a kitchen counter. Next, take some modeling clay, make a base, and build another tepee. Which one was easier to build and lasted longer?
- Every time you memorize Scripture and obey God, you build part of a foundation for your life in him. How will you build that foundation this week?

PRAY
Praise God for his love for you. Thank him for the Bible, which tells us about him and what he wants us to do.

MEMORIZE
He will be your sure foundation, providing a rich store of salvation, wisdom, and knowledge. The fear of the LORD will be your treasure. Isaiah 33:6

WHAT'S THE POINT?
We can't always see a foundation, but everything depends on it. God gives us a solid foundation for our lives. *LF*

MAY 8
Lost in a Maze

"I can make it through the maze faster than you," Lewis challenged his friend Amber. Their Pioneer Clubs group was on a field trip. The owners of the farm had created a maze out of stacked bales of hay.

"Start counting!" Lewis yelled. *This is going to be easy,* he thought as he made one turn and then another. His next turn surprised him. It was a dead end.

He turned around. He made a right turn. Another dead end! He knew one pathway through the maze would get him to the other end, but at the moment, all he could see was hay.

READ
Acts 4:8-12. Peter had just healed a crippled man through God's power. The people in charge were angry. Peter told them about Jesus.

THINK
- Who is the only one who can save us? What do we need to be saved from?
- What other ways to heaven do some people believe in? What would you tell them?
- Finish the story, showing how Lewis's adventure helped him understand this passage. Then read the possible ending at the back of the book.

DO
- Make a maze out of building blocks. Place some blocks crosswise to create dead ends. What are the dead ends for people—paths they take that can't lead to salvation in the end?
- Talk with your family about how to turn to Jesus to be saved from the penalty for sin.

PRAY
Thank God for loving you so much that he sent Jesus and has a plan for you to be with him in heaven.

MEMORIZE
There is salvation in no one else! God has given no other name under heaven by which we must be saved. Acts 4:12

WHAT'S THE POINT?
Lewis realized there was only one way out of a maze, and there was only one way to heaven—Jesus. *LF*

MAY 9
I Love You

"Mom loves me more," Jonah teased. Of course, he knew it wasn't true. But his younger sister, Jen, wasn't so sure. *Jonah is older and helps out more at home,* thought Jen. She came up with an idea. For the next week, she'd be a "super helper." Then maybe Mom would love her more.

"Mom, did you notice how clean my room is?" Jen asked. "And I fed Miss Kitty twice today."

"Thanks, honey," her mom said. It was her usual "thanks." In fact, all Jen's extra effort didn't seem to make a difference. What was she doing wrong?

READ
Ephesians 3:17-19. God's love for us is so huge that we can't fully understand it. It doesn't depend on what we do. It depends on God, who *is* love.

THINK
- How would you describe how big God's love is for us?
- How do you know that God loves you?
- Finish the story, showing how the verses could help Jen understand God's character—and his love for her. Then read the possible ending at the back of the book.

DO
- Verse 17 talks about our "roots" growing down into God's love. Water a plant. Think of how the plant's roots drink up the water.
- Choose a way that you will let your "roots" drink up God's love today: sing a song about his love; tell someone about God's love; admire something in nature and remember that he made it for you to enjoy; pretend to give God a big hug; or think of your own idea.

PRAY
Thank God for his huge love for you, which doesn't depend on how you behave.

MEMORIZE
Your roots will grow down into God's love and keep you strong. And may you have the power to understand, as all God's people should, how wide, how long, how high, and how deep his love is. Ephesians 3:17-18

WHAT'S THE POINT?
Jen started to realize that love isn't earned. God's big love for you, like a good parent's love, isn't based on what you do. *LF*

MAY 10
The Birthday List

Even though his birthday was weeks away, Quinn was working on his wish list. Nearly every night, he'd scratch out one item and add a couple more. Under his bed was a growing stash of store sales flyers that had arrived in the mail.

"Mom, do we have some blank paper and glue?" Quinn asked. After an hour of cutting out pictures and gluing, Quinn's wish list was a work of art.

"What do you think of my great list?" Quinn asked. His mother folded it over and said, "There's another birthday list I'd like to read to you; it was in the newspaper today. It's from a kid in a town where many people have lost their jobs."

READ
Luke 12:15-21. Our world encourages greed. We're told more is better. God doesn't think so. He knows that the stuff that fills our toy boxes or closets isn't nearly as important as our relationship with him.

THINK
- How could the man in Luke 12 have been more rich in God's view?
- What makes you feel greedy—TV commercials or friends, maybe?
- Finish the story, showing how Quinn might want to change his list after learning from the verses. Then read the possible ending at the back of the book.

DO
- This coming week when you want something, ask yourself if that thing is a "want" or a "need."
- Choose a way to become richer with God: read the Bible more; pray more; do something kind for someone; forgive someone; say something nice when you'd rather call someone names; or pick another idea of your own.

PRAY
Ask God to help you focus on him and not your possessions.

MEMORIZE
Beware! Guard against every kind of greed. Life is not measured by how much you own.
Luke 12:15

WHAT'S THE POINT?
Greed prevents us from caring for others. It focuses on our possessions. When we put greed aside, we can focus on God and others. *LF*

MAY 11
Talking Trash

"You're such a baby! Need a bottle?" Kirby hollered when the kid on first base threw down his baseball glove over an unfair call.

Kirby always tells it like it is, thought Gabe. If someone acted stupid, he heard about it. In a way, Gabe found himself admiring Kirby's daring attitude. After all, pro sports players were good at talking trash, and they seemed cool.

Later in the game, a fly ball soared past a teammate's glove. As Gabe raced to catch it, he yelled to his teammate, "You idiot—why did you miss it?" Calling someone a name happened so easily. It just rolled off his tongue. Then Gabe noticed the kid looking miserable and staring at the ground.

READ
Romans 12:2. God wants Christians to be different in the way we think and act. God wants us to behave in ways that please him, not in ways that others might think are popular or cool.

THINK
- When do you find it hard to behave like a Christian?
- What things can you do to resist the temptation to behave in ways some friends might think are cool but God says are wrong?
- Finish the story, showing how Gabe could follow the teaching of the verse. Then read the possible ending at the back of the book.

DO
- With a family member, find a Bible verse that reminds us how to act—maybe one about kindness, forgiveness, or love.
- In the week ahead, look for specific ways you can live out this verse.

PRAY
Ask God to help you change to live up to his standards and not the world's.

MEMORIZE
Don't copy the behavior and customs of this world, but let God transform you into a new person by changing the way you think. Romans 12:2

WHAT'S THE POINT?
Gabe's memory verse helped him tell the difference between ways of talking that God would and wouldn't like. He decided to follow God's ideas instead of the world's. *LF*

MAY 12
And the Fight Was On

"Is it ever going to stop raining?" Rocío wondered. Her family's plans for a day at her favorite park were off. The apartment felt small, and everywhere she went, Miguelito was nearby.

"Quit following me," she demanded of her younger brother. She was drawing a picture when Miguelito showed up again. As he asked what she was drawing, his drink splashed across her work of art.

Rocío let out a shriek. Miguelito yelled. Rocío gave her brother a shove. The fight was on. The cat hid under the couch just as their mother rushed into the room. "What is going on?" she asked.

READ
Romans 12:17-19. Peace doesn't come naturally. For it to happen, we have to think of others, not ourselves.

THINK
- Why do you think God wants us to live in peace?
- Why doesn't God want us to get back at someone?
- Imagine an ending for this story, showing how Rocío could pursue peace in her family. Then read the possible ending at the back of the book.

DO
- Make a poster by tracing around each family member's hand. Title it "Give Peace a Hand!"
- On the poster, have each family member write a way he or she will try to be a peacemaker the next time another family member upsets him or her.

PRAY
Ask God to help you be a peacemaker and not to take revenge.

MEMORIZE
Do all that you can to live in peace with everyone. Romans 12:18

WHAT'S THE POINT?
When bad things happen, we have a choice. We can make things worse by choosing a sinful response, one that doesn't consider the other person. Or we can do our best to stay at peace with the person by remembering that we care about him or her and choosing to work toward peace. *LF*

MAY 13
Twice a Day

"Have you brushed your teeth?" At least twice a day, Caitlyn's mom reminded her to brush her teeth. Several times she even added, "Did you remember to floss?"

On Friday Caitlyn had a dental appointment. She wasn't afraid of the dentist. What she didn't like was that he could always tell if she had forgotten to follow her mom's reminders.

"Why are teeth so important anyhow?" she asked Dr. Lambert.

"The teeth you're getting are your permanent teeth; they need to last your whole life. You'll need them to chew and to talk normally, for starters," he explained.

"I get busy and forget," explained Caitlyn. Dr. Lambert opened up a drawer and pulled out something special for patients like Caitlyn.

READ
Proverbs 4:13. This verse tells us that we should listen to wise instruction and not forget it. It will help us have a healthy and safe life.

THINK
- Why does God want us to listen and remember to follow wise instruction?
- How can following good advice help us be healthier, happier, and more obedient to God?
- Finish the story, showing how Caitlyn could benefit from knowing this verse. Then read the possible ending at the back of the book.

DO
- What is some good advice that you have gotten from a doctor, teacher, or parent?
- Did you remember to follow the advice? Make a chart with columns labeled Sunday through Saturday. Each day that you follow the advice, put a check mark in the right column.

PRAY
Thank God that he gave you wise people like parents and doctors to give you good advice on how to take care of yourself and be healthy and safe.

MEMORIZE
Take hold of my instructions; don't let them go. Guard them, for they are the key to life. Proverbs 4:13

WHAT'S THE POINT?
God uses other people in our lives to give us good advice on how to live wisely. We should listen and not forget to follow their advice. *LF*

MAY 14
The Spelling Test

Every school week ended with something Zander dreaded—a spelling test. All week long he would study the fifteen words Mrs. Foster gave him. He would even take a practice test with his mother every Thursday night. "I'm not going to do good," he told himself every Friday morning.

"Does everyone have a pencil and paper?" Mrs. Foster asked on Friday. "Please number from 1 to 15 on your paper." Zander gripped his pencil tightly. He could almost feel the words float out of his brain.

"The first word is 'legislature,'" Mrs. Foster announced. Rather than start to write, Zander started to squirm in his chair and breathe faster. Soon he was so nervous that he had trouble thinking at all.

READ
Psalm 118:5-6. When we're upset, God wants us to pray instead of becoming so afraid that we forget about him. When we worry, we stop accepting God's help.

THINK
- What thought keeps the psalm writer from being afraid?
- What does it mean to trust God? How is worry the opposite of trust?
- Finish the story, showing how Zander could take these verses to heart. Then read the possible ending at the back of the book.

DO
- Learn a simple prayer to say when you feel afraid, such as "God, I trust you. Help me with _____."
- Say the prayer now about something that you're afraid of or worried about.

PRAY
Ask God to help you give him your worries. Ask him to help you trust in him to give you peace.

MEMORIZE
In my distress I prayed to the LORD, and the LORD answered me and set me free. Psalm 118:5

WHAT'S THE POINT?
God loves us. One way that he shows his love is by encouraging us to pray rather than worry. He listens to our needs. We can trust in him to give us peace. *LF*

MAY 15
Wow, New Comic Books

"Let's hang out at your house today," Theresa said to her friend Corinne. Theresa liked Corinne's house the best. Corinne had two older sisters and they had cool stuff that they shared with Corinne and Theresa.

"Wow, new comic books," Theresa said as she noticed a stack of them on the kitchen table.

"My sisters are always reading those," Corinne said, giggling. "They're scary."

Theresa paged through a comic book. While some of the pages were fun and colorful, others had mean, scary images that she felt uncomfortable seeing.

READ
Philippians 4:8. What we put into our minds makes a difference to God. He wants us to fill our minds with good and true things.

THINK
- Why would God want us to think about good things?
- What happens when we spend our time thinking about things that aren't good or true?
- Finish the story, showing how Theresa could begin to apply the instruction in today's verse. Then read the possible ending at the back of the book.

DO
- Find filters in your home. Here's a hint: Check out a coffeemaker. Or ask a parent about the furnace. Filters let good things through and keep bad things out, like coffee grounds or dust.
- Create your own "life filter" by asking yourself, "Is whatever I'm going to see or do true, right, and good?" Think of several things you will look at or do this week. Ask yourself the question about them. Do them only if the answer is "yes."

PRAY
Ask God to help you filter what you see and do.

MEMORIZE
Fix your thoughts on what is true, and honorable, and right, and pure, and lovely, and admirable. Think about things that are excellent and worthy of praise. Philippians 4:8

WHAT'S THE POINT?
God knows that when we put good things in our minds, good things come out of our lives. He also knows that the memory he gave us is powerful. He wants to protect us, and that's why he warns us to be careful. Things can get stuck in our minds even when we don't want them to stick! It's better to have good things stick. *LF*

MAY 16
A Job Well Done

Shelley carefully glued the last map onto her social studies project. "There! I'm almost done!" she said with satisfaction. Shelley had been working steadily on this project for two weeks. It was due tomorrow. She was hoping Mr. Barnes would give her a good grade.

"Wow, Shelley!" her mom exclaimed. "That looks amazing! I'm sure Mr. Barnes is really going to like what you've done."

The next day Shelley was shuffling onto the bus with her project. She saw Amanda sitting in one of the seats with her social studies project resting on her lap. As Shelley looked it over, she started to feel discouraged. *Amanda is so creative! She has so much more information on her project. What if Mr. Barnes thinks I didn't do enough?* Shelley glumly stared out the window.

READ
Galatians 6:4. If we work hard, we'll have the satisfaction of a job well done. Then we won't need to be anxious and compare ourselves to anyone else. Even if someone else seems more talented, we can know we've done our best, and that is good enough for God.

THINK
- Why do people compare themselves to others?
- How do you feel when you compare yourself to a friend or brother or sister?
- Make up an ending for the story, showing how Shelley could find wisdom in today's verse. Then read the possible ending at the back of the book.

DO
- Remember a time when you worked hard at something and received praise for it. Write about it or draw a picture.
- Think of a way you tend to compare yourself unfavorably to someone else. Write yourself a note from God's point of view, encouraging you to simply do your best and not compare.

PRAY
Ask God to help you work hard and wisely when you do projects or schoolwork.

MEMORIZE
Pay careful attention to your own work, for then you will get the satisfaction of a job well done, and you won't need to compare yourself to anyone else. Galatians 6:4

WHAT'S THE POINT?
When we compare ourselves to others, we can become insecure about our own efforts; this happened to Shelley. Paying attention to our own work and working hard will pay off with the satisfaction that we've done our best. *LF*

MAY 17
I Don't Lie All the Time

Mariel couldn't pull herself away from the TV. Tonight's episode of her favorite mystery show had her guessing until the end.

"Mariel, did you unload the dishwasher?" her mother asked as the show reached the most exciting part.

"Yes," Mariel responded, without even looking up.

As she was going to bed that evening, Mariel's mother stopped her. "I looked in the dishwasher just now, and all the dishes are still in it," Mom said.

"Oh, I guess I was wrong. I forgot that I didn't do it," Mariel answered.

"You lied to me, honey," said Mom.

"Well, I don't lie *all* the time," answered Mariel.

READ
Ephesians 4:25. God wants us to tell the truth—all the time, not just when we feel like it or it is convenient.

THINK
- What is truth? Why is it important?
- Why do you think people lie?
- Finish the story, showing how Mariel could follow the direction given in today's verse. Then read the possible ending at the back of the book.

DO
- People who tell the truth are trustworthy. Make a T-shirt design showing the benefits of being trustworthy.
- Write the names of several people who count on you to be trustworthy. This week think of them when you are tempted to lie.

PRAY
Ask God to help you always speak the truth—even if you are concerned about the consequences.

MEMORIZE
Stop telling lies. Let us tell our neighbors the truth, for we are all parts of the same body. Ephesians 4:25

WHAT'S THE POINT?
God knows that lying hurts relationships. He wants us to live together in peace and trust. Telling the truth to each other is one of the ways we can do that. *LF*

MAY 18
I Don't Want to Work

Luke shoved the vacuum back and forth as he daydreamed about the expensive new sneakers he was saving up to buy. Getting paid for doing extra chores was taking a long time. When his mom went upstairs, he hurriedly took out her wallet and removed a dollar bill.

"What are you doing?" his mom asked. Luke jumped. How could he have not heard her coming back?

"Nothing," he stammered.

"So that's where my money's been going. How long have you been doing this?"

"A couple of months, I guess."

"Why?" Mom demanded.

"It's taking too long to earn money for my shoes. I need them now!" he said desperately.

READ
Ephesians 4:28. Like lying, God knows that stealing damages relationships. God gives us a choice. We can use our hands for doing good things or for doing bad things.

THINK
- What do you think God would say about taking something without asking? Why?
- What do you think God would say about shoplifting? Why?
- Finish the story, showing how today's verse could change Luke's life. Then read the possible ending at the back of the book.

DO
- Sketch something you have stolen. Have you made excuses, thinking it's not really stealing?
- Make a plan to ask forgiveness and make up for what you have stolen. There may still be consequences, but God will be pleased.

PRAY
Ask God to help you work for what you want, not steal.

MEMORIZE
If you are a thief, quit stealing. Instead, use your hands for good hard work, and then give generously to others in need. Ephesians 4:28

WHAT'S THE POINT?
Luke understood the seriousness of what he had done. God forbids stealing. Luke took the first step toward making things right. *LF*

MAY 19
Swinging High

With only five minutes until recess, Benjamin carefully positioned himself so he'd be first outside. Today he was going to get one of the swings for sure. Other kids tended to hog them, so he didn't get a turn.

His plan worked, and soon he was swinging high. Gordy arrived a minute later, and all the swings were gone.

"I got one today!" Benjamin shouted. "It's about time."

"Can I have a turn?" Gordy asked.

"But I finally got my turn," Benjamin said. "Maybe someone else will get off."

READ
Psalm 143:10. God wants to teach us to do the things that please him.

THINK
- What kinds of actions please God?
- Which of these actions would you need God's help to want to do?
- Finish the story, showing how God's Spirit might help Benjamin make good choices. Then read the possible ending at the back of the book.

DO
- Discuss with your family: Can we see or feel God's power in us? How can we know it is there?
- Take turns telling about an action that would please God but is hard for you to do. Pray for each other, asking for God to work in all of you to want to do what's right.

PRAY
Talk to God about how you feel about pleasing him in all you say and do. Ask for his help.

MEMORIZE
Teach me to do your will, for you are my God. May your gracious Spirit lead me forward on a firm footing. Psalm 143:10

WHAT'S THE POINT?
Our desire to please God comes from the Holy Spirit living in us. When we know what is right to do but don't feel like doing it, we can ask God for his help. *LF*

MAY 20
The Shouting Match

"Loser!" Ross yelled to a classmate on the playground. "Just shut up!"

"You shut up," was the response. Marcus wasn't sure what had started the shouting match. He couldn't seem to stop watching the two guys as they said meaner and meaner things to each other. Soon bad names were flying back and forth.

"What are you staring at?" Ross said, as he turned and glared at Marcus. "What's your problem?"

Marcus felt his heart beat faster. "Shut up" was on the tip of his own tongue.

READ
Colossians 3:8. God wants us to avoid hurtful behavior and words.

THINK
- How can bad names and unkind words hurt people?
- Why should we be careful how we use our words?
- Finish the story, showing how Marcus could live by the teaching of today's verse. Then read the possible ending at the back of the book.

DO
- Think of how people talk to one another on the playground, in the classroom, and in stores. Discuss with your family: are people generally kind, or do they often speak in ways that are hurtful or negative?
- Write a minus sign (-) to stand for mean or bad words you're sometimes tempted to say. This week, will you stop yourself and see if you can say something positive instead? If so, turn the – sign into a + sign. Maybe you'll make somebody's day!

PRAY
God knows that sometimes it's hard to do the right thing. Ask him to help you use kind words each day.

MEMORIZE
Now is the time to get rid of anger, rage, malicious behavior, slander, and dirty language. Colossians 3:8

WHAT'S THE POINT?
Each day Jesus wants us to behave in loving and kind ways. One way to do that is with the words we choose. *LF*

MAY 21
You Did That on Purpose!

"You broke my favorite camping chair!" Vince said.

"I'm sorry; forgive me," his older brother said. "I didn't mean to."

"You did it on purpose!" Vince was angry.

"It was an accident!" Jakob said.

Vince stomped away. The chair couldn't be replaced, and his brother shouldn't have sat on it the wrong way. He wasn't going to talk to him for the rest of the campout.

"What happened to your chair?" Vince's dad asked at the evening campfire.

"Jakob broke it—on purpose," Vince said. "He said he was sorry, but I don't believe him."

READ
Matthew 5:7. *Mercy* is kindness toward someone who doesn't deserve it or someone who has wronged you.

THINK
- Why do you think the verse says that when we're merciful, we'll find mercy?
- Who has already shown us great mercy?
- Make up an ending for this story, showing how Vince could show mercy. Then read the possible ending at the back of the book.

DO
- With your family, talk about why we often jump to the conclusion that someone hurt us on purpose. How would this affect whether we're willing to be merciful?
- Think of someone who wronged you. Choose how you will show mercy this week: forgive the person; let the person know you're still friends; stop bringing up the wrong; do something kind for them; believe it when the person says it wasn't done on purpose; or think of another idea of your own.

PRAY
Thank God that he loves you so much that he forgave all of your sins. Ask him to help you forgive the wrongs of others and be able to show mercy.

MEMORIZE
God blesses those who are merciful, for they will be shown mercy. Matthew 5:7

WHAT'S THE POINT?
God shows us what mercy is like by forgiving us and loving us even though we're sinners. When we forgive each other, we pass along God's love and kindness. *LF*

MAY 22
Fix It, Mr. Cricket

"Mr. Cricket can fix it," Mrs. Johnson said, looking at the broken shelf in the reading nook of the classroom. "Let's save him some time and take the books off now."

Josh got to work. Besides having a fun name, Mr. Cricket was a fun person. He knew every student's name. He always smiled and asked kids how they were doing.

Even more important, when things broke or a student accidentally made a mess, he never got angry. Kennedy Elementary School was blessed to have a janitor who really liked his job.

At the end of the school day, Josh ran into Mr. Cricket as he was hauling garbage to the dumpster. "Mr. Cricket, that smells terrible," Josh said. "Don't you hate your job?"

READ
Colossians 3:23. Our work is a gift from God, whether it's going to school each day or keeping a school building clean. It's our special way to serve the Lord.

THINK
▣ Why should we focus on working for God instead of people?
▣ What are some jobs you have, such as schoolwork and chores?
▣ Make up an ending for the story, showing how Josh could learn from the verse. Then read the possible ending at the back of the book.

DO
▣ Sketch a job that you don't like to do and remember that when you do it, you are doing it for God.
▣ Sketch a gift box around the job sketch to show God you are giving this job as a gift to him.

PRAY
Thank God for a way to serve him. Ask him to help you do your job for him and not just for people.

MEMORIZE
Work willingly at whatever you do, as though you were working for the Lord rather than for people. Colossians 3:23

WHAT'S THE POINT?
Mr. Cricket knew that no matter what God has called us to do, we can do it for him. *LF*

MAY 23
Three's a Crowd

All the kids in Lina's neighborhood liked to play together, but this summer was different. The new girl, Sydney, was taking away Lina's best friend.

When Lina visited Becky's house, Sydney was there. "Three's a crowd," Becky told her. The tears started to sting in Lina's eyes. It hurt to be excluded.

As Lina walked back to her house, the tears ran down her cheeks. Becky and Sydney were so mean. As she neared her yard, she wondered what she could do that would make them feel just as terrible as she felt right now.

READ

1 Thessalonians 5:15. When we are hurt by another person's actions, our human response is to want to hurt that person back. God challenges us to do the opposite.

THINK

- Why do you think Christians can struggle with wanting to get even?
- What are some ways that you can "try to do good" even when you don't feel like it?
- Finish the story, showing how Lina could choose her actions to obey this verse. Then read the possible ending at the back of the book.

DO

- Remember a time when your feelings were hurt. What caused it, and how did you respond?
- Write the name of an adult who you can feel comfortable pouring out your feelings to. (Don't forget God! He cares about our feelings.)
- In the coming week, if someone does or says something that upsets you, count to one hundred to cool down. Look for someone to help you work through your feelings. Then pray that God will help you get your feelings under control so you can respond in a Christlike way.

PRAY

Thank God that he shows us what love looks like. Ask him to help you to be kind even when it's hard.

MEMORIZE

See that no one pays back evil for evil, but always try to do good to each other and to all people. 1 Thessalonians 5:15

WHAT'S THE POINT?

When we try to get even, God knows the result will be more wrong being done. As Christians, we are asked to do good, no matter what the situation or how we feel. *LF*

MAY 24
Me, My Dog, and God

"Up," said Jonathan, and his bulldog, Meatball, leaped onto the bed. Jonathan got his Bible and sat with Meatball's head in his lap. He scratched the dog's ears while he read a story about Jesus. "I like to have my devotions when I'm curled up with you, Meat," he said. "It helps me think that Jesus likes to curl up with me and talk to me through the Bible."

Jonathan's dad came in and rubbed Meatball's tummy. "I think you feel closer to God when you're with animals," Dad said.

Jonathan said, "That sounds funny!"

READ
James 4:8. God is with us every day. One of the best ways to connect with him is through reading his Word—the Bible—and praying. We can each find our own special way to do that.

THINK
- What helps you feel that God is close by and involved in your life?
- Why is it good that God is with you?
- Imagine an ending for this story, showing how the verse can make a difference for Jonathan. Then read the possible ending at the back of the book.

DO
- Plan a way to remind yourself when you're having devotions that God meets you there. Ideas: post a sign with James 4:8 written on it in your room; snuggle under a blanket to remind yourself that you're surrounded by God's love; sit outside in the nature that God made; share the time with a family member who loves you as God does.

PRAY
When you are spending time with God, tell him how it feels to know that he's always with you.

MEMORIZE
Come close to God, and God will come close to you. Wash your hands, you sinners; purify your hearts, for your loyalty is divided between God and the world. James 4:8

WHAT'S THE POINT?
God is always eager to be with us. We need to do our part as well. God gave us the Bible to be read regularly. He gave us the gift of being able to talk directly to him. *BA*

MAY 25
Spray Paint

"Look what I found," Parker said to his neighbor Tristan. He held up two cans of green spray paint. "They're from when my dad painted the patio furniture."

Tristan shook a can. "What should we do with it?"

"Let's paint some stuff on that old guy's garage across the street. It's practically falling down. He never uses it."

"I think that's against the law," Tristan said doubtfully.

"It'll be fine," Parker said. "Let's go."

The boys had fun spray painting the garage. They had just started spray painting each other when they saw a police officer coming through the yard toward them. "Hold it, you kids!" he called.

"Yikes!" hollered Parker, and he took off through the trees.

READ
1 Peter 2:13-15. God wants us to obey the law and the people who make the laws. Authorities are the people in charge of us and the rules we need to live by.

THINK
- Why do you think God gives us authorities?
- What does the verse say about why we should obey them?
- Finish the story, showing how the truth of today's verses might help Tristan act wisely. Then read the possible ending at the back of the book.

DO
- Make a matching game. Write some authorities in your life on separate pieces of paper. Write some things they tell you to do on other pieces of paper. See if your family can match the authorities with what they say. For example, "Put your dirty clothes in the hamper" might match with "Mom."
- Choose one thing an authority says that you're tempted not to obey. Make a deal with Jesus that you will obey it this week.

PRAY
Ask God to help you obey authorities this week.

MEMORIZE
For the Lord's sake, respect all human authority—whether the king as head of state, or the officials he has appointed. 1 Peter 2:13-14

WHAT'S THE POINT?
Tristan made a poor decision to spray paint the garage. But he made a good decision to obey the police officer and make up for his wrong choice. God wants us to obey our authorities. *BA*

MAY 26
Shop till You Drop

Preparing for the "Shop till You Drop" event at Toby's church involved nearly one hundred people. In the months before the May event, clothes, shoes, food, and toys were collected. Families in the community who were having a hard time were invited to "shop" for what they needed.

This year Toby's Pioneer Clubs Trailblazer group would help unload two school buses full of donations. "Take the boxes to the sorting area with a sign that matches the label on the box," explained his club leader.

Toby and his friends worked for three hours. Amazingly, the gym turned into an organized store. "Ask your parents if you can come back on Saturday; we need more help the day of the event," his leader said.

READ
1 John 3:17-18. Love is more than a word. It is an action. What we say and do shows God's love to others.

THINK
- How does God want us to use our possessions?
- How can we show love by actions and not just by saying "I love you"?
- Finish the story, showing how Toby could put love into action. Then read the possible ending at the back of the book.

DO
- Why does God want us to help those in need?
- Sort through your toys or clothes and donate some to a resale store, church garage sale, homeless shelter, or another charity.

PRAY
Ask God to help you develop the desire to help people in need.

MEMORIZE
If someone has enough money to live well and sees a brother or sister in need but shows no compassion—how can God's love be in that person? Dear children, let's not merely say that we love each other; let us show the truth by our actions. 1 John 3:17-18

WHAT'S THE POINT?
God wants us to love with actions, not just with words. When we share our time and possessions with those who have less than we do, we show God's love to others. *LF*

MAY 27
Close Call

Jocelyn's father put out an arm to hold her back on the curb. They were waiting to cross the busy city street as cars, buses, and taxis raced by. Jocelyn was eager to get home and play with her friends.

"Be patient, Jocelyn," her father said, as she stepped off the curb again. "Wait until I say 'go.'"

Jocelyn looked both ways, as she'd been taught. The road looked clear. Cars were slowing down for the yellow light. She ran into the crosswalk just as a taxi ran the yellow light and came straight at her. The taxi's horn blared. Her father yelled.

READ

Colossians 3:20. God has our best interests in mind when he gives us instructions. He wants parents to have our best interests in mind too. He wants us to obey.

THINK

- Do you think it's hard or easy to be a parent? Why?
- Why do you think God wants us to obey our parents?
- Finish the story, showing how obeying the instruction in today's verse could save Jocelyn's life! Then read the possible ending at the back of the book.

DO

- Write down some instructions your mom or dad wants you to obey. Put a 1 by the ones that are hard to obey, a 3 by the ones that are easy to obey, and a 2 by the medium ones.
- Circle an instruction you rated 1 that you will plan to do this week without complaining or putting off until later.

PRAY

Thank God for your parents (or the person who's like a parent to you). Ask God to help you obey them.

MEMORIZE

Children, always obey your parents, for this pleases the Lord. Colossians 3:20

WHAT'S THE POINT?

God wants parents to protect and care for us. They know more about the world, so they can give us instructions that help us when we obey. *LF*

MAY 28
What's the Matter with the Batter?

"Trust me, I know how to follow a recipe," Harrison said. "We learned about cooking at Pioneer Clubs."

His sister, Lori, wasn't quite so sure. "Have you ever made this recipe before?" she asked.

"Once before, and Mom only kind of helped," Harrison said with confidence. Lori watched as Harrison measured out the ingredients. She'd watched her mother cook, and Harrison wasn't doing everything the same way.

"Mom doesn't do that," Lori remarked. "She usually adds the flour last."

"Don't worry. I know what I'm doing," said Harrison, a little disturbed by his sister's comments.

When the batter was ready, it didn't look anything like Harrison remembered.

READ
Proverbs 19:20. God puts wise people in our lives who have good advice. We can listen to them to avoid trouble.

THINK
- What can happen when we avoid good advice?
- If you wanted to make a good choice, what steps would you take?
- Make up an ending for the story, showing how Harrison might follow the verse. Then read the possible ending at the back of the book.

DO
- Write a list of people you can turn to for good advice.
- Think of a choice you need to make. Ask at least one person from your list for advice this week.

PRAY
Ask God to help you know good advice when you hear it and to help you listen.

MEMORIZE
Get all the advice and instruction you can, so you will be wise the rest of your life.
Proverbs 19:20

WHAT'S THE POINT?
Harrison realized that his knowledge about cooking was limited. Listening to his sister's advice and then asking his mom for help would have prevented his cooking disaster. *LF*

MAY 29
Let Me in the Tent!

"You're too little to play with us," Roberto's older brother, Guillermo, told him. Then Guillermo started to zip up the opening to the tent.

"Mamá said you had to include me!" Roberto said. "Let me in!"

All day long Roberto had looked forward to the backyard campout. Now Guillermo and his friends were being a pain.

"Let me in!" he shouted again. He could hear the older boys inside laughing.

Roberto clenched his fists. He looked at the tent pegs that held the sides of the tent upright. If he couldn't be included in the fun, then he was going to stop the fun.

As his hand reached for the first tent peg, he heard his mother call his name.

READ
Proverbs 29:11. When we feel left out or someone hurts our feelings, it's natural to feel angry. We can let our anger control us or we can control our anger.

THINK
- When we let anger control our actions, what can happen to our relationships?
- What kinds of actions would be foolish when we're angry?
- Finish the story, showing how Roberto could apply what he knows from this verse. Then read the possible ending at the back of the book.

DO
- When we slow down and take time to think rather than react, what might happen to our angry feelings?
- When you feel angry this week, ask yourself why. If the reason is that your feelings are hurt, talk things over with an adult instead of acting on your anger.

PRAY
Ask God to help you recognize when you are getting angry, then act in a way that is pleasing to him.

MEMORIZE
Fools vent their anger, but the wise quietly hold it back. Proverbs 29:11

WHAT'S THE POINT?
God made us with many wonderful emotions, but he also knows we need to learn to control them. Thinking things through can stop us from acting in a way that doesn't please God. *LF*

MAY 30
Hide It in Your Heart

Whenever Jack practiced his memory work for Pioneer Clubs, he always messed up a word or two.

"Perfection isn't the goal," said Mrs. Camp, his club leader, as she encouraged Jack to keep working hard. "You're doing the best you can, and God is pleased." He tried again and got almost all the words right.

At the end of club time, club members shared prayer requests. "I'm worried about my uncle Bill," Ivan said. "He's on a big trip to Singapore for work, and I hope he'll be safe."

"Hey, I know what to do when we're worried," Jack said. "God wants us to give our cares to him."

READ
Psalm 119:11. When we memorize God's Word, the Bible, it fills our minds and changes us to be more like God.

THINK
- Why are we less likely to sin when we have God's Word in our minds?
- What are some ways we can memorize the Bible?
- Finish the story, showing how knowing the verse is helping Jack. Then read the possible ending at the back of the book.

DO
- With your family, think of a creative way to memorize today's verse, such as a game, song, or rap.
- Take turns practicing memory verses from weeks ago. Tell how any of them have helped you.

PRAY
Thank God for the gift of the Bible. Thank him for how it can work in us to shape our actions and thoughts.

MEMORIZE
I have hidden your word in my heart, that I might not sin against you. Psalm 119:11

WHAT'S THE POINT?
God's Word guides us; it helps us do the things that please God. That's why it is important to memorize verses, so they will always be available when we need their guidance. *BA*

MAY 31
Sorting Beans

"I've never helped at a food pantry," Jesse said. "What's there to do?"

The outreach project at Jesse's church for May was to spend a day helping organize canned food donations. More and more people needed food these days, and all helpers were welcome. Convinced it would be boring, Jesse wanted to stay home.

His good friend Jimmy finally talked him into joining the group. When they arrived at the food pantry's office, Jesse could not believe the boxes and boxes of food that needed to be sorted.

"No way," Jesse groaned as he grabbed the first can of beans.

"Let's dive in," Jimmy urged. "We can finish our section in less than two hours!"

Soon the boys had a rhythm going, and they stopped only once for some water.

READ

Hebrews 13:16. A sacrifice is something special that we give to God. By nature, we human beings like to serve ourselves. But thinking of others is like giving God a gift.

THINK

- How does God feel when we think of others and do good for them?
- See how many ways you can list that we can do good and share with others.
- Make up an ending for this story, showing how Jesse lived out the teaching of the verse. Then read the possible ending at the back of the book.

DO

- With your family, practice doing good by giving each other some compliments.
- Tell your family something good you will do for someone this week.

PRAY

Ask God to help you care about the needs of others.

MEMORIZE

Don't forget to do good and to share with those in need. These are the sacrifices that please God. Hebrews 13:16

WHAT'S THE POINT?

When we serve God by serving others, we often feel happiness and joy. God gives special blessings to those who help other people! *LF*

JUNE 1
Ugh! Dirty Feet

Dennis was not about to go to the foot-washing ceremony at his church. "Who wants to wash someone's stinky, dirty feet?" he said to his mom. Not only that, he didn't want anyone to wash his feet. It would be embarrassing.

That night at dinner, his family talked about foot washing. Dennis's sister said, "It was neat last year that I got to wash my best friend's feet." His brother added, "Yeah, you were lucky. I had to wash the feet of the guy who teases me about being short. But the worst thing is that he washed my feet too."

Dennis could not imagine getting on his knees with a pan of water to wash someone's feet. It definitely did not seem like a cool thing to do.

READ
John 13:3-5, 8, 12-15. God's Word shows Jesus washing his disciples' feet. He told them he had given them an example to follow.

THINK
- Why did Jesus wash his disciples' feet?
- Do you think it was strange that Jesus would do something like wash the disciples' feet?
- What "example" was Jesus talking about?
- Imagine an ending for this story, showing how the verses could make a difference for Dennis. Then read the possible ending at the back of the book.

DO
- Have a small foot-washing ceremony with your family.
- Discuss what Jesus' message of serving others could mean for your family.

PRAY
Ask God to help you serve someone this week.

MEMORIZE
Since I, your Lord and Teacher, have washed your feet, you ought to wash each other's feet. I have given you an example to follow. Do as I have done to you. John 13:14-15

WHAT'S THE POINT?
Jesus gave us an example of serving others rather than feeling as though we're too important to serve. *BC*

JUNE 2
God, Can You Hear Me Now?

Bridget was sure she couldn't pray out loud in front of the whole Sunday school class. She begged her mom, "Please call Mrs. Frizzle and tell her I can't pray for the class next week." There was no doubt in her mind that she would stutter, stammer, turn red, and choke on her own words.

"Well," said her mom, "I think it would be a good experience for you. Mrs. Frizzle must have thought you could do it, or she wouldn't have asked you to pray." She suggested that Bridget talk to God about it.

"I don't think God will be able to help me. He has a lot more important things to do," Bridget told her mom.

READ
Psalm 86:6-7. In these verses, the writer asks God to hear his prayer and trusts that God will answer.

THINK
- What does God expect us to do when we're afraid or in trouble?
- What have you been asked to do that you felt you could not do? How did you do it? Did you ask God to help you?
- Finish the story, showing how the verses could encourage Bridget. Then read the possible ending at the back of the book.

DO
- Talk with a parent about how God helps you when you feel as though you can't do something or you're afraid.
- Create a sticker from a sheet of labels that says, "God hears my prayers!" Color the sticker and put it someplace where it will remind you to pray.

PRAY
Ask God to remind you to turn to him first in prayer either when you are afraid, feel as though you can't do something, or have a need.

MEMORIZE
I will call to you whenever I'm in trouble, and you will answer me. Psalm 86:7

WHAT'S THE POINT?
Bridget took her problem to God. God's power helped her to do what she felt she could not do. *BC*

JUNE 3
Raggedy Anne

Yikes! Why is Anne wearing a jacket with a hole in the back? Dustin was taking a test and was trying to figure out a tricky math problem. As he stared into space, his eyes fell on the girl in front of him. Suddenly, he saw something else besides the hole in her jacket: the sleeves were stained and had frayed cuffs.

Anne was different. She lived in a run-down part of town. Kids thought she was weird and talked about her on the playground. Why did she always wear that dumb jacket even when it was hot? Why didn't she go through the lunch line like everyone else? And why did she come to school in stained clothes?

Dustin couldn't wait till recess to tell the other kids about it.

READ
Romans 15:25-26. These verses give us an example to follow of believers who helped others in need.

THINK
- What had the believers in Macedonia and Achaia done for the believers in Jerusalem?
- What was the Macedonians' attitude about giving to the Achaians?
- How have you helped someone in need?
- Finish the story, showing how the verses could inspire Dustin with some good ideas. Then read the possible ending at the back of the book.

DO
- Consider volunteering with your family at a resale shop or food pantry.
- Do something kind for a neighbor or friend whose parents are out of work or are struggling financially.

PRAY
Talk to God about how he can use you to help those in need.

MEMORIZE
Blessed are those who are generous, because they feed the poor. Proverbs 22:9

WHAT'S THE POINT?
Dustin cared about someone else's feelings. He knew what it was like to be in need. God's Word tells us to reach out to others who are in need. *BC*

JUNE 4
Wonder-Working Power

Kendra's Grammy encouraged her to talk about Jesus. She said, "Jesus has wonder-working power. Nothing is too hard for him." She told about how he had healed her after a heart attack.

"But, Grammy, didn't the doctors and nurses take care of you and make you well?" Kendra asked.

Grammy explained that the doctors and nurses did help her. "They have been trained to know what to do and how to take care of sick people. But there came a time when they didn't know what else to do for me. That's when God stepped in and healed me."

It was Grammy's belief in Jesus that led her to talk about him whenever she had a chance. Kendra wanted a faith that gave her confidence to talk about who Jesus is and about his wonderful power.

One night at a slumber party, the girls were talking about God. Becca asked Kendra, "What do you believe?" Kendra wasn't sure what everyone would think of her if she told them. She could ignore the question—or tell them she believed in Jesus.

READ
Acts 3:11-13, 17-19; 1 Peter 3:15. In these verses from Acts, God had just used Peter to heal a man whose legs didn't work. The crowd was excited. Peter used this opportunity to talk about Jesus.

THINK
- What did Peter want the people to know about Jesus and God?
- How would you explain the hope that Jesus gives you?
- Finish the story, showing how the verses could help Kendra speak out for Jesus. Then read the possible ending at the back of the book.

DO
- What are some things you know about Jesus that you can share with someone?
- With a family member, role-play a conversation you could have with someone about Jesus when the opportunity comes.

PRAY
Talk with God about sharing Jesus with others. Ask him to give you the right words.

MEMORIZE
Worship Christ as Lord of your life. And if someone asks about your Christian hope, always be ready to explain it. 1 Peter 3:15

WHAT'S THE POINT?
Kendra had a strong faith and wanted to tell others about Jesus, just like her Grammy and Peter had. *BC*

JUNE 5
Doing What's Best

Sunday school had just ended. Nolan ran to his mom to see if Vito could come over to play after church. "Sure," his mom said. "But only if it's okay with Vito's mom."

Later at Nolan's house, the boys were wondering what to play. "I've got it! Let's watch Action Rangers on TV. It's my favorite cartoon!" Nolan said.

Vito hesitated. "My mom doesn't let me watch Action Rangers—too much kicking and punching, she says."

"It's okay; my mom let's *me* watch it!" Nolan said. "Besides, your mom's not here." Vito still looked uncomfortable. But Nolan was sure he could talk Vito into watching the show.

READ
1 Corinthians 10:32-33. These verses talk about how we should not do anything that would encourage another follower of Jesus to sin.

THINK
- How could something be okay for you to do but not okay for someone else?
- What do the verses say about how we should act when this happens?
- Finish the story, showing how Nolan could apply the teaching of the verses. Then read the possible ending at the back of the book.

DO
- Using puppets, act out a scene with a family member where one character wants to do something that would not be good for the other character. Show what happens.
- Discuss how our choices can encourage each other to act in ways that please God.

PRAY
Ask God to give you wisdom to know how to be a good example.

MEMORIZE
Don't give offense to Jews or Gentiles or the church of God. 1 Corinthians 10:32

WHAT'S THE POINT?
Nolan realized that by talking Vito into watching the TV show, he'd be encouraging Vito to disobey his mom, which is wrong. *BC*

JUNE 6
False Gods

Dawson squirmed at his desk. For Art Appreciation, Arjun's mother had brought in a fancy picture with lots of golds and reds and oranges. The figure in the picture looked like a person, but with four arms and a trunk like an elephant. "This is our god, Ganesh," she explained. "In our Hindu religion, we pray to Ganesh."

"I like the colors," said Liita.

"Why does he have a broken tusk?" Wally asked.

As Mrs. Patel talked about the painting, Dawson felt uncomfortable. He started to pray. *Jesus, I know Ganesh isn't a real god. So praying to him is worshiping an idol, right?*

At recess, Dawson said to his friends, "Who believes in Jesus?" Some of the kids raised their hands.

"There are many gods," said Arjun.

READ
Matthew 28:18-20. Jesus told his followers to go into all the world and tell people about him so they could become his followers too.

THINK
- Why do people need to know about Jesus?
- How can Jesus help us tell others about him?
- Finish the story, showing how the verses could help Dawson figure out what to do. Then read the possible ending at the back of the book.

DO
- Name some things you know about Jesus, what he has done for you, and how to accept him as your Savior.
- With your family, role-play ways to tell others what you know about Jesus.

PRAY
Ask God for an opportunity to tell someone something you know about Jesus.

MEMORIZE
Go and make disciples of all the nations, baptizing them in the name of the Father and the Son and the Holy Spirit. Matthew 28:19

WHAT'S THE POINT?
Dawson followed Jesus' command to tell others about him. Dawson knew Jesus would be with him and help him because Jesus promised to be. *BA*

JUNE 7
Sharing a Lunch Table

Callie was different. She never talked to anyone and rarely looked at others when they talked to her. She ate lunch alone at the end of the lunch table. But the worst thing was the clothes she wore—they looked faded and worn and didn't fit right. Everyone avoided her.

Some of the kids whispered behind her back, "I heard she doesn't have a place to live and sleeps in her car. That's why she's the way she is." Shari didn't know if that was true, but she remembered what Jesus had said in the Bible about treating others kindly. *I guess I should give it a try,* she thought.

The next day at lunch Shari put her lunch tray down across the table from Callie. "Hi! Umm, could I eat with you?" Callie looked up at her through a thick fringe of bangs and nodded. Shari took a deep breath and sat down.

READ
Luke 8:26-39. These verses tell how Jesus healed a demon-possessed man and told him to tell everyone what God did for him.

THINK
- How was the man freed from the demons?
- How did meeting Jesus make a difference? What did Jesus tell the man to do?
- Make up an ending for the story, showing how Shari lived out the teaching of the verses. Then read the possible ending at the back of the book.

DO
- With a parent, discuss the great things God has done for you and your family over the years.
- Choose a friend or family member to tell about what God has done for you.

PRAY
Ask God to help you share about Jesus and what he has done for you so you can help others.

MEMORIZE
"Go back to your family, and tell them everything God has done for you." So he went all through the town proclaiming the great things Jesus had done for him. Luke 8:39

WHAT'S THE POINT?
Shari knew God had taken care of her family. She wanted Callie to know that God could take care of her family too. *BC*

JUNE 8
I've Lost It!

Tammy wanted to take her grandmother's ivory cross made out of an elephant's tusk to Sunday school. She told her grandmother, "Grandma, we're studying about the church in Africa. Can I take your cross and show it?"

Her grandmother said, "Yes, but be careful with it. It's very special to me." Tammy agreed to guard it carefully.

When Tammy got home from church, Grandma asked, "Did the class enjoy the ivory cross?" Tammy reached into her pocket to return it. *Oh no, where is it?* thought Tammy. *What do I do now?* She was sure the church would be locked up by now. How would she ever find it?

Her mother quickly called the church. She suggested Tammy pray that God would show her where it was.

READ
2 Kings 6:1-7. These verses talk about a man of God, Elisha, who cared enough about his followers to find an ax head that had been lost in the water.

THINK
- What is Elisha called in verse 6? Why is that important?
- How did Elisha make the ax head float?
- Imagine an ending for this story, showing how the verses could make a difference for Tammy. Then read the possible ending at the back of the book.

DO
- Write a list of all the times you remember God taking care of you through others.
- Write another list of prayer requests that you currently have.

PRAY
Pray through your prayer request list. Ask God to use others to help you.

MEMORIZE
The LORD directs the steps of the godly. He delights in every detail of their lives.
Psalm 37:23

WHAT'S THE POINT?
The pastor cared about Tammy and wanted to help her. Like Elisha finding the ax head, he was able to find what she had lost. God often uses other people to help us. *BC*

JUNE 9
Love? Who?

Tori was confused about who God wanted her to love. She loved her parents more than anyone. What about Pumpkin, her kitten, and Gran and Gramps?

Her Sunday school teacher had said, "Love your enemies! Do good to them." Her teacher said that was what Jesus told us.

Tori asked her, "How can I love my enemies? What if they're mean to me?" She remembered when she had lent Clarice one of her model horses. Clarice never returned it, even after Tori asked her several times. *Am I supposed to love her, too?* she thought.

READ
Luke 6:32-36. Jesus talked about the importance of loving others who may not be easy to love.

THINK
- Why did Jesus say you shouldn't get credit if you just love those who love you or just do good to those who do good to you?
- Who did Jesus say we should also love? Why?
- Finish the story, showing how the verses can affect Tori's relationship with Clarice. Then read the possible ending at the back of the book.

DO
- Write down a person who reminds you of each of the situations in these verses.
- Discuss with a family member how you could show love to the people whose names you wrote down.

PRAY
Ask God to help you love people in your life who are hard to love.

MEMORIZE
You must be compassionate, just as your Father is compassionate. Luke 6:36

WHAT'S THE POINT?
Jesus tells us to love our enemies. If we ask him, he will help us to show love even when our feelings don't seem ready. *BC*

JUNE 10
Hopscotch on the Clouds

Mrs. Larsen asked her Sunday school class, "What do you think heaven is like?"

The kids went around the room, giving their ideas. Cal said there would be streets of gold. Meyer hoped there would be lots of video games. Lila thought there would be ice cream every day. Monica looked forward to playing hopscotch on the clouds.

Giggles filled the room as they thought about life in heaven. Mrs. Larsen smiled too. Then she said, "You know, Anya isn't here today. Her grandmother died last week. She is in heaven, and I would like for you to think of things about heaven that she will experience so we can encourage Anya."

As the class tackled the question in a serious way, they concluded they didn't know much about heaven. "What *will* it be like?" they wondered.

READ
Revelation 21:1-5. Discover some things about what heaven will be like.

THINK
- What do the verses say about God's presence in heaven?
- What part of the description of heaven do you like best?
- Finish the story, showing how the class can be affected by these verses. Then read the possible ending at the back of the book.

DO
- Talk with family members about their ideas about heaven based on these verses.
- Name someone you know who is in heaven and be glad for him or her.

PRAY
Thank God for preparing a place for you someday in heaven.

MEMORIZE
He will wipe every tear from their eyes, and there will be no more death or sorrow or crying or pain. All these things are gone forever. Revelation 21:4

WHAT'S THE POINT?
The class wanted to comfort Anya by telling her about heaven. The Bible's descriptions of heaven can be a big comfort and encouragement for us. *BC*

JUNE 11
Role Reversal

Christine just knew she was perfect to play the lead role in the community theater's play. The Saturday after tryouts, she couldn't wait to see if she had been assigned the part. As she rushed to see the list, she collided with her best friend, Gina. Christine was stunned when she saw Gina's name at the top. Her best friend had gotten the part she wanted. She almost cried.

She glared at Gina and said, "Why did you try out for that part? I will never forgive you! I should have gotten it."

Later Christine learned she would be doing artwork for the scenery. At least she would have the opportunity to use her artistic gifts, but it didn't make her feel much better.

READ
Romans 12:4-8. These verses explain that God gives each of us different gifts to be used for his glory.

THINK
- What do these verses say about God giving us gifts?
- How does God want us to use our gifts?
- Make up an ending for this story, showing how the verses could make a difference for Christine. Then read the possible ending at the back of the book.

DO
- Create a booklet by stapling paper together. At the top of each page, write a talent or ability you have. Draw a cartoon of how you can use your gifts to help others.

PRAY
Ask God to show you what gifts he has given you. Ask for wisdom about how to use them.

MEMORIZE
In his grace, God has given us different gifts for doing certain things well. Romans 12:6

WHAT'S THE POINT?
Christine realized she had used her gifts to help make the play a success, and so had Gina. God's Word reminds us that we all have different gifts. We should use our gifts and appreciate the gifts he has given others. *BC*

JUNE 12
Sharing Is Awesome

Kirk had worked hard to earn the five-dollar bill he was holding. He had pulled weeds in his neighbor's garden in the hot sun. "I'm going to save till I get enough to buy the building set I've been wanting," he told his mom.

The next Sunday his class watched a video about kids in Haiti. They looked hungry; some had no clothes, and no one had shoes. The teacher said, "The church is collecting money to buy food for them. It will be our way of sharing Jesus with them."

Kirk thought about his five dollars and the building set he wanted. *I'm not going to give my money,* he thought. He'd find some other way to share Jesus' love.

READ
Acts 2:41-47. These verses talk about sharing with others and how great that can be.

THINK
- What are some of the things the early believers shared with one another?
- How have you felt when someone shared with you?
- Imagine an ending for this story, showing how the verses might change Kirk's feelings about giving. Then read the possible ending at the back of the book.

DO
- Talk with your family about what it would be like to be in a church where there is no sharing.
- Find a gift tag. Write on it something you will share this week.

PRAY
Ask God to help you be willing to share with others.

MEMORIZE
All the believers devoted themselves to the apostles' teaching, and to fellowship, and to sharing in meals (including the Lord's Supper), and to prayer. Acts 2:42

WHAT'S THE POINT?
When Kirk saw how he had been blessed because others had shared with him, he wanted to share what he had with others. *BC*

JUNE 13
The Grumpy Day

Bella wasn't feeling particularly joyful this Sunday morning. She had stubbed her toe on the way to the kitchen for breakfast. Her younger brother had eaten the last of her favorite cereal, and the outfit she wanted to wear wasn't clean.

Bella told her mom, "I don't want to go to church today. I'm not in a good mood, and I don't think I should go to church when I'm grumpy."

Her mother put her arms around Bella. She said, "I know how hard it is to do things like worship God when we're feeling grumpy. God understands." She explained to Bella, "Sometimes when we're obedient and praise him even when we don't feel like it, God can surprise us and fill us with his peace and joy."

Bella thought about what her mother had said. It didn't make a whole lot of sense to her.

READ
Psalm 100. This psalm gives us reasons to worship God and be thankful.

THINK
- What enables you to worship God with joy?
- Does worship depend on circumstances—whether we're sad or happy? Explain.
- Finish the story, showing how obeying these verses might change Bella's feelings. Then read the possible ending at the back of the book.

DO
- Play a ball-toss game with your family. Toss a ball from person to person. Each catcher names one reason given in Psalm 100 to worship God.
- Play again, naming ways to respond to God from the psalm. Choose one and do it now.

PRAY
Ask God to give you a thankful, worshiping heart in all circumstances.

MEMORIZE
Enter his gates with thanksgiving; go into his courts with praise. Give thanks to him and praise his name. Psalm 100:4

WHAT'S THE POINT?
Bella discovered that God is good and faithful and his love never fails, no matter what she was feeling. *BC.*

JUNE 14
The Crybaby

Shane didn't know if his mom would ever have time to spend with him. Ever since his baby brother, Sean, was born a month ago, his mother never seemed to have a free moment. Sean always needed something—to be fed, have his diaper changed, have a bath—there was no end to Sean's needs! Mom used to spend extra time helping Shane with his homework, doing puzzles with him, or just talking.

"Why can't you just put Sean in his crib and leave him alone?" Shane asked his mom.

"Shane, Sean is a baby—he can't do things for himself the way you can," she said. "It will get easier as he grows. I'll have time for you again."

Shane decided that he wasn't going to have anything to do with Sean since he was an annoying, helpless crybaby who was keeping his mom from spending more time with him.

READ
Colossians 3:12. This verse tells how belonging to God makes a difference in how we treat others.

THINK
- What does the verse say about being chosen by God?
- How can you "clothe" yourself with the qualities listed in the verse?
- Finish the story, showing how the verse could affect Shane's feelings about his baby brother. Then read the possible ending at the back of the book.

DO
- Think of someone you may not always treat well.
- Come up with a plan for how you can follow the verse to treat the person better.

PRAY
Ask God to help you be kind, gentle, and patient with others no matter who they are.

MEMORIZE
Since God chose you to be the holy people he loves, you must clothe yourselves with tenderhearted mercy, kindness, humility, gentleness, and patience. Colossians 3:12

WHAT'S THE POINT?
Shane realized that his thoughts and actions weren't kind toward his baby brother. When we belong to God, he wants us to be gentle and patient with others. *BC*

JUNE 15
Whose Child Are You?

"Hey, Dad," Campbell said, "I've got a question. What does it mean to live in a foster home?"

"Well, it means you live with people who are not your biological parents," Dad said. "They have agreed to take care of you when your birth parents can't."

Campbell thought about what living with people who were not his biological parents would be like. He wondered if they would love him. Could he love them? Would they have fun together?

"Dad, the Bible says that God loves us so much that we can be called his children. Does that mean that we're like God's foster children?"

Campbell's dad smiled. "No, Campbell, it's not like that," he said. Campbell wondered what it *was* like, then.

READ
1 John 3:1. This verse tells us about the relationship God wants to have with us.

THINK
- What does God call those who know him, according to this verse?
- How does he feel about them?
- Imagine an ending for this story, showing how the verse can help Campbell understand his relationship with God. Then read the possible ending at the back of the book.

DO
- Discuss with family members how God's love is like that of a perfectly great parent. Talk about what it means to be a child of God.
- Are you a child of God? How do you know?

PRAY
Thank God that he loves you so much that you are called one of his children.

MEMORIZE
See how very much our Father loves us, for he calls us his children, and that is what we are! But the people who belong to this world don't recognize that we are God's children because they don't know him. 1 John 3:1

WHAT'S THE POINT?
Campbell was glad he knew God and that God loved him and called him his child. *BC*

JUNE 16
Beanbag Toss

"Oh no! What's *he* doing here?" Franklin whispered to Marcy.

"I don't know, but it means trouble," Marcy responded.

Lars had just shown up at their church's June picnic. He was the troublemaker in the neighborhood. The other kids were afraid of him. What were they supposed to do now?

When Lars walked toward them at the beanbag toss, Franklin and Marcy looked the other way and pretended they didn't see him. Lars said, "Hi! Can I play? I promise I won't pick on you or anything."

Yeah, right, Franklin thought to himself. But Marcy said, "How can we be sure you won't?"

READ
Acts 9:1-6, 26-28. Persecuting people means hurting them. Saul (another name for Paul) hurt the Christians badly. But he changed when he met Jesus. Read 2 Corinthians 5:17.

THINK
- Why did the believers change their minds about Saul?
- How did Saul have the power to change?
- Finish the story, showing how the verses could make a difference for Franklin and Marcy. Then read the possible ending at the back of the book.

DO
- Think of someone you know who needs to be changed by Jesus. Pray for that person.
- Sometimes Jesus changes us all at once. Sometimes he works with us to change us little by little. Tell a family member what attitude or behavior you want Jesus to change about *you*.

PRAY
Thank Jesus for making you a new person. Ask him to work with you to change the attitude or behavior you thought of.

MEMORIZE
Anyone who belongs to Christ has become a new person. The old life is gone; a new life has begun! 2 Corinthians 5:17

WHAT'S THE POINT?
It was hard for the kids to believe Lars had changed until the youth pastor told them that Lars had met Jesus. When people meet Jesus, they become new people. Jesus starts changing them. *BC*

JUNE 17
Division Multiplies

"I have a riddle for you to solve," Kip's mom announced. "When does division lead to multiplication?"

Kip thought and finally said, "I don't know!"

"Check out Acts 6:1-7, and you'll find the answer."

"Okay, I'll check it out after I play baseball," Kip said, and he hurried out.

When Kip met his friends, they discovered that Andy couldn't play because he had yard chores to do. One of the guys said, "Let's help Andy, and then he can play too." So the guys divided the chores. They finished fast, and then ran to the field to play ball.

Kip walked home thinking about his mom's question. A lightbulb flashed on in his head as he thought about what he and the guys had done. *Hmm*, he thought, *we divided the work, and then our fun multiplied.* He wondered if that solved Mom's riddle. After a big gulp of water, he opened the Bible to figure out the answer.

READ
Acts 6:1-7. In the church that began when Jesus went back to heaven, the leaders were overwhelmed with many tasks to do. So they divided them up. Now read Ephesians 4:16. This verse uses the word picture of body parts to describe all the people in a church working together.

THINK
- What could the church leaders concentrate on once they divided up the tasks?
- How did this help the believers multiply?
- Finish the story, showing how Kip applied the verses. Then read the possible ending at the back of the book.

DO
- Choose a job at church or at home that can be divided up to make the work go faster. Find out what part you can do, and do it.
- Talk with the other people who helped about how you all made a difference.

PRAY
Ask God to help you be willing to do your share to make big jobs less overwhelming.

MEMORIZE
He makes the whole body fit together perfectly. As each part does its own special work, it helps the other parts grow, so that the whole body is healthy and growing and full of love. Ephesians 4:16

WHAT'S THE POINT?
In the early church, and with Kip's friends, dividing up the tasks made the work go smoothly and quickly. *BC*

JUNE 18
Fighting with Family

"Jerk!" Marie yelled at her brother.

"I am not!" Leon yelled.

"You are too, and you always will be!" Marie stormed down the stairs.

"Loser!" he shouted after her. Then he sat on the stairs and fumed. Why did he always fight with his sister?

Their dad overheard the yelling. "You know how I feel about the two of you calling each other names."

"I know." Leon sighed. "But sometimes I can't help it. I thought Jesus was supposed to change me now that he's in my life."

Mr. Montaigne sat beside him and put an arm around his shoulder.

READ
Acts 2:38-39. God sends his Holy Spirit to live in each person who accepts Jesus as their Savior. The Holy Spirit comforts us, teaches us about God, and helps us change to be the kind of person God wants us to be.

THINK

- How do you know if the Holy Spirit lives in you?
- Which of the things in today's Bible reading do you want the Holy Spirit to do for you?
- Finish the story, showing how the verses could change Leon's day. Then read the possible ending at the back of the book.

DO
Write down one thing you keep doing wrong that you'd like to change. Ask the Holy Spirit to help you begin changing.

PRAY
Thank God for his gift of the Holy Spirit.

MEMORIZE
Each of you must repent of your sins and turn to God, and be baptized in the name of Jesus Christ for the forgiveness of your sins. Then you will receive the gift of the Holy Spirit. Acts 2:38

WHAT'S THE POINT?
Leon's dad helped him learn that God promises us the Holy Spirit. The Holy Spirit would help him change little by little. *BC*

JUNE 19
First Sunny Day

Carson turned off his buzzing alarm clock, looked out the window, and yelled, "Yay! Sunshine!" For two long rainy weeks, he had been praying for a sunny day. "Mom," he shouted. "Did you see the sun? Let's go to the beach! I want to build sand sculptures."

His mom poked her head into the room. "Did you forget this is Sunday? You can build sand sculptures after church."

Carson didn't want to wait. He began to think of a way to stay home. He could fake a stomachache. He could bribe his mom with the promise to do his chores this week without complaining. All he could think of was getting out in the sun and sand—*now*!

He dragged himself to breakfast. "I'm not happy about going to church," he loudly announced to everyone.

READ
Psalm 122:1. The "house of the LORD" is church. In the psalm writer's time it was called a temple. It was a place to praise and worship God. That is still what church is today.

THINK
- Why do you think God wants us to be happy about going to church?
- How do you feel about going to church? Why?
- Make up an ending for the story, showing how the verse could make a difference for Carson. Then read the possible ending at the back of the book.

DO
- With your family, list all the things that go on in church. Why might they be things to be glad about?

PRAY
Ask God to give you joy about going to church and worshiping him.

MEMORIZE
I was glad when they said to me, "Let us go to the house of the LORD." Psalm 122:1

WHAT'S THE POINT?
Carson realized sunshine is God's creation and is not more important than God. He loved the sunny day, but honoring God comes first and brings good things. *BC*

JUNE 20
Gentle Sheep or Greedy Goat?

Elise was visiting her aunt and uncle on their farm. She stood by the fence watching the sheep and goats grazing in the field. "What's the difference between sheep and goats?" Elise asked her uncle.

"Sheep are gentle and good followers of a shepherd," Uncle Bob replied. "Goats can be selfish and greedy." Then he remarked, "The Bible says some people are like sheep and some are like goats."

Elise remembered shutting her bedroom door in her little sister's face, and the times she stuck out her tongue at her brother, and the times she whined when she didn't want to do something.

"How can I know if I'm a sheep or a goat?" she asked.

READ
Matthew 25:31-40. These verses explain how God's people are like sheep.

THINK
- When we do kind things for others, who are we really doing them for?
- What reward is there for God's people in this story?
- Finish the story, showing how the verses can help Elise figure out whether she is a sheep or a goat. Then read the possible ending at the back of the book.

DO
- After reading the Bible story, how do you feel about doing good things for people? Draw a face showing that feeling.
- Write down a way you will do something kind for Jesus today by doing something kind for someone else.
- If you're not sure you're a sheep, talk to a Christian adult about how to know.

PRAY
Ask God to help you be a good follower of Jesus.

MEMORIZE
The King will say, "I tell you the truth, when you did it to one of the least of these my brothers and sisters, you were doing it to me!" Matthew 25:40

WHAT'S THE POINT?
Elise found out that God's followers are like sheep, not goats. She learned how God's followers show they are his sheep. *BC*

JUNE 21
Getting the Cast Off

Austin swung himself along on his crutches into the grocery store. "Two more days and the cast comes off," his mom said.

"Cool!" said Austin. It had been two months since he broke his leg. He couldn't wait.

"Let's have a little party to celebrate God healing your leg!" Austin's mom said. "We can shop for whatever snacks and dessert you want. And let's get candles and balloons."

"Cool!" Austin said again. "Can I have pizza and a giant chocolate chip cookie?"

"That's quite a combination!" Mom laughed. "Yes, you can have those."

Two days later the cast was off. In the evening, Austin's family gathered for the party. Austin's dad prayed, "Father God, thank you for healing our guy. We want to celebrate your healing power tonight."

Austin said amen with the others. Then he said, "Why are we celebrating God? Didn't my leg just heal on its own?"

READ
Genesis 21:1-3, 6-7. God kept his promise and gave Abraham and Sarah a son. The name they chose for him means "laughter."

THINK
- How did Abraham and Sarah feel about what God had done for them?
- How did the name Isaac celebrate what God had done for them?
- Make up an ending for this story, showing how the verses could affect Austin. Then read the possible ending at the back of the book.

DO
- With your family, choose something God has done for you. It can be an everyday thing or a big, exciting thing. Plan a way to celebrate what God did. Ideas: make up a song to him, have a party, make up a cheer, post your story on the Internet (with a parent's permission).

PRAY
Thank God for several things he has done for you.

MEMORIZE
The LORD kept his word and did . . . exactly what he had promised. Genesis 21:1

WHAT'S THE POINT?
Abraham and Sarah chose a special baby name to celebrate what God had done. Austin's family had a party to celebrate how God healed his leg. *BA*

JUNE 22
Grouchy Old Grouch

"Grouchy old grouch" was what the kids called Mr. Snead. He took care of the church building and yard. His favorite word was "don't." Don't walk on the grass. Don't park your bike there. Don't. Don't. Don't.

Most of the kids just kept on doing what he said not to do. One Sunday after church, they decided to play tag on the grass.

Mr. Snead appeared out of nowhere. He shook his head in disbelief, shrugged his shoulders, and walked away. All the kids except Barnaby laughed. He had helped Mr. Snead one Saturday. He knew how hard Mr. Snead worked to take care of the lawn.

Barnaby said, "Hey, guys, let's play in the parking lot." There were only grunts and groans from the other guys.

READ
Galatians 6:9-10. "The family of faith" means other Christians—people who have Jesus in their lives.

THINK
- Who does the verse say to do good to? Does it say there are any exceptions?
- Blessings are good gifts and approval from God. What blessings do you think could come from doing good?
- Imagine an ending for this story, showing how the guys could follow the verses. Then read the possible ending at the back of the book.

DO
Make a chart listing two or three people across the top. Along the side, list a good thing you could do for each of them. Put a check mark in the middle of the chart when you do each thing.

PRAY
Ask God to show you how pleased he is when you do good for others.

MEMORIZE
Whenever we have the opportunity, we should do good to everyone—especially to those in the family of faith. Galatians 6:10

WHAT'S THE POINT?
When we do good to someone, we are doing what God asks us to do. God doesn't want us to get tired of doing good, even if the other person seems grouchy, like Mr. Snead. God will help us, and he'll be pleased with us. *BC*

JUNE 23
Hospital Project

Colin got a new game player for his birthday, so he sold his old one. "Fifty dollars! Cool!" he said. Then he mowed the lawn for seven dollars and did other yard chores for five dollars. He was admiring his earnings when his mom called all the boys for a family meeting.

"Our church will be supporting a mission hospital in an area where the people can't afford medical care," said Dad. Mom and Dad explained that they would get overtime pay for the next month at work. Part of that would go to the hospital project. "You boys have been earning extra money too," Mom said. "How would you like to help?"

Colin's younger brother, Gavin, said he would give half of what he made weeding the next week. Colin's older brother, Adrian, said he would give four hours' worth of babysitting money.

"What are you interested in giving, Colin?" asked Mom.

Colin felt frustrated. "It's not fair! I earned my money! It's mine!" he said. Nothing Mom or Dad said could change his mind.

READ
Acts 4:32-37. These verses talk about how God blesses unselfishness.

THINK
- What good came from the believers' unselfishness?
- How would the story be different if the believers looked out only for their own needs?
- Finish the story, showing how the verses might soften Colin's feelings. Then read the possible ending at the back of the book.

DO
- Ask family members to point out ways that you are unselfish.
- Make a pledge card. Write "My Pledge" at the top. Write "I pledge to _____."
  Fill in the blank with something you will do or give unselfishly this week.

PRAY
Talk to God about an area in your life where you may be selfish. Ask him to help you change selfishness to generosity.

MEMORIZE
All the believers were united in heart and mind. And they felt that what they owned was not their own, so they shared everything they had. Acts 4:32

WHAT'S THE POINT?
Colin became willing to listen to the idea that God wants us to share what we have with others. Then he would have a decision to make about the money he earned. *BC*

JUNE 24
I Want to Be a Star

Renee and Stacy were having a sleepover. A song by their favorite singer was playing. "I want to be a star like her," said Renee.

"But you sound like a sick cow when you sing," Stacy said. "I want to be an Olympic gymnast."

"You can barely do a cartwheel." Renee giggled.

They went to the kitchen to get a snack. "Mom, what can we do that will make us famous? We must have been hiding in the closet when God passed out talents."

"God doesn't always give talents that make a person famous," Mrs. Gilbert replied. "God often helps people make a difference in quiet, seemingly unamazing ways."

Renee thought *that* sounded dull.

READ
Acts 9:32-42. Look for two people in this passage who made a difference in very different ways.

THINK
- What did God help Peter do? What talents did God give Dorcas?
- What difference do you think each of them made in the world?
- Finish the story, showing how the verses might change Renee's and Stacy's dreams for the future. Then read the possible ending at the back of the book.

DO
- Ask a parent about people who made a difference in his or her life in seemingly small ways.
- Write down an ability God has given you. Write how you could use it to make a difference in the world right now. It's okay with God if it's a small, quiet difference! Maybe you could help a parent with a chore, or help the new kid feel welcome, or give someone a compliment.

PRAY
Ask God to help you make a difference using the ability you thought of.

MEMORIZE
Tabitha . . . was always doing kind things for others and helping the poor. Acts 9:36

WHAT'S THE POINT?
God healed people through Peter. That was exciting! God helped Dorcas make clothes—maybe not as exciting. But the people Dorcas helped said she made a big difference. God can help each of us make a difference, even if it's in small ways. *BC*

JUNE 25
The Last Red Pipe Cleaner

"A red pipe cleaner will finish my design perfectly," said Hayden as he grabbed the last one. At the same moment, Makayla grabbed the other end of the pipe cleaner.

"I need a red one too," she announced. Making colorful designs at their Pioneer Clubs meeting started out as fun, but now Hayden was frustrated.

"I had it first," Hayden said. "It's mine."

Makayla wouldn't let go. The tug-of-war continued as they stared at each other.

"Miss Hicks," they both yelled to their club leader. "Help us!"

READ

Proverbs 2:6-8. Wisdom, or good judgment, is like a treasure—far more important than things we might own.

THINK

- How do you think "common sense" is like a treasure?
- Think of someone you know who is wise, maybe a grandparent, a teacher, or a coach. What actions and words help you know that this person uses good judgment?
- Finish the story, showing how Hayden and Makayla could apply the verses you read. Then read the possible ending at the back of the book.

DO

- With your family, create a short skit where some kids have a problem and one of them finds a wise solution.
- Tell your family about a situation where you need wisdom to know what to do. See if they have some ideas.

PRAY

God promises to give wisdom to those who ask him for it. Ask him right now to give you wisdom for the tricky situation you face.

MEMORIZE

The LORD grants wisdom! From his mouth come knowledge and understanding.
Proverbs 2:6

WHAT'S THE POINT?
God gave Miss Hicks a wise idea to solve the problem. God is pleased when we ask him for wisdom. *BC*

JUNE 26
Knee or Knuckle?

"Your body is like an airplane," Mr. Andrews, Akira's science teacher, said.

"Huh?" said Akira.

"Every part of an airplane works together to get the plane to fly. Every part of your body works together to get you to school each day. It doesn't matter if it's a knee or a knuckle."

So an airplane is like a body, Akira thought. His Sunday school teacher said the church is like the body of Christ. That puzzled him. To him, the church was made up of a lot of different people, not a bunch of body parts.

READ
1 Corinthians 12:12, 14-18, 27. Each person who believes in Jesus as his or her Savior is an important part of the church.

THINK
- Think of the church as the "body of Christ." What do these verses say it takes to make a complete church?
- What do the verses say about which people are more important in the church?
- Finish the story. How do you think Akira will figure out how the church is like a body? Then read the possible ending at the back of the book.

DO
- You are an important part of your church! Choose some things you can do for your church: be friendly; bring someone new; pay attention; give money; pray for someone; play an instrument; encourage someone; or think of another idea of your own.
- Write a thank-you note to someone in your church. Thank the person for the part he or she plays in your church.

PRAY
Ask God to show you how to be a useful part of Jesus' body, the church.

MEMORIZE
All of you together are Christ's body, and each of you is a part of it. 1 Corinthians 12:27

WHAT'S THE POINT?
The church has many people doing different things. They work together to be the "body of Christ" to do his work. *BC*

JUNE 27
Lost on a Hike

Sergio was a little scared. He had never been away from home. Now he was waiting for the church bus to pick him up for a week at church camp. *What if I get homesick? What if the kids don't like me?* he thought.

When all the kids were on the bus, Mr. Mattas prayed for fun at camp, for the kids to learn about God, and that God would keep them safe.

Sergio loved swimming, canoeing, and cooking over a fire. On a long hike, Sergio spotted a cool bug. As he examined it, the rest of the group went on without him. When he finally looked up, no one was in sight. And the path forked up ahead. Which way had they gone? Sergio was lost and alone. Then he remembered how Mr. Mattas had prayed, so he said, "Please help someone come back for me, God!"

READ

Acts 12:5-11. Discover how Peter escaped when he was put in prison just for being a Christian.

THINK

- Why do you think God rescued Peter?
- What difference do you think the church people made in this story?
- Finish the story, showing how prayer could alter Sergio's circumstances. Then read the possible ending at the back of the book.

DO

- What can you do when someone has a problem? Sketch something you've learned from this story.
- Pray for someone who has a problem—it could be you or someone else.

PRAY

Thank God for loving us enough to hear and answer when you or someone you care about has troubles.

MEMORIZE

While Peter was in prison, the church prayed very earnestly for him. Acts 12:5

WHAT'S THE POINT?

God is glad to hear and answer when we pray and when others pray for us. He answers because of his great love for us! He may not always answer just the way we want, but we can always trust him to care for us. *BC*

JUNE 28
No Way Could She Be a Christian!

Finn's Sunday school class had a visitor who was Indian. Her name was Shreya. Everything about her was different—her name, the way she talked, and her clothes. Finn thought, *There's no way she could be a Christian.* He had learned in school that people from India believe in many different gods.

The teacher was talking about becoming God's child. She asked, "Does anyone want to share with the class about how people can know if they belong to Jesus?"

Shreya raised her hand.

Finn snorted. *She's probably never even heard of Jesus,* he thought.

READ
Galatians 3:26-28. We are told that everyone can be a child of God, no matter who we are or where we are from.

THINK
- Why did God send Jesus to earth?
- Who can become God's child?
- Finish the story, showing how the verses could make a difference in Finn's thinking. Then read the possible ending at the back of the book.

DO
- You can become God's child no matter who you are or where you're from. If you're ready, pray something like this: "Dear God, I know I have disobeyed you and done wrong things. Thank you for sending Jesus to die in my place and to come back to life. Please forgive me and make me your child. Thank you!" Be sure to tell someone you've prayed this prayer. This is an exciting step for you.
- If you're not ready to pray the prayer, talk to God about why you aren't. If you have already become God's child, thank him for giving you a new life.

PRAY
Thank God for wanting people of every size, shape, and color to be his children.

MEMORIZE
There is no longer Jew or Gentile, slave or free, male and female. For you are all one in Christ Jesus. Galatians 3:28

WHAT'S THE POINT?
Finn learned that people of all types can be God's children. It only depends on whether or not they have accepted Jesus' offer of forgiveness and asked him into their lives. *BC*

JUNE 29
Waiting for a Baby

Just twenty more days! Chelsea was counting the days until she would have a baby sister. Then she started worrying. Her friend Ronnie had a little sister in a wheelchair. Chelsea asked her mother, "What if my baby sister is not okay? What if she can't learn to walk or talk or play with me?"

Her mother explained that God loves each person, no matter what. "God promises to make each person like him in some ways. He says each person is worthwhile."

Chelsea had a hard time believing what her mom said about God. She couldn't see the baby. How could she trust God?

READ
Genesis 15:5-6. Descendants are our children's children's children and more. What God told Abram was especially amazing because Abram didn't even have one child. Abram had to trust, even though he could not see what God would do. And God's promise came true! When we have faith (believe God), God is pleased.

THINK
- *Righteous* means "right with God." What did Abram do to make him right with God?
- What can you do when it is hard to have faith (believe God)?
- Make up an ending for the story, showing how the verses can help Chelsea. Then read the possible ending at the back of the book.

DO
- Talk to family members about something you're having trouble trusting God about.
- With your family, think of promises from God that would be helpful in that situation, such as "I am with you always" (Matthew 28:20). Practice trusting God's promises when you're faced with a difficult circumstance.

PRAY
Ask God to grow your faith so you can believe him, no matter what.

MEMORIZE
Abram believed the LORD, and the LORD counted him as righteous because of his faith. Genesis 15:6

WHAT'S THE POINT?
Chelsea believed her baby sister was a part of God's plan. She was learning to have faith and trust God. We can't always see what God is doing in our lives. Faith has to do with believing what we can't see. God can be trusted. He is pleased when we believe him. *BC*

JUNE 30
Wind and Fire

Pentecost! Francisco's mom had told him, "Our church is going to celebrate Pentecost next Sunday."

Pentecost was a mystery to Francisco, but it sounded exciting. A sound from heaven like the roaring wind, flames of fire touching everyone's head, the Holy Spirit filling people so they spoke different languages! Wow!

"People from lots of different countries were there that day, right?" Francisco asked his mom.

"Yes," she said. Francisco knew how they must have felt, since he was living in a country where the people didn't speak his language. Sometimes he felt his ears were stuffed with cotton when others spoke to him.

But at Pentecost all the people understood in their own language what was being said! *How can that be?* he wondered. *Did God have a special language everyone could understand?* He went to church full of questions.

READ
Acts 2:1-11. Pentecost happened right when the church began, after Jesus went back to heaven. Jesus had promised his helpers that the Holy Spirit would come to them.

THINK
- What did all the people hear in their own language?
- Why do you think God wanted his helpers to speak many different languages that day?
- Finish the story, showing how the verses can help Francisco understand Pentecost. Then read the possible ending at the back of the book.

DO
- Learn John 3:16 or the phrase "Jesus loves you" in another language.
- Pray for God to send people to tell people of every language in the world about Jesus.

PRAY
Ask God to speak to you in a way you will understand.

MEMORIZE
Everyone present was filled with the Holy Spirit and began speaking in other languages, as the Holy Spirit gave them this ability. Acts 2:4

WHAT'S THE POINT?
Francisco learned that God is for all people. God understands all languages, and his Good News is being spread to people around the world in different languages. *BC*

JULY 1
I Have Two Good Legs

Mrs. Rodriguez took Vivian aside. "A new student is coming. Would you introduce her to your friends?"

Vivian nodded eagerly and imagined how jealous the other girls would be when they heard that Mrs. Rodriguez had asked her for help.

"Her name is Livvy." The teacher's forehead wrinkled. "She uses a walker to get around."

Vivian frowned. She didn't want to hang around with a girl who couldn't walk. Everyone would stare and make fun of them. She knew it would happen because once when the teachers weren't around, she and her friends had teased a boy with leg braces and a girl who talked funny. Vivian felt bad about it and wished she hadn't been so mean.

Mrs. Rodriguez continued. "Vivian, I chose you because Livvy deserves a chance to make friends, and you can help her do it. Will you be her friend?"

READ
Leviticus 19:14. God says we should not be unkind to people with disabilities. Our unkindness makes their lives harder.

THINK
- How do you think God wants us to treat people with disabilities?
- "Fearing" God means respecting him. What do you think respecting God has to do with treating people kindly?
- Finish the story, showing how Vivian could respect God through her friendship with Livvy. Then read the possible ending at the back of the book.

DO
- Write the name of someone you know who has some kind of disability.
- Ask that person if you can interview him or her about what everyday life is like. Ask how he or she wants to be treated and what you can do to help people with disabilities.

PRAY
Ask God to show you ways to be a friend to people with disabilities.

MEMORIZE
Do not insult the deaf or cause the blind to stumble. You must fear your God; I am the LORD.
Leviticus 19:14

WHAT'S THE POINT?
Vivian's mom taught her to appreciate her abilities and use them to help others. When we use our strengths to help those in need, we show respect for God. He gave us our strengths, and he loves the people we're helping. *JP*

JULY 2
On Your Feet, Boys!

Dixon picked up his bag. The people on the floats had thrown so much candy that his bag was full. "Scoot over," he told his brother. Kenton wriggled closer to Mom, and Dixon squeezed in beside Dad.

The boys opened their bags and sorted candy. They were unwrapping bubble gum when Dad tapped their shoulders. "On your feet, boys."

The boys stood. Everyone clapped and cheered as a group of older men rode by. Dixon read the words on the side of the float: Former POWs. "What does POW mean, Mom?"

"It's short for 'prisoner of war,'" Mom said. "When those people were younger, they were soldiers, captured while fighting for our country. They were in prison camps until the war ended."

"Life in the prison camps was hard," Dad went on. "Some of the prisoners didn't have enough to eat. They lived in tiny cells. Some of them were badly hurt."

"That's why we stand up when they go by," Mom explained. "We want to show them respect."

"I wish we could do more for them," Dixon said. "But what?"

READ
Leviticus 19:32. This verse says we show respect to God when we show respect to older people.

THINK
- ▸ What does Leviticus 19:32 say is one way to show respect to older people?
- ▸ How else could you show respect for older people?
- ▸ Imagine an ending for this story, showing how Dixon might live out the instruction of the verse. Then read the possible ending at the back of the book.

DO
- ▸ Tell someone some ways an older person has made your life better.
- ▸ Make an encouraging card for an older person you know. Or ask an older person to tell you about his or her childhood and family, work and adventures.

PRAY
Thank God for an older person you thought of for one of the "Do" activities.

MEMORIZE
Stand up in the presence of the elderly, and show respect for the aged. Fear your God. I am the LORD. Leviticus 19:32

WHAT'S THE POINT?
Dixon's family showed respect to the older POWs by standing up and by sending cards. God is pleased when we honor people who have lived a long time. *JP*

JULY 3
The New Kid

Darrell eyed the new kid standing on the sidelines. The kid was watching their soccer game as if he wanted to play too. Darrell was about to ask him to join them when his friend Reggie whispered, "You aren't going to ask him to play, are you? He's from Italy—another country. His name is Carlo. He doesn't even speak English very good."

Reggie was right. When Darrell went over to say hi, the new boy nodded and said, "Hello," with a strong accent. The new boy's hair was shorter than everyone else's, and his sneakers were different too. If he joined their team, the other guys might tease them. Better to ignore him until he went away.

Then Carlo smiled and pointed at the soccer ball. "Play—me, too?" he struggled to ask.

"Ignore him," Reggie whispered as he walked past. So Darrell returned to the game.

Carlo shrugged and walked away. He looked sad and lonely. Darrell chewed on his lower lip nervously. Maybe Carlo would make friends when school started. But did Darrell want him to wait that long?

READ
Leviticus 19:33-34. God wants us to treat people from other countries kindly.

THINK
- What do these verses say about how we should treat people from other countries who live in our towns and nation?
- How can we understand how they feel?
- Make up an ending for the story, showing how Darrell could obey the teaching of the verses. Then read the possible ending at the back of the book.

DO
- Think of someone you know from another country who lives near you. Plan a way to help the person feel welcome.

PRAY
When kids move near you, ask God to show you how to treat them with kindness, even if they're not just like you.

MEMORIZE
Do not take advantage of foreigners who live among you in your land. Leviticus 19:33

WHAT'S THE POINT?
When Darrell remembered how lonely he'd been, he knew how to help Carlo. God wants us to love people who move to our towns and country. *JP*

JULY 4
A Worker I Can Trust

Ivy knew stealing was wrong, but she didn't have enough money for candy. So yesterday Ivy waited until the store owner, Walt, wasn't looking and stole a candy bar.

Now she wished she hadn't stolen from her friend. "Ivy, you're a worker I can trust," Walt told her every Friday after she swept the floor of his convenience store. Then he gave her a can of pop.

I'll sneak the candy bar back into the store, Ivy told herself. *Walt will never know.*

Ivy did as she'd planned, but she didn't feel any better. The next Friday she swept as usual. But when Walt said, "Now there's a worker I can trust," and handed her a can of pop, Ivy couldn't look him in the eye. *If he knew the truth, he wouldn't trust me.*

READ
Proverbs 28:13. When we admit our wrongs and stop doing them, we can receive forgiveness even though we don't deserve it. (We'll still have to make things right, though.)

THINK
- In this verse, what does God say about why telling the truth is important?
- When we admit our sins (wrongs) and stop doing them, why do you think God will be kind to us even though we don't deserve it?
- Finish the story, showing how this verse might help Ivy find some relief from her guilty feelings. Then read the possible ending at the back of the book.

DO
- When you've done something wrong, do you admit it and try to change? Why or why not?
- Think of a sin you haven't admitted. Admit it to God now. Make a plan to change. Plan to admit your sin to the person you have wronged.

PRAY
Ask God to give you courage to confess to the people you have wronged. Thank him for his kindness when you admit your wrongs.

MEMORIZE
People who conceal their sins will not prosper, but if they confess and turn from them, they will receive mercy. Proverbs 28:13

WHAT'S THE POINT?
Admitting her wrong helped Ivy begin repairing her friendship with Walt. God knows sins can destroy a friendship. He shows kindness when we tell the truth. *JP*

JULY 5
A Cool-Tempered Plan

Louis high-fived his best friend, Dante. They saw both their names on the same basketball team roster. But when Louis saw Alberto's name there also, he groaned. "Oh no," he told Dante. "If Alberto annoys me at practice and I lose my temper, the coach will throw me off the team."

"So don't let Alberto get to you," Dante said.

"I can't help it. He likes to do dumb things like trip me when I'm not looking and call me from across the court by yelling, 'Loooeee!' in this high-pitched voice."

Dante nodded. "Yeah, I know, but to stay on the basketball team, you can't be fighting with someone."

"How can I keep from fighting with him when he bugs me?"

"Maybe we can think of a way to stop him next time he starts," Dante suggested.

"But how?" Louis asked.

READ
Proverbs 15:18. This verse explains that losing our tempers starts arguments, but controlling them ends fights.

THINK
- Does God want us to be hot- or cool-tempered? Why?
- Why should people who love Jesus stop fights instead of start them?
- Finish the story, showing how Louis could get an idea from the verse. Then read the possible ending at the back of the book.

DO
- How can you create a plan to control your temper? Talk to your cool-tempered friends about how they choose to control their tempers. Use their ideas to help you keep your temper under control.

PRAY
Ask God to show you ways to stay cool-tempered and not start fights.

MEMORIZE
A hot-tempered person starts fights; a cool-tempered person stops them. Proverbs 15:18

WHAT'S THE POINT?
Louis's plan made it easier for him to control his temper. God wants us to think ahead and stay cool instead of fighting. *JP*

JULY 6
Bring Right from Wrong

Usually Pamela loved Pioneer Clubs. But for weeks Sadie had been driving Pamela crazy. Sadie always had the answers during the Bible Exploration and wouldn't let anyone else answer. And whenever anyone else tried to talk, Sadie would interrupt, even after the club leader asked her not to.

At first, Pamela was nice to her. But after a while, she kept hoping that Sadie would quit coming to club. During one activity, Sadie was so hyper and loud that she spilled a bottle of glitter glue all over Pamela's project. She didn't even apologize.

That's it! Pamela thought. *I am going to tell her not to come back!*

READ
Proverbs 19:11. God wants us to be patient and not be quick to react in anger when someone insults us or makes us angry.

THINK
- If someone does something wrong to you, why would God say to overlook it?
- Where do we get the wisdom that gives us patience?
- Finish the story, showing what ideas Pamela might find in today's verse. Then read the possible ending at the back of the book.

DO
- Brainstorm with your family a list of phrases you can tell yourself to help you not be so hard on people. Ideas: People give me breaks, so I can give someone else a break. Nobody's perfect. God still loves me and that other person. God forgives me, so I can forgive.
- Think of someone who often drives you nuts. Plan a way to be more patient the next time you're annoyed with the person.

PRAY
Ask God for more wisdom that leads to patience.

MEMORIZE
Sensible people control their temper; they earn respect by overlooking wrongs.
Proverbs 19:11

WHAT'S THE POINT?
Pamela realized it's wiser to be patient than lose her temper. God wants us to respect others. *JP*

JULY 7
Hungry People

"The teacher made me sit by Lance today." Ty made a face as he rode down the street with his dad. "His clothes look really old. And they're so wrinkled I think he sleeps in them."

Dad stopped at a red light. "Do you know where he lives?"

"I asked him at lunch, but he just asked if he could finish my sandwich." Ty frowned. "Then he scarfed it down."

"Could he be homeless or hungry?" Dad drove on when the light changed.

"I don't know. But if he is, there's nothing I can do about it. Hey, I thought we were getting ice cream." Dad drove past the ice cream shop and pulled into the church parking lot. "Why are we here?" Ty asked.

"We'll get ice cream later. Right now we're going to see what we can do for hungry people."

Dad steered him past a line of people and into the kitchen, where he held out an apron. "Want to help serve supper to homeless people?"

READ
Proverbs 14:31. Oppressing people means treating them badly.

THINK
▶ Who is the Maker referred to in the verse? How would treating people badly insult him?
▶ What are some ways that kids might treat poor people badly?
▶ Finish the story, showing how Ty might act because of today's verse. Then read the possible ending at the back of the book.

DO
▶ Draw a face to show how you feel about people who are homeless or hungry. If you need to change your attitude about them, how could you do that?
▶ With your family, find out what programs your community, church, or school offers to help homeless or hungry families. See if you can volunteer at one of them.

PRAY
Ask God to help you honor him by treating poor people with kindness.

MEMORIZE
Those who oppress the poor insult their Maker, but helping the poor honors him.
Proverbs 14:31

WHAT'S THE POINT?
Ty learned that people without homes and food need kindness, not complaints. God is pleased when we help people who don't have much. *JP*

JULY 8
Trusting God's Will

Nadia was tired of washing dishes. For days, her counselor, Maggie, had assigned her to the kitchen crew. Maggie knew Nadia hated it and wanted to be on the crew that fed the horses. Why didn't Maggie just let her do what she wanted?

"Hey, Nadia. How's it going?" Maggie picked up a towel.

Nadia glared at the counselor. "How come you don't like me?"

Maggie looked surprised. "But I do like you. Why do you think I don't?"

Nadia threw the dishcloth in the water. "Because you make me work in the kitchen even though you know I want to feed the horses."

Maggie dried dishes as she talked. "Almost everyone wants to feed the horses. What would happen if every camper got her way all the time?"

"The horses would get fat, and the dishes wouldn't get done," Nadia mumbled.

"I promise that when the time comes, you'll get your turn feeding the horses. Will you trust me on this one?" Maggie asked.

READ
Matthew 6:9-10. In these verses, Jesus teaches the disciples how to pray. He teaches them to pray for God's will to be done.

THINK
- What do you think it means to ask for God's will to be done?
- Where does this passage say God's will is already being done? Where should we ask for it to be done?
- Finish the story, showing how Nadia could get an inspiration from today's Bible passage. Then read the possible ending at the back of the book.

DO
- What are things you want, but may not be God's will?
- Make a prayer notebook and write those things in it. Pray to know which are God's will.

PRAY
Ask God to change you until his will is what you want to do.

MEMORIZE
Pray like this: Our Father in heaven, may your name be kept holy. May your Kingdom come soon. May your will be done on earth, as it is in heaven. Matthew 6:9-10

WHAT'S THE POINT?
Nadia trusted Maggie once she understood the counselor cared about everyone's needs, not just Nadia's. God wants us to obey his will because he is concerned about our needs as well as everyone else's. *JP*

JULY 9
More than Enough

Martin's arms were tired. All morning, he and Darcy had hauled vegetables to the road where they would sell them at their family's fruit and vegetable stand. He added another basket of beans to the growing pile. "You know how Dad asks God to give us food for each day? Well, this year he's given us more than enough."

Darcy nodded. "Yeah, it's weird. We have plenty to eat, but kids in other countries are starving."

At supper Martin said, "Dad, it doesn't seem fair for God to give us so much food when kids in other countries are starving."

Dad set down his fork. "Well, maybe God wants us to be the answer to someone else's prayer."

Darcy looked puzzled. "How can we do that?"

Dad showed them a magazine ad. "This group feeds children in other countries and builds schools for them."

"How do they pay for it?" Martin asked.

"They ask people to sponsor children and send a monthly donation for their food and schooling," Dad explained. "Would you two be interested?"

READ
Matthew 6:11. In this verse from the Lord's Prayer, Jesus shows that we can ask God to provide food and other needs for each day.

THINK
- According to this verse, who provides for our needs each day?
- How does God use people to provide food, shelter, and medicine for others?
- Finish the story, showing how Martin and Darcy could use the gifts God is providing for their family to help others. Then read the possible ending at the back of the book.

DO
- How can God use you to provide for someone?
- Use coupons to save money on groceries. Buy extra food with the savings and donate it to a food bank. Or ask your family to sponsor a child in another country.

PRAY
Thank God for providing for your needs every day. Ask him to show you who to help when he provides more than enough.

MEMORIZE
Give us today the food we need. Matthew 6:11

WHAT'S THE POINT?
Martin and Darcy understood that God provided plenty so they could help others. God is pleased when we share what he gives us with those in need. *JP*

JULY 10
Forgiveness and Trust

Pete couldn't excuse Dewayne for what he'd done. Dewayne was his best friend, but that didn't mean he could take Pete's skateboard to the park without permission. What if he'd busted it?

The phone rang. "Pete, it's Dewayne," Mom called from the living room.

Dewayne probably wanted to say he was sorry again. But Pete wasn't ready to forgive him. He ignored Mom.

Mom came into the kitchen. "When you didn't come to the phone, I told Dewayne I couldn't find you. Why didn't you come when I called?" Pete poked at his cereal with his spoon. Mom sat down. "What's wrong?"

Pete couldn't hold in his anger any longer. He told Mom what had happened. "If I forgive him, then I have to trust him. But I don't trust him, not after what he did."

Mom sighed. "What Dewayne did was wrong. But God says you're to forgive him just as God forgives you. You don't have to trust him again right away. Dewayne needs to earn back your trust. Can you give him time?"

READ
Matthew 6:12. In this verse from Jesus' prayer, Jesus explains that God forgives us just as he wants us to forgive others.

THINK
- What has God forgiven you for?
- Is it hard for you to forgive sometimes? Why? What could help?
- Make up an ending for the story, showing how the verse could make a difference for Pete. Then read the possible ending at the back of the book.

DO
- On a piece of paper, write a word that stands for something you need to forgive someone for.
- Each time you ask God to forgive you, ask him to show you who you need to forgive. Ask him to give you courage to forgive.

PRAY
Thank God for forgiving your sins. Ask him to help you forgive others.

MEMORIZE
Forgive us our sins, as we have forgiven those who sin against us. Matthew 6:12

WHAT'S THE POINT?
Pete learned that forgiveness doesn't mean allowing a wrong thing to happen again. God forgives and gives us another chance to do what's right. That's what he wants us to do for others too. *JP*

JULY 11
I Can't Eat That

Juliana couldn't believe her friend's news. "You have diabetes? What does that mean?"

Karina explained. "It's a disease, but you can't catch it from me. I have to take medicine. And I have to eat healthy food. Sweets or soda can make me really sick."

"But we always snack on candy and soda during sleepovers. What are you going to do?" Juliana asked.

"Well," Karina said slowly, "I can have popcorn, and you can eat what you want. But it'll be hard with all the candy around."

Juliana leaned forward. "Maybe you could have just a little."

"No." Karina shook her head. "I can't."

Juliana tried to imagine what it would be like for Karina to watch her eat sweets when she couldn't. What if Karina couldn't resist the temptation? How could Juliana help her stay strong?

READ
Matthew 6:13. In this part of Jesus' prayer, he teaches us to ask God to protect us from choosing to do wrong things. Temptation is wanting to do wrong things. The evil one is Satan, who wants us to do those wrong things.

THINK
- Why do we need God's help to resist doing wrong?
- What temptations do you need God to help you resist?
- Finish the story, showing how Juliana could find an idea in today's verse. Then read the possible ending at the back of the book.

DO
- How could God use friends or family members to help you stay strong when you're tempted?
- Talk to God about a way you're tempted. Ask a family member to help you too.

PRAY
Ask God to protect you from temptation. Ask him to help you do your part to resist.

MEMORIZE
Don't let us yield to temptation, but rescue us from the evil one. Matthew 6:13

WHAT'S THE POINT?
Juliana knew it would be easier for Karina to eat right if someone ate healthy food with her. God often provides people to help us resist doing the wrong thing. *JP*

JULY 12
The Orphanage

Simon couldn't take his eyes off the pictures of the AIDS orphanage in Africa. There were kids from toddlers to teenagers. Their clothes didn't fit, their food looked gross, and their school was crowded. Still, the kids were smiling.

The Pioneer Clubs guest speaker explained, "The kids don't have parents—they're orphans. They have few toys or books. But they love to tell other kids about God. Sometimes they find kids who need food and want to learn about Jesus, and they bring them to the orphanage."

Simon raised his hand. "But where do you get money for everything?"

The speaker smiled. "We ask God to provide what we need. Almost every time, somebody makes a donation so we can buy what's needed."

Simon was amazed. His family had enough money, he could go to all the fun places he wanted to go, and he could buy what he wanted to buy. The orphans trusted God to provide food and clothes, things he never worried about. How could God use him to help them?

READ
1 Timothy 6:17. This verse says God is pleased to give us what we need. But he wants us to trust in him, not in money.

THINK
- According to this verse, what does God want us to think about? Why?
- Which do you think more about: your money and things you want, or how to live for God?
- Finish the story, showing how Simon could trust God as much as needy kids in an orphanage did. Then read the possible ending at the back of the book.

DO
- Ask your family to sit down together. Name something you can trust God to give you that money can't buy. Then tag the next family member to name something else, and so on.
- Plan a way to thank God for what he gives you—both money and things money can't buy. Ideas: Make up a song for him. Give something to someone in need. Give some money back to God in the church offering.

PRAY
Ask God to help you put your trust in him, not money.

MEMORIZE
Teach those who are rich in this world not to be proud and not to trust in their money, which is so unreliable. Their trust should be in God, who richly gives us all we need for our enjoyment. 1 Timothy 6:17

WHAT'S THE POINT?
Simon learned how the orphans trusted in God. God had provided a lot for Simon, so Simon showed his trust in God by sharing. *JP*

JULY 13
That Sounds like Work

Adele was so excited during her first student council meeting, she barely heard Mrs. Lamb's instructions. "It's a big responsibility," the teacher explained. "You get to do cool stuff, like organize the fun nights and the spring carnival. But you'll also volunteer an hour a week on our service projects."

"Service projects?" Adele asked.

"Yes, student council members pick up litter around the school, plant and weed the flower beds, organize a food drive, and write thank-you notes to people who work at the school."

Adele frowned. That sounded like work, not nearly as fun as having her picture on the student council bulletin board and sitting on a special platform during assemblies.

"But I thought the student council ran things. Why do we do so much work?"

Mrs. Lamb smiled. "Because the best leaders are the ones who put other people first."

Adele slumped down. If student council was this much work, did she really want to be in it?

READ
Mark 10:35-45. In this account Jesus tells James and John that leading others is about serving them, not about being important and powerful. In verse 45, he is talking about himself.

THINK
- What did James and John think leaders do? What does Jesus say leaders do?
- How can a leader also be a servant?
- Finish the story, showing how Adele might follow Jesus' example in these verses. Then read the possible ending at the back of the book.

DO
- Create a bumper sticker about one of the points in verse 43 or 45.
- Think of a leader of a group you're in who is a good example of serving others. Make a thank-you card for this person.

PRAY
Ask God to help you learn to be a leader and servant.

MEMORIZE
Even the Son of Man came not to be served but to serve others and to give his life as a ransom for many. Mark 10:45

WHAT'S THE POINT?
As a leader who put others first, Mr. Ross was a good example for Adele. Jesus wants leaders to serve others. *JP*

JULY 14
The More the Merrier

"Addison and I are walking to the park." Mom buckled Wendell's little sister in the stroller. "Do you want to come?"

"Nah," Wendell shook his head.

Mom raised her eyebrows. "You don't want to go to the park? What's going on?"

Wendell hesitated. He didn't want his mom to know he and his buddies didn't go to the park anymore, not since some new kids had started hogging the soccer field. Wendell and his friends played them once, but the other team beat them badly. Wendell and his friends felt like major soccer "losers." Now Wendell and his group of friends avoided them and played basketball at the school playground instead.

"Tell me what's up."

Wendell knew his mom would keep bugging him, so he told her the whole story.

"Sounds as if you're missing out on some fun," Mom said. "If you and your friends got over losing to them you could still play soccer together, and you could all play basketball too." She pushed the stroller out the door. "So do you want to come?"

READ
Mark 1:40-45. In Bible times, people with leprosy were considered "unclean." Other people stayed away from them. By healing the leper's body, Jesus brought people back into the man's life too.

THINK

- How did being healed change the leper's life in other ways?
- Why did Jesus go near the leper when he could have stayed away?
- Make up an ending for the story, showing how Wendell could learn from the example in the verses. Then read the possible ending at the back of the book.

DO
- When is it tempting to stay away from people?
- Think of people you avoid because you think they're different or you feel uncomfortable around them. Introduce yourself to one or two of them and get to know them.

PRAY
Ask God to show you ways to get to know people you have avoided until now.

MEMORIZE
Jesus reached out and touched him. . . . Instantly the leprosy disappeared. Mark 1:41-42

WHAT'S THE POINT?
Wendell realized that avoiding others hurts relationships, while including them heals relationships. In God's eyes, healed relationships are as important as healed bodies. *JP*

JULY 15
A Ministry Team

Whitney rushed home from school. "Is he here yet?" she shouted up the stairs to her mom.

"Is who here yet?" a deep voice said from the living room.

"Uncle Sal!" she exclaimed. Her mom's brother was her absolute favorite uncle. He was fun and never got tired of playing with her. He was the missions and outreach pastor at his church. He was visiting them before heading to the inner city to lead a ministry team.

"Uncle Sal, what's a ministry team, and why are you going to the city?" Whitney asked.

"A ministry team is a group of people who want to help others and tell them about Jesus. We're going to the city because there are people there who are homeless, have done wrong things, or have other problems and need to hear about Jesus."

Whitney frowned. "Why do you want to be around people like *that*? Why not stay home and just tell the people in your church about Jesus?"

READ

Luke 5:27-32. In this story, the religious leaders think Jesus shouldn't be friends with sinners. But Jesus says he was sent to save people who need to learn about him.

THINK

- Why did the leaders and teachers complain about Jesus' friends?
- Why did Jesus say he came to call sinners instead of the leaders and teachers to follow him?
- Finish the story, showing how Whitney could learn what Uncle Sal already knows from these verses. Then read the possible ending at the back of the book.

DO

- Who do you know who needs to hear about Jesus? Ask God to help you find a way to tell him or her about Jesus.

PRAY

Ask God to bring friends into your life who will want to hear about Jesus.

MEMORIZE

I have come to call not those who think they are righteous, but those who know they are sinners and need to repent. Luke 5:32

WHAT'S THE POINT?

We need to tell people, no matter how sinful they seem to us, about Jesus because God loves them too. God wants them to ask forgiveness and accept Jesus as their Savior. *JP*

JULY 16
The Crabbiest Guy in the Neighborhood

Mateo ran down the block, in a hurry to get to his friend's place. Should he run across Mr. Ho's corner yard for a shortcut? Old Mr. Ho was the crabbiest guy in the neighborhood, but he didn't seem to be in sight. Mateo jumped the flower bed and started across the lawn.

"Stop, you kid!" Mr. Ho called out, coming out the door onto the front porch. He shook his cane. "What's the matter with you? Why are you on my grass?"

"Uh, it was just a shortcut," Mateo stammered.

"Get out of here before I call someone!" Mr. Ho bellowed, looking down the stairs at Mateo. He sat down in a chair with a painful moan.

Mateo wondered if Mr. Ho's back hurt all the time, like Grandpa's. Maybe that's why he was so crabby. He turned to hurry down Mr. Ho's walk and tripped over three newspapers.

READ

Luke 10:25-28. Jesus explained which of God's laws are most important: to love God completely and to love other people the way we love ourselves.

THINK

- How can you love God with all your heart and soul and strength and mind?
- How can you love others as much as you love yourself?
- Finish the story, showing how Mateo might change his actions to fit these verses. Then read the possible ending at the back of the book.

DO

- Play a "Trading Places" game with family members. One family member will "be" you and you will "be" that family member. Ask each other, "What would you like me to do for you today?" Try to answer as the other person would. Then you will know something you can do to show each other love.
- Do one thing you thought of in the game for a family member.

PRAY

Think of some people who show you love. Thank God for them.

MEMORIZE

"You must love the LORD your God with all your heart, all your soul, all your strength, and all your mind." And, "Love your neighbor as yourself." Luke 10:27

WHAT'S THE POINT?

By understanding what other people need and helping them, we obey Jesus' command to love our neighbors as we love ourselves. *BA*

JULY 17
Cutting the Grass

Roxy picked up sticks while Dad cut the grass. It was hot, and sweat dripped into her eyes. Finally she flopped under a tree. Dad stopped the mower and sat beside her. "Tired?"

She blew her bangs from her forehead. "How come we're mowing the Hoovers' yard? They're so rich they could pay somebody to do it."

Dad mopped his forehead. "Well, Mr. Hoover called and said his wife will be in the hospital for a few weeks and asked if I would mow until he found someone else. I told him I'd do it as long as he needed."

"But I want to go swimming on Saturdays, not mow lawns."

"Yeah," Dad agreed. "I want to go swimming too. But ever since the Hoovers moved next door, I've been praying for a way to show them I care. But you can go to the pool, and I'll join you after I'm done. Would you like that?"

READ
Luke 10:29-37. Jesus told this story about a man who went out of his way for someone he didn't even know. Jesus wants us to serve each other.

THINK
- Why do you think the Samaritan helped the beaten man when the church leaders didn't want to?
- Who do you think Jesus would say is *your* "neighbor"?
- Finish the story, showing how the example of the Good Samaritan might make a difference for Roxy. Then read the possible ending at the back of the book.

DO
- Write three ways you could follow Jesus' idea of serving others.
- Put a star by one thing you will do this week.

PRAY.
Ask God to help you do the thing you chose.

MEMORIZE
"Which of these three would you say was a neighbor to the man who was attacked by bandits?" Jesus asked. The man replied, "The one who showed him mercy." Then Jesus said, "Yes, now go and do the same." Luke 10:36-37

WHAT'S THE POINT?
Dad's love for the Hoovers showed Roxy how to serve them and want to help them. God uses Jesus and people around us to show us how to serve others. *JP*

JULY 18
How to Be a Friend

"There's a new boy at school." Jeff licked his ice cream. "His family moved here from Argentina. He dresses like us, but he doesn't speak any English."

"He must be lonely." Mom stirred the ice cream in her bowl. "He needs some new friends."

"Yeah." Jeff nibbled at his cone. "But how can we make friends with him? He goes to a special English class sometimes, but it will take a long time before he can talk to us."

"Hmm." Dad finished his ice cream. "It's a challenge. But maybe you already know how to be his friend."

"No." Jeff was surprised. "I don't have a clue."

"Well, how would you want to be treated in his place?" Dad asked. "How would you want people to treat you if you couldn't talk their language?"

READ
John 13:35. Jesus is talking in this verse. "Disciples" means Jesus' followers who believe in him.

THINK
- How would treating others with love show people that we are Jesus' followers?
- What do you think treating someone with love means?
- Finish the story, showing how Jeff might prove he's a disciple, as the verse says. Then read the possible ending at the back of the book.

DO
- Think of someone who could use some care and understanding.
- If you were in this person's place, what would you want people to do? Visit you? Make a gift? Help around the house? Play a game? Do one thing for the person that you would want done for you.

PRAY
Ask Jesus to show you ways to love others.

MEMORIZE
Your love for one another will prove to the world that you are my disciples. John 13:35

WHAT'S THE POINT?
Jeff imagined himself in the other boy's place and knew what to do. Jesus did that when he came to earth. That's what he wants us to do too. *JP*

JULY 19
Secret Friends

Iris loved her best friend Maci. They told each other everything and promised not to tell another soul their secrets. Until now, Iris had kept her promise.

But Iris had a new friend, Tina. Tina was fun and invited Iris to play laser tag with her family. Now they called each other every night. Yesterday, when Iris mentioned that she and Maci told each other everything, Tina got huffy. "But I'm your friend too," she said. "And friends don't keep secrets from one another. I don't want to be your friend if you don't tell me everything too."

Iris didn't know what to do. She didn't want to break her promise to Maci. But if Tina thought friends weren't supposed to keep secrets, who was right? Finally, she called Maci and told her what Tina had said.

Maci's answer surprised her. "Well, if Tina's a good friend of yours, I guess you can tell her our secrets. We'll still be friends."

Iris thanked her, hung up, and then paused before calling Tina.

READ
John 15:13. Jesus says love and friendship are about giving of ourselves.

THINK
- Who gave us the best example of following this verse?
- What kinds of things might you give up for your friends?
- Make up an ending for the story, showing how the verse could affect Iris. Then read the possible ending at the back of the book.

DO
- This week, practice showing your friends how much you care. Let them go first, play their favorite games, or give them the biggest cookies on the plate. (Remember, God wants them to do the same for you.)

PRAY
Thank Jesus for laying down his life for you.

MEMORIZE
There is no greater love than to lay down one's life for one's friends. John 15:13

WHAT'S THE POINT?
When Iris compared Maci's and Tina's words with what Jesus said and did, she saw which girl was a true friend. God wants us to be that kind of friend. *JP*

JULY 20
Challenger Buddies

Coach worked the team hard during baseball practice, and Julio was tired afterward. "Gather 'round," Coach hollered. They all sat on the bench. "Have any of you heard of the new Challenger Baseball League?"

All the boys shook their heads, and Coach explained. "It's a league we're starting for kids who are in wheelchairs or need walkers or leg braces to get around."

"But how can they play baseball?" Julio wondered out loud.

"That's were you come in." Coach smiled. "So far, twelve kids are signed up, and they need Challenger Buddies to help them bat and run the bases during their games. They'll be practicing indoors every Thursday night. Anybody interested?"

Several hands shot up, but not Julio's. Then a friend elbowed him. "How come you aren't raising your hand?"

How could Julio admit he didn't want to miss his favorite TV show every Thursday?

READ
Acts 3:1-10. In this story, a disabled man asked two of Jesus' helpers for money. But Peter showed the love and power of Jesus by healing him instead.

THINK
- How did Peter and John show love to the disabled man?
- What did being healed teach him about who Jesus is?
- Imagine an ending for this story, showing how Julio could learn from the verses. Then read the possible ending at the back of the book.

DO
- Sketch some activities you can do with someone who's disabled. (If you don't know someone who's disabled, choose someone who's sick or hurt or an older person who can't get around well.)
- Plan an activity with a disabled person in the near future.

PRAY
Ask God to show you how to include disabled kids in activities and games.

MEMORIZE
Peter said, "I don't have any silver or gold for you. But I'll give you what I have. In the name of Jesus Christ the Nazarene, get up and walk!" Acts 3:6

WHAT'S THE POINT?
Julio realized he could give Petey a valuable gift, the chance to play baseball. God wants us to use our abilities to help disabled people. Doing so shows them God's love. *JP*

JULY 21
Remembering Grandpa

"Who is Uncle Paul?" No matter how many times Meredith asked, she couldn't figure out how she was related to him.

"He's your great-uncle, your Grandpa Joe's older brother. Uncle Paul's been begging me to visit ever since Grandpa Joe died."

Meredith and her brother, Perry, exchanged glances. Would Mom and Uncle Paul spend all afternoon crying? Mom had been crying a lot since her dad, Grandpa Joe, died, and Meredith was getting worried about her.

Mom pulled up beside an apartment building. An old man sat outside on a bench, holding a bat and a baseball. "There's Uncle Paul." Mom cried when she ran and hugged him.

Paul patted her shoulder. "I miss Joe too. But he knew Jesus, so we'll see him again someday. Anyway, I was thinking we should play some baseball. It was Joe's favorite game." He handed them each a baseball glove.

Meredith and Perry looked at Mom. What would Mom think if they laughed and played while they remembered Grandpa?

READ
1 Corinthians 13:1-7. This description of love says that love always hopes and never gives up, no matter how difficult life gets.

THINK
- What are three things these verses say about how to show love?
- What are three things they say don't show love?
- Finish the story with your ideas about how Meredith and Perry can express hope and sadness and love at the same time. Then read the possible ending at the back of the book.

DO
- Think of someone who is lonely or sad.
- Choose a way to cheer that person up, such as visiting him or her, sending a card, or calling.

PRAY
Thank God for people in your life who are hopeful and don't give up.

MEMORIZE
Love never gives up, never loses faith, is always hopeful, and endures through every circumstance. 1 Corinthians 13:7

WHAT'S THE POINT?
Uncle Paul was sad, but God's love made him hopeful. His example helped Meredith share hope with her mom. When we share the hope of Jesus, we keep others from giving up. *JP*

JULY 22
Freedom to Love

Josie was babysitting Nora again after school. That meant Nora couldn't do all the fun stuff she wanted to do.

"Nora," Josie called, "come help with supper."

"I have to finish my homework," Nora replied. Actually, her homework was done. But she wanted to talk on the phone, not help with supper.

Later, Josie called again. Nora dragged herself into the kitchen. How come her parents expected her to help Josie fix supper instead of letting her do what she wanted?

"You don't look happy." Josie handed her a pitcher.

Nora made the lemonade. "How come I'm supposed to do stuff like this, but my parents won't let me use their computer to chat with my friends or surf the Internet?"

"Have you asked them why?"

"They say I have to learn to use my time more wisely. They think I'll spend more time on the computer than I should when they're not around. If I show them I will make good choices, then I can have more freedom."

READ
Galatians 5:13. This verse reminds us that Jesus gives us freedom to make our own choices but not to sin. We should love and serve others.

THINK
- Why does God warn us against using freedom to sin?
- How does serving others show we know how to use our freedom well?
- Finish the story, showing how Nora could follow the commands given in this verse. Then read the possible ending at the back of the book.

DO
- How can you serve others in love?
- Decide three ways that you will serve others this week, such as read a book to a younger child, run errands for a parent, do your chores without being reminded, or another idea you think of.

PRAY
Thank Jesus for giving you the freedom in him to make choices. Ask Jesus to help you make choices that honor him and serve others in love.

MEMORIZE
Don't use your freedom to satisfy your sinful nature. Instead, use your freedom to serve one another in love. Galatians 5:13

WHAT'S THE POINT?
Nora realized God wanted her to serve her family instead of doing only what she wanted. When we use our freedom to love and serve others, they will see God at work in us. *JP*

JULY 23
Growing Fruit

Howie and Trent raced for the apple tree. As usual, Trent, who was older and faster, got there first. Howie's shoulders slumped. No matter how hard he tried, he couldn't outrun his big brother.

But when Howie reached the ladder, Trent was waiting at the bottom. "You want to go first?" He held out the bucket.

Howie didn't show his surprise. "Sure." He snatched the bucket and hurried up the rungs before Trent could change his mind.

When he'd picked every apple within reach, he tried to climb down, but the bucket was too heavy. Would Trent call him a weakling?

"Here, I'll help you," Trent said. "Stay where you are and hand me the bucket."

Howie followed his brother's instructions a bit cautiously. "Want to pick some more?" Trent asked.

Howie was suspicious. "Why are you being so nice?"

Trent blushed. "At Pioneer Clubs, we've been talking about the fruit of the Spirit. I prayed that God would help me have more of the fruit of the Spirit in my life. Kindness is part of that."

Howie stared at Trent. Could God really help his brother change?

READ
Galatians 5:22-25. These verses say that God helps grow the fruit of the Holy Spirit in us as we obey him.

THINK
- Who guides us as we develop the fruit of the Spirit?
- Whose life in the Bible is the perfect example of one that produces fruit?
- Finish the story, showing how Howie could follow his brother's example and the instruction in these verses. Then read the possible ending at the back of the book.

DO
- Which of the fruit mentioned do you see evidence of in your life?
- Choose one quality from the list in verses 22 and 23. Ask God to grow that fruit in you.

PRAY
Ask the Holy Spirit to guide you so you produce good things.

MEMORIZE
The Holy Spirit produces this kind of fruit in our lives: love, joy, peace, patience, kindness, goodness, faithfulness, gentleness, and self-control. Galatians 5:22-23

WHAT'S THE POINT?
The changes Howie saw in Trent made him want to change. God uses the fruit he grows in us to draw people to him. *JP*

JULY 24
Teamwork

Grant loved football. He could run faster and throw better than anybody on his flag football team. Since he'd become quarterback, Grant had scored all the team's touchdowns.

As usual, Grant was the first kid at the field. He liked the coach to see he was there before his teammates.

"Hey, Grant." Coach threw him a football. "I'm glad you're early. I'd like to talk to you for a few minutes."

"Sure." Grant tossed the ball back and ran over to him.

Coach held the ball. "The scouts were on the sidelines at the last game. They chose kids to draft onto the city all-star team."

Grant had been waiting for this day. "Great! When do we start practice?"

Coach held onto the ball and just looked at him. "Grant, you didn't make it."

"What do you mean? I'm one of the best players on the team!"

"Since you became quarterback, you've thrown or rushed for every touchdown. But the scouts don't choose hotshots for their teams. They choose kids who help the whole all-star team work well as a group. Unless you start doing that, you're going to be passed over for teams like this one. There's always next season." He handed the football to Grant.

READ
Proverbs 11:2. This verse warns us that when we're proud, sometimes it can lead to bad consequences.

THINK
- What does this verse say comes when we're proud? What does humility bring?
- Think of someone you know who is humble. What makes that person different?
- Finish the story, showing how Grant might make changes in his teamwork because of today's verse. Then read the possible ending at the back of the book.

DO
- When is it hard for you to be humble? Talk with your family about ideas that could help.
- Repeat Proverbs 11:2 to yourself when you're tempted to show off.

PRAY
Ask God to make you confident of his love so that you're not tempted to brag.

MEMORIZE
Pride leads to disgrace, but with humility comes wisdom. Proverbs 11:2

WHAT'S THE POINT?
Grant saw how his selfishness hurt the team and himself. God wants us to be humble because it helps others and it helps us. *JP*

JULY 25
Knitting Lesson

Celia and her mom boarded the train. There were only two empty seats left. "I'll take the back one," her mom said. "You sit up here."

As Celia set her backpack down, her elderly seatmate looked up from her knitting and smiled. "Get comfortable, honey. It's a long ride."

Celia wanted to listen to music, not talk to a stranger. She put in her earbuds and turned on her MP3 player. The lady smiled again, so Celia closed her eyes and bobbed her head to the songs. When one ended, she looked up and noticed the woman's knitting. Earlier it had been only a few inches long. Now it was a long stretch of midnight blue background sprinkled with white snowflakes. Without thinking, Celia stroked it. "That's beautiful."

"Would you like a knitting lesson?"

Celia looked at her MP3 player. This train trip was her best opportunity to listen to music. Did she want to give that up?

READ
Philippians 2:4. God wants us to care about what matters to other people, not only about what's important to us.

THINK
- Does this verse say it's wrong to look out for what we like, or that we should think about what other people like too?
- How could caring about others' interests help you get to know other people better?
- Finish the story, showing how Celia might follow the instructions in this verse. Then read the possible ending at the back of the book.

DO
- See if you can name a favorite hobby of everyone in your family. If that's easy, try to do it for kids at school too.
- Ask someone to tell you about his or her hobby or teach you how to do it.

PRAY
Thank God for hobbies and interests. Ask him to help you be interested in others.

MEMORIZE
Don't look out only for your own interests, but take an interest in others, too.
Philippians 2:4

WHAT'S THE POINT?
The trip with Grandpa showed Celia the importance of being interested in someone else. God wants us to use our interests to share our lives with each other. *JP*

JULY 26
Babysitting

Dad was painting the basement and Mom was out. They were paying Christian to watch his little sister, but it wasn't going to be easy. Jayla could be a pest, and this afternoon she'd been terrible. When he told her they couldn't go outside, she made a face. He explained, "Mom said we have to stay inside until she gets home. Then we'll all go to the park."

Jayla stomped her foot. "I want to go now."

When Christian went to get her a graham cracker, she ran outside. When Christian caught up to her, she said, "I told you I want to go to the park *now*!"

Christian yelled, "How could you be so dumb?" He told her to take a time-out. "You can sit there until Mom gets home!"

"Well, you're dumb, too, for not taking me to the park!" Jayla screamed. Christian rolled his eyes. *I'm turning out to be a lousy babysitter,* he thought. Maybe he should just give Jayla everything she wanted and then she wouldn't complain. But then he wouldn't be doing what his mom wanted.

READ

Genesis 39:1-6. Joseph was sold as a slave. Even so, he decided to be so responsible that Potiphar trusted him enough to be in charge of his entire house. Also read Matthew 25:21.

THINK

- What do these verses show us about Joseph? How was Potiphar blessed because of Joseph?
- How can being responsible when someone trusts you with something be a blessing to others?
- Make up an ending for the story, showing how Christian could find encouragement in the verses. Then read the possible ending at the back of the book.

DO

- Write three things that you are responsible for at home, at school, or somewhere else.
- Write a grade by each thing to show how responsible you act in that area. If you need to improve in an area, plan to do so.

PRAY

Thank God for the responsibilities that you are entrusted with. Ask him to help you act wisely when doing them.

MEMORIZE

The master was full of praise. "Well done, my good and faithful servant. You have been faithful in handling this small amount, so now I will give you many more responsibilities. Let's celebrate together!" Matthew 25:21

WHAT'S THE POINT?

Christian realized that he was entrusted with watching Jayla. He needed to be responsible or his mother wouldn't continue to trust him. *JP*

JULY 27
Gold Medalist

Tanya and her neighbor Marlee loved to watch the gymnastics Olympic competition. When the show ended, they pretended they were gymnasts. After they did their tumbling routines, they had an awards ceremony. They made medals out of cardboard and foil.

They waved to the imaginary crowd. They did interviews, pretending to thank their imaginary coaches, parents, and friends who had supported them, just as the gymnasts did.

Today after the Olympic medal ceremony, the gold medalist was interviewed. She said she was thankful to Jesus, who gave her all her athletic skills. "Jesus is Lord!" she said.

Tanya felt kind of embarrassed. Why praise Jesus in front of all those people?

READ
Philippians 2:8-11. God has honored Jesus, and one day everyone on earth will honor him too.

THINK
- How did God honor Jesus?
- What do these verses say we can do to honor Jesus? What are some other ways you can think of?
- Finish the story, showing how Tanya could also give Jesus the place of honor. Then read the possible ending at the back of the book.

DO
- Play a reporter and interview your family members on reasons to honor Jesus.
- Use cardboard and foil to make a medal of honor for Jesus.

PRAY
Praise God for Jesus.

MEMORIZE
God elevated him to the place of highest honor and gave him the name above all other names. Philippians 2:9

WHAT'S THE POINT?
When Tanya thought of what Jesus had done for her, she wanted to praise him. When we praise him now, it's a small taste of what it will be like someday when everyone in the world praises him. *JP*

JULY 28
The Gift

When Chloe went in the candy store, she saw the card she'd made for Mr. Martz on display beside the cash register. Theo's card, which was way better than hers, was there too. Theo was such a gifted artist that she felt jealous.

Mr. Martz beamed. "Hello, Chloe. These cards brightened my hospital stay. Thank you for remembering me."

"Are you better now?"

"I'm great! And every time I look at these cards, I feel even better." He picked up both of them.

"My card isn't nearly as nice as Theo's."

Mr. Martz looked puzzled. "What do you mean?"

"His drawing is really good."

"Yes," he agreed. "Theo's drawing is stunning." Then he opened her card. "But your poem brings tears to my eyes each time I read it. God has given you the gift of encouraging words."

Chloe stared at Mr. Martz. Did he mean what he said, or was he just trying to make her feel better?

READ

1 Peter 4:10. God gives each of us different gifts and talents. He wants us to use them to affect the lives of others.

THINK

- Does God give everyone the same gifts? Why or why not?
- Why do you think God wants us to use our talents to serve others?
- Imagine an ending for this story, showing how the verse could make a difference for Chloe. Then read the possible ending at the back of the book.

DO

- Ask family members to help you think of talents God has given you.
- Ask for suggestions about how to use your talents to help others. Write down something you will do.

PRAY

Thank God for the gifts he's given you.

MEMORIZE

God has given each of you a gift from his great variety of spiritual gifts. Use them well to serve one another. 1 Peter 4:10

WHAT'S THE POINT?

Mr. Martz's compliment helped Chloe see the gift God had given her. She realized she could use that gift to help others. *JP*

JULY 29
Don't Take Off the Training Wheels!

Nash was tired of teaching his little brother, Evan, how to ride a bike. They'd been practicing since June. Here it was the end of July, and Evan still panicked whenever Nash suggested ditching the training wheels.

The boys stood on the sidewalk. "You can do it." Nash hoped he sounded patient. "I promise to hold on to the bike and run beside you."

"What if you let go?" Evan's lip trembled. "I could fall and get hurt."

Nash tightened Evan's helmet and handed him elbow pads and knee pads. "Put on this gear, and you'll be safe." Nash began to unscrew the training wheels with a wrench. "I promise I won't let go."

"No!" Evan wailed. "Please, Nash, don't take them off!"

Nash was sure the neighbors were staring at them. He wanted to throw down the wrench, grab his little brother, and shake him. Instead, he closed his eyes and prayed, *Please, God, help me not to lose my temper.*

READ
1 John 3:23. This verse says we are to love one another because Jesus told us to do so.

THINK
- What are the two things this verse tells us to do?
- When is it hard to follow the command to love others? What could help?
- Finish the story with your ideas about how Nash could apply the instructions in the verse. Then read the possible ending at the back of the book.

DO
- Play "Toss and Tell." Toss a ball from family member to family member. Each catcher says a loving thing to the person who threw it.
- Tell your family how other people have obeyed the command by loving you.

PRAY
Thank God for sending Jesus to love us and to show us how to love.

MEMORIZE
This is his commandment: We must believe in the name of his Son, Jesus Christ, and love one another, just as he commanded us. 1 John 3:23

WHAT'S THE POINT?
After he prayed, Nash passed on to Evan what Dad had done for him. God uses the loving acts of others to show us how to love one another. *JP*

JULY 30
In the Dirt

Rosalind ran to the swing set at the church playground, hoping she would get to the last available swing first. Tessa was always pushing Rosalind out of the way to get what she wanted. No matter how much Rosalind tried, she just couldn't get along with Tessa. "Hey, Rosalind! I called that swing first!" Tessa yelled behind her.

"Tough! I got here first!" Rosalind yelled back. Tessa lunged for the swing and tried to dump Rosalind off.

"Hey, cut it out!" Rosalind said. "I'm going to fall in the dirt!" And just as she had predicted, the swing dipped and Rosalind ended up in a pile underneath. Tessa jumped on the swing and tried to push Rosalind away with her feet. Rosalind grabbed Tessa's feet and pulled her off the swing.

"Ow!" Tessa screamed. Rosalind kept holding on to her feet and dragged her all the way to sandbox.

"There! See how that feels!" Rosalind said smugly.

Tessa looked up at her with tears in her eyes. "You're just mean. I don't like you!"

READ
1 John 4:19-21. The way Christians treat each other proves whether or not they love Jesus.

THINK
- According to these verses, why do we show love to other Christians?
- Is it harder for you to love the people you see or the God you can't see? Why?
- Finish the story, showing how Rosalind and Tessa might learn something together from today's verses. Then read the possible ending at the back of the book.

DO
- Have you been unloving toward another Christian? Ask that person for forgiveness.

PRAY
Ask God to help you love your Christian brothers and sisters.

MEMORIZE
We love each other because he loved us first. 1 John 4:19

WHAT'S THE POINT?
Rosalind and Tessa realized that the best way to prove that they loved Jesus was to change the way they acted. When we love God, he gives us power to love others. *JP*

JULY 31
No Matter What

Chandler was excited. His big sister was coming to visit. Winnie had been at college for two months, and Chandler had missed her. But he was nervous too. What if she had changed?

A horn honked outside, and he looked out the window. Winnie was home! He held the door while she lugged in her stuff.

"Thanks, Squirt. What have you been eating since I left? You've gotten so tall." She took off her stocking cap and coat.

Chandler stared. Winnie looked so different. Her hair was dyed a weird shade of red and was cut all raggedy. Her clothes were baggy, and her ears had four new piercings. What had happened to his pretty, blonde-haired sister?

Winnie grinned. "What do you think of the new me?"

Chandler thought she looked kind of scary. Suddenly he didn't want to be around her. "I need to do my homework." He fled to his room. How was he supposed to act around this new Winnie?

READ
1 John 4:11-12. Real love starts with God, who loves us so much that his love in us should be shown to others.

THINK
- What are some ways that God has shown his love to us?
- If God loves us and we love him, how does this help us love others?
- Finish the story with your advice about how Chandler can use the truths in these verses to help him relate to his sister. Then read the possible ending at the back of the book.

DO
- Who do you know who you could show God's love to through your actions?
- Draw a heart and write today's verses in it. Hang it on a bulletin board or the refrigerator to remind yourself to love others at all times.

PRAY
Thank God for loving you. Ask him to help you love others more.

MEMORIZE
Dear friends, since God loved us that much, we surely ought to love each other. 1 John 4:11

WHAT'S THE POINT?
Chandler realized his love for Winnie didn't come from what she did or how she looked. When we understand how much God loves us, we have plenty of love for others. *JP*

AUGUST I
Who's the Boss?

"Are you *done*, Megan?" Tamika was about to burst. Outside her bedroom window, the sky shone blue. Inside, her friend Megan was carefully fitting the saddle onto a plastic horse by a miniature castle. Small figures and other items lay scattered across the rug.

"Megan!" Tamika jumped up. "Let's go out *now*! We can draw something cool on the driveway with my new sidewalk chalk."

Megan found a knight. "I'd rather stay here." She picked up a shield and helmet.

"Well, it's *my* house," Tamika snapped.

Megan's eyes left the castle to meet Tamika's angrily. "So what if it's your house? You're not the boss! Why do we always have to do what *you* want, anyway?" She stomped to the bedroom door.

Tamika swallowed hard.

READ
1 Samuel 18:1-4. After David won the battle against the giant, Goliath, David and the king's son Jonathan became good friends. Now read Philippians 2:3. Being humble is the opposite of being stuck up.

THINK
- Why did Jonathan do the things in these verses for David? Do you think it was hard or easy?
- Remember some times when you and friends disagreed about what to do. What happened? Who was being humble or unselfish?
- Finish the story, showing how Tamika could change if she followed the teaching in the memory verse. Then read the possible ending at the back of the book.

DO
- How humble or unselfish a friend are you? Not so much? Average? Very much? Ask family members to rate you as well.
- Let a friend choose what you do together this week.

PRAY
Ask God to help you act unselfishly toward your friends.

MEMORIZE
Don't be selfish; don't try to impress others. Be humble, thinking of others as better than yourselves. Philippians 2:3

WHAT'S THE POINT?
Good friends think of others, not just themselves. Tamika was asking for God's help and trying to do better. *SG*

AUGUST 2
Playing on the Oak Team

"No way, Moshe!" Denny nudged the soccer ball into the air with his toe and caught it. "I know *you're* good, so I want *you* on the Oak team, but I don't want *that* kid."

What a mess, Moshe thought. It was the first day of camp, and the Oak cabins were going to play the Spruce cabins. He could see his cabinmate, Archie, standing at the edge of the field. He didn't look athletic, but Moshe thought he would make a good friend.

When Denny let the ball drop again, Moshe stuck his foot out. The two of them jostled for it, laughing, until finally Moshe got control. He looked back at Archie.

READ
1 Samuel 19:1-7. King Saul was jealous of David and wanted to kill him! Jonathan risked standing up for his friend. Now read Proverbs 18:24.

THINK
- Why do you think Jonathan stood up for David? Think of two reasons.
- Though it's good to stand up for a friend, some problems are serious or dangerous. In what situations might it be good to get adult advice or help?
- Finish the story, showing how Moshe could follow Jonathan's example in the Bible passage. Then read the possible ending at the back of the book.

DO
- What might make it hard for you to stand up for a friend?
- With a family member, act out scenes about someone putting down a friend. Practice what you might say to stick up for him or her.

PRAY
Ask God for courage to support your friends even when it's hard. Ask him to help you know when to ask adults for help.

MEMORIZE
A real friend sticks closer than a brother. Proverbs 18:24

WHAT'S THE POINT?
The Bible says friends go out of their way to help each other. Moshe spoke up for Archie even though he risked missing the game himself. *SG*

AUGUST 3
The Flying Potato Chips

Keenan tried not to stare. The new boy's twisted body rocked awkwardly from side to side as he walked. It seemed to take forever for him to cross the lunchroom to an empty table and sit down.

A woman assistant followed him with a cafeteria tray. "Here you go, Curtis." She cheerfully set it in front of him. "I'll be back. I forgot the napkins."

After she left, the boy started in on his lunch, and Keenan went back to eating. But he soon saw that Curtis's arms flailed around as he reached for his hot dog. Ketchup landed on his baseball shirt. Some kids were whispering. Then Curtis's elbow knocked his bag of chips flying onto the floor. Someone laughed.

Keenan looked around. The woman assistant was nowhere in sight.

READ
2 Samuel 9:1-7 and Proverbs 19:17. David's friend Jonathan had died, leaving his disabled son without support. David promised to help Mephibosheth.

THINK
- Do you think it was easy or hard for David to help Mephibosheth? Explain your answer.
- Why do you think God wants us to help people in need?
- Finish the story, showing how David's good example in these verses could make a difference for Keenan. Then read the possible ending at the back of the book.

DO
- With your family, list some people who could use help and friendship (because of problems with health, money, loneliness, and so on).
- Do something kind for someone on your list.

PRAY
Ask God to help you see the needs of others and then act with kindness.

MEMORIZE
If you help the poor, you are lending to the LORD—and he will repay you! Proverbs 19:17

WHAT'S THE POINT?
God wants us to be kind to people in need. Although Keenan felt a little uncomfortable around Curtis, he reached out anyway. The more Keenan gets to know him, the more comfortable he'll be. *SG*

AUGUST 4
Hairy Problem

Noelle picked up her overnight bag and waved as her big sister drove away. Parties at Annika's were fun. After pizza and a movie, all four girls headed for Annika's room.

Annika's mom stuck her head in. "We're going to bed, but you can stay up until midnight."

When her mom was gone, Annika whispered, "Look! I have a surprise!" She pulled out a bag and dumped four packages of hair dye on the bed. "These were really cheap!"

"Do you really think we should dye our hair?" Noelle wondered.

"Why not?" Annika shrugged. "The package says it'll wash right out."

Noelle felt uneasy. "Maybe I'll call my sister and see what she thinks." The other girls weren't listening.

"I can't decide between redhead and brunette!" Annika giggled.

READ
1 Kings 12:1, 3-11, 16, 19. Rehoboam listened to bad advice. Soon most of his kingdom turned against him. Read Proverbs 12:15. God encourages us to get good advice from people we trust.

THINK
- Why should Rehoboam have listened to the older men instead of the young men?
- We make choices every day about what to think and do. What makes someone or something a good source of ideas? a bad source?
- Make up an ending for the story, showing how Noelle might learn from the Bible verses. Then read the possible ending at the back of the book.

DO
- Draw three stick people. Label them with the names of people you feel you can trust for good advice.
- Talk to someone on the list when you need to make a decision this week.

PRAY
Ask God to show you good friends and adults to ask for advice.

MEMORIZE
Fools think their own way is right, but the wise listen to others. Proverbs 12:15

WHAT'S THE POINT?
The Bible says to listen to good advice. Noelle realized that her sister could have given her good advice to help her avoid following her friends. *SG*

AUGUST 5
A Place to Go

Diana spun the spinner. "A four! I win!"

"Great!" Sunisa said. "Let's eat." Diana liked going to Sunisa's. They played games and ate spicy noodles or peanut butter toast.

Diana looked at Sunisa nibbling. "You look like my hamster, Skipper, when he's eating a carrot," she giggled.

"I want to see Skipper sometime," Sunisa answered, her mouth full.

Diana fell silent. *What should I do, God? Should I have Sunisa over?* She thought about her tiny apartment with her mother inside taking care of her grandmother, who was sometimes crabby and sometimes asleep. "I've got to go," she said abruptly.

Sunisa felt bad. She wondered what she'd said wrong.

READ
2 Kings 4:8-17. A family welcomed Elisha into their home, and he showed his thanks. Read Romans 12:13. Hospitality has to do with generously welcoming guests.

THINK
- Why do you think the woman invited Elisha in? Why did Elisha want to help her?
- If you can't invite someone to your home, how else could you show hospitality?
- Finish the story, showing how Diana and Sunisa could solve their problems by learning from the Bible story. Then read the possible ending at the back of the book.

DO
- With your family, discuss ways to help others feel cared for or welcome.
- Clean your room and invite someone over (or plan another place to play).

PRAY
Ask God to help you welcome others.

MEMORIZE
When God's people are in need, be ready to help them. Always be eager to practice hospitality. Romans 12:13

WHAT'S THE POINT?
Sunisa welcomed Diana to her home, and Diana found a way to show appreciation, like Elisha and the woman in the Bible story. *SG*

217

AUGUST 6
Trashed!

LaToya straightened up from filling her trash bag and wiped her forehead. A long-sleeved shirt and work gloves felt hot, but her Pioneer Clubs leader had insisted.

"I don't want anyone cut on broken glass or scratched with a rusty nail."

Across the empty lot, other kids were picking up cans and bottles. LaToya's brother Davon was loading larger trash into a bin. Tomorrow they'd sweep and wash, and later paint the fence—and eventually have a playground!

They were just leaving when three boys came by on bikes. "Need help? Here!" They threw bottles onto the asphalt and rode off, laughing.

LaToya looked at the broken glass, stunned.

"That's okay, kids," Miss Constance said quietly. "We'll take care of it tomorrow." But some of the club members were grumbling.

LaToya felt discouraged. "I'm not going back, Mom!" she said at home. "I don't know if Miss Constance will either."

READ
Nehemiah 2:17-18; 4:10-14; and 6:15-16. Nehemiah encouraged the people, and they rebuilt the wall around Jerusalem in spite of their enemies' threats.

THINK
- How did Nehemiah cheer his people on? How did others discourage them?
- Who did the enemies realize was helping Nehemiah and his people?
- Finish the story, showing how LaToya could follow Nehemiah's example. Then read the possible ending at the back of the book.

DO
- With your family, list some big projects going on in your church or community.
- Write a note, bring a snack, or pitch in to encourage someone in his or her work.

PRAY
Ask God to help you speak and act to encourage others.

MEMORIZE
When our enemies and the surrounding nations heard about it, they were frightened and humiliated. They realized this work had been done with the help of our God. Nehemiah 6:16

WHAT'S THE POINT?
The club members were tempted to give up on the project. Like Nehemiah, LaToya decided to keep going and give her friends a boost too. *SG*

AUGUST 7
River Explorer

Corey looked restlessly out the window. In the main room of Grandpa's farmhouse, his cousins were doing a puzzle. Others were playing a game. Though Corey loved the family reunions here every summer, there were times when he just wanted some peace and quiet.

Maybe I can sneak out to the river, he thought. He knew his parents didn't want him wandering around Grandpa's farm alone, but he didn't see why not.

"Hey, what are you doing?" The voice of his cousin Hughie broke in.

"Uh, heading for the bathroom," Corey stammered. He ducked into the little room and shut the door. *Now maybe Hughie will go away and I can sneak out,* he thought.

READ
Ecclesiastes 4:12. This verse gives us a word picture about facing an enemy, but we face many other situations in life where two or three people are better than just one.

THINK
- According to this verse, what are some benefits of teamwork?
- How would *you* finish the verse? "Two or three people are better than one because _____."
- Finish the story, showing how Corey could find some inspiration in this verse. Then read the possible ending at the back of the book.

DO
- With your family, pantomime activities (both work and fun) that are better when done with someone else. Let the others guess what the actor is doing.
- Ropes made of three pieces braided together are stronger than one. Braid three pieces of string. Knot the ends. Use it as a bookmark or friendship wristband to remind yourself of the value of being with others.

PRAY
Ask God to help you include others often in your work and play.

MEMORIZE
A person standing alone can be attacked and defeated, but two can stand back-to-back and conquer. Three are even better, for a triple-braided cord is not easily broken. Ecclesiastes 4:12

WHAT'S THE POINT?
Though there are times for being alone, Corey realized that some activities are better and safer when done with others. *SG*

AUGUST 8
Smashing a Sand Castle

"I'm tired of the water. Let's go build a sand castle," Kinzie said irritably.

What's her problem today? Elena wondered. She shrugged and followed her friend out of the pool and across the concrete to the sand area. On their way, they passed their little brothers splashing in the kiddie pool. Their mothers sat on the pool's edge, talking.

For a while the girls worked quietly together, pressing the wet sand into buckets and molds, forming walls and towers. Elena was carefully extending the wall on her side of the project when her friend seemed to explode.

"Stupid sand!" Kinzie kicked over a crumbling tower. "Who cares, anyway!" She threw her shovel down and started bashing in the walls with a bucket. Her face looked angry, but her eyes were filled with tears. Elena didn't know what to do.

"Hey, this is my castle too!" she called out. She wondered if she should tell Kinzie's mom.

READ
2 Corinthians 1:3-7. Talk together about how God has comforted you in the past—and how you can comfort others.

THINK
- When have you been very angry or upset in the past? What comforted you? Who helped comfort you?
- What kinds of words would *not* help a friend who's upset?
- Imagine an ending for this story, showing how Elena might find advice in these verses. Then read the possible ending at the back of the book.

DO
- With your family, act out ways to encourage a hurting person.
- Write the name of someone you know who may be going through a hard time. Think of something you could say or do that would encourage the person.

PRAY
Ask God to help you act sensitively when people around you are hurting.

MEMORIZE
He comforts us in all our troubles so that we can comfort others. When they are troubled, we will be able to give them the same comfort God has given us. 2 Corinthians 1:4

WHAT'S THE POINT?
God wants us to comfort those who hurt. Elena asked what was bothering her friend and then showed she cared. *SG*

AUGUST 9
It's a Secret!

"I don't get it." Fernando squinted at his friend. "You're coming here Friday evening, going home to sleep, and then coming back in the morning? Are you afraid of sleeping in the tent? There'll be four of us. It'll be fun!"

Conrad glanced around nervously. "Listen, you can't tell anyone, but I have this problem with, um, wetting at night," he stammered. Fernando was startled.

"Mom says it's a medical thing," Conrad continued awkwardly, "and I'm seeing a doctor, but . . ."

"But you'd rather sleep at home," Fernando finished. "That's okay."

Friday came, and Fernando's parents set up the tent. The boys played in the yard until dark and then went in the tent with flashlights.

"Conrad, your dad's here!" a voice called from the yard.

"I gotta go! See you in the morning!" Conrad darted quickly out.

"What's his problem?" another boy asked.

READ
Proverbs 11:13, which talks about the importance of keeping secrets. Gossiping means telling people personal things about others.

THINK
- If you have a secret, why would you want a trustworthy friend?
- According to the verse, how does gossiping hurt a friendship?
- Finish the story, showing how Fernando could find wisdom in this verse. Then read the possible ending at the back of the book.

DO
- Discuss with your family which kinds of secrets should stay quiet and which should be told (such as if someone is being hurt).
- Lay a piece of paper on a zipper and rub a crayon over the texture. Write "Zip your lip. Proverbs 11:13." Hang it as a reminder.

PRAY
Ask God to help you be a trustworthy friend.

MEMORIZE
A gossip goes around telling secrets, but those who are trustworthy can keep a confidence.
Proverbs 11:13

WHAT'S THE POINT?
Sharing someone's secret might make you feel important. Fernando realized it was better to be a trustworthy friend. *SG*

AUGUST 10
Cookie Disaster

"This will be great!" Deena bounced with excitement. "We'll make lots of money selling cookies!" The girls took turns reading the recipe and adding ingredients to the dough. Deena worked fast and sort of messily, while Mallory measured everything slowly and carefully. "Come on, Mallory, hurry up!" said Deena.

Soon the cookies were baked. The chocolate chips smelled great! But when they each took a bite, the cookies didn't taste very good. "Are you sure you read the recipe correctly?" Mallory's mom asked. The girls looked at the book.

"Oh no!" Deena's face turned red with embarrassment. "I didn't put in enough sugar. I put in a *half* cup instead of *one and a half* cups."

"What?!" All kinds of mean remarks popped into Mallory's head.

READ
Proverbs 12:18. This verse talks about the power of words used for either good or bad.

THINK
- Remember a time when someone was mad and said something to you that hurt. How did that affect your friendship?
- Think about some ways you can speak more carefully next time you're angry: count to ten; remember how the other person feels; pray; remember that God cares about the other person's feelings too; remember that cutting words hurt others; or come up with another idea of your own.
- Finish the story, showing how Mallory could use what she knows from this verse. Then read the possible ending at the back of the book.

DO
- Pretend to be a reporter. Interview family members about how to express anger without using "cutting" words.
- Pick one idea in the "Think" list to use this week when you're upset.

PRAY
Ask God to help you control your tongue so you don't say mean words to others.

MEMORIZE
Some people make cutting remarks, but the words of the wise bring healing. Proverbs 12:18

WHAT'S THE POINT?
Although Mallory was angry with Deena, she realized God didn't want her to use mean words. Her kind words helped their friendship. *SG*

AUGUST 11
The Flying Burrito

"I'm a pretty good cook. These burritos are great," Rory bragged with his mouth full.

Across the table, his friend Jordan laughed. "Yeah, you're good at heating things in the microwave!"

Rory's two-year-old brother, Timmy, laughed too. This was Jordan's first visit to their house, but Timmy seemed to think he was funny.

"Hey, pass me another burrito!" Rory called out.

Jordan grabbed a burrito and assumed a quarterback stance. "It's a long bomb!"

Timmy squealed with delight as the burrito flew across the table. Rory grabbed for it, and his elbow knocked over a glass. It hit the floor and smashed, spilling lemonade and scattering pieces of glass across the floor.

The kitchen was suddenly quiet. Then Jordan said, "You could tell your mom that Timmy broke it. He can't talk much yet, so no one would know."

Rory looked at Jordan, thinking over what his friend said.

READ
Proverbs 12:5. This verse means that godly people do right things but ungodly people give advice that can't be trusted.

THINK
- Why do you think God wants us to be careful about listening to advice from friends?
- Have you ever had a friend try to get you to do something wrong? What did you do?
- Finish the story, showing how Rory could find advice in this verse. Then read the possible ending at the back of the book.

DO
- Talk with your family about how to tell if someone is giving you bad advice.
- Role-play ways to say no to a friend who's trying to get you to do something foolish or wrong.

PRAY
Ask God to help you make wise choices about friends and advice.

MEMORIZE
The plans of the godly are just; the advice of the wicked is treacherous. Proverbs 12:5

WHAT'S THE POINT?
Rory knew he was getting bad advice from Jordan, and he chose not to follow it. *SG*

AUGUST 12
Who's Playing Games?

"I don't like Belinda anymore," Tabitha's new friend Ria announced. She dumped the contents of the game box onto Tabitha's rug. "Belinda says we're losers because we still like board games."

Tabitha glanced over from the game board she was setting up. "Really?"

"Yeah!" Ria continued. "I guess she thinks she's too cool for us."

Tabitha frowned as she placed pieces on the board. She'd known Belinda for a long time, but she hadn't played with her for a while. Maybe Belinda didn't want to be around her now.

Ria leaned forward. "I'm glad we're friends, aren't you? Who needs Belinda, anyway!"

Tabitha didn't know what to say.

READ
Proverbs 16:28. *Strife* means trouble and arguments. Gossip is spreading personal information or rumors behind someone's back.

THINK
- According to the verse, why might a person spread stories or gossip about someone else?
- Why do you think God doesn't want us to gossip?
- Make up an ending for the story, showing how the verse can make a difference for Tabitha. Then read the possible ending at the back of the book.

DO
- Play "Toss and Tell." Toss a ball from one family member to another. Each catcher tells a way to check if a story someone tells about someone else is true.

PRAY
Ask God to help you resist gossiping about others behind their backs.

MEMORIZE
A troublemaker plants seeds of strife; gossip separates the best of friends. Proverbs 16:28

WHAT'S THE POINT?
Tabitha knew it wasn't good to spread rumors or share personal information about friends behind their backs. She resisted name-calling, and she talked to Belinda directly about what was true. *SG*

AUGUST 13
Crash Landing

Thoughts of yesterday still made Reed queasy. On the playground, he'd heard a thud and a loud yell. He'd whirled around to see Marshall on the ground by the slide, howling in pain, one leg twisted in an odd direction.

Reed winced at the memory as he dialed the phone. Marshall answered. "How are you doing?" Reed asked.

"Not great," Marshall answered weakly. "My leg still hurts, even inside the cast. I guess that's how it is when you break something."

"Hey, do you still want to go to the park with my dad and me to watch those little radio-controlled airplanes?" Reed continued. "I thought maybe you might like to get out."

The phone was silent. "Thanks anyway," Marshall finally replied, "but I'm not up to going anywhere today."

"Okay. See you later." Reed hung up. "Bummer," he muttered.

READ
Proverbs 17:17. This verse talks about sticking with friends.

THINK
- Define a true friend based on this verse.
- Why might it be hard to stick with someone who is having problems?
- Finish the story, showing how Reed might get an idea from this verse. Then read the possible ending at the back of the book.

DO
- List some ways you could show friendship to people who are hurt, sick, or have some other problem.
- Call, e-mail, or visit someone who's hurt or sick, or bring over a card or treat.

PRAY
Ask God to help you care for your friends even when they're having troubles.

MEMORIZE
A friend is always loyal, and a brother is born to help in time of need. Proverbs 17:17

WHAT'S THE POINT?
A true friend doesn't disappear during times of trouble. Reed realized that it was more important to cheer up Marshall than to watch planes. *SG*

AUGUST 14
Mad Messages

From her spot in line for the roller coaster, Eleanor could see Shauna up on the Ferris wheel with her head bent down.

She's probably texting someone, Eleanor thought irritably.

Text messages had been flying all morning at the amusement park. Pretty soon the club members would meet Vickie, their adult leader, for lunch—if they could stand being at the same table with one another. It was a bunch of "She said this" and "Her hair's gross" and "Aren't those pants ugly?"

It's stupid! Eleanor grumbled to herself—although she'd added a couple jabs of her own about Shauna's T-shirt.

Finally, she climbed into the roller coaster car. The girl next to her tapped her arm. "Shauna says you need braces 'cause you look like—"

"I don't want to hear it!" Determined, Eleanor bent over her cell phone.

READ
Proverbs 26:20. *Quarreling* means arguing or making mean comments to each other.

THINK
- This verse compares quarreling to a fire. Why?
- When two people are quarreling, what happens if friends join in?
- Finish the story, showing how Eleanor could find some wisdom in this verse. Then read the possible ending at the back of the book.

DO
- Draw a campfire. As a caption, write how someone might help "put out" a quarrel. Draw a circle with a slash through the campfire if you will say no the next time you're asked to join an argument or pass along hurtful words.

PRAY
Ask God to help you resist passing on quarrelsome words.

MEMORIZE
Fire goes out without wood, and quarrels disappear when gossip stops. Proverbs 26:20

WHAT'S THE POINT?
Eleanor realized she had contributed to the quarreling at the amusement park. She bravely chose to follow the leader's instructions and apologize. *SG*

AUGUST 15
Zoo Trip

Flynn gazed at the leafy rainforest exhibit, his favorite one at the zoo. Brilliantly colored birds soared above, tiny monkeys swung from branches, and frogs hopped in quiet pools. But the scene behind him was not so peaceful.

"I still say he's the best baseball player ever!"

"Are you kidding? He's a jerk!" Flynn's friends Doug and Renaldo had been arguing all through the zoo.

"How would *you* know, loser? Ow!" Someone had started shoving.

"Would you guys just *cut it out!*" he yelled. He thought of adding that *they* belonged in a cage. Doug and Renaldo stopped in surprise.

READ
James 3:18. James is encouraging all believers to work toward peace.

THINK
- What kind of person would be good at making peace?
- What might make peacemaking hard to do?
- Finish the story, showing how the encouragement from this verse could make a difference for Flynn. Then read the possible ending at the back of the book.

DO
- With your family, brainstorm ways to calm an argument.
- Using one of your ideas, create a skit with two friends arguing and a third one trying to help.

PRAY
Ask God to help you value peace and work toward it.

MEMORIZE
Those who are peacemakers will plant seeds of peace and reap a harvest of righteousness.
James 3:18

WHAT'S THE POINT?
Instead of giving up on his friends, Flynn tried to stop their arguing. Peacemaking may not be easy, because we don't have control over what other people decide to do. But Jesus is proud of us when we try. *SG*

AUGUST 16
Picking Tomatoes

With towels over their shoulders, Brock and his two friends headed down the dirt road on their bikes. It was a hot, muggy day—perfect for the swimming hole. They reached the paved road and turned toward their friend Damien's house.

Damien's bike was propped against the farm stand by the road. His mother was inside it, waiting on customers. "Where's Damien, Mrs. Vance?" Brock called out.

"In the garden," she replied.

They found Damien picking tomatoes and carefully placing them in a bag around his neck. "Sorry, guys!" he said. "Mom just asked me to pick more stuff. We've had a lot of customers this morning. I guess I'll have to come later."

"Yeah, too bad," said Brock. "We'll see you soon." The other two boys climbed back on their bikes and started off. Brock hesitated a moment and then rode after them. "Guys, wait!" he yelled.

READ
Matthew 7:12. Jesus talked about treating others the way we'd like to be treated.

THINK
- Jesus said this rule sums up all of God's laws. What do you think that means?
- What might make it hard to be giving or helpful to others? What could help?
- Finish the story, showing how Brock could follow the commandment in this verse. Then read the possible ending at the back of the book.

DO
- Discuss with your family: if all the people in the world treated others the way they wanted to be treated, what would be different?
- Trace around a shoe on a piece of paper. Write, "Put yourself in their shoes. Matthew 7:12." Hang it up as a reminder.

PRAY
Ask God to help you think of others and take action.

MEMORIZE
Do to others whatever you would like them to do to you. This is the essence of all that is taught in the law and the prophets. Matthew 7:12

WHAT'S THE POINT?
Jesus said to treat others as we would like to be treated. Brock knew Damien wanted to swim as much as he did—and could get there sooner with help. *SG*

AUGUST 17
This Skateboard's Mine!

Philip parked his bike and ran into the sports supply store, money in hand. He couldn't wait to buy the skateboard he'd been saving for! Sure, it was used, but it was one of the best. He could never afford a new one. This was a lucky find!

"Have a nice day," he heard the cashier say. He looked over to see his friend Maury heading for the door—carrying *his* skateboard!

Philip exploded. "What are you doing? I wanted that board, and you knew it! I just had to earn a little more money!"

Maury's eyes narrowed. "I guess you took too long!"

Philip wanted to punch him, but the clerk was watching. Philip lowered his voice. "Some friend you are! I'm never going to forget this!"

"Fine, but the skateboard's still mine!" Maury clutched the board and walked out.

READ
Matthew 18:21-33. Jesus told a story about forgiveness. God is like the king who forgives us for the huge numbers of wrongs we have done.

THINK
- Do you think the king's actions in verse 27 were *fair* or *generous*? Explain. What about the servant's actions in verses 28-30?
- Remember a time you were upset with someone. What did it take to forgive him or her?
- Make up an ending for the story, showing how the verses could make a difference for Philip. Then read the possible ending at the back of the book.

DO
- Rate how forgiving God has been to you: not much; some; a lot.
- Write the name of someone you're mad at. Forgive the person by "giving up" feelings of hate or bitterness.

PRAY
Ask God to help you love and forgive others as he loves and forgives you.

MEMORIZE
Peter came to him and asked, "Lord, how often should I forgive someone who sins against me? Seven times?" "No, not seven times," Jesus replied, "but seventy times seven!" Matthew 18:21-22

WHAT'S THE POINT?
Jesus taught that we should forgive others as God forgave us. Philip realized it was wrong to hold a grudge against Maury. *SG*

AUGUST 18
The Race

"Time to walk for a while," Hilary panted, slowing down. They were on a blocked-off street, partway through the "Shuffle for the Shelter" 5K run and fund-raiser.

"Finally!" Debbie gasped and stopped in her tracks. "This is hard."

"Don't stop! It's better to keep moving slowly," Hilary advised. She liked to run, and she thought they were making good time so far. "The homeless shelter is a good cause," she went on encouragingly. "Think about all the pledges we got!"

"I'm trying," Debbie muttered. The girls walked silently down a shady stretch of the course. A few other "Shufflers" jogged by.

Soon Hilary was ready to go. "Time to run again!" She started to jog.

"You go ahead." Debbie waved her on. Her face was red. "I can't. Sorry!" She headed for the curb. More runners went by, and Hilary felt torn. It would be faster to run without Debbie.

READ
Mark 2:1-5, 11-12. The paralyzed man's friends were faced with a big problem when they tried to help him, but they kept going and solved it. Now read Galatians 6:9. God is pleased when we do good.

THINK
▪ Why do you think the men kept on trying to bring their friend to Jesus?
▪ Helping others can be hard. Why might you want to give up? What could help?
▪ Imagine an ending for this story, showing how Hilary could learn from the verses. Then read the possible ending at the back of the book.

DO
▪ With your family, list some neighbors, friends, or others facing tough challenges.
▪ Plan to do a chore, run an errand, or bring a treat to encourage one of them.

PRAY
Ask God to give you strength so you can keep on helping others, even when it's tough.

MEMORIZE
Let's not get tired of doing what is good. At just the right time we will reap a harvest of blessing if we don't give up. Galatians 6:9

WHAT'S THE POINT?
Hilary knew God wants us to help others. He smiles on our efforts. *SG*

AUGUST 19
Bully on the Block

Walker rounded the corner on his bike and suddenly saw Silas. He briefly considered turning around before the big kid noticed him. Silas was at work with a weed digger next to a pile of uprooted dandelions.

That Bible verse about loving your enemy sounds great until you have a real enemy, Walker thought nervously. He remembered the times Silas had pushed him off his bike after school last spring. Walker and some of Silas's other victims had ended up in the principal's office, and Silas's parents had been called. *Maybe it's all over now,* Walker thought. He kept riding.

Silas looked up and glared as Walker came near. Then he poked the digger extra hard at a big weed. The pointed tool slipped and stabbed into Silas's leg. "Aaaaah!" he yelled. Blood started oozing from the cut.

Walker froze. Should he try to help, or would Silas slug him?

READ
Luke 6:27-28, 31. Jesus tells us how to treat enemies (or people who are mean or mad at us).

THINK
- What is surprising about Jesus' words?
- If you followed these verses, what bad things might happen? What good things?
- Finish the story, showing how Walker could follow the directions given in these verses. Then read the possible ending at the back of the book.

DO
- Make a list of people to pray for, including family, friends, and people you have trouble getting along with.
- Pray for someone who's mad at you or doesn't like you.

PRAY
Ask God to change your feelings toward enemies as you pray for them.

MEMORIZE
Love your enemies! Do good to those who hate you. Bless those who curse you. Pray for those who hurt you. Luke 6:27-28

WHAT'S THE POINT?
Jesus tells us to love our enemies. Walker overcame his fear of helping when Silas needed it. *SG*

AUGUST 20
Funniest Guy

"Listen up, everybody!" Ms. Huffman called out above the chatter echoing in the big room. "I have the list of all your parts in our final theater-camp program."

Mitch adjusted his glasses and ran his hands through his red hair nervously. Then he grinned at the other kids at his table. Why should he worry? He was a naturally funny guy.

"The other directors and I think we have a great show for your families to see," Ms. Huffman went on. "As you know, we're having a dramatic section, a short musical, and a comedy sketch."

Mitch leaned toward the kids next to him. "I'll be the lead in the comedy sketch for sure," he whispered. "I'm the funniest guy here!"

The others looked at him and frowned.

READ
Luke 14:1, 7-11. Jesus tells a story about guests looking for seats at a formal dinner. Exalting yourself means bragging about how important you are.

THINK
- Why did the guests in the story try to get special seats?
- What might kids do or say today to seem important to others?
- Finish the story, showing how the verses could make a difference for Mitch. Then read the possible ending at the back of the book.

DO
- Discuss with your family what it means to brag or be arrogant. How is it like blowing up a balloon?
- Blow up a balloon (or draw one). Write "Don't brag—be humble" on it with a permanent marker. Hang it in your room.

PRAY
Talk to God about a way you are tempted to brag. Ask him to help you be humble (not exaggerating your importance).

MEMORIZE
Those who exalt themselves will be humbled, and those who humble themselves will be exalted. Luke 14:11

WHAT'S THE POINT?
Jesus taught that it's unwise to brag. Mitch backed off, and later he received a compliment from the director. *SG*

AUGUST 21
Some Kind of Monster

"Here's one for you, Janet!" Gayle's friend Jodie was carrying a pile of envelopes and handing them out at recess. She stopped by Gayle and flipped through the stack. "Sorry, there isn't one for you!" she exclaimed as if surprised. Then she moved on to other girls.

Gayle's face turned bright red as the other girls were reading their party invitations. *I can't believe she said that! Ever since Jodie started hanging out with that new girl, she's turned into some kind of monster! This really hurts, God!*

On the way back to class Jodie walked past Gayle. Gayle thought about calling her a mean name. Or she could act as if Jodie didn't exist.

READ
Luke 17:3 explains the process of forgiveness. *Rebuking* means pointing out a wrong. *Repenting* means being sorry and trying to change.

THINK
- Why might it be important to rebuke someone before forgiving that person?
- If the person repents, how does that help you get ready to forgive?
- Finish the story, showing how Gayle could get good ideas from this verse. Then read the possible ending at the back of the book.

DO
- Rebuking isn't yelling or being mean, but calmly explaining the truth. Imagine talking to someone who's wronged you: "When you _____, then I felt _____."
- Talk to someone who wronged you this week. Be willing to rebuke and forgive, using the ideas above.

PRAY
Ask God to help you rebuke and forgive this person instead of being angry.

MEMORIZE
Watch yourselves! If another believer sins, rebuke that person; then if there is repentance, forgive. Luke 17:3

WHAT'S THE POINT?
Gayle was tempted to give up on Jodie, but instead she followed God's plan to rebuke and forgive. *SG*

AUGUST 22
Tagging Along

Joel hurried onto the white church bus and grabbed a spot in front by Chen. Out the window, he could see Mischa in line, talking loudly. *He probably thinks he's an expert on baseball like everything else,* he muttered to himself.

Joel felt excited about watching a minor-league game. But at church outings like these, Mischa always stuck to him like glue. Sure, they'd known each other since they were little. But sometimes Joel got tired of Mischa tagging along.

Soon Mischa climbed up the bus steps. He seemed briefly disappointed that the front seats were full. "I'll go in the back," he said to Joel. "See you at the game!"

"He is so weird." Chen snickered. "He's not going to sit with us, is he?"

The bus lurched onto the road. *Now what do I do?* Joel wondered.

READ
Luke 19:1-10. Jesus visited the home of Zacchaeus, a hated tax collector.

THINK
- Why was Zacchaeus unpopular (verses 2, 8)? What makes kids unpopular today?
- Why did Jesus want to spend time with Zacchaeus?
- Make up an ending for the story, showing how the verses could make a difference for Joel. Then read the possible ending at the back of the book.

DO
- Why might it be hard to act kindly toward someone who's unpopular? Talk to your family about what could help.
- Brainstorm some group events (video games, park outing, and so on) where you could include a less popular kid. Use one of your ideas to reach out to someone.

PRAY
Ask God to help you care about unpopular kids just as he does.

MEMORIZE
The Son of Man came to seek and save those who are lost. Luke 19:10

WHAT'S THE POINT?
Jesus cared about Zacchaeus even though others didn't like him. Joel realized he needed to change his behavior toward Mischa. *SG*

AUGUST 23
Berry Picking

April chose a pail from the stack that they'd brought to the berry patch. Each had a metal handle plus a loop of leather strap attached, so that you could hang the pail around your neck and pick berries with both hands. "What's your favorite way to eat strawberries?" she asked.

Her friend Lisa grabbed another pail. "Strawberry shortcakes are good," she said. "Strawberry pie is even better."

Some of the berries were green, some pink, some red. The deep red ones were ripe. April popped a couple into her mouth. "I like them plain, straight off the plant!"

The girls worked steadily, carefully pulling berries one by one checking under the leaves on each plant. Soon all the pails were full. "These are going to be heavy," Lisa observed.

April looked at their stash: five pails. "Someone's going to have to carry three," she said slowly.

READ
John 15:12. This verse is Jesus' command to love.

THINK
- When Jesus talked about *love*, do you think he meant *feelings* or *actions* or *both*? Explain.
- When Jesus lived on earth, how did he show love to others?
- Finish the story, showing how April could live out the directions of the verse. Then read the possible ending at the back of the book.

DO
- Draw a cartoon of yourself doing a chore or favor to help someone.
- Do this chore or favor this week.

PRAY
Ask God to help you show love in action, even if it means hard work.

MEMORIZE
This is my commandment: Love each other in the same way I have loved you. John 15:12

WHAT'S THE POINT?
Jesus wants us to love each other with a "giving" love, the way he loves people. April could have avoided the heavier load, but she found a creative way to be kind to her friend. *SG*

AUGUST 24
He Doesn't Speak English

Graham dribbled to the corner, whirled around, and shot. The ball bounced off the rim, but his friend Winston got the rebound and made the basket.

"All right!" Graham high-fived Winston and jogged down the court. Off to the side, he could see a boy watching from under a tree. When the other team's pass went out of bounds, the boy caught it and tossed it to Graham.

"Thanks!" Graham said. "Hey, do you want to play? We could use more guys." The boy smiled, but didn't move or say anything.

"Don't bother," said Winston. "He doesn't speak English. He probably doesn't know basketball rules, anyway."

READ
Romans 15:7. God made people with many differences. He wants us to be accepting of others.

THINK
- This verse talks about Jesus welcoming or accepting us. Finish this sentence: "Jesus accepts me in spite of _____."
- The opposite of *accept* is *reject*. Have you ever been rejected by someone? How did it feel?
- Imagine an ending for this story, showing how Graham could follow the verse. Then read the possible ending at the back of the book.

DO
- Are you accepting or welcoming to people who are new or different? Ask someone to rate you in this area and explain his or her answer.
- Reach out to someone who is different from you this week by helping him or her join an activity or learn something new.

PRAY
Ask God to help you notice others who need acceptance and then welcome them.

MEMORIZE
Accept each other just as Christ has accepted you so that God will be given glory.
Romans 15:7

WHAT'S THE POINT?
It was extra work to help the new boy, but Graham chose to be accepting and welcomed Temo onto the team. *SG*

AUGUST 25
Kitchen Duty

Maxwell and Deonte slumped on Deonte's couch, enjoying the breeze from the fan nearby. "What do you want to do now?" Deonte asked. Maxwell shrugged.

"Hey, Mom, can you make us some lunch?" Deonte called out.

His mom stuck her head out of the laundry room. "I'm working on the laundry, and I'm tired. I think you boys are quite capable of making your own lunch," she commented. "There's plenty of food in the refrigerator."

The washing machine started up, and Maxwell rolled his eyes. "My mom's always saying stuff like that," he grumbled.

Deonte and Maxwell headed for the refrigerator. *Aren't moms supposed to take care of kids?* Deonte thought irritably. On the other hand, his mom *did* look tired.

READ
Philippians 2:5-7. This passage tells about Jesus' attitude when he left heaven for earth.

THINK
- What do you think it means that Jesus became a servant? Who did he serve?
- Why would it be good to follow Jesus' example?
- Finish the story, showing how Deonte could follow Jesus' example. Then read the possible ending at the back of the book.

DO
- Make a list of some tasks that friends or other family members do.
- Volunteer to help with one, even if you don't have to.

PRAY
Ask God to help you help others, as Jesus did.

MEMORIZE
Have the same attitude that Christ Jesus had. Philippians 2:5

WHAT'S THE POINT?
Philippians 2:5-7 shows Jesus giving up his rights to serve us instead—to help us unselfishly. Deonte chose to be helpful rather than demanding. *SG*

AUGUST 26
Too Good to Be True

"Since you're new here," Gwen said to Talia mysteriously, "there's a lot you don't know. But *I* can help you." The other girls walking home from school giggled.

Talia didn't know what to think of Gwen. "What do you mean?"

Gwen gestured across the street. "See that little store? My aunt owns it," she explained. "She lets me and my friends get things for free—little stuff like gum and lip gloss. You can just take them. She doesn't mind."

Talia looked confused.

"Since you're my friend now, you can do it too—just try!" Gwen insisted. She grabbed Talia by the arm. Soon Talia found herself in the little store. Gwen and the others waited outside, watching through the window. Talia looked at the woman behind the counter. Then she picked up some strawberry lip gloss.

READ
1 Thessalonians 5:21-22. This means to check out things people say. That way you will know if their words are good or not.

THINK
- How could you check out something you hear to see if it is good or evil?
- What can you do if you "test" someone's idea and find out it's not good?
- Finish the story, showing how Talia could learn from the passage. Then read the possible ending at the back of the book.

DO
- With a partner, act out a scene where one friend has a bad plan, but the other is unsure and asks questions. Then switch roles.
- Plan to ask questions and get more information the next time you're unsure of an idea that a friend suggests.

PRAY
Ask God to help you ask questions and avoid bad situations.

MEMORIZE
Test everything that is said. Hold on to what is good. Stay away from every kind of evil.
1 Thessalonians 5:21-22

WHAT'S THE POINT?
When Talia felt unsure about Gwen's idea, she decided to test it and find out more. The Bible tells us to test things in order to avoid evil. *SG*

AUGUST 27
Hole in the Snare Drum

As Drew crossed the basement, he couldn't believe his eyes. There was his new drum set—with a hole in the snare drum! Alan was standing next to it with a pair of drumsticks, looking upset.

"I can't believe it!" Drew exploded. "I leave you alone for a while, and you break it!"

"I didn't—" Alan began.

Drew cut him off. "You're always goofing around! Now you banged so hard on the drum that it broke!" he yelled. Alan didn't say anything. He looked hurt. *He deserves it,* Drew thought angrily.

READ
James 1:19-20. God knows that a lot of problems can be helped by listening instead of getting angry and saying things we may regret.

THINK
- Why is it a good idea to *listen* first if you're getting angry?
- How does it feel when someone won't listen to your side of the story?
- Make up an ending for the story, showing how Drew could learn from the verses. Then read the possible ending at the back of the book.

DO
- Make a paper traffic light. Write "quick to listen" on the green circle, "slow to speak/be angry" on the yellow, and "angry words" on the red. Draw a slash through the "angry" words.
- Our beliefs add to our anger. If we believe that the other person is hurting us on purpose, we'll get angrier. But if we believe it's possible to work things out, we can understand the person better. Think about this the next time you start feeling angry.

PRAY
Ask God to help you listen to others and control angry words.

MEMORIZE
My dear brothers and sisters: You must all be quick to listen, slow to speak, and slow to get angry. James 1:19

WHAT'S THE POINT?
God knows that angry words make disagreements worse. Drew didn't listen, and he found out he'd been wrong about his brother. *SG*

AUGUST 28
Rich Kid

"You've got a voice mail," Kay's mom said when Kay got home. "Quinlan wants to know if you can come over this afternoon."

Kay plunked into a kitchen chair. "I don't think I want to," she grumbled. "Quinlan doesn't have any good stuff—just boring board games and an old dollhouse."

Her mom looked surprised. "Don't you usually have fun there?"

Kay shrugged. "I'd rather go to Niki's. She's new here, and she wears the coolest clothes. She has computer games and these stuffed animals that you can program!"

"Has Niki invited you over?" her mom asked.

"No," Kay admitted, "but maybe if I call her she will." She picked up the phone.

READ

James 2:1-4, 8-10. *Favoring* and *discriminating* have to do with treating some people better than others.

THINK

- Why do you think showing favoritism breaks God's law of loving your neighbor as yourself?
- What causes some kids to be treated better than others? Explain why this is unfair.
- Finish the story, showing how Kay might by influenced by the story in these verses. Then read the possible ending at the back of the book.

DO

- Think of how you choose friends. On a sheet of paper, put a big *L* by the following things that matter a *lot*. Put a little *l* by things that matter only a *little*: their toys and games; home; popularity; sports ability; appearance; personality; faith.
- Write the name of someone you or other kids play favorites against. Plan a way to include the person this week.

PRAY

Ask God to help you care about people whether they're rich or poor, popular or unpopular.

MEMORIZE

My dear brothers and sisters, how can you claim to have faith in our glorious Lord Jesus Christ if you favor some people over others? James 2:1

WHAT'S THE POINT?

Kay planned to give up an old friend for a new, richer one until she remembered the Bible's warning against favoritism. *SG*

AUGUST 29
Talent Tryout

Dad was taking Juliet to try out for the talent show at the fair. "Allelu, alleluia!" They sang a praise song happily in the car. But at the big tent, Juliet was dismayed by the number of other kids trying out. "Tough competition," her dad agreed.

When Juliet's turn came, she eyed the judge, a woman writing rapidly on a sheet of paper. Juliet's voice wavered nervously at first but got better.

She and two other kids waited for results. They could hear more tryouts as they sat. Then an assistant said, "None of you made the talent show. Here are the judge's comments." He handed out the score sheets and left.

Juliet was stunned. The others started griping about the "stupid judge," and Juliet was ready to join in.

READ
James 3:8-10. These verses mention our tongues and what we say. Cursing someone is bad-mouthing him or her.

THINK
- Why should praising and bad-mouthing not come from the same mouth?
- How could remembering that the person you're about to bad-mouth is made by God help you to be like him in some ways?
- Finish the story, showing how Juliet could take these verses to heart. Then read the possible ending at the back of the book.

DO
Ask a family member how often you say negative things about others (not often; sometimes; a lot?). Talk about how you could do better.

PRAY
Ask God to help you honor him with your words.

MEMORIZE
Blessing and cursing come pouring out of the same mouth. Surely, my brothers and sisters, this is not right! James 3:10

WHAT'S THE POINT?
Juliet remembered that God wants Christians to watch their words. *SG*

AUGUST 30
Canoe Racers

Lake water splashed in Rafael's face as he swept his paddle out and back. "Turn right, turn right!" he shouted.

"I'm trying!" his friend Eli called from his seat in the back of the canoe. "But you keep doing weird stuff up there!"

Rafael was pretty good at canoeing. But if this practice was any clue, they'd be a disaster at the camp canoe race tomorrow. "Loser," Rafael grumbled.

"You don't know everything," Eli said. "Just shut up and paddle!"

But after a few more minutes of weaving back and forth, Rafael had had enough. "We're switching, and I'm steering!"

"No way!" Eli yelled. Rafael stood up. The canoe rocked dangerously.

READ
1 Peter 3:8-9. God has great ideas about how to get along with each other.

THINK
- Draw a chart with two columns. Label them YES and NO. Under YES, write the things the verses say to do. Under NO, write the things the verses say not to do.
- How would the YES things help during an argument with a friend? How would the NO things make it worse?
- Finish the story, showing how Rafael could follow the teaching in these verses. Then read the possible ending at the back of the book.

DO
- With a partner, act out ways to say no to insults and say yes to working as a team.
- Tell your partner which one of these ideas you will try the next time you have a disagreement with a friend or family member.

PRAY
Ask God to help you avoid exchanging insults and work as a team with friends.

MEMORIZE
Don't repay evil for evil. Don't retaliate with insults when people insult you. Instead, pay them back with a blessing. That is what God has called you to do, and he will bless you for it.
1 Peter 3:9

WHAT'S THE POINT?
Rafael and Eli both felt irritated and kept putting each other down. The counselor helped them realize they could stop the insults and try working together. *SG*

AUGUST 31
Burned Out!

Matthias turned from side to side. *It's no use. I can't sleep,* he thought irritably. He got up from the sleeping bag and tiptoed out of his room, past the five-year-old twins sleeping on his double bed.

In the kitchen, he reached for the Choco Crunchers, but the box was empty! *First, Chico and Chaz move into my room, and I end up on the floor. Now they eat up my favorite cereal!* Out the window, the sky was still hazy with smoke from the recent wildfires. At first, Matthias had felt good about hosting a family whose home had burned down. Now, after three nights, it was getting old.

Little Chaz appeared in the doorway. "Mmm, Choco Crunchers! I love those!"

"Yeah, I noticed," Matthias snapped. "They're all gone."

Chaz looked at him uncertainly.

READ
1 Peter 4:9. Sharing what we have with guests is a way to pass along God's awesome love for us.

THINK
- Why might we invite someone over but not be cheerful about it?
- What kind of attitude do you think God wants us to have about our home, belongings, and food when we invite someone over? Why?
- Finish the story, showing how Matthias could change his attitude in order to follow the verse. Then read the possible ending at the back of the book.

DO
- How good are you at sharing your home and belongings with guests? Make a scale from 1 to 5 with 1 being "Not good" and 5 being "Really good." Circle the number that describes how well you share.
- Invite a friend over this week, if it's okay with your mom or dad. Use some of your own money or work to provide a treat to eat. (If you can't have someone over, bring a treat to someone at school or in the neighborhood.)

PRAY
Ask God for an attitude that welcomes guests.

MEMORIZE
Cheerfully share your home with those who need a meal or a place to stay. 1 Peter 4:9

WHAT'S THE POINT?
Matthias was annoyed at having to put up with guests. Then he remembered 1 Peter 4:9 and decided he could share. SG

SEPTEMBER 1
Night and Day

"I think your mom just wanted to get us off the computer; that's why she sent us outside to play," Emilio mumbled to Timothy as they stood in the backyard.

"Yeah," said Timothy, "let's go exploring in the woods out back. We can look for salamanders down by the creek."

"Or tadpoles," Emilio added as he raced toward the woods.

Both boys reached the creek and began peering under rocks and logs. "I found one!" yelled Timothy. "I'm really glad the sun is out today, or we wouldn't be able to find anything in the woods back here. The trees make it so shady."

As the afternoon wore on the boys lost track of time as they looked for salamanders and tadpoles and made boats out of twigs and raced them in the water. Before they knew it, the sun was slipping behind the horizon.

"It's starting to get dark," Emilio said. "We should go home."

"Not yet," said Timothy. "Let's see if we can find minnows in the water."

READ
Genesis 1:1-8. These verses introduce us to God's power and wisdom. God speaks and creates night and day. He also separates the sky and the earth.

THINK
- Why do you think God said light was good? Why is night also good?
- Discuss God's wisdom in having water in the sky as well as on the ground in rivers, lakes, and oceans.
- Finish the story, showing how Emilio and Timothy might begin to appreciate God's creation of light and darkness. Then read the possible ending at the back of the book.

DO
- How are our lives shaped by the existence of day and night?
- Start a "creation book." Under day one, draw a picture of night and day.

PRAY
Thank God for creating light, for the pattern of day and night, and for the cycle of water that gives life to the world.

MEMORIZE
God said, "Let there be light," and there was light. And God saw that the light was good. Then he separated the light from the darkness. Genesis 1:3-4

WHAT'S THE POINT?
While playing outdoors, the boys learned that God's creation of light and darkness was good. *SP*

SEPTEMBER 2
Potting Soil and Peat Pots

Heidi and Devlyn looked at the crowded workbench with excitement. Heidi's grandmother had set out what they needed to start seeds for her new indoor herb garden. Heidi handed a tray of peat pots to Devlyn and opened a big plastic bag of potting soil.

"Why do we use that instead of just digging up some dirt from your yard?" Devlyn asked Heidi's grandmother.

"You could, but seeds need lots of good organic material for the seedlings to grow strong and big."

"What else do seeds need?" Heidi asked.

Grandma said, "Once we plant the seeds, they need the right temperature and just enough water. Enough to sprout, but not so much that the new sprouts rot."

Devlyn studied a few seeds. "How do the seeds know what kind of plant to grow into?"

READ
Genesis 1:9-13. God continues to enjoy creating. He calls the dry land, the seas, and the plants "good."

THINK
- Why is it important that God created dry land?
- How are trees and plants that have seeds "good" creations from God?
- Imagine an ending for this story, showing what the girls can learn from the verses. Then read the possible ending at the back of the book.

DO
- Tell your family which nuts, vegetables, or fruits you think are especially good.
- With an adult, pick a recipe using favorite plants. Cook something for your family or friends to help them enjoy God's creation of plants.

PRAY
Praise God for beautiful—and yummy—fruits, nuts, and vegetables.

MEMORIZE
God said, "Let the land sprout with vegetation—every sort of seed-bearing plant, and trees that grow seed-bearing fruit. These seeds will then produce the kinds of plants and trees from which they came." And that is what happened. Genesis 1:11

WHAT'S THE POINT?
The girls were learning just how carefully God created seeds and plants. *SP*

SEPTEMBER 3
Tons of Stars

"Sawyer! Leo! Come out to the lake!" Sawyer's uncle, who was also Leo's dad, called the boys to join the rest of the family on the shore. The cousins were excited to be outside at night where no man-made lights could be seen.

"Look up," Leo's mother said as they reached the sand. The boys did, and their jaws dropped.

Sawyer finally managed a stunned, "Wow!" In the city they could see maybe a few dozen stars. Here, the stars looked like someone had spilled silver glitter on black velvet. The Milky Way glowed across the sky.

"God did a good job, didn't he?" Leo's mom said.

Leo nodded. "With these tons of stars that I'm not used to seeing, I can't find any constellations. Where's north?"

READ
Genesis 1:14-19. God made the sun, moon, and stars to be both beautiful and useful.

THINK
- What is your favorite thing to do when the sun is out? How about when the moon and stars are out?
- What would the world be like without the sun?
- Finish the story, showing how the verses could make a difference for the cousins. Then read the possible ending at the back of the book.

DO
- Tonight check the shape of the moon. Have you seen how the moon changes shapes? What does that mean?
- Learn something new about how God made the sun, moon, or stars.

PRAY
Tell God which is your favorite creation—sun, moon, or stars—and why it's your favorite.

MEMORIZE
God made two great lights—the larger one to govern the day, and the smaller one to govern the night. He also made the stars. Genesis 1:16

WHAT'S THE POINT?
Sawyer and Leo admired God's work and understood how God's sun, moon, and stars help us find direction and tell the time of year. This helped them appreciate God's amazing creation. *SP*

SEPTEMBER 4
The Fall Bird Count

Mercer and Jordi shoved their hands into their jacket pockets in the chilly morning air. The sun had just come up over the cliffs by the river. It was the start of the fall bird count. Their job was to count the different types of birds as they flew past for the fall migration.

Mercer and Jordi were matched up with an experienced bird-watcher, an older woman named Marilyn. "It's time," she said. "Let's do it!" And the counting began. Flocks and flocks of birds flew by as they counted. Hundreds of birds. Thousands!

Awesome! Jordi thought. *It feels like all the birds in the whole world are coming by.*

Marilyn must have been feeling the same sense of awe. "Isn't the universe amazing?" she said. "The universe somehow lets these birds know exactly when and where to migrate."

READ
Genesis 1:20-25. God created animals to fill the skies and seas and land.

THINK
- Why do you think God told the sea creatures and the birds to multiply?
- What are your favorite sea creatures, land animals, and birds?
- Finish the story, showing how the verses can help Mercer and Jordi know how the birds know when and where to migrate. Then read the possible ending at the back of the book.

DO
- Talk with your family: What do birds, sea creatures, and land animals need to multiply? How can people help them do so?
- Choose a project to do by yourself or with your family that will help God's animals. Ideas: take on an extra chore for your pet, walk a neighbor's dog, build or mount a birdhouse, set out a bird feeder, clean a stream.

PRAY
Thank God for wild animals and those we keep as pets or on farms.

MEMORIZE
God said, "Let the waters swarm with fish and other life. Let the skies be filled with birds of every kind." Genesis 1:20

WHAT'S THE POINT?
Mercer and Jordi remembered that God made the animals. They appreciated the creative job he did. *BA*

247

SEPTEMBER 5
Lumpy Self-Portraits

Paulo and Sebastian looked at the big lumps of clay sitting in front of each of them. Sebastian said, "I've never made a *person* before."

"Me either," said Paulo to his younger brother. "Just plaques and little pots." He started rolling the clay into a log. Their homeschool project for the morning was making "impressionist self-portraits."

"What do you think that means?" Sebastian asked, picking up his clay.

"Well, Mom said to make something that represents something about us, not necessarily a figure that *looks* like us."

READ
Genesis 1:26-31. God created people as the final act of Creation; human beings were made in God's own image.

THINK
- How can all people be created in God's image when individual people look so different from each other?
- What are some ways we're made in God's image?
- Make up an ending for the story, showing how the verses could help Paulo and Sebastian understand what it means to be made in God's image. Then read the possible ending at the back of the book.

DO
- Talk with your family: How should being made in God's image affect how you treat yourself? How should it affect how you treat others?
- Make a poster about yourself. Label some ways you are made in God's image.

PRAY
- Thank God for loving us so much that he wanted to make you and everyone else like him in some ways.

MEMORIZE
God created human beings in his own image. In the image of God he created them; male and female he created them. Genesis 1:27

WHAT'S THE POINT?
Being created "in God's image" doesn't mean people are patterned after what God looks like but after what God *is* like. Like him, we can create, love, reason, and understand. We can be generous and helpful. We can love nature and music and more. *SP*

SEPTEMBER 6
God Created Man and Woman

Meg looked angry. Her friend Ariana asked, "What's bugging you?"

"Kaden and his friends won't let us into his tree house. No girls allowed!"

"That's not fair." Ariana said.

"He said 'Girls are useless—that's why.' Then he pulled up the rope ladder so that we can't get in." Meg grumbled.

"Oh yeah? Well let's go back there and show them that girls are not useless. In fact, I've got an idea!" Ariana said.

READ

Genesis 2:18-23. This account emphasizes the connection of men and women to each other in God's plan.

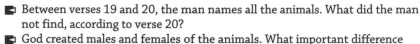

THINK

- Between verses 19 and 20, the man names all the animals. What did the man not find, according to verse 20?
- God created males and females of the animals. What important difference marked the creation of the woman in these verses?
- Finish the story, showing how Meg and Ariana might help Kaden and the other boys to appreciate them. Then read the possible ending at the back of the book.

DO

- What do you appreciate about the boys/men and girls/women in your family?
- Draw a diagram of how different family members help each other.

PRAY

Thank God for creating both men and women to be partners and help each other.

MEMORIZE

The LORD God said, "It is not good for the man to be alone. I will make a helper who is just right for him." Genesis 2:18

WHAT'S THE POINT?

Women and men were created by God to help each other. Both are equally useful and necessary. *SP*

SEPTEMBER 7
People Name Animals

Ron said, "My favorite part of the school year is coming up next week—the trip to the zoo!"

Jasper agreed. "I love going to the zoo. My family has a membership, and we go at least once a month."

"I like watching the big cats move," Ron said. "What do you like best?"

"Hard question!" said Jasper. "The otters are fun. But reptiles look amazing, and the poison dart frogs are so shiny and colorful!"

Ron asked, "How many animals can you name?"

READ
Genesis 2:19-20. This Bible account tells how Adam named all the animals.

THINK
- These verses say that God wanted "to see what he would call them." How does this show God enjoying his creation and Adam?
- How might naming the animals show Adam's creativity?
- Finish the story, showing Ron and Jasper's understanding of God's creativity in making the animals. Then read the possible ending at the back of the book.

DO
- How many animals can you name?
- Have fun with family members making up your own names for several animals.

PRAY
Thank God for giving us the gift of creativity and for all of God's creation. Ask God to help you appreciate and protect what he created.

MEMORIZE
The LORD God formed from the ground all the wild animals and all the birds of the sky. He brought them to the man to see what he would call them, and the man chose a name for each one. Genesis 2:19

WHAT'S THE POINT?
When you name something, you use the creativity that God gave you. When you enjoy God's creation, you celebrate his creativity. *SP*

SEPTEMBER 8
How Far Is the East from the West?

Joshua and four-year-old Joey raced around the yard. Joshua tackled him just as Mom looked out the window.

"Joshua! I've told you over and over—don't wrestle with Joey! He's too little. You might hurt him."

"Okay, Mom," Joshua said. Then Joey pushed him, and Joshua pushed back. Joey fell. His head hit the concrete step, and suddenly there was blood everywhere. Joshua felt guilt crash over him like a tidal wave. *Idiot!* he said to himself. *Why don't you think for a change!* "Mom, come quick!"

That night Dad found Joshua moping in his room. "I feel like a jerk," Joshua mumbled. "I disobeyed Mom, and Joey had to get stitches."

Dad pointed out the window to the left and right. "How far is the east from the west?"

Joshua shrugged. "As far as you can get, I guess."

READ

Psalm 103:11-14. God knows we are human. He knows that as humans, we sin—over and over. In these verses he uses his creation to show us the size of his love and forgiveness.

THINK

- What words would you use to describe the size of God's love and forgiveness?
- Which word picture in the verses means the most to you? Why?
- Finish the story, showing how the verses can help Joshua. Then read the possible ending at the back of the book.

DO

- Think about a sin that is weighing you down. Write some words to tell God how you feel about it.
- Ask God for forgiveness.

PRAY

Ask God to help you understand how far he removes your sins from you when you ask. Thank him for doing that so you can feel right with him, with others, and with yourself.

MEMORIZE

He has removed our sins as far from us as the east is from the west. Psalm 103:12

WHAT'S THE POINT?

God wants us to feel bad about what we've done but not bad about ourselves. He always loves us and is eager to forgive us. *BA*

SEPTEMBER 9
Tornado Warning

"Beep, beep, beep!" A notice started to scroll across the bottom of the TV screen as Gareth and his teenage sister, Christina, were watching a cartoon. Outside the rain slashed at the windows. "It's a tornado warning," Christina said. "Get your stuff, and let's go to the basement."

Gareth nervously grabbed a flashlight, the battery-powered radio, and a game, and they both went downstairs. "I wish Mom and Dad were here," Gareth said.

Christina turned on the radio. "We'll just sit tight and listen for notices on the radio." They both jumped as a tree branch hit a window.

"Let's pray," said Gareth.

READ
Genesis 8:15-22. God sent a flood long ago to destroy all life on the earth because human beings were so evil. God saved Noah, his family, and animals in a huge boat that Noah built. Find out what Noah did after he got out of the boat.

THINK
- Why do you think Noah's first action was to worship God?
- What are ways God helps people today?
- Finish the story, showing how the verses can make a difference for Gareth and Christina. Then read the possible ending at the back of the book.

DO
- We don't sacrifice animals or birds anymore, as Noah did. How do you worship and give thanks to God?
- Make up a song of praise to God for a time he has helped you. Use a familiar tune such as "Mary Had a Little Lamb" or create your own.

PRAY
Sing your song as a prayer to God.

MEMORIZE
As long as the earth remains, there will be planting and harvest, cold and heat, summer and winter, day and night. Genesis 8:22

WHAT'S THE POINT?
Like Noah did so long ago, Gareth, Christina, and the neighbors realized God had kept them safe. They wanted to worship him for his care. *BA*

SEPTEMBER 10
Making Rainbows

Verity walked around the house to where her friend Julia stood watering the flower garden with the nozzle of the hose set to a fine spray. "Hi!" Julia said.

"Don't squirt me!" Verity demanded.

"I won't. Look what happens when I point the nozzle the right way." Julia twisted the hose and nozzle until a beautiful rainbow danced on the surface of the spray.

"That's cool," Verity said. "Let me try." Julia showed her how to hold the hose, and soon Verity had a rainbow too.

"I suppose you can make rainbows with the hose anytime," Verity said. "You need to be lucky to see a rainbow after a storm."

Julia said, "It's more than luck."

READ
Genesis 9:8-17. After the Flood, God told Noah and his family about a covenant—a promise or contract—that God would make with all people and all living creatures. He would never again destroy the world with a flood.

THINK

- Why do you think God gave us a sign that we could see (rainbows) to stand for his promise?
- How do you know that we can trust God to keep his promises?
- Finish the story, showing how the verses can affect Verity and Julia. Then read the possible ending at the back of the book.

DO
- Set a piece of paper on a table. Put a glass of water at the far end of the paper. Shine a flashlight down through the water at an angle to see a rainbow on the paper. With your family, take turns naming your favorite promises God has made.
- Which promise do you think helps you the most? Plan to think of it often.

PRAY
Thank God for rainbows and the promise they stand for.

MEMORIZE
When I see the rainbow in the clouds, I will remember the eternal covenant between God and every living creature on earth. Genesis 9:16

WHAT'S THE POINT?
The girls found out that rainbows are not only beautiful but that they also stand for God's promise to them and to all of us. *SP*

SEPTEMBER 11
Deer and Dogs

Rich and Zachary slowly moved through the woods as quietly as they could. Suddenly a tree branch cracked loudly under Zachary's shoe. "Shh!" Rich whispered. "We don't want to scare them away." Both boys peered through the trees at a group of deer that were grazing. One of the does lifted her head and froze, looking straight at them.

"Uh-oh," Zachary whispered. "I think she saw us." At that moment a crow above them began cawing loudly. Startled, the deer turned, and leapt through the brush. "Oh no!" Zachary exclaimed. "Now we'll never catch up to them."

Rich nodded, "Yeah, I guess not. Come on, let's go back to my house."

READ
Genesis 9:2. This verse says that God caused the creatures of the earth to fear us and that we have power over them.

THINK
- What types of creatures does God mention in this verse? What does he say about them in regard to us?
- This verse says that God has placed animals in our power. What does this mean in terms of our responsibility toward them?
- Finish the story, showing how this verse can help Rich and Zachary better understand how animals and other creatures relate to us. Then read the possible ending at the back of the book.

DO
- What are some ways that you can show respect for God's creatures?
- Choose an activity to do this week that reminds you to care for God's animals.

PRAY
Ask God to increase your love and respect for all animals in his creation.

MEMORIZE
All the animals of the earth, all the birds of the sky, all the small animals that scurry along the ground, and all the fish in the sea will look on you with fear and terror. I have placed them in your power. Genesis 9:2

WHAT'S THE POINT?
God has given people permission to take charge of his creatures, but he holds us accountable for treating them with respect. *SP*

SEPTEMBER 12
God Holds Us in His Hands

Trevor entered the room quietly. "Hey, Terrence. Your mom told me about Biscuit."

Terrence blurted out, "She was only three years old. I didn't even know dogs could *get* sick."

Trevor shook his head in sympathy. "So what happened?"

"We thought she had a cold or something. Then she wouldn't get up. When we took her to the vet, it was too late. She died a few days later."

"She was a cute little dog," said Trevor. "That's really terrible."

READ
Job 12:4-10. In this passage Job says that often good people suffer while evil people don't, but ultimately the fate of every animal and human is in God's hands.

☁ THINK
- What was it that Job thought God's creation could teach us?
- Job lost his family and everything else, but not his faith in God. What does he say about God's power and authority?
- Finish the story, showing Terrence's understanding of God's authority over all life. Then read the possible ending at the back of the book.

DO
- How can looking to God's creation help you know God is in control when you're very sad?
- Discuss with family members aspects in nature that show God's power and planning.

PRAY
Ask God to comfort you when you're sad; thank God for having everything under his control.

MEMORIZE
The life of every living thing is in his hand, and the breath of every human being. Job 12:10

WHAT'S THE POINT?
Animals and people we love will sometimes have bad things happen to them. But we can learn from them to trust that God is in control of the events of our lives—when we are born, when we die, and everything in between. *SP*

SEPTEMBER 13
S'mores under the Stars

William raced over to his friend Khalil's house. "My dad set up the tent for us to camp out tonight. I can't wait! He says we can even have a bonfire!" he said.

Khalil smiled. "Great! My mom bought stuff for us to make s'mores."

Later that evening, as they stood around the bonfire roasting marshmallows with William's family, William glanced up at the sky.

"Wow! Look at all the stars," he said.

Khalil stared at the sky. "My science teacher told us that some of the stars we're looking at actually died out years ago and that all we're seeing is the light from them."

"I keep thinking that there are so many stars, plants, animals, and people that it's hard to believe that God even thinks about you or me at all," William said.

READ
Psalm 8. This psalm of David explores the greatness of God in light of God's creation, including us humans.

THINK
- What do verse 1 and verse 9 tell you about how the psalmist feels toward God and creation?
- According to the psalm, how do humans fit in to God's plan for his creation?
- Finish the story, showing what William and Khalil might learn to appreciate about God's creation and how God views humans. Then read the possible ending at the back of the book.

DO
- How can we show respect for God's creation, since God has given us "authority" over it?
- Choose one creation-loving action and set a time to do it. Some ideas might include planting a butterfly garden, helping clean up outside your church or in a local park, recycling, or conserving energy by turning off lights and household appliances.

PRAY
Thank God for certain plants, animals, or people that he created. Ask God to help you be responsible with the creation that he's entrusted to you.

MEMORIZE
O LORD, our Lord, your majestic name fills the earth! Your glory is higher than the heavens. Psalm 8:1

WHAT'S THE POINT?
Even though God created thousands of stars, plants, animals, and people, he loves each one of his people individually and created us to have authority over creation. *SP*

SEPTEMBER 14
Storm Chasers

Kaya and Leslie sat on the edge of the couch watching a storm chaser TV show. The chase vans barreled down a country road, trying to get as close as they could to a massive thunderstorm. "I would be so scared!" Kaya said as the people piled out of the vans in heavy rain to look at the thunderclouds and the lightning flashing across the sky.

Kaya's dad came through the family room. "You could do your own storm chasing just by sitting on the porch right now," he said.

Kaya and Leslie ran outside with Dad and sat down. The sun was setting in a sky filled with building thunderclouds. Kaya pointed to a particularly impressive cloud. "Look! A huge horse, rearing up on its hind legs."

"I don't look for cloud pictures much," Leslie said. "But I love the color and the brightness of sunsets. Look at the reds and golds!"

Dad said, "The Bible says the heavens are speaking. What is the sky saying to you right now?"

READ
Psalm 19:1-4. This psalm of David says the heavens—the sky and everything we see in it—tell us about God and show us what God has done.

THINK
- What does the psalmist think the "voice" of the heavens is saying? What do you think "voice" means here?
- What is your favorite thing the skies tell you about God?
- Make up an ending for the story, showing how the verses can affect the girls. Then read the possible ending at the back of the book.

DO
- Go look at the sky right now. What does it say to you about God?
- With your family, be like the sky and praise God now in a way you choose.

PRAY
Give thanks to God for the glories of the sky, which remind us of God's own glory.

MEMORIZE
The heavens proclaim the glory of God. The skies display his craftsmanship. Psalm 19:1

WHAT'S THE POINT?
Whether it's clouds or weather, sun or stars, the beauty and power of the sky remind us to praise God. *SP*

SEPTEMBER 15
Power and Love

"We just got back from the Maine coast," Domingo told his friend Ray.

"How is the ocean different from a big lake—other than being salty?" asked Ray.

"It's really different off northern Maine," said Domingo. "For one thing, the water stays pretty cold even in August. But the biggest difference is the tide."

Ray had forgotten about tides. "The water moves higher and lower on the beach?"

"Twice a day," said Domingo. "In the Bay of Fundy, the tide changes by twenty feet or more."

"That's almost as tall as our house! No way!"

READ
Psalm 33:6-9, 18. Fear of God is not panic or terror, but a form of awe and reverence for God's glory and power, which leads to obedience and trust.

THINK
- What aspects of Creation does the psalmist pick to demonstrate the power and glory of God?
- How does knowing about the power of God affect our hope in God's love and help?
- Finish the story, showing how Ray and Domingo understand that God's power over creation is matched by God's love for us. Then read the possible ending at the back of the book.

DO
- How does loving and respecting someone affect how much you are willing to do things for that person?
- Using a familiar tune, write a song praising God for his unfailing love and power.

PRAY
Praise God for being the Creator of the whole universe. Thank God for showing his faithful love to those who trust and follow him.

MEMORIZE
Let the whole world fear the LORD, and let everyone stand in awe of him. For when he spoke, the world began! It appeared at his command. Psalm 33:8-9

WHAT'S THE POINT?
God's power, demonstrated through nature, caused the psalmist to call on people to fear and revere God, but also to trust that God's love is unfailing. *SP*

SEPTEMBER 16
All Creatures Great and Small

Courtney called over her shoulder to Brynn, "Race you to the climbing tree!" They took off running across the field toward the woods.

When Courtney reached the climbing tree she stopped suddenly. "Look, Brynn! There's an injured bird in the grass!" Both girls knelt on the ground and inspected the small brown bird that was struggling with an injured wing.

"Do you think he'll ever be able to fly again?" Brynn asked.

"I don't know, but maybe we can help him." Courtney gently cradled the bird in her hands, and the girls walked back to her house.

READ
Psalm 50:10-11. In these verses, the psalmist speaks with God's voice, and declares that God cares about every animal and that all creation is his.

THINK
- How does God see creation in relation to himself?
- What does God's attitude toward living things tell us about how we should care for animals, birds, and other creatures?
- Finish the story, showing how Courtney and Brynn could apply what Psalm 50 says about God's interest in and love for different creatures to their injured bird. Then read the possible ending at the back of the book.

DO
- How does knowing that God created and owns all animals make you want to care for them?
- Take a trip to a zoo—in person or on the Internet. Notice the amazing creativity God used when he created so many kinds of animals. Pick a few favorites.
- If you have an animal in your care, make a checklist of feeding, grooming, and cleanup responsibilities. Ask God to make you a good steward of his creation.

PRAY
Praise God the Creator for the love and concern he shows his creatures.

MEMORIZE
All the animals of the forest are mine, and I own the cattle on a thousand hills. Psalm 50:10

WHAT'S THE POINT?
God knows his creation personally and cares about each creature. We can ask God for help and healing for animals, especially when they're in our care. *SP*

SEPTEMBER 17
Lights in the Sky

Clay and Terry couldn't contain their excitement. That night, they would be staying up late and driving out into the country to see a meteor shower. They'd been checking the weather all week, afraid that cloudy weather might cancel their plans.

Terry said, "Tell me again how we know we'll see shooting stars tonight?"

"Mom found out about it from an astronomy Web site," said Clay.

Terry asked, "But how can anyone predict a meteor shower?"

"I don't know," Clay admitted.

READ
Psalm 89:8-13. This psalm focuses on God as Creator, his power, and the praise and honor that he receives for his greatness.

THINK
- Who does the psalm say that the heavens and earth belong to?
- What does it tell us about God to know that even though he is all-powerful, people and creation praise him? Should we praise him too?
- Finish the story, showing how the predictability of meteor showers reminds the boys about God's power and love. Then read the possible ending at the back of the book.

DO
- Discuss with family members things in nature that demonstrate God's power.
- God is powerful and also deserves trust and love. Write a psalm of your own about God's power demonstrated in nature. Remember to praise him in your psalm.

PRAY
Thank God for being powerful, loving, and trustworthy. Ask for God's help to trust him more.

MEMORIZE
O LORD God of Heaven's Armies! Where is there anyone as mighty as you, O LORD? You are entirely faithful. Psalm 89:8

WHAT'S THE POINT?
Psalm 89 tells us that the wonders of earth and sky can remind us of God's faithfulness and love as well as God's might. *SP*

SEPTEMBER 18
God Rules

Katelyn and Ellie were walking home from the park when Katelyn pointed out the dark clouds. "It looks like it's going to rain any second. There might even be a storm!"

"I love watching lightning," said Ellie. "But only when I'm indoors."

As the first drops of rain started falling, Katelyn shouted, "Quick! Run! I think it's going to pour!" Just as the girls reached the house, rain fell in sheets from the sky.

Once the girls were indoors, a bolt of lightning struck the top of a tree in the neighbors' yard. "Wow! Did you see that? That was scary!" said Ellie.

"Yeah, that was almost as scary as the hurricane we escaped from on our last trip to Florida. The winds were so powerful they ripped the roofs off of houses!" said Katelyn.

"Really? I guess that would be worse than lightning," said Ellie. "Sometimes nature scares me!"

READ
Psalm 97:1-6. God's glory and power are demonstrated in nature in forces like storms, lightning, floods, and other natural events.

THINK

- What is awesome about the power of storms, lightning, fire, and volcanoes?
- To what characteristics of God do these natural wonders point?
- Finish the story, with Katelyn showing Ellie how to enjoy God's power and glory. Then read the possible ending at the back of the book.

DO
- What is the most powerful or amazing part of nature that you've ever seen?
- Draw a picture of it to remind you of God's power.

PRAY
Praise God for showing his glory and power through nature. Thank God for being in control.

MEMORIZE
The LORD is king! Let the earth rejoice! Let the farthest coastlands be glad. Psalm 97:1

WHAT'S THE POINT?
The power of creation in such natural events as volcanoes and storms reminds us that nothing created has more power than the Creator—God himself. Nature's power shows God's glory. *SP*

SEPTEMBER 19
Bibles and Bookmarks

Hakim ran downstairs for breakfast. "Mom! I can't wait for the Pioneer Clubs hike and picnic. Morgan said he could come, and my club leaders said that they would be talking about Jesus!" Hakim came to a halt in front of the kitchen window. "Oh no! It's pouring! What if they cancel it?"

"Honey, I'm sorry. I just got a call from the club coordinator, and the hike and picnic have been canceled," said Hakim's mom.

Hakim slumped into one of the kitchen chairs. "Just great!" he grumbled. "Now how is Morgan going to hear about Jesus?"

"Well, he's gone to Pioneer Clubs with you a few times, and you gave him a Bible with a bookmark about Jesus," his mom said.

"Yeah, so?" Hakim shot back. "How is reading about Jesus on a bookmark or in the Bible going to help him without someone there to explain everything?"

"God's there," Hakim's mom said, but Hakim just rolled his eyes.

READ
Isaiah 55:10-11. In this passage the rain and the snow watering the earth and causing plants to grow are compared to God's words in the Bible being able to make belief grow in the hearts of people.

THINK
- How are God's words in the Bible like the rain the verse mentions?
- What does it mean when the verse says that God's Word produces fruit?
- Finish the story, showing how Hakim comes to realize that God's Word can help people believe wherever it goes. Then read the possible ending at the back of the book.

DO
- Create a bookmark to give to a friend that explains how to follow Jesus.
- Role-play how you might tell others about Jesus.

PRAY
Thank God for the go-everywhere power of his Word, the Bible.

MEMORIZE
It is the same with my word. I send it out, and it always produces fruit. It will accomplish all I want it to, and it will prosper everywhere I send it. Isaiah 55:11

WHAT'S THE POINT?
Hakim realized that God's words in the Bible have the ability to change people's hearts and to accomplish God's will. *SP*

SEPTEMBER 20
God Provides for All Needs

Cami stared at Marianne's backyard and said, "I've never seen anything like this. Your grandfather planted all this?"

"He raised olives, grain, and goats with his father before coming to America." Marianne realized she took these gardens for granted, even though few of her friends had gardens.

"He doesn't live with you, though," said Cami.

"No," agreed Marianne. "But he has a condo without a yard; he just has a balcony. So he comes over here. My dad helps with the digging, and I'm learning how to mulch and weed. My grandfather even let me plan my own garden area this year."

"He thinks working this hard is *fun*?" Cami wondered.

READ
Psalm 104:14-23. Our God not only created everything, but he provides food, shelter, and everything else creation needs to exist and grow.

THINK
- Identify all the ways God takes care of plants and animals and people.
- How does the change from day to night provide for both people and wild animals?
- Finish the story, showing how Marianne could explain the way gardening helps her understand how God takes care of everything. Then read the possible ending at the back of the book.

DO
- How have you seen the way God provides for us in nature?
- Write a rap song praising God for all the ways nature can provide for our needs. Some examples include food, clothing (cotton, wool), medicines, etc.

PRAY
Thank God for creating a world that provides so much for us.

MEMORIZE
You cause grass to grow for the livestock and plants for people to use. You allow them to produce food from the earth. Psalm 104:14

WHAT'S THE POINT?
People might say they support themselves, but everything that lives, including the food we eat, lives because God created what plants and animals need to grow and multiply. *SP*

SEPTEMBER 21
The Deep Blue Sea

"Sailing to Nantucket Island last summer was freaky, Anthony," Kai said.

"How come?" Anthony asked.

"Most of the way, we were totally out of sight of land. My mom got nervous not being able to see anything besides sky and water. But Dad knew how to read the chart, plot a course, and steer by the compass, so there was no problem."

Anthony really wished he could have gone with Kai. "Did you see any whales?"

READ

Psalm 104:24-27. The psalmist writes about the greatness of God, which is demonstrated in the size of the ocean and all the sea creatures that live in it.

THINK

- The ocean is enormous and contains the largest animals on earth, yet what does verse 27 say about their relationship and greatness compared to God?
- What does verse 24 tell you about God?
- Finish the story, showing how the ocean has reminded Kai about God's wisdom and power. Then read the possible ending at the back of the book.

DO

- What's the biggest, strongest, or most amazing sea creature that you've seen? What impressed you about it?
- Make plans to visit the ocean, the zoo, or a local aquarium soon. Pick one fish or sea creature that interests you. Take a photo or draw a picture and put verse 24 or 25 underneath it as a caption.

PRAY

Join the psalmist in praising God and all that God has created.

MEMORIZE

O LORD, what a variety of things you have made! In wisdom you have made them all. The earth is full of your creatures. Psalm 104:24

WHAT'S THE POINT?

Kai and Anthony made the connection between God and his greatness by remembering the size and power of the ocean and the many sea creatures he created. *SP*

SEPTEMBER 22
Birds Sing and Mosquitoes Whine

Savannah looked up at the green tunnel of trees over the bike path she and Karen were walking on. "Do you come out here often?" Savannah asked her friend.

"This path goes out past my cousins' house," Karen said. "I can walk or bike there whenever I want as long as I tell my parents where I'm going and take someone with me. I'm glad you could come."

"It's pretty here," said Savannah. "And quiet, except for the birds who are singing their heads off."

READ
Psalm 148. This psalm tells us that all of nature praises God and people should do the same.

THINK
- ◗ The psalm tells us that all of nature praises God. What are all created things praising God for?
- ◗ What is it about sea creatures, mountains, plants, and wild animals that show praise to God?
- ◗ Imagine an ending for this story, showing how the girls see nature praising God on their walk. Then read the possible ending at the back of the book.

DO
- ◗ What can you think of in nature that might remind you to praise God?
- ◗ Gather some pictures of things in nature from magazines or the Internet. Glue them to paper or paper plates and hang them from sticks or a wire hanger with string to make a mobile. Write one thing about each pictured plant, animal, or sea creature that you can praise God for.

PRAY
Ask God to use the glory of nature to help you remember to praise him.

MEMORIZE
Let them all praise the name of the LORD. For his name is very great; his glory towers over the earth and heaven! Psalm 148:13

WHAT'S THE POINT?
The sights and sounds in the woods reminded the girls of how Psalm 148 tells us everything in creation leads to praising God because it all displays God's splendor. *SP*

SEPTEMBER 23
Soaring on Wings like Eagles

Sun Hee and Nicole leaned on the rail at the lookout point where Nicole's family had stopped to check out the view. "Wow! Look at those eagles. I've never seen them this close in the wild before," said Nicole.

But Sun Hee was feeling gloomy. She was glad that Nicole had invited her to come on her family's road trip out West, but she was envious. Without even noticing the eagles, she said, "Your family is the greatest, and your dad does fun things like teach you how to throw a softball and fix things. I hate it that my dad died when I was little. My mom never takes me on road trips."

"But your mom is great," said Nicole. "She bakes really yummy brownies and is always so friendly."

"Yeah, but sometimes I worry about what might happen in the future," said Sun Hee. "What if something happens to my mom like it did to my dad?"

READ
Isaiah 40:28-31. These verses talk about God as the Creator, who gives strength to those who are tired, worried, and feeling hopeless.

THINK
- Have there ever been times when you felt tired, worried, and hopeless?
- What do these verses say God offers to those who feel this way? What animal does God say people will be like when they trust in him? What does he renew in them?
- Finish the story, showing how Sun Hee can learn to trust in God. Then read the possible ending at the back of the book.

DO
- What worries you about the future or a situation you're facing?
- Role-play how God might help you trust him in that situation.

PRAY
Thank God that he is in control of all things. Ask for the ability to trust him even when you're worried or feeling sad. Ask him to strengthen you and give you peace.

MEMORIZE
Those who trust in the LORD will find new strength. They will soar high on wings like eagles. They will run and not grow weary. They will walk and not faint. Isaiah 40:31

WHAT'S THE POINT?
God wants us to trust him with all of our worries and troubles. He promises to be there and strengthen us so that we can "soar high on wings like eagles." *SP*

SEPTEMBER 24
Morning in the Mist

Samuel and Bradley watched wisps of early morning mist rise from the lake as the oars from the boat that Bradley's dad was rowing dipped gently into the water.

"I think this is a good spot, boys. Now remember to keep quiet or you'll scare the fish away," Bradley's dad said.

"The mist makes everything look kind of spooky, doesn't it, Samuel?" whispered Bradley.

"Yeah, but the sun is rising. I don't think it will be spooky for long."

"Mist evaporates pretty quickly, doesn't it, guys?" whispered Bradley's dad. "Did you know that mist is mentioned in the Bible?"

READ

Isaiah 44:22. Isaiah is speaking a message from God about his forgiveness of sins and how he redeems those who repent.

THINK

- In this verse, how do the images of clouds and mist help you understand your sins being forgiven?
- When the verse says that "I have paid the price to set you free," what do you think was the price that was paid? Who paid the price to set you free?
- Finish the story, showing how the boys might learn about God's forgiveness through the weather. Then read the possible ending at the back of the book.

DO

- What happens when you boil water? Where does the water go?
- Check out a book from the library on clouds. Learn how evaporation, mist, clouds, and rain work. Compare how this process relates to this verse, and remember the illustration of God forgiving your sins being like clouds that are swept away.

PRAY

Ask God to forgive any sins that you need to tell him about. Thank him for forgiving you.

MEMORIZE

I have swept away your sins like a cloud. I have scattered your offenses like the morning mist. Oh, return to me, for I have paid the price to set you free. Isaiah 44:22

WHAT'S THE POINT?

Samuel and Bradley are reminded of how God forgives and forgets our sins by watching how quickly the mist evaporates from the lake. *SP*

SEPTEMBER 25
Part of God's Plan

Lizzie and Meghan peered into the bathroom mirror. "Mom says I can cut my hair short, but I'm not sure how I want it cut," said Lizzie.

"I've heard it depends on how your face is shaped. I have a narrow face and you have a round one, so maybe you should ask the hairdresser," said Meghan.

Lizzie frowned and made a face. "I hate the way my face is shaped. Why did God make it that way? I wish I had a narrower face like yours," she sighed.

READ
Isaiah 45:9-12. God's message through Isaiah is that he planned every aspect of creation. We should appreciate, not criticize, what God has made.

THINK
- A potter uses clay to make pots. What does verse 9 say about how we (the clay) should respond to the potter (God) about how we were created?
- What reason is given in verse 12 for why we should trust how God made us?
- Finish the story, showing how Lizzie might accept God's plan for how she was made. Then read the possible ending at the back of the book.

DO
- Discuss with family members the things that make you special. Examples could be that you have brown hair, your eyes are blue, you're good at drawing, etc.
- Write a thank-you note to God telling him how much you appreciate what's special about you and thanking him for creating you the way he did.

PRAY
Ask God to help you appreciate what makes you special and not to be critical of yourself. Thank God for making you the way he did.

MEMORIZE
I am the one who made the earth and created people to live on it. With my hands I stretched out the heavens. All the stars are at my command. Isaiah 45:12

WHAT'S THE POINT?
Lizzie realized that God had created her according to his plan and she could appreciate and be thankful for how she looked. *SP*

SEPTEMBER 26
Sowing Seeds

As Casey and Karl sat down at their Sunday school table, they could hardly wait for their teacher to let them see the seeds the class had planted. The strange thing was how their teacher had told them to plant some of the seeds!

The class eagerly crowded around the trays. One had seeds lying on the bottom of the container with no soil, one had seeds planted on rocks, one was planted with a bunch of weeds, and the last was planted in rich dark soil.

"Okay, everyone, look at the trays. Can anyone tell me which container has the most sprouting plants?" said their Sunday school teacher.

READ
Matthew 13:1-9, 18-23. This is a parable, a story told to teach a lesson, about a farmer who plants seeds and how the seeds grow. The parable teaches what happens when different people hear God's truth about salvation through Jesus.

THINK
- Why is the place where you plant seeds important? What do you think the seeds stand for in the parable?
- Which type of soil do you think you are?
- Finish the story, showing what Casey and Karl learned from the parable. Then read the possible ending at the back of the book.

DO
- How could you use a plant to show someone God's love?
- Plant different seeds in a container indoors. Watch to see if all the seeds sprout plants. For those seeds that do not grow, remind yourself that the dirt stands for people who do not believe or follow God's truth and therefore can't grow spiritually.

PRAY
If you have not asked Jesus to be your Savior by asking him to forgive your sins and come into your life, consider if now is the right time to do this. If Jesus is already your Savior, thank him.

MEMORIZE
The seed that fell on good soil represents those who truly hear and understand God's word and produce a harvest of thirty, sixty, or even a hundred times as much as had been planted! Matthew 13:23

WHAT'S THE POINT?
Casey and Karl learned that those who believe in and follow Jesus are like the seeds that were scattered on the rich soil in the parable. *SP*

SEPTEMBER 27
Creation Points to Jesus

Hope turned on the television. She and her friend Tara found themselves watching a woman draping strands of brightly covered flowers over a golden statue and bowing and laying food in front of it. Hope quickly grabbed the remote and turned to the channel they wanted. "Tara, how long before the movie starts?" she asked.

"We've got about ten minutes," said Tara. "What were we just watching before you changed the channel?"

"I don't know. It looked like a woman worshiping a statue of a god," said Hope.

"Why do people worship gods that aren't real instead of Jesus?" Tara asked.

"Maybe because they don't know about Jesus or maybe because it's easier for them to worship a statue in front of them instead of Jesus, who is in heaven," said Hope.

READ
Acts 14:8-17. Barnabas and Paul were upset with the people of Lystra, who wanted to worship them as gods because they had healed a crippled man.

THINK
- Why do you think the people of Lystra found it easier to believe that Paul and Barnabas were gods than to believe in Jesus Christ, who Paul and Barnabas told them about?
- What aspects of creation in these verses do Paul and Barnabas point to as proof that God is real?
- Finish the story, showing how Hope and Tara can learn about proof of God's existence in creation. Then read the possible ending at the back of the book.

DO
- Talk with your family about how creation can help people believe in God.
- The last part of verse 17 talks about how God gives us "food and joyful hearts." Do something that makes you joyful and thank God for it.

PRAY
Praise God for leaving proof in nature that he's real.

MEMORIZE
He never left them without evidence of himself and his goodness. For instance, he sends you rain and good crops and gives you food and joyful hearts. Acts 14:17

WHAT'S THE POINT?
People too easily begin to give the worship that belongs to God to an image or person that they follow. But only Jesus is the source of life and joy. *SP*

SEPTEMBER 28
The Invisible Guy

Grayson didn't look up as his friend Vic walked into his room. "Good book?" Vic asked.

"The main character is invisible. He's trying to sneak in someplace he shouldn't be," Grayson said. "It's not as easy as he thought."

Vic sat on the bed. "If no one can see him, sneaking in somewhere should be easy."

"Maybe," Grayson agreed. "But he's nearly been caught a couple of times already." He put the book down and picked up a flying disc. "Wanna go play some disc golf?"

"Wait," Vic said. "How do they even know to look for the guy if he's invisible?"

READ
Romans 1:20. The apostle Paul wanted the Christians in Rome to know God and worship him.

THINK
- According to this verse, how can we know God exists and what he's like?
- What is there about creation that would prove these things?
- Make up an ending for the story, showing how the verse could make a difference for the boys. Then read the possible ending at the back of the book.

DO
- With your family, make up a skit where you use nature to show someone that there's a God.
- Carry a leaf or pebble in your pocket. Every time you feel it, tell God, "I'm glad you're real!"

PRAY
Tell God three reasons you're glad he's real.

MEMORIZE
Ever since the world was created, people have seen the earth and sky. Through everything God made, they can clearly see his invisible qualities—his eternal power and divine nature. So they have no excuse for not knowing God. Romans 1:20

WHAT'S THE POINT?
The universe God created shows God's power and all sorts of qualities about God. We can know he's there because of his detailed creation. *SP*

SEPTEMBER 29
Earning Extra Credit

Thanne and Cara were busy raking leaves for their neighbor, Mr. Atkins, who had just had knee surgery. "My mom was really surprised when I suggested we do this for Mr. Atkins. 'You're earning extra credit in heaven,' she said." Thanne laughed.

Cara paused and leaned on her rake. "You don't really think you can earn extra credit in heaven, do you?"

"Well, it can't hurt," said Thanne. "I mean, I'm a good person, so I'm sure I'm going to heaven, but why not rack up a few extra points?"

Cara frowned. *The Bible doesn't say if you're good, you'll go to heaven! What should I tell Thanne?*

READ
Ephesians 2:8-10. These verses tell us that we're saved because of God's grace given to all who believe in Jesus, not because of good things we do.

THINK
- Why do these verses say we can't take credit for our salvation?
- What do you think verse 10 means when it says you are God's masterpiece? How do you feel knowing that long ago God planned good things for you to do?
- Finish the story, showing how Cara could tell Thanne why doing good things doesn't earn her a place in heaven, only God's grace does. Then read the possible ending at the back of the book.

DO
- What good things can you do for God's glory (*not* to earn salvation) this week?
- Make a list of kind and helpful things you can do for others this week. Pick one or two items to do this week.

PRAY
Thank God for his gift of salvation through Jesus. Ask him to reveal to you the good works he has planned for and created you to do.

MEMORIZE
We are God's masterpiece. He has created us anew in Christ Jesus, so we can do the good things he planned for us long ago. Ephesians 2:10

WHAT'S THE POINT?
Doing good things does not save us; God's grace saves us when we follow Jesus. God created us for good, so we respond to salvation by doing good. *SP*

SEPTEMBER 30
God Controls Wind and Water

A strong gust of wind made Alexander and Jerome glance up from the bicycle they were working on. Alexander said, "Wow! That's a dark, dangerous-looking bunch of clouds out to the west."

"The forecast this morning did say there might be a tornado watch later," Jerome said as he thought about biking home. "Do you think your mom could give me a ride?"

"Or maybe you can stay for supper. The tornado watch is supposed to be over by then." Alexander grinned. "That way we'd get lots more done."

"Wouldn't it be wild if those clouds suddenly poured snow instead of rain? Or if water flooded everything, like it did with Noah?" imagined Jerome out loud.

READ
Psalm 104:1-9. This passage reminds us of Genesis 9, where God made a covenant promise to Noah that another flood would never destroy earth.

THINK
- What do the first six verses of Psalm 104 tell about how God controls the weather?
- How does God's control over nature bring order and peace?
- Finish the story, showing what the boys understand about God's power over the weather. Then read the possible ending at the back of the book.

DO
- What kinds of weather do you like best?
- Check weather reports in the newspaper, on TV, or on a weather Web site. Keep track and see how many passages in the Bible mention the weather pattern you've found (rain, mist, storms, floods, etc.).

PRAY
Thank God for being in control of wind and water and making the weather predictable. Ask God to help you trust him during the "stormy" times in your life.

MEMORIZE
Let all that I am praise the LORD. O LORD my God, how great you are! You are robed with honor and majesty. Psalm 104:1

WHAT'S THE POINT?
We can predict the weather and count on weather patterns because God controls the weather. *SP*

OCTOBER I
Up a Climbing Wall

Alexis tightened her helmet and stood with the other campers at the climbing wall. It was forty feet tall, but to Alexis it looked like a skyscraper.

"There's nothing to fear if you follow the directions," said the instructor. "This belay system will catch you if you let go of the wall or slip. Now let's put on the harness."

Alexis's heart pounded as she followed the steps. *Put your feet through the big loops. Pull the harness up. Make sure nothing is twisted. Tighten the buckles.*

The instructor told the boy in front of her, "Your harness is twisted. Go back and fix it."

Alexis was next. The instructor clipped her harness to a long rope. "If you get tired or slip, just let go." He smiled. "We'll get you down safely!" He pointed to a counselor holding the other end of the rope.

Alexis started to climb. Soon her arms and fingers ached. She looked down. The ground was a long way away!

READ
Joshua 1:1-9. God instructed Joshua to obey and be brave.

THINK
- How might Joshua have felt about the big job of taking over a new land?
- How would obeying God's law help Joshua be brave?
- Imagine an ending for this story, showing how Alexis could learn from the verses. Then read the possible ending at the back of the book.

DO
- Choose something you're nervous about doing. Choose one of God's laws that would help you if you obeyed it: be truthful; trust God; pray instead of worrying; love others; remember what God has done in the past; or something else.
- Write out Joshua 1:7 in your own words, putting your name at the beginning. Read it aloud.

PRAY
Ask God to help you obey and be brave.

MEMORIZE
Study this Book of Instruction continually. Meditate on it day and night so you will be sure to obey everything written in it. Only then will you prosper and succeed in all you do. Joshua 1:8

WHAT'S THE POINT?
Alexis followed the rules and was braver at the climbing wall. She learned that obeying rules can help us be brave. *SG*

OCTOBER 2
The Woman in 3F

Helena slung the basket over her arm and marched cheerfully into the hallway.

"Smile, offer a muffin and a flyer, and ask how they are," her mom reminded her, heading down another hall. "Some of these folks would like a ride to church. Others are just lonely."

This outreach to the retirement center is fun, Helena thought. Most people seemed happy to see her. A few even signed up for rides.

Not apartment 3F. They'd knocked there four Saturdays in a row. No answer. They had left flyers and treats anyway. Helena's mother had asked a neighbor if the person who lived in 3F was sick. The man had frowned: "No. She's just grumpy."

Helena's march slowed as she approached 3F. *Why should I even knock? I could eat the muffin myself.*

READ
Joshua 6:1-5, 15-16, 20 and 2 Thessalonians 3:13. Joshua kept obeying God, marching around Jericho for seven days.

THINK
- If you were Joshua, would it be hard to keep following God's unusual plan, day after day? Explain.
- What do you think would have happened if Joshua had gotten tired of obeying and only marched around Jericho five days?
- Finish the story, showing how Helena could learn from today's verses. Then read the possible ending at the back of the book.

DO
- With a partner, pretend to be Israelites: One of you wants to keep marching around Jericho, and the other wants to quit. What will you say to each other?
- Think of something good you have trouble doing. Circle seven days on your calendar. Ask God to help you obey all week. Put a check mark for each day you obey.

PRAY
Ask God to help you keep obeying even when you want to quit.

MEMORIZE
Never get tired of doing good. 2 Thessalonians 3:13

WHAT'S THE POINT?
Helena wanted to quit reaching out to the grumpy resident. After she remembered Joshua, she decided to keep obeying God. *SG*

OCTOBER 3
Cleaning Up after Rusty

"Seth," his mom called out to the yard, "have you cleaned up after Rusty yet?"

Seth patted their big rust-colored dog and groaned. He had been looking forward to the big family cookout tonight. He loved eating burgers and playing with his cousins. He did *not* like the chore of cleaning up after Rusty in the backyard.

"Why can't Shannon do it, Mom?" he complained.

"Your sister is helping me in the kitchen," she replied.

Seth squinted at the grass. Hadn't he done this chore not long ago? There might not be many messes out there. Maybe no one would notice if he skipped cleaning up.

His dad appeared, carrying some long poles. "Is the yard ready? I thought I'd set up our new volleyball net for everyone."

Seth swallowed and thought about what to say.

READ
2 Kings 5:1-15 and Deuteronomy 6:18. To be healed, Naaman had to obey God's prophet Elisha and dip himself in a river.

THINK
▶ What clues show you that Naaman is an important person?

▶ Why do you think Naaman didn't want to obey Elisha?

▶ Make up an ending for the story, showing how the verses could make a difference for Seth. Then read the possible ending at the back of the book.

DO
▶ Talk with your family about tasks you find unpleasant or boring. What would happen if they didn't get done?

▶ Write a note to God saying what you will do the next time you are asked to do one of those tasks.

PRAY
Ask God to help you do what's right even when it's not fun.

MEMORIZE
Do what is right and good in the LORD's sight, so all will go well with you.
Deuteronomy 6:18

WHAT'S THE POINT?
Seth disliked cleaning the yard, but he knew the Bible teaches us to obey even when it's not fun. *SG*

OCTOBER 4
Mystery Present

"We're done with the birthday cake. Now it's time for presents!" Eliana's mom announced.

Eliana raced to the pile of gifts with her cousins close behind her. One package was very large. Eliana opened each present: a shirt, a new game, socks, a stuffed cat, a book, fuzzy slippers. Soon the only package left was the large mystery gift.

Eliana read the tag: "From Uncle Pedro!" Her uncle had a big smile on his face. When she tore the paper open, she gasped. Inside was a huge wooden dollhouse, painted pale yellow, with two floors, a roof and chimney, and lots of rooms.

"He made it himself," Eliana heard someone say. Her cousins crowded in, admiring the stairway, fireplace, and windows. She thought her favorite part was the porch with its fancy railing. "Let's take it to my room and play with it now," she said to her cousins.

As they picked it up, she noticed her uncle. He had a funny look on his face.

READ
1 Chronicles 16:34. King David's song tells people to thank God.

THINK
- What are some ways God shows his goodness and love to us?
- This verse is a command. Why might God want us to thank him?
- Finish the story, showing how Eliana might get an idea from the verse. Then read the possible ending at the back of the book.

DO
- Draw two columns with the headings "ask" and "thank." Write numbers to show about how many times you have *asked* God for things and *thanked* God for things this week. Which do you do more? Why?
- Plan to thank God for something every day this week.

PRAY
Ask God to give you a thankful heart.

MEMORIZE
Give thanks to the LORD, for he is good! His faithful love endures forever.
1 Chronicles 16:34

WHAT'S THE POINT?
Eliana remembered that thankfulness is important. People appreciate being thanked when they've done something good for us, and so does God. *SG*

OCTOBER 5
Left Out

It was a beautiful day, but no one else seemed to be outside. Alvaro decided to get his bike out and ride. Down the block he saw a bunch of kids playing touch football in Jon's backyard. He stopped his bike and watched. A couple of guys noticed him, but no one said anything.

Furious, Alvaro rode home. *Jon always does this! He plans fun stuff and leaves me out!* He came in the house and slammed the door.

His mom looked up. "What's wrong?"

"I don't want to talk about it!" Alvaro yelled as he stomped up the stairs.

READ
Psalm 62:4-8. King David writes in these verses about leaning on God.

THINK
- Do you think King David wrote this during a time of happiness or trouble? Explain.
- In your own words, explain what "pouring out your heart to God" means.
- Finish the story, showing how Alvaro could find comfort and encouragement by following the teaching of this psalm. Then read the possible ending at the back of the book.

DO
- Pour water out of a pitcher into a sink. Picture God being like the sink as he listens and "catches" the feelings you pour out to him.
- Pouring out our angry or sad thoughts and feelings to God can be a way to keep from acting on them in a bad way. Talk to God now about thoughts and feelings you have about a problem in your life. He loves you, so he will listen.

PRAY
Thank God that he wants to hear about your fears and problems and that he can help.

MEMORIZE
O my people, trust in him at all times. Pour out your heart to him, for God is our refuge. Psalm 62:8

WHAT'S THE POINT?
Alvaro knew that God wants to hear about all of our feelings, whether we're sad, glad, or mad. He even tells us to pour them out to him. *SG*

OCTOBER 6
Slow Motion

"Cassie, this is the second time I've asked you to put away the dishes!" her mom called down the hall.

"Okay, Mom!" Cassie bent over the new jigsaw puzzle on her desk. The picture on the box showed a herd of galloping horses. When the puzzle was done, her dad would glue it onto some cardboard and hang it on her wall. Cassie had put the edge pieces together already. Now she was working on a white horse.

"Cassie?" her mom called again.

"Just a minute, Mom," Cassie said. Her eyes scanned the desk, looking for pieces with white. *Here's one. There's another one.* She was concentrating so hard she barely heard the doorbell.

A moment later, her mom stood in the doorway. "That was Crystal, wanting to play. I told her you're not allowed out right now."

"Why not?" Cassie pouted. "I didn't do anything wrong!"

READ
Psalm 119:59-60. The psalmist's past experiences have made him eager to obey what he finds in God's Word.

THINK
- Why might someone *delay* obeying instead of *hurrying* to obey?
- Finish the story, showing how Cassie could take today's verses to heart. Then read the possible ending at the back of the book.

DO
- With your family, create a T-shirt design on the theme of "Obey, don't delay!"
- Make a deal with your mom or dad that you will obey quickly all day tomorrow. Seal the deal with a handshake.

PRAY
Ask God to help you be eager to obey him.

MEMORIZE
I will hurry, without delay, to obey your commands. Psalm 119:60

WHAT'S THE POINT?
Whether it's God or a parent giving the command, obeying too slowly is like disobeying. *SG*

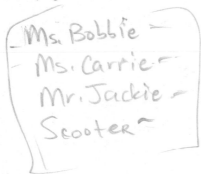
Ms. Bobbie —
Ms. Carrie —
Mr. Jackie —
Scooter —

OCTOBER 7
Football or Soccer?

The football flew end over end across the park, and Gideon backed up to catch it. "Nice punt, Scottie!" He let the football drop and kicked it back, but it didn't travel far. His friend caught it on the first bounce.

"Let me show you how to do it," Scott offered, walking over.

"You're a good punter," Gideon said. "I should have known it after seeing those long passes you do in soccer!"

"Yeah." Scott made a face. "I'd like to sign up for junior football. But then I'd have to give up soccer. I don't know what to do!"

"That's a tough choice," Gideon agreed.

"My aunt said I should *pray* about it," Scott continued. "Isn't that weird? I go to church on Sundays, but what does that have to do with sports?"

READ
Proverbs 3:5-6. God wants us to turn to him in all areas of our lives. He wants us to ask what he wants us to do.

THINK
- The verses describe God giving us directions or a "path" to take. What do you think that means?
- Why is depending on God better than depending on ourselves?
- Finish the story, showing how Gideon might help his friend learn the truth in these verses. Then read the possible ending at the back of the book.

DO
- List your responsibilities and activities. Do you talk with God about decisions you need to make about them? Why or why not?
- Walk on a path (or walk through your home pretending you're on a path). As you walk, talk to God about one decision you need to make. Tell him you trust him to guide you.

PRAY
Thank God that he knows about everything and promises to guide you.

MEMORIZE
Trust in the LORD with all your heart; do not depend on your own understanding. Seek his will in all you do, and he will show you which path to take. Proverbs 3:5-6

WHAT'S THE POINT?
Gideon and Scott learned that God wants to give us wise guidance about everything in our lives. *SG*

· Caleb Scholar Bowl Comp. 23ʳᵈ

Ms Bobbie" search for piano.

OCTOBER 8
Chicken Chores

From the school bus window, D.J. could see his father out in the cornfield driving the combine. The huge machine rumbled steadily down the rows, slicing down the stalks and pulling them inside. Next to the combine, D.J.'s brother steered a truck, catching the stream of shelled corn as the harvester spit it out.

D.J. frowned. His father and brother would be working late. That meant more chores for him.

In the kitchen, his little sister, Hailey, was sitting at the table, eating cookies. His mom turned to him. "D.J., since your brother's helping Dad, I need you to—"

"Don't say it! I already know!" D.J. popped a cookie into his mouth, picked up his boots, and headed for the chicken coop. The chickens were out in their yard, pecking at the grass. *Stupid, smelly birds.* D.J. uncoiled the hose and pulled it over to the henhouse.

"Boo!" Suddenly Hailey jumped out at him, grinning. She had smeared lipstick on her nose and poked straw into her hair and sleeves. "Hey, D.J., I'm a scarecrow!"

READ
Proverbs 15:30 tells about two things that can create a cheerful attitude.

THINK
- How does a cheerful look affect other people?
- Remember a time when someone cheered you up. What did he or she do or say?
- Imagine an ending for this story, showing how the verse could make a difference for D.J. Then read the possible ending at the back of the book.

DO
- Make a thank-you card for someone whose cheerful attitude has helped you.
- Try hard to smile at others this week. Notice if they smile back at you.

PRAY
Ask God for a cheerful heart. Thank him for those who cheer you up.

MEMORIZE
A cheerful look brings joy to the heart; good news makes for good health. Proverbs 15:30

WHAT'S THE POINT?
D.J. felt grumpy about doing extra chores. His sister's attitude helped him feel better. *SG*

OCTOBER 9
A Mountain of Leaves

"Time for a break!" Danielle said to herself, leaning her rake against a tree. Where she had already worked, the green grass showed, but the rest of the yard was blanketed with yellow and brown leaves. Down the block, a boy was also outside with a rake. Instead of working, he was throwing leaves in the air.

Danielle's mom peeked out the front door. "How's it going?"

"Okay, I guess," Danielle answered. "But it would be more fun to play in the leaves!"

"You've been working hard," her mom observed. "If you get all the leaves raked into one pile, you can jump in them for a while with a friend."

"Okay, great!" Danielle went back to raking, determined to get done quickly. The leaf pile grew bigger and bigger. *It'll be a mountain!*

Her mother leaned out the front door again. "Danielle, you have a phone call," she said in a surprised voice.

READ
Proverbs 20:11 says that a person's actions show something about the person's character.

THINK
- According to this verse, how can you really know what someone is like?
- If someone watched your actions, what might he or she learn about you?
- Make up an ending for the story, showing how Danielle could learn from the verse. Then read the possible ending at the back of the book.

DO
- With your family, list people who see your actions (for example, neighbors; store clerks; referees). Create a skit about what a kid's actions could tell one of these people about the kid.
- Make a plan to honor God with your actions around one of these people this week.

PRAY
Ask God to help you honor him by acting in ways that please him.

MEMORIZE
Even children are known by the way they act, whether their conduct is pure, and whether it is right. Proverbs 20:11

WHAT'S THE POINT?
Danielle kept on raking, even though she wanted to play. A neighbor watched her at work and asked to hire her. Danielle learned that actions tell others a lot. *SG*

OCTOBER 10
Far from Home

Levi dragged his big bag of hockey gear down the motel hallway.

"Levi, Nicholas, and Bryan—you're in this room with Bryan's dad!" the coach barked. Their team had traveled here for a tournament. "You guys are excited," the coach continued, "so you can have fun for a while before we turn out the lights."

Levi squeezed his bag through the doorway. He didn't know if he'd sleep. It was his first time in a motel without his family.

Nicholas and Bryan turned on the TV and found the video games. "Let's play Blood Weapons!" Bryan said. More boys came in.

Levi felt uneasy. He wasn't allowed to play those violent games at home. Bryan's dad was talking on his cell phone and didn't seem to care.

READ
Daniel 1:5-6, 8, 12-19. The king of Babylon had fought against Jerusalem and won. He captured some young men to make into servants. The king's food may have been offered to idols. Daniel and his friends faced tough choices.

THINK
- Daniel and his friends were far from home, in a country where people didn't believe in God. Why was their belief in God in danger?
- Why might the king's food be hard for Daniel to resist?
- Finish the story, showing how Levi could find wisdom in the example of the boys in today's Bible story. Then read the possible ending at the back of the book.

DO
- With your family, discuss places or situations where it's hard to obey God. Think of ideas to help you follow God.
- Make a poster. Draw or cut out pictures of places or situations from your list. Write "God is with me everywhere."

PRAY
Ask God to help you obey him even when you're away from home.

MEMORIZE
I thank and praise you, God of my ancestors, for you have given me wisdom and strength. Daniel 2:23

WHAT'S THE POINT?
Levi was away from home and tempted to do wrong. Remembering Daniel gave him courage. *SG*

OCTOBER 11
Gymnastics Practice

Sierra walked slowly to the middle of the balance beam. Stretching her arms out to the side, she lifted her front leg as high and straight as she could. She wobbled a bit, but she didn't fall.

"Good job!" the instructor said. "Remember to point your toe!"

Across the gym, a whistle blew. Sierra hopped down to join the other girls on the mat. "You all should have talked with your parents about extra practices before our first meet," the head coach was saying. "You could come on Wednesday night or Thursday night or both." She got out her clipboard. "Who can come on Wednesday?"

Gabrielle looked over at Sierra with a sneer. "*Sierra* can't come on Wednesdays," she whispered to the girls around them. "She always has to go to *church*. She's a churchy weirdo!"

Sierra felt her face turning red.

READ
Daniel 3:8-28. These three young men were willing to face death rather than worship a fake god.

THINK
- How might the three young men have felt when they were brought to the king?
- Why do you think the young men were willing to stand up for God whether he saved them or not?
- Finish the story, showing how Sierra could find encouragement in these verses. Then read the possible ending at the back of the book.

DO
- With a partner, act out someone being mean or teasing someone else for being a Christian. How could the Christian respond?
- Act out how you might respond if someone teased you for your faith.

PRAY
Ask God to give you courage when others mock your faith.

MEMORIZE
The God whom we serve is able to save us. Daniel 3:17

WHAT'S THE POINT?
When Gabrielle teased her about church, Sierra was tempted to deny her faith. The courage of the young men in the furnace helped her have courage too. *SG*

OCTOBER 12
Crushed

Gretchen let the backpack slide off her shoulders onto the apartment floor. She knew it held a watercolor painting that the art teacher had marked with a star. But it also held another poor test score in reading. She went to her room without even saying hello to her mom and lay down on the bed.

What's wrong with me? It takes me so long to read stuff, and then I can't even remember it! Why can't everything be as fun and easy as art? Gretchen's thoughts felt like heavy rocks piled on her, crushing her down.

Her mom came in with the backpack. "Honey, your watercolor is beautiful! And the teacher loved it."

"What about the reading test?" Gretchen sniffled.

Her mom sighed. "That's disappointing, I know. But we can keep working on it."

"No, we can't!" Gretchen burst out. "Nobody can help me!"

READ
Matthew 11:28-29. Jesus offers rest to those who are tired and weighed down.

THINK
- Jesus is not talking about physical loads. What might feel like a "heavy load" in your mind or soul?
- A yoke holds cattle together as they work. What does Jesus promise to those who "take his yoke" (obey him)?
- Finish the story, showing how Gretchen could find hope in these verses. Then read the possible ending at the back of the book.

DO
- Write a few words to stand for some problems that "weigh you down." Do you pray about them? Why or why not?
- Carry some heavy books around and then put them down. How does that feel? Turn over some of your problems to Jesus now.

PRAY
Thank God that he wants to help with your burdens.

MEMORIZE
Jesus said, "Come to me, all of you who are weary and carry heavy burdens, and I will give you rest. Take my yoke upon you. Let me teach you, because I am humble and gentle at heart, and you will find rest for your souls." Matthew 11:28-29

WHAT'S THE POINT?
When Gretchen felt discouraged about reading, her mom reminded her that Jesus wants us to give him our burdens. *SG*

OCTOBER 13
Tumble on the Trail

Ned and Colleen, the Pioneer Clubs leaders, led the kids up the rocky trail. "Bird watching is great in the fall, because so many birds are migrating," Colleen explained.

I'd rather explore on my own, Ahmed thought unhappily, trudging along at the back of the group. When the others rounded a bend, Ahmed stepped back. *They probably won't even notice I left! I thought I heard water back there. Maybe there's a stream.*

Ahmed followed the trail for a while and then left it to head for the sound. Suddenly his foot slipped on some loose rocks, and he tumbled down a steep slope. When he tried to stand, stabbing pain shot through his knee.

READ
Matthew 18:12-14. Jesus compared God to a shepherd with lost sheep.

THINK
- What could happen to the one lost sheep? Why does the shepherd bother to look for it when he has ninety-nine others?
- According to Jesus, how is God like this shepherd?
- Finish the story, showing how Ahmed could take heart from the truth of these verses. Then read the possible ending at the back of the book.

DO
- Based on the Bible story, how much would you say God loves you? With your family, come up with some words or actions to show how much he loves you.
- Count out 100 pennies, pebbles, or other objects. Pick up one from the pile. Remember that God has many children, yet he still cares about you personally. Carry the object in your pocket as a reminder.

PRAY
Thank God for creating millions of people, yet still loving you.

MEMORIZE
It is not my heavenly Father's will that even one of these little ones should perish.
Matthew 18:14

WHAT'S THE POINT?
Every single person is important to God, who is like a good shepherd, loving and looking for his lost sheep. *SG*

OCTOBER 14
A Bucket of Seashells

Jasmine sifted through gobs of seashells in the big bucket. First she held up a white fan-shaped shell, speckled with purple. "This is a scallop," she explained. "And this dark gray one is called a turkey wing."

Jasmine had loved collecting seashells on her vacation. Now she got to show them in Sunday school! "Thank you, Jasmine," said Mrs. Durant as Jasmine sat down.

"Could I have a shell, Jasmine?" Magda whispered. "I've never been to the ocean!" Jasmine scowled. "No! This is my *collection*."

Mrs. Durant continued. "We've been talking about creation. God made a beautiful world, but then sin ruined it. Can anyone explain what sin is?"

Jasmine raised her hand. "Sin is stuff like lying, stealing, and killing. I don't think I've sinned, though."

READ
Mark 10:17-25. A rich man asked Jesus about having life forever.

THINK

- The man wondered if he could get to live forever by keeping the law. How did Jesus answer?
- Jesus saw what the man really wanted. What did the man love most?
- Imagine an ending for this story, showing how Jasmine could learn from this story about Jesus and a rich man. Then read the possible ending at the back of the book.

DO
- Gather some of your favorite toys or sketch some of your favorite fun activities. Do you ever act mean, crabby, or selfish because of them?
- Draw a cross on another sheet of paper. If you will remind yourself to put God and others before your favorite toys or activities, put the cross picture on top of the toys you gathered.

PRAY
Ask God to show you if you are putting things ahead of him and others.

MEMORIZE
It is easier for a camel to go through the eye of a needle than for a rich person to enter the Kingdom of God! Mark 10:25

WHAT'S THE POINT?
Jasmine didn't recognize that her selfishness about her seashell was sinful. Her teacher pointed out that Jesus showed sin as an attitude. *SG*

OCTOBER 15
Picnic Problem

Sara picked up the big platter of brownies and started carefully across the grass to the park shelter.

"Don't eat any yet!" her mom called after her. Tables of food were already spread out for the church picnic: fried chicken, cornbread, potato salad, and more. Everything smelled delicious, and Sara was starving!

She set the platter on the dessert table and took off the plastic wrap. The brownies were stacked in a huge pyramid. Sara's mouth watered. She looked around. *No one will notice if I take just one,* she thought.

READ
Luke 16:10. God thinks little things are important.

THINK
- Finish the sentence: When you *trust* someone, you know he or she will do what's right even if _____.
- The verse says that small sins can lead to big ones. How might that happen?
- Finish the story, showing how Sara might learn something important from the verse. Then read the possible ending at the back of the book.

DO
- With your family, pantomime little things that your parents or other adults trust you to do or trust you not to do. See if the others can guess what you're doing.
- Write one of the things you pantomimed on a piece of paper. Plan to be *trustworthy* in that area this week. Seal the paper in an envelope. Address it to yourself. Open the envelope at the end of the week and think about how you did.

PRAY
Ask God to help you obey him even in small things.

MEMORIZE
If you are faithful in little things, you will be faithful in large ones. But if you are dishonest in little things, you won't be honest with greater responsibilities. Luke 16:10

WHAT'S THE POINT?
Sara thought it wasn't so bad to sneak one brownie, but that small action harmed her mother's confidence in her. She learned that it is important to be trustworthy even in little things. *SG*

OCTOBER 16
The Candy Bar

Toshiko pushed the shopping cart and followed her dad. He was looking for nails, but the big store also sold clothes, food, and even computer games. Today they saw costumes on display: pirates, skeletons, princesses, ghosts, and more.

Toshiko remembered a question she'd thought of. "Dad, I heard someone talking about the Holy Ghost. What's that?"

Mr. Takahashi peered at the nails on display. "*Holy Ghost* is another way of saying the *Holy Spirit*, who is part of God. A spirit is invisible. God sends his Holy Spirit to be inside Christians and help them do what's right."

God's Spirit inside me? Toshiko believed in Jesus, but she hadn't heard much about the Holy Spirit before.

They headed to the checkout. While her dad paid the cashier, Toshiko noticed a candy bar that had fallen off the display. She bent to pick it up. *I could slip it in my pocket, and no one would notice,* she thought.

READ
John 14:15-17. God sends the Holy Spirit to us.

☁ THINK
- Find the name that Jesus called the Holy Spirit. What do you think this name means?
- How would having the Holy Spirit inside you help you do what's right?
- Finish the story, showing how these verses could help Toshiko. Then read the possible ending at the back of the book.

DO
- Talk with your family about questions you have about the Holy Spirit.
- Think of a problem you have or a decision you need to make. Ask the Holy Spirit to counsel you.

PRAY
Thank God for sending his Holy Spirit to be with you every day.

MEMORIZE
I will ask the Father, and he will give you another Advocate, who will never leave you.
John 14:16

WHAT'S THE POINT?
When Toshiko was tempted to do wrong, the Holy Spirit reminded her of what the Bible says. *SG*

OCTOBER 17
Poor Dog!

Breanna threw the old shoe across the back lawn. The family's new dog, Cocoa, ran after it. She picked it up, shook it back and forth, and growled.

Breanna's friend Suzi giggled. "She's so funny!"

Next door, the neighbor kid came out to his front yard with his dog. Cocoa barked and scratched at the fence. The other dog barked too.

Suzi jumped up. "They really want to see each other. Why don't you let Cocoa out to play with Bam Bam in the front yard?"

"Cocoa isn't trained to stay in our yard yet. She has to have a fence."

Suzi frowned. "Poor dog! I think that's mean! Bam Bam is free to run wherever he wants."

READ
Isaiah 48:17-18. God teaches us for our good. He gives us rules to help us.

THINK
- Based on these verses, explain why you think God has a right to tell us what to do.
- Do you usually let God lead you or do you dislike following his rules?
- Make up an ending for the story, showing how the verses could make a difference for Breanna. Then read the possible ending at the back of the book.

DO
- Play a tag game where one person names one of God's rules and then tags someone. The person tagged has to say a reason the rule is good for us. Then he or she names a rule and tags someone else, and so on.
- Close your eyes and let someone guide you around the room. Tell why you need God to guide you in your life.

PRAY
Ask God to help you follow him in his good ways so you will have peace.

MEMORIZE
This is what the LORD says—your Redeemer, the Holy One of Israel: "I am the LORD your God, who teaches you what is good for you and leads you along the paths you should follow." Isaiah 48:17

WHAT'S THE POINT?
The fence wasn't mean; it was keeping Cocoa safe. God's guidance and his rules are for our good too. *SG*

OCTOBER 18
Police Trouble

Tommy and Nathaniel rode their bikes down the sidewalk into town for a snack at Happy Jack's. As they turned a corner, they saw a police car parked on the main street. An officer inside was watching the people and traffic.

"See that cop?" Nathaniel whispered. "That's the one who busted Zach for riding across the street here. He even had Zach sit in the squad car. Jerk!" As the boys rode by the squad car, Nathaniel stuck his tongue out.

"Why did you do that?" Tommy gasped.

Nathaniel shrugged. "He wasn't looking. Let's cut across the street to Happy Jack's."

Tommy glanced back. The policeman was facing the other way. There didn't seem to be much traffic.

READ
Romans 13:1-7. These verses talk about obeying authorities. Authorities are the people in charge of us.

THINK
- Why does God give us authorities?
- List some authorities in your school and community (teachers, police, and so on). What attitudes do kids have toward them?
- Finish the story, showing how Tommy could make a good decision based on today's verses. Then read the possible ending at the back of the book.

DO
- Pretend to be one of the authorities you listed. Have a family member play a reporter and interview you on why kids should obey you.
- Choose someone from your list. Choose a way to show respect to him or her this week: obey without complaining; don't make fun of the person; smile; write a thank-you note; or something else.
- *Note*: if any authority asks you to disobey God, talk to another adult you trust.

PRAY
Ask God to help you have the right attitude toward people in authority.

MEMORIZE
Everyone must submit to governing authorities. For all authority comes from God, and those in positions of authority have been placed there by God. Romans 13:1

WHAT'S THE POINT?
Though Nathaniel talked rudely about the policeman and his rules, Tommy realized that God gave us authorities for our good. *SG*

OCTOBER 19
Prank Calls

"Call us when you need a ride home!" Destiny's mom called from the car. Destiny waved from the doorway of Ginger's town house. She was excited to be there. Ginger had more videos than Destiny had ever seen. Two other girls were already popping in a disk.

They settled down in front of the TV with popcorn. Suddenly Ginger pointed at the screen. "That kid looks just like Claudia! We were just talking about her."

"Who's Claudia?" Destiny asked, reaching for the popcorn.

"The weird kid who lives down the street," one of the others explained. "I think we should write 'Ugly Weirdo' on her sidewalk! Or we could do something to her bike." The others laughed.

Destiny felt herself getting excited. She jumped up. "No, no! Let's do prank phone calls!"

READ
1 Corinthians 10:13. God helps us when we're tempted.

THINK
- What things does God promise us when we're tempted?
- Remember a time you were tempted. What way out did you have? Did you take the way out?
- Finish the story, showing how the verse could help Destiny resist temptation. Then read the possible ending at the back of the book.

DO
- Role-play some temptations (such as watching a bad TV show) and ways out (such as turning it off or suggesting something else to do).
- Plan to use some of your ideas this week when you're tempted.

PRAY
Ask God for help in finding ways to escape temptations.

MEMORIZE
The temptations in your life are no different from what others experience. And God is faithful. He will not allow the temptation to be more than you can stand. When you are tempted, he will show you a way out so that you can endure. 1 Corinthians 10:13

WHAT'S THE POINT?
The girls were planning a mean prank. God helped Destiny resist and think of a way out. *SG*

OCTOBER 20
The Missing Shields

Darius watched the drama practice from the side of the classroom. The two knights held up their cardboard shields and clashed their wooden swords.

"That's right!" Mr. Murphy called out. "Plan those moves, and no one gets hurt. Keep practicing!"

He turned to Darius. "How are the real shields coming along?"

Darius looked down awkwardly. Mr. Murphy grasped his shoulder. "I'm counting on you, Darius. You'll do a great job of painting those shields! You know, I'm proud of you. In the past, you wouldn't have volunteered to spend so much time doing something for someone else."

Darius looked worried when his mom came to get him. "Mr. Murphy needs me to finish the shields," Darius said, "but I haven't even started! He should have given them to someone else."

READ
Philippians 2:13. God is at work in us.

THINK
- Why might God need to work on someone?
- How does it feel to know that God will help you *want* to please him?
- Imagine an ending for this story, showing how the verse could encourage Darius. Then read the possible ending at the back of the book.

DO
- Write one way God might want to work on *you*. Around the edges of the paper, draw a hammer, nails, and a paintbrush. Write, "God is working on me!"
- Ask God one way he would like *you* to work with him on this. (Ask a family member for ideas too.) Plan to do what he tells you this week.

PRAY
Thank God that he is working on you to help you become a better person.

MEMORIZE
God is working in you, giving you the desire and the power to do what pleases him.
Philippians 2:13

WHAT'S THE POINT?
Mr. Murphy and Mom helped Darius see how God was at work in him to change him for the better. God works in all of us to help us please him. *SG*

OCTOBER 21
I Want to Wear Makeup

Lola dug through the newspaper ads at breakfast. Finally she found the pharmacy flyer. "Look, Papá!" she said. "The makeup is on sale. Look at these beautiful colors!"

Her dad glanced at the ad. "We've talked about this, Lola. Your mother and I don't want you to wear makeup yet."

"Liliana does!" Lola objected. "Why can't I?"

"Every family is different. I've told you we think you're too young."

Lola stomped upstairs. She sneaked into her parents' room and opened her mother's makeup drawer. If she put some on, she could go out the back door to catch the bus to school. Papá wouldn't see her. He'd never know.

READ
Hebrews 2:18. Jesus helps us face temptation.

THINK
- Based on the verse, do you think it was easy or hard for Jesus to be good when he lived on earth? Explain.
- Imagine Jesus as a child. What might he have been tempted to do?
- Finish the story, showing how Lola could learn from the verse. Then read the possible ending at the back of the book.

DO
- Draw a cross to stand for Jesus. Did he ever give in to temptation? How do you know?
- Glue (or draw) a picture of yourself next to the cross. Next time you're tempted, picture Jesus by your side, helping you to resist.

PRAY
Ask Jesus to help you remember that he's with you when you're tempted.

MEMORIZE
Since he himself has gone through suffering and testing, he is able to help us when we are being tested. Hebrews 2:18

WHAT'S THE POINT?
Even though Lola was frustrated and disappointed, she was discovering a better way to handle it than by rebelling or sneaking; she could talk with God about any problem. *SG*

OCTOBER 22
Hanging in There

Ramiro and Malcolm walked out of the church service and stood in the lobby. "When I'm a teenager," Ramiro commented, "my parents will let me decide if I go to church or not. I'll probably quit."

Malcolm felt stunned. "Don't you believe in God?"

"I guess so," Ramiro said. "But church isn't very important." He waved good-bye.

Malcolm sat down in one of the lobby chairs, waiting for his family. The pastor walked over. "How's it going?"

"Not so good," Malcolm admitted. "What would you say to someone who wants to quit church?"

The pastor sat next to him. "Good question. Look around for a minute. What would your friend be missing?"

READ
Hebrews 6:12. Many people are good examples to us of what it means to hold firm in our faith in God.

THINK
- How might someone act lazy or bored about his or her faith in God?
- What good things might be promised in the verse if we continue with our faith?
- Finish the story, showing how Malcolm could find wisdom in today's verse. Then read the possible ending at the back of the book.

DO
- With your family, think of some Christians (from the present or from history) who are good examples of not giving up on their faith. How can you imitate them?
- Learn more about someone on your list by reading, seeing a video, or listening to the person. Tell someone one thing you learned that will help you be strong in your faith.

PRAY
Ask God to help you stick with your faith and follow the good examples of others.

MEMORIZE
Then you will not become spiritually dull and indifferent. Instead, you will follow the example of those who are going to inherit God's promises because of their faith and endurance. Hebrews 6:12

WHAT'S THE POINT?
Malcolm's friend planned to quit church, but Malcolm could already recognize great reasons to stay in fellowship with other Christians. *SG*

OCTOBER 23
I Don't Want to Be Here

"Mom, I don't want to go," Mackenzie repeated as they arrived at church.

"I know it would be easier to stay home." Mrs. Breckenridge patted her on the arm. "But sometimes we really need to be here. I need to go to my women's group—tonight more than ever! I'll see you later."

Mackenzie made her way to the gym and slumped in the hallway outside it. Through the door she could hear the Pioneer Clubs kids playing a game. She was not in the mood to run and yell.

She could still picture her parents' grim faces from yesterday. She'd been surprised to see her dad home when she came back from school. Then she heard why: He'd lost his job! She wondered what would happen to them now.

One of the club leaders, Alicia, came out to the drinking fountain. "Mackenzie, what are you doing out here? Is something wrong?"

"I'd—I'd just rather not come in," Mackenzie whispered.

READ
Hebrews 10:25. God knows we need other Christians.

THINK
- What factors might make someone stop meeting with other Christians?
- Why might we need encouragement from other Christians?
- Finish the story, showing how Mackenzie might be glad to obey the instructions of the verse. Then read the possible ending at the back of the book.

DO
- With your family, talk about Christians at church who have been kind to you, taught you, or helped you.
- Make a thank-you card for one of them. Then you will be encouraging the person for encouraging you!

PRAY
Thank God for other believers who encourage you and your family.

MEMORIZE
Let us not neglect our meeting together, as some people do, but encourage one another, especially now that the day of his return is drawing near. Hebrews 10:25

WHAT'S THE POINT?
Mackenzie felt terrible when her dad lost his job, but she discovered that other Christians could be a source of support and encouragement. *SG*

OCTOBER 24
I Know Planes Can Fly

Wyatt watched the flight attendant carefully as he pointed to the plane's emergency exits and showed the passengers how the seat belt and oxygen mask worked. Across the aisle, his sister and parents were watching too. They were on their way across the country to a family reunion.

Soon the engines started to screech, and the plane started rolling. Wyatt looked past the older woman next to him so he could see out the window. "It's my first plane flight!" he explained.

"You don't seem worried," she commented. "I always get scared when I fly."

Wyatt looked at her. Her face did seem a little pale. "Well, maybe you could pray," he suggested.

She sighed. "I don't think I believe in God," she said. "Some things are just too hard to understand."

READ
Hebrews 11:1-2. Since we can't see God, we need to have faith to know he's there.

THINK
- What helps you have faith in God and what he will do?
- Why do you think the Old Testament people were praised for their faith?
- Finish the story, showing how Wyatt could explain what faith really is. Then read the possible ending at the back of the book.

DO
- Turn on a fan. How does it help you know air is real?
- Write some ways you know your invisible God is real. Show them to someone.

PRAY
Thank God that he is real. Thank him for the faith that he helps you have.

MEMORIZE
Faith is the confidence that what we hope for will actually happen; it gives us assurance about things we cannot see. Hebrews 11:1

WHAT'S THE POINT?
Wyatt didn't have all the answers to give the woman who didn't believe in God, but he still was able to share his own experience of faith in God. *SG*

OCTOBER 25
Cat Fight

Ian was irritated. His friend Yoshi had shown up at school with the exact kind of new sneakers Ian wanted—that his parents said were too expensive. He clenched his fists. *I don't think Mom and Dad care about me!*

His sister Linnea was lying on the couch with their fluffy gray cat, Misty, on her lap. Ian ran over and scooped up the cat. "My turn for Misty!"

"It is not!" Linnea yelled. "She's comforting me after my fight with Mia!" Linnea grabbed at Misty. The cat yowled, twisted out of Ian's grasp, and streaked out of the room.

Their mother came in. "What's going on?"

"Ian took the cat!" Linnea said.

"She was hogging her!" Ian yelled.

Their mom looked at each of them. "Is that the whole story?"

READ
James 4:1-3. These verses talk about what causes quarrels.

THINK
- What wrong desires inside us might lead us to fight with others?
- Have you ever felt mad or jealous and then taken it out on someone else? Explain.
- Make up an ending for the story, showing how Ian and Linnea could learn from the verses. Then read the possible ending at the back of the book.

DO
- Have a family member play a reporter and interview the rest of you: How can you tell when you're grumpy or jealous? How can you stop your feelings from starting a fight?
- Use one of your ideas this week when you feel like quarreling.

PRAY
Ask God to help you deal with what's inside you before you hurt others.

MEMORIZE
"Don't sin by letting anger control you." Don't let the sun go down while you are still angry. Ephesians 4:26

WHAT'S THE POINT?
Ian and Linnea realized that their own angry feelings had started the fight. They thought of ways to deal with angry feelings rather than taking them out on others. *SG*

OCTOBER 26
Real or Fake?

The last customers left the pumpkin stand. Dallas carried the cash box over to his dad, who was changing their roadside sign to say, "Closed."

"Look, Dallas!" His dad held up a twenty-dollar bill from the box. "This one might be counterfeit."

Dallas fingered the bill. "What's *counterfeit*?"

"It means *fake*," his dad explained. "People print their own money and use it to buy things. It can be hard to tell the counterfeit from the real thing, but the bank will know." As they drove to town, his dad continued, "There are lots of fakes out there—like fake medicines. They do a lot of harm! There are even fake Christians."

Dallas felt disturbed. "How can you tell if something's a fake?"

READ
1 John 2:3-6. These verses describe the mark of a true Christian.

THINK
- In verse 4, what's more important, words or actions? Why?
- How does obeying God show love?
- Finish the story, showing how Dallas could know the difference between what's true and what's not based on today's verses. Then read the possible ending at the back of the book.

DO
- Think of a coach, teacher, or leader you especially like. Draw a face to show how you feel about obeying him or her. Draw a face to show how you feel about obeying God.
- Draw a big heart. In it, write "I obey God because . . ." Fill in reasons that you love and admire God. (If you obey because you're scared of God, talk to a Christian adult you trust.)

PRAY
Ask God to help you love and obey him.

MEMORIZE
Those who obey God's word truly show how completely they love him. That is how we know we are living in him. Those who say they live in God should live their lives as Jesus did.
1 John 2:5-6

WHAT'S THE POINT?
Dallas determined not to be a counterfeit Christian, but the real thing. *SG*

OCTOBER 27
Unwelcome Guest
Part 1 of 5

Peyton heard the splintering crash and ran to his room, with his sister Lydia close behind. Clothes were thrown all over the floor and toys knocked off the shelves. His cousin Brody stood by the closet door—which had a big hole in it. He looked ready to punch someone.

"What did you *do*?" Peyton sputtered.

"I got mad!" Brody said angrily. "I kicked a few things around. Who cares?"

Peyton couldn't believe it. "I care! This is *my* room! I'm not the one who invited a *maniac* to move in with me!"

"Well, you're not Mr. Perfect!" Brody snapped.

Just then Peyton's dad arrived. "Brody," Mr. Howard said quietly, "we told your mother that you could live with us for a while. But when you break the rules, there are consequences. Let's talk in the kitchen."

After they left, Lydia turned to Peyton. "Brody's right, you know."

READ

Romans 3:23. Sin is doing wrong things that displease God.

THINK

- This verse says *everyone* sins. What wrong things would kids your age do?
- Think of the most loving, unselfish person you know. How does this compare with the "glory" of a perfect God?
- Imagine an ending for this story, showing how the kids could learn from the verse. Then read the possible ending at the back of the book.

DO

- Draw a picture of your favorite shirt with a stain on it. How is the stain like sin?
- Write Romans 3:23 on the picture. Post it in your room so you can remember it next time you think sin isn't bad.

PRAY

Ask God to help you understand that you sin against him.

MEMORIZE

Everyone has sinned; we all fall short of God's glorious standard. Romans 3:23

WHAT'S THE POINT?

Peyton was angry when his cousin wrecked his room, but he realized he wasn't perfect either. *SG*

300

OCTOBER 28
Undeserved Gift
Part 2 of 5

Lydia burst into the kitchen the next afternoon. "Mom, Brody got in trouble at school!"

Brody was already there, sitting at the table. One eye was black and puffy. "What did the other kids say?" he asked.

Peyton joined them. "They said *you* started a fight."

"Maybe I did," Brody sighed. "It always happens. Someone says something, and I get mad, and then *bam*! I thought I'd do better here at a new school, but . . ." He sighed again. "If I keep messing up, I'll end up in juvie."

"What's *juvie*?" Peyton asked.

"It's short for *juvenile detention*," his mom explained. "That's a place some kids have to live when they're in trouble with the law."

She turned to Brody. "None of us can change or become better people on our own. We need Jesus."

"I don't think Jesus could help me," Brody said.

READ
Romans 6:23. We have a choice between death and life forever.

THINK
- According to the verse, why is there death?
- What does God's gift of life forever mean to you?
- Finish the story, showing what the kids understand about the choice between life and death described in the verse. Then read the possible ending at the back of the book.

DO
- Remember a time you received a gift. Why did the person give it to you? Why might God offer the gift of life forever to us?
- Wrap (or draw) a gift box. Write a tag: "God loves me and has a gift for me."

PRAY
Thank God that he wants to give you life forever.

MEMORIZE
The wages of sin is death, but the free gift of God is eternal life through Christ Jesus our Lord. Romans 6:23

WHAT'S THE POINT?
Brody was worried that he kept sinning. Mrs. Howard explained that he could have new life in Jesus as a gift. Peyton wondered if Brody deserved it. *SG*

Brody's cloth squeaked as he rubbed it across the window outside the house. "What are you doing?" Lydia asked, joining him.

"Your dad gave me some chores," Brody explained. "That's how I'm paying for the closet door I broke."

"Wow! Our house will look great," Lydia said. Brody moved his bucket to the next window.

"You're nice, Lydia," he said after a while. "Have you ever done that stuff about new life in Jesus?"

Lydia was startled. "Yes, I have."

"What's it like?" Brody asked.

"Well, I told Jesus I was sorry for the wrong things I do," Lydia remembered. "I thanked him for dying on the cross and coming back to life to pay the penalty for my sins."

"*Your* sins!" Brody laughed. "You've got to be kidding!"

"Sins don't have to be big," Lydia explained. "They can be stuff like selfishness, or talking behind someone's back. Jesus took our punishment for all that. Then he forgives us, and we get a new life. We're not perfect, but Jesus can help us get better every day."

"Hmmm." Brody scrubbed at the window. "Do you think Peyton's ever done that with Jesus?"

READ
1 John 1:8–2:2. Jesus paid the price for our sin. *Sacrifice* and *atone* mean that Jesus gave his life to pay the penalty for our wrongs.

THINK
- The verses show crime and payment. Who did something wrong?
- Why do you think Jesus paid the penalty for our sins?
- Finish the story, showing how the kids' lives could be changed by the truth in today's memory verse. Then read the possible ending at the back of the book.

DO
- In your own words, write how to become right with God (see chapter 1, verse 9).
- Practice explaining the words of this verse to someone.

PRAY
Ask God to help you understand how Jesus saves us.

MEMORIZE
If we confess our sins to him, he is faithful and just to forgive us our sins and to cleanse us from all wickedness. 1 John 1:9

WHAT'S THE POINT?
Lydia explained that Jesus took our punishment, and he will forgive us when we ask. Brody was interested, but Peyton wasn't. *SG*

Surprise Party
Part 4 of 5

"Surprise!" Lydia and her parents yelled and flipped on the lights. Brody and Peyton blinked, startled to see the kitchen decorated with balloons. A large pizza sat in the middle of the table.

"What's this for?" Peyton asked.

Mr. Howard pointed to Brody. "A week ago, this young man asked Jesus to forgive his sins. That means he has a *new life*. So we thought we'd celebrate with a birthday party!" He pointed to the counter.

Peyton looked over and saw a cake with one candle in it. *This is ridiculous,* he thought.

Brody seemed uncomfortable too. "I'm not sure we should party," he said. "I know I prayed, but I didn't have a very good week at school. God might not be so happy with me."

READ

Luke 15:10. There is a special celebration in heaven when a person becomes part of God's family.

THINK

- Every person needs to choose between accepting God's forgiveness for his or her sins or ignoring it. How does God feel about each choice?
- How does God show his joy in this verse? Use your imagination to picture the scene in heaven.
- Finish the story, showing how the kids could share in the joy described in the verse. Then read the possible ending at the back of the book.

DO

- Act out how you felt during a time you found something that was lost, or when you had something fixed that was broken. Compare that with God's feelings about people who come to him and ask forgiveness for their sins.
- Have a family party to celebrate with God over people accepting his forgiveness. Think about God rejoicing with you.

PRAY

Thank God that he loves and wants you so much.

MEMORIZE

There is joy in the presence of God's angels when even one sinner repents. Luke 15:10

WHAT'S THE POINT?

The Howards knew that God was celebrating in heaven because Brody was now God's child. *SG*

OCTOBER 31
Music from the Trees
Part 5 of 5

The yellows and reds of the fall trees reflected on the river. Lydia and Brody ran to the water's edge and tried to skip rocks. Peyton set the picnic basket down. "It's beautiful!" his mom exclaimed. "Days like this definitely help me believe in God!"

Mr. Howard put down the cooler. "It's even more amazing that the Creator cares about folks like us."

Peyton felt uneasy. He'd been running away from God, saying he didn't need him. Now he had to admit that he *did* need help.

Mrs. Howard joined Lydia and Brody by the water.

"Dad, can we talk for a minute?" Peyton asked.

READ
Isaiah 44:22-23. Creation rejoices because God forgives us!

THINK
- According to these verses, what does God do to our sins when we ask for forgiveness? Explain in your own words.
- These verses describe creation's joy. How should people respond when God forgives them?
- Make up an ending for the story, showing how Peyton could share in the celebration, just like his cousin. Then read the possible ending at the back of the book.

DO
- If you have not accepted God's forgiveness and new life, you can pray right now: "Dear Jesus, thank you for dying to take the punishment for my sins. I'm sorry for the wrong things I've done. Please forgive me and give me new life. Thank you!"
- If God has already taken away your sins, rejoice with him and the mountains and forests and trees!
- If you are not ready, think of someone you can talk to about your questions.

PRAY
Ask God to help you feel his joy over you.

MEMORIZE
Sing, O heavens, for the LORD has done this wondrous thing. Shout for joy, O depths of the earth! Break into song, O mountains and forests and every tree! For the LORD has redeemed Jacob and is glorified in Israel. Isaiah 44:23

WHAT'S THE POINT?
Peyton realized he needed Jesus to forgive him. His dad explained that God loved and rejoiced over him too. *SG*

NOVEMBER 1
Too Young?

Raul walked over to his friend Gregory who was standing by the vending machines. "There's nothing healthy in these stupid machines," Gregory complained.

Raul shrugged. "I don't really care." He put in money and pulled out a bag of chips.

"Well, I do!" Gregory said as they carried their trays to the lunch table. "You know, some schools have vending machines that sell healthy stuff. Our school should get one."

"Well, ask the principal or something," Raul said, stuffing some chips in his mouth.

"No one will listen. I'm just a kid."

Raul liked a challenge. "I memorized this verse in the Bible once that said—"

"The *Bible*?" Gregory made a face. "Who cares what's in the Bible? It's just some old church book!"

READ
2 Timothy 3:14-17. These verses remind us that the Bible is special and not like ordinary books.

THINK
- Whose words are in the Bible?
- Based on the verses, give two examples of things the Bible is good for.
- Finish the story, showing how the verses could make a difference for Raul. Then read the possible ending at the back of the book.

DO
Play a ball-toss game with your family. Throw a ball to someone. Each "catcher" says one thing he or she has learned from the Bible during these devotions and one way he or she will use that information in everyday life.

PRAY
Ask God to show you how to read Scripture to learn from it.

MEMORIZE
All Scripture is inspired by God and is useful to teach us what is true and to make us realize what is wrong in our lives. It corrects us when we are wrong and teaches us to do what is right. 2 Timothy 3:16

WHAT'S THE POINT?
Raul helped Gregory see that the Bible is from God and it's helpful in our everyday lives. *BA*

NOVEMBER 2
Truth or Dare

"Time for Truth or Dare," Piper's friend Alana announced at her sleepover. Piper was excited. She'd never played before.

"Be sure you stick to the G-rated questions and dares we found on the Internet," Alana's mom reminded them, handing Alana two bags with slips of paper in them. "Good night, girls," she added, and left the room.

"Me first!" Sandy called out. "I choose 'dare'!" The other girls giggled as Sandy drew a slip out of the Dare bag.

"Walk around the room three times, flapping your wings and clucking like a chicken!" she read. The girls hooted with laughter as Sandy clucked around the room.

"Me next!" Piper shouted. "I choose 'truth.'" She reached into the Truth bag and drew out a question. "Do you believe the Bible is true?" she read. Piper felt her face flush. *I do believe your Word is true, Lord,* she prayed. *But what if they tease me?*

READ
Psalm 33:1-4. God wants us to sing and shout for joy because his Word is true.

THINK
- How much of the Bible can you believe? How can you tell?
- Why is the truth of God's Word a reason to be joyful?
- Finish the story, showing how the verses could give courage to Piper. Then read the possible ending at the back of the book.

DO
- Play "Toss the Ball" with your family. Toss a ball to someone. The catcher names something in the Bible that he or she is glad is true. Then the catcher tosses the ball to someone else, and so on.
- Pick a tune you know. Write your own song of joy that the Bible is true. Sing it with your family.

PRAY
Thank God that we can believe his Word.

MEMORIZE
The word of the LORD holds true, and we can trust everything he does. Psalm 33:4

WHAT'S THE POINT?
Piper knew that God promises us that the Bible is true. We can sing for joy because we can believe his Word. *BA*

NOVEMBER 3
Snake Facts

Paul and Shawn searched for snake facts for a school project using Paul's family computer. "Dad, did you know a rattlesnake can chase you for ten minutes?"

Paul's dad looked over their shoulders. "Where did you find that?"

"In this blog, see?" said Paul.

Mr. Kim said, "Sometimes bloggers post things without checking whether what they write is true. Some people even make things up. I was reading a blog the other day that said the Bible was written by aliens."

Shawn made a "too weird" face. "How do we know what to believe, then?"

READ

Deuteronomy 10:1-5. God directly wrote the Ten Commandments on stone tablets.

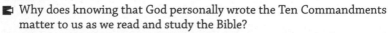

THINK

- Why does knowing that God personally wrote the Ten Commandments matter to us as we read and study the Bible?
- How do you think you would have felt if you were Moses and you saw God writing his own words on the stone tablets?
- Finish the story, showing how the verses can matter to Paul and Shawn. Then read the possible ending at the back of the book.

DO

- How do you feel about the Ten Commandments, knowing God wrote them?
- In the next few days, you'll study the Ten Commandments. Write a note to God explaining what your attitude toward them will be.

PRAY

Thank God for taking the time to write his words down for us.

MEMORIZE

You must always obey the LORD's commands and decrees that I am giving you today for your own good. Deuteronomy 10:13

WHAT'S THE POINT?

Knowing that God actually wrote the Ten Commandments gives us confidence that the Bible can be trusted. *SP*

NOVEMBER 4
Can't We Wait till Later?

Claire and Brent raced into the family room and turned on the TV. Claire flopped on the couch, and Brent lay on the floor with his arm around the dog.

From the kitchen, their mother called, "It's time for family devotions."

Claire smacked the couch. "But, Mom! It's time for the game to start!"

Brent called, "Can't we wait till later for devotions?"

Dad stuck his head in the family room. "You know this is our time every day. I have to go out right afterward, so we can't wait."

Both kids howled louder. "Aw, Mom!" "Come on, Dad!"

Mom shut off the TV. "We're going to talk about the first two of the Ten Commandments today. I think you'll find them interesting."

READ
Deuteronomy 5:1-8. God gave the Israelites his Ten Commandments. Verses 7 and 8 are the first two.

THINK
- Why do you think God wants to be our only God?
- What are some things that kids your age might make more important than God?
- Finish the story, showing how the verses can make a difference in Claire's and Brent's attitudes. Then read the possible ending at the back of the book.

DO
- Why do you think worshiping only the one true God comes first in the Ten Commandments?
- Sketch something you think you make more important than God. Above it, write a way you will make God more important in your life, like starting your day with prayer.

PRAY
Give thanks for God's Ten Commandments that help us learn how to live.

MEMORIZE
You must not have any other god but me. Deuteronomy 5:7

WHAT'S THE POINT?
Mom and Dad helped the kids see that God wants to come first in our lives. *BA*

NOVEMBER 5
The Toad Race

Andre drew blue starting and finish lines on the sidewalk. Orlando and Ellen picked up boards and held them along the edge of the grass to keep the racers on the course.

"Let the toad races begin!" said Orlando.

Henry and Andre picked up their toads and held them at the start line. Ellen made sounds like a crowd cheering.

"On your mark, get set, go!" Orlando yelled. Henry and Andre let go of their toads and picked up little sticks to prod them along gently. Henry's toad leaped ahead.

"Oh my g—! My toad's ahead!" Henry shouted.

Andre cringed. His family didn't use God's name that way. The toads kept hopping. Suddenly Henry's toad veered off to the right.

"He's going the wrong way!" Henry yelled. "Oh my g—! Stop!"

"*You* stop! Quit saying that!" Andre blurted out.

READ
Deuteronomy 5:11. This is the third of God's Ten Commandments.

THINK
- When do kids tend to misuse God's name?
- Why do you think God feels so strongly about this that he put it in the Ten Commandments?
- Finish the story, showing how Andre and his friends might obey this commandment. Then read the possible ending at the back of the book.

DO
- Draw a stick figure with an open mouth. Add some speech balloons. Write some things you could say when you're excited or mad instead of misusing God's name.
- If you've developed a habit of using God's name in a casual way, ask a friend or a sibling to give you a quiet reminder—maybe a hand signal you make up together—whenever you use it without thinking.

PRAY
Ask God to help you to use his name only when you purposely want to talk to him or about him. Ask him to help you make habits that are respectful to his name.

MEMORIZE
You must not misuse the name of the LORD your God. The LORD will not let you go unpunished if you misuse his name. Deuteronomy 5:11

WHAT'S THE POINT?
Andre helped Henry see that the third commandment is important to God. God wants it to be important to us too. *BA*

NOVEMBER 6
Goal!

Rosita dribbled the soccer ball across the grass, aimed, and kicked. The ball flew past her dad's outstretched arms and into the net. "Goalllllll!" she shouted and danced around.

"Good shot!" said Dad. "You're a natural."

As they sat down at the picnic table at the park, Rosita took a deep breath. "That's what I want to talk to you about, Dad," she said. "I really, really want to play in the park district soccer league next season."

"*Mi hija*, my daughter," Dad began, "your mom said the games will be on Sundays. We can't make it to the games in time after church."

"My life will be ruined if I can't play soccer!" Rosita exclaimed.

READ
Deuteronomy 5:12. The fourth commandment says that God wants us to respect him by celebrating a special day each week. Keeping this day *holy* means keeping it *set apart* for God or *devoted* to him.

THINK
- What are things we can do on the Sabbath day to keep it set apart for God?
- Why does worshiping God by going to church fit in with keeping the Sabbath day holy?
- Make up an ending for the story, showing how the verse can make a difference for Rosita. Then read the possible ending at the back of the book.

DO
- Give yourself a grade on how well you think you keep the Sabbath day holy.
- Write something you could do to respect God more on the Sabbath.

PRAY
Pray that your Sabbath day will help you reconnect with God.

MEMORIZE
Observe the Sabbath day by keeping it holy, as the LORD your God has commanded you.
Deuteronomy 5:12

WHAT'S THE POINT?
Dad helped Rosita understand the importance of church in keeping the Sabbath day holy. *BA*

NOVEMBER 7
Crash!

"Mom!" Penny called. "Can we sled on our hill?"

"Sure," Mrs. Washington said. "Be sure to put the hay bale in front of the street-light at the bottom so you don't crash into it."

Soon kids were sledding down the hill that Penny's house sat on. One boy bailed out at the bottom just before he hit the streetlight. *I'd better get that hay bale,* Penny remembered. *I'll go down one more time first.* As she rode screaming down on her stomach, she turned her head to yell at her neighbor Colton, "I'm gonna beat you!"

Crash! Pain shot through Penny's forehead, and the sled stopped dead. "You hit the streetlight with your head!" Colton yelled, running toward her.

Penny lay in the snow crying as her mom came running out. "I forgot to look where I was going!" she sobbed.

"And you didn't put the hay bale out like I told you to," Mom said.

READ
Deuteronomy 5:16. This fifth commandment tells us how to treat our parents.

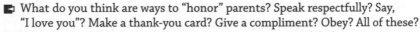

THINK
- What do you think are ways to "honor" parents? Speak respectfully? Say, "I love you"? Make a thank-you card? Give a compliment? Obey? All of these?
- Why do you think God wants us to honor our moms and dads?
- Imagine an ending for this story, showing how the verse can make a difference for Penny. Then read the possible ending at the back of the book.

DO
- Think of a way you sometimes disobey your mom or dad or the person who's like a parent to you.
- Make a card that tells your mom or dad that you will obey in this way this week.

PRAY
Ask Jesus to help you honor your mom or dad.

MEMORIZE
Honor your father and mother, as the LORD your God commanded you. Then you will live a long, full life in the land the LORD your God is giving you. Deuteronomy 5:16

WHAT'S THE POINT?
Penny realized that her mom had a good reason for asking her to obey. God is pleased when we honor our parents. *BA*

NOVEMBER 8
He'll Never Miss Four Bucks

Judah's class filed into the library to look at the books that were going to be for sale at the book fair. "I don't have any money," Judah said. But he went to look anyway.

"That comic book's awesome," said Victor. "I'm getting that for sure."

"Me, too," said Pablo. "You gotta get it, Judah! It's only four dollars."

That night Judah was trying to figure out how he could get the money when his older brother came into their room. T.J. got a box out from under the bed and dumped out some money. "Yesss!" he said after counting it. "I've finally saved enough for the ATV tour with Uncle Warren." He ran back out of the room.

Judah stared at the box. *T.J. would never miss four dollars,* he thought.

READ
Deuteronomy 5:19. The eighth commandment shows us God's opinion of stealing.

THINK
- If Judah takes the money, is it okay, since T.J. has more than he does? Explain.
- If Judah takes the money and pays T.J. back later, is it still stealing? Explain.
- Finish the story, showing how the verse could provide wisdom for Judah. Then read the possible ending at the back of the book.

DO
- Have you stolen something? Make a plan to make things right with God and the other person.
- Write a few things you could tell yourself when you feel like stealing to help yourself not do it.

PRAY
Ask Jesus to help you respect others' property.

MEMORIZE
You must not steal. Deuteronomy 5:19

WHAT'S THE POINT?
God was at work on Judah through his conscience. He realized he had stolen T.J.'s money, and he found a way to make things right. *BA*

NOVEMBER 9
Look What You Made Me Do!

Camilla's little sister, Clara, was drawing at her desk. Camilla sneaked up behind her. "What are you doing?" she asked.

"It's private!" Clara flung her arms out to cover her picture so fast that she shook the desk. Her glass cat teetered and fell. *Smash!* Clara started to cry. "My cat! Look what you made me do! I'm telling!" She pushed past Camilla and ran out of the room.

"I didn't do anything!" Camilla yelled after her. But soon she heard Mom calling her. She went to the living room. Mom looked from one girl to the other.

"Clara says you broke her cat on purpose," Mom said.

READ
Deuteronomy 5:20. The ninth commandment means not to tell lies about each other.

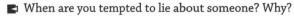

THINK
- When are you tempted to lie about someone? Why?
- What bad results come from lying about someone?
- Finish the story, showing how the verse could help both Camilla and Clara. Then read the possible ending at the back of the book.

DO
- Have you lied about someone? Ask God how you can make things right.
- Has someone lied about you? Ask God to help you talk it over with the person.

PRAY
Ask Jesus to help you value the truth at all times.

MEMORIZE
You must not testify falsely against your neighbor. Deuteronomy 5:20

WHAT'S THE POINT?
Clara's lie about Camilla hurt Camilla and damaged relationships between the girls and their mom. God gives us a law against lying to protect us. *BA*

NOVEMBER 10
Whose MP3 Player?

"Hey, Kristi, look at my new MP3 player," Lissa said by their lockers. "I just found it."

Kristi looked it over. "It looks just like Angie's," she said slowly. "She reported it missing this morning."

Lissa clenched her fists. "It's mine!" she yelled. "Angie threw hers away because she wanted a new one!"

Their teacher looked out the door. "Lissa, I need to talk to you," he said.

Lissa leaned nearer to Kristi. "You're not my friend anymore!" she hissed angrily.

Kristi's hand shook as she closed her locker. She walked out to the bus, feeling miserable. "Can I sit by you?" she asked her older brother, Dave. Kristi told him what happened. "Why did she get so mad at me?" she asked with a sniffle.

READ
Deuteronomy 5:21. The tenth commandment has to do with jealously wanting something that belongs to someone else.

THINK
▣ How does the tenth commandment involve treating someone with respect?
▣ What good actions could you take when you want something that belongs to someone else?
▣ Finish the story, showing how Kristi understands this verse. Then read the possible ending at the back of the book.

DO
▣ What is something someone else has that you really, really want?
▣ Plan a step you will take this week to keep from coveting: save to buy one of your own; ask God to help you not covet; ask to borrow it (and be sure to give it back!); thank God for the things you *do* have; or think of your own idea.

PRAY
Ask God to give you self-control when you want something that belongs to someone else.

MEMORIZE
You must not covet your neighbor's wife. You must not covet your neighbor's house or land, male or female servant, ox or donkey, or anything else that belongs to your neighbor. Deuteronomy 5:21

WHAT'S THE POINT?
God knows that coveting leads to bad thoughts and often to bad actions. He wants us to respect what belongs to someone else. *SP*

NOVEMBER 11
No-Peanut Zone

"Beginning today, school is a no-peanut zone," Maria's teacher announced. "We have students with severe peanut allergies. This new rule is one way we can keep the commandment that Jesus said was one of the two most important: Love your neighbor as you love yourself."

Maria scowled. Her favorite lunch was peanut butter-and-banana sandwiches. How could they tell her she couldn't have them anymore?

The next day at school she looked to see what her mom had packed her. *Ham. Gross,* she thought. Grumpily, she began to eat. Across from her, Sonya was also complaining about not being able to eat peanut butter.

Suddenly they heard raised voices across the room. A boy was standing up, wheezing. A teacher was dialing 911 and asking for help.

Openmouthed, Maria stared. "What's going on?" asked Sonya.

READ
Psalm 119:24. God gave us rules in the Bible to guide us. They help us choose wisely as we make decisions.

THINK
- How can rules give you advice?
- Do rules please you or annoy you? Why?
- Finish the story, showing how Maria might learn something new from this verse. Then read the possible ending at the back of the book.

DO
- Role-play a kid having trouble making a decision and then using one of God's rules to guide him or her.
- Talk with your family about one of God's rules that's hard for you. Brainstorm how you could look at the rule differently so you would be pleased to have it.

PRAY
Thank God for giving you guidance through his rules. Ask for help with being pleased to have his guidance.

MEMORIZE
Your laws please me; they give me wise advice. Psalm 119:24

WHAT'S THE POINT?
Maria learned that school rules and God's rules are there to guide us and protect us, not spoil our fun. *BA*

NOVEMBER 12
Sneaking In

Alec and Braeden stood at the gate of the fairgrounds, looking across the carnival midway to their left. They could hear the 4-H animals mooing and grunting and baaing to their right. Alec counted his money. "Do you think we could get into the fairgrounds by going through the fence behind where the trailers are parked?" he asked.

Braeden looked surprised. "Don't you have enough money to buy a ticket?"

"Sure, but I'd rather save it for food or rides."

Braeden hesitated. "That sounds the same as stealing a ticket to me."

Alec rolled his eyes. "Think of the corn dogs, pizza, and nachos. It's not the same as stealing, and anyway, who cares about stealing a cheap ticket?"

READ

2 Kings 22:1-2. God's Temple was broken down in King Josiah's day. People were worshiping false gods. Josiah gave orders for the Temple to be rebuilt. They found a surprise in it. Read 2 Kings 22:8, 11. The Bible they found told how the people were not following God. Josiah was very upset. Read 2 Kings 23:1-3.

THINK

- What did King Josiah want the people to do? What did they decide to do?
- Why do you think Josiah was described as doing what was right in God's sight?
- Finish the story, showing how young King Josiah could be a good example for Alec. Then read the possible ending at the back of the book.

DO

- Discuss with your family one way you haven't followed God's law, and what would help you correct this.
- Josiah and the people renewed their "covenant" with God. That's a written agreement—a deal. Write a covenant with God that you will obey him in the area you have been disobeying.

PRAY

Ask God to use the Bible to change your mind about any behavior that doesn't please him.

MEMORIZE

He did what was pleasing in the LORD's sight and followed the example of his ancestor David. He did not turn away from doing what was right. 2 Kings 22:2

WHAT'S THE POINT?

The Bible helped the Israelites change their minds and obey God. The Bible can help us change our minds when we're tempted to do wrong. *SP*

NOVEMBER 13
Don't Splash Me!

Latham thought it was cool to be driving to a water park in November. Where they used to live, he would have been sledding and making snowballs.

"Why don't we review Bible memory verses for Sunday school tomorrow? After that, we'll be almost there," Mom suggested.

Latham and his little sister, Luciana, rattled off some verses. "Last week's was 'Children, obey your parents because you belong to the Lord,'" Latham finished.

Finally they got to the water park. "Don't splash me, Latham!" Luciana said as they waded in a wave pool. But Latham did anyway. Luciana started to cry.

"Latham, she doesn't like water in her eyes," said Mom. "Don't splash her anymore." Latham resisted until they were floating down the lazy river. Up ahead, a little waterfall splashed into the river. When Luciana was even with it, Latham pushed her tube with his foot. She floated right into the waterfall and got drenched. Latham laughed.

"Latham!" Mom snapped. "What did I tell you?"

READ
James 1:22-25. As believers in Jesus, we should change the way we act to show what we've learned from the Bible.

THINK
- Imagine looking in a mirror, seeing your face is dirty, and then walking away without washing it. Why might someone see something in the Bible that God wants us to do and then not do it?
- Why do we need to do more than read and know about what God teaches?
- Finish the story, showing how the verses might affect the way Latham treats his sister. Then read the possible ending at the back of the book.

DO
- Write a word or two to stand for something that the Bible says to do that you're not doing.
- Plan one way to improve this week.

PRAY
Ask God to help you *do* what Jesus wants and not just *hear* it.

MEMORIZE
Don't just listen to God's word. You must do what it says. Otherwise, you are only fooling yourselves. James 1:22

WHAT'S THE POINT?
Just reading something in the Bible isn't enough, but doing something to use what you've learned helps you change to become more like Jesus. *BA*

NOVEMBER 14
The Secret Weapon

Michelle went over to Jennifer's house after school. The girls called hi to Jennifer's mom and ran upstairs. They dropped their backpacks on the floor and flopped onto the bed.

"What should we do?" Michelle asked.

"I know," said Jennifer, digging in her nightstand drawer. She handed Michelle a pack of Bible verse cards. "Help me review my memory verses for Sunday school. I want to get a prize this week."

Michelle said, "I don't understand why you have to remember Bible verses in Sunday school."

"I don't *have* to, but memorizing is a challenge. Besides, I have to understand what they mean first, and that part is interesting."

Michelle made a smug face. "It's really all about the prizes you get, isn't it?"

READ
Matthew 4:1-11. Satan thought he could tempt Jesus to do wrong, but Jesus had a secret weapon.

THINK
- What was Jesus' secret weapon?
- Why do you think Jesus used Scripture to say no to Satan instead of just using his own words?
- Finish the story, showing how the verses could make a difference for Jennifer and Michelle. Then read the possible ending at the back of the book.

DO
- Choose a verse and make up a skit with your family. Act out a situation you find yourself in regularly. Use the verse to show how to resist doing the wrong thing.

PRAY
Thank God for giving you a secret weapon—the Bible—to help you fight temptation.

MEMORIZE
People do not live by bread alone, but by every word that comes from the mouth of God.
Matthew 4:4

WHAT'S THE POINT?
Jennifer wanted to follow Jesus' example of using Scripture to fight temptation. *SP*

NOVEMBER 15
Treasure Hunt

Clinton and Maddie shone their flashlights around the dark corners of Grandma's attic. "You never know what treasures you might find up there!" Grandma had said.

Maddie turned her flashlight to the right and stared. "An old trunk!"

"If there's a treasure, this is where it would be," Clinton said. The lid creaked as they lifted it. Inside was an old book. "It's a Bible," Maddie said. She carefully turned crackly brown pages. "Look, it says 'Our Family' in the front with a bunch of names."

"With a Bible verse by each one," Clinton said. "There's Grandma's name. Who are these other people?"

READ
Psalm 19:7-11. The writer finds wisdom and joy in God's teaching.

THINK
- What reasons are given for putting a high value on God's laws and commands?
- Which reason means the most to you? Why?
- Finish the story, showing how Clinton and Maddie could understand the verses. Then read the possible ending at the back of the book.

DO
- Ask your mom or dad to help you choose a life verse. Write it in your Bible.
- Make a poster with the following sentence to remind yourself of the value of God's Word; then, fill in the blank on the poster with something you value: *God's words are more precious than _____.*

PRAY
Ask God to give you the joy and wisdom in the Bible that the verses describe.

MEMORIZE
Reverence for the LORD is pure, lasting forever. The laws of the LORD are true; each one is fair. They are more desirable than gold, even the finest gold. Psalm 19:9-10

WHAT'S THE POINT?
Grandma helped the kids understand that the Bible is full of wisdom and value for us. *BA*

NOVEMBER 16
The Scary Old House

Gracia and her friend Lindsey kicked through the fallen leaves on the way home from school. Suddenly Gracia pointed. "Look! People are moving into that scary old house!"

"It was empty for a really long time," Lindsey said. A man and woman carried some furniture inside. Bright curtains hung in each window.

"It doesn't look scary anymore," Gracia said wonderingly. "I mean, the house is still the same shape and size, but it all feels so different—so happy."

They told Gracia's mom about the change when they got to her house. "A new family moving in is just what that old house needed. They'll give it a new life now," Mom said. She set out some fresh-baked cookies and paused. "I just reminded myself of something!" She grinned. "That old house can help us think of what happens when the Holy Spirit moves into our lives."

READ
John 14:25-26. Jesus is speaking in these verses. He would soon be going back to heaven. He told his followers to expect the Holy Spirit to come live in them.

THINK
- Who is the Holy Spirit? How do we get him to live in us?
- What kinds of things do you think he will teach us and remind us of?
- Finish the story, showing how Gracia might learn something from these verses. Then read the possible ending at the back of the book.

DO
- What is something you would like the Holy Spirit to remind you of this week from the Bible? When would you need this reminder?
- Pick a partner to pray with you about what you chose. At the end of the week, tell each other what the Holy Spirit did for you.

PRAY
Thank God for the gift of his Spirit.

MEMORIZE
When the Father sends the Advocate as my representative—that is, the Holy Spirit—he will teach you everything and will remind you of everything I have told you. John 14:26

WHAT'S THE POINT?
When God's Holy Spirit lives in us, he teaches us how to live to please God. *SP*

NOVEMBER 17
Birthday Presents

Victoria and Ramona rushed into Victoria's apartment after school, hanging up their wet coats by the door. "There's a package for you on the table," Mom said to Victoria.

Victoria and Ramona ran to look. "It's from Grandma and Grandpa," Victoria exclaimed.

"It must be for your birthday tomorrow," Ramona guessed.

"Can I open it now, Mom? Please, please, please, please?"

"Okay," Mom said. "But your other gifts have to wait." Ramona helped Victoria pry open the box. They lifted out another box wrapped in birthday paper. Victoria ripped the wrapping off and opened it.

"It's a new Bible with my name in it!" Victoria said. "And another book."

"That's a daily devotional book, Victoria," Mom said. "It has stories that help you study the Bible."

Ramona looked confused. "Is it important to study the Bible? I don't even have one."

READ

Psalm 119:97-99. The psalm writer can help us love God's Word by explaining why he valued it.

THINK

- Why do you think the psalm writer thought about God's commands so much?
- How have the verses you've discussed in this devotional book made you wiser or given you understanding?
- Finish the story, showing how the verses could affect Victoria and Ramona. Then read the possible ending at the back of the book.

DO

- Write how many times a week you have devotions with God.
- Pick one thing you need to improve: how often you read the Bible; how much you love the Bible; or how much you act on the wisdom you find in the Bible. With your family, discuss how you could improve.

PRAY

Thank God for giving you the wisdom written in the Bible. Ask him to help you love the Bible.

MEMORIZE

I have more insight than my teachers, for I am always thinking of your laws. Psalm 119:99

WHAT'S THE POINT?

The girls were beginning to understand that we can love the Bible as God helps us become wise through it. *BA*

NOVEMBER 18
I Didn't Steal Anything

"Hey, Owen, how about helping me put up this new picture?" Dad called. Owen liked helping Dad. He went to get a hammer and nail.

"Okay, hold the picture up so I can decide how high it should go," said Mr. Moran. Owen picked up the picture. "We're hanging up the Ten Commandments?" he asked.

"Yes, your mom and I thought it would be a good reminder," Mr. Moran said. "Okay, here's where to put the nail." Owen pounded it partway in.

"Perfect," Dad said. "You know, speaking of a reminder, the eighth commandment reminds me of something I just heard about between you and your sister."

Owen read the eighth commandment: "You must not steal." He thought it over. "I didn't steal anything from Kendall," he said.

READ
Deuteronomy 6:20-25. God wants parents to teach their kids about the Bible.

THINK
- Name some ways your mom or dad has taught you about God or other truths.
- What is something that you are confused about that you could ask your mom or dad about? Parents like to be helpful.
- Make up an ending for the story, showing how Owen could understand the verses. Then read the possible ending at the back of the book.

DO
- Ask your mom or dad one thing he or she is trying to teach you that you should pay more attention to. Tell your mom or dad how you will try to improve. Ask your mom or dad to tell you how he or she can help you. Shake on it.

PRAY
Ask God to help you pay attention when your mom or dad tries to teach you.

MEMORIZE
We will be counted as righteous when we obey all the commands the LORD our God has given us. Deuteronomy 6:25

WHAT'S THE POINT?
Mr. Moran followed God's command to parents to teach their children what he says in his Word. God wants us to obey. *BA*

NOVEMBER 19
It Would Take a Miracle

Jay and his friend Reilly sat down at the dinner table with Jay's mom. "I'm glad you could come over, Reilly," said Mrs. Davis. "How's your dad?"

Reilly's eyes welled up with tears. "His truck got shot at," he said. "He's wounded. I hope the Army brings him home soon."

"Oh, hon, I'm really sorry," said Mrs. Davis. "Let's pray for him before we eat." She and Jay bowed their heads. "Dear God, please bring Reilly's dad home soon."

When they opened their eyes, Reilly looked sad. "I don't know if I believe in Jesus," he said. "I don't think he can really help. It would take a miracle for the Army to send Dad home."

"Jesus *does* miracles," Jay said.

READ
John 20:30-31. Jesus performed many miracles when he lived on earth. We can be glad that people wrote them down to help us believe in him today.

THINK
- What kinds of miracles did Jesus do when he lived on earth?
- Why do Jesus' miracles prove that he's the Son of God?
- Imagine an ending for this story, showing how the verses might encourage Reilly. Then read the possible ending at the back of the book.

DO
- Tell your family what Jesus' miracles help you believe about Jesus.
- Practice telling your family something Jesus has done for you. Who else could you tell? Even if it wasn't a big miracle, it might be just what someone you know needs to hear to believe in Jesus.

PRAY
Thank Jesus for three things he's done for you.

MEMORIZE
These are written so that you may continue to believe that Jesus is the Messiah, the Son of God, and that by believing in him you will have life by the power of his name. John 20:31

WHAT'S THE POINT?
Jesus' miracles helped Reilly start believing that Jesus is God and could help him and his dad. *BA*

NOVEMBER 20
Out with the Old—In with the New

Tricia and Alison were sitting together during Sunday school and working on their class projects. "Did you have fun during Christmas break?" Alison asked.

"It was great. We went to Florida to visit my grandparents," Tricia replied.

"Awesome! My family stayed here, but I got a lot of cool things for Christmas—like this new Bible. It even has pictures in it," Alison said.

Tricia picked up Alison's Bible and flipped through it. She put it down with a thud and picked up her own Bible. "I only read the New Testament," Tricia said.

Alison looked puzzled. "Why?"

"Because, silly, the Old Testament was written before Jesus came. Why read it now when you can just read the words of Jesus?" Tricia went back to painting.

READ
Colossians 3:16. This verse tells us to read the words of Jesus, as well as singing psalms, hymns, and spiritual songs.

THINK
- Why is it important to let Jesus' message fill your life?
- A psalm is a spiritual song about God. Where are the Psalms found in the Bible? Are they found in the New or the Old Testament?
- How do you know the Old Testament and the New Testament are closely connected?
- Finish the story, showing how the verse can help Tricia get interested in the whole Bible. Then read the possible ending at the back of the book.

DO
- Choose an Old Testament verse from the Scripture index in the back of this book. Memorize it. How will you put it to work in your life this week?
- Pick a psalm and sing it to the tune of a popular song.

PRAY
Thank God for giving us his words in both the Old and the New Testaments.

MEMORIZE
Let the message about Christ, in all its richness, fill your lives. Teach and counsel each other with all the wisdom he gives. Sing psalms and hymns and spiritual songs to God with thankful hearts. Colossians 3:16

WHAT'S THE POINT?
Tricia and Alison learned that God intends for us to read and learn about both the Old and New Testaments. *HP*

NOVEMBER 21
The Lighthouse Verse

Alexandra opened the back door. "Hi, Mom. I'm home!"

"Hi, hon," Mom said. "Come try this new pizza recipe with me."

"Cool!" Alexandra ran to the bathroom to wash her hands. Right above the bowl of seashells on the toilet tank and the lighthouse hand towels, she saw a new picture on the wall. A lighthouse shone on a rocky cliff, with a Bible verse printed next to it. "'He is my loving ally and my fortress,'" Alexandra read, "'my tower of safety.' Psalm 144:2."

"Mom! Why do we have a Bible verse in the bathroom?"

"Well, I thought it went really well with our lighthouse theme," Mom said, holding out a bag of shredded cheese for Alexandra to open. "And do you know what God says we should do with his Word?"

READ

Deuteronomy 11:18. God wants us to know Scripture well enough that the words and ideas become part of our everyday life. In Bible times, some Jewish people really tied Scripture to their arms and foreheads in little boxes.

THINK

- We don't tie little boxes to our heads. What are ways we can have God's Word around us and with us all the time?
- What do you think it means to commit yourself to God's Word?
- Finish the story, showing how the verse could affect Alexandra. Then read the possible ending at the back of the book.

DO

With your family, decorate a poster of any Bible verse special to you or your family. Tell each other what the verse means to you. Post it somewhere you can read it every day.

PRAY

Ask God to help you make Scripture part of your everyday life.

MEMORIZE

Commit yourselves wholeheartedly to these words of mine. Tie them to your hands and wear them on your forehead as reminders. Deuteronomy 11:18

WHAT'S THE POINT?

God knows that the more we read and talk about Scripture, the more we will remember it and do what it says. *BA*

NOVEMBER 22
The Reasons behind the Rules

"What's the next answer?" Mr. Collins asked the class. Myles answered 426. "No, not quite!" Mr. Collins replied.

Gage snickered in the third row. "Loser!" he said under his breath.

Mr. Collins heard. "Gage, I need to speak to you at recess."

When the other kids went out, Mr. Collins sat Gage down. "We've talked before about calling other kids names," he said.

"They're just words," Gage said grumpily. "They don't mean anything."

"When you call other kids names, it means something to *them*. It hurts their feelings. And besides that, what rule did you break?"

Gage sighed. "No talking out of turn."

Mr. Collins studied him. "I like you a lot, Gage. How can I get you to understand the importance of changing your behavior?"

READ
Psalm 119:33-35. The psalm writer wants to understand God's laws. God is always ready to help us when a command is hard to understand or follow.

THINK
- Why does understanding God's commands help us obey?
- Why do you think we can find joy in following God's commands?
- Finish the story, showing how the verses can make a difference in Gage's life. Then read the possible ending at the back of the book.

DO
- Which of God's commands do you have trouble understanding or following?
- Write the name of someone you trust who you will go to for help.

PRAY
Thank God for loving you so much that he will help you obey him.

MEMORIZE
Give me understanding and I will obey your instructions; I will put them into practice with all my heart. Psalm 119:34

WHAT'S THE POINT?
Understanding the rules helped Gage be more ready to follow them. God loves us enough to help us understand the reasons behind his rules. *BA*

NOVEMBER 23
Searching for Answers

Luz booted up the computer, eager to check out something the teacher said in class. "Dad, she said some plants live *half a century* before they bloom, and then they die!"

"I can see why you want to check it out. That *is* hard to believe," said Mr. Powell.

"Here it is!" Luz exclaimed after a few minutes. "The *Agave Americana* can bloom in fifteen years in Mexico, but plants growing in greenhouses farther north may take fifty years to grow big enough to bloom."

"Cool!" said Dad. "That reminds me of something *I* wanted to check out. My coworker said that God removes our sins from us as far as the east is from the west. I've never heard that before. Maybe you can check that out for me."

"Okay. Let me think how," Luz said.

READ
Acts 17:10-12. Paul told the Berean people about Jesus and how he died and came back to life for them. The Berean people searched God's Word when they weren't sure whether they could believe Paul.

THINK
- Why do you think the Bereans were eager to check out Paul's teachings?
- Why do you think they used Scripture (our Old Testament) to check out Paul's claims?
- Finish the story, showing how Luz might "search the Scriptures." Then read the possible ending at the back of the book.

DO
- Write some questions you have about God or the Christian life.
- Ask a family member to be your partner in finding the answers in God's Word.

PRAY
Talk to God about some of your questions now.

MEMORIZE
They searched the Scriptures day after day to see if Paul and Silas were teaching the truth. Acts 17:11

WHAT'S THE POINT?
You may hear many different ideas about Jesus. You may have questions about him. Checking the Bible can help you find out the truth. *SP*

NOVEMBER 24
The Flying Shoe

"I'm going to the garage to sort through boxes," Christa's mom called. "Don't fight with your brother."

Christa's little brother, Caden, stuck out his tongue at her. "Let's ignore him," her friend Jacki suggested. They continued playing their board game.

"Can I play?" Caden begged.

"You're too little. Go away!" Christa said.

Caden went away and came back with the cat. Caden dropped Snarla onto the board. "Oops," he said, as the cat scrambled to get away. Caden ran after her, laughing.

"Now our game's all messed up," Christa yelled. "You did that on purpose!" She threw her sneaker after her brother. It hit the lamp instead. *Crash!* The lamp landed on the floor in a million pieces.

"What was that?" called Mom,

"Tell her Caden did it," Jacki hissed.

READ
Psalm 119:105. We can turn to God's Word to know how we should act and what we should do.

THINK
- Imagine taking a flashlight on a hike through some dark woods. How could your life be like the path?
- How could the Bible be like a light for you?
- Make up an ending for the story, showing how Christa could look to God's Word for guidance. Then read the possible ending at the back of the book.

DO
- With your family, take turns sharing some decisions you need to make. Brainstorm what Bible verses could help you decide.

PRAY
Thank God for his Word that shows us how to live.

MEMORIZE
Your word is a lamp to guide my feet and a light for my path. Psalm 119:105

WHAT'S THE POINT?
Christa used God's Word as her guide to help her know she should tell the truth. *BA*

NOVEMBER 25
God's Word Is Alive

Tori turned to her friend Rebekah. "Oh, look! The drugstore has all of its candy on sale! Let's get some," she said as she tugged on Rebekah's coat sleeve.

"Wait!" Rebekah called. "I don't have any money."

"That's okay!" Tori called over her shoulder. "I have the change from my lunch money left."

Rebekah ran to catch up with Tori. "Aren't you supposed to give the change back to your mom? She gave you a ten dollar bill—that's gotta be a lot of change!"

"Yeah, but I'll just tell her I lost it. The candy I don't finish eating, I'll hide in my backpack. She'll never know." Tori laughed. Both girls ran inside the drugstore and bought bags of chocolate with the money Tori had.

READ
Hebrews 4:12-13. The writer of Hebrews tells us that God's Word reveals our hidden thoughts and motives and that we can't hide our actions from God.

THINK
- How is God's Word (the Bible) like a sword?
- How can God's Word affect our thoughts and attitudes when we read it?
- Finish the story, showing how Tori is affected by what she reads in God's Word. Then read the possible ending at the back of the book.

DO
- If the Bible can tell us when we have wrong thoughts and actions, what should we do when this happens?
- In a Scripture journal, write down how the Bible verses you've read and studied have made you think about and change your actions.

PRAY
Ask God to reveal your actions and thoughts that need changing.

MEMORIZE
The word of God is alive and powerful. It is sharper than the sharpest two-edged sword. Hebrews 4:12

WHAT'S THE POINT?
The Bible can reveal our hidden thoughts and motives so that we can ask forgiveness, change our actions, and obey God. *HP*

NOVEMBER 26
The Gossip Queen

Katherine got into the lunch line behind Sofia and her friends. They were laughing about what a geek Ernesto was. *Sofia's such a gossip queen,* Katherine thought. But she was happy they were including her, so she laughed too.

Suddenly ahead of them, Charles spilled his drink off his lunch tray. As he bent to pick it up, he dropped the whole tray. "What a klutz!" Sofia hooted. Katherine joined in.

Sofia turned to go to a table. "Come on, Katherine, sit with us," she said. "I want to tell everyone who I just found out Corina has a crush on. She doesn't think anyone knows."

"Okay," Katherine said. *I really shouldn't, though. They're just going to say mean things about people.*

READ
Psalm 119:9-11. Knowing what God teaches us keeps us on the right path in life.

THINK
- List all the ways the psalmist uses God's words to avoid doing wrong.
- How can you know that you have hidden some part of God's Word in your heart?
- Finish the story, showing how the verses could help Katherine. Then read the possible ending at the back of the book.

DO
- With your family, create a TV commercial that tells people how to use a Bible verse to help them live God's way.
- What is one thing you will do this week because you know what to do from God's Word?

PRAY
Ask God to help you choose *his* way when tough situations come up. Thank God for the wonderful guidebook he has given.

MEMORIZE
How can a young person stay pure? By obeying your word. Psalm 119:9

WHAT'S THE POINT?
Memorizing Scripture is a way to hide it in our hearts so that we can know how to follow God and not sin. *BA*

NOVEMBER 27
Decorating the Tree

Stephen opened a big box of Christmas ornaments. "I love decorating our tree!" he said happily.

His friend Oscar said, "Thanks for letting me help." He picked up a felt cat and hung it on the tree.

Stephen grabbed a red-and-white, glittery candy cane and hung it next to the cat. Oscar reached for a little package wrapped in tissue paper. He carefully unwrapped it and held up a miniature manger scene. "What's this?" he asked.

Stephen was surprised. "Baby Jesus and Mary and Joseph," he said, "in the stable."

"What were they doing in a stable?" Oscar asked.

Stephen did his best to explain. That night he told his grandma what had happened. "I don't think Oscar knows anything about Jesus," he said worriedly. "I know his family doesn't go to church. How can I explain more about Jesus?"

READ

Acts 17:1-4. Paul used Scripture to help the Jewish people understand about Jesus.

 THINK
- Why do you think Paul used the Bible to tell about Jesus?
- What were the results?
- Finish the story, showing how Stephen could help Oscar by using Paul's approach. Then read the possible ending at the back of the book.

DO
- With family members, find some Bible verses you could use to help someone understand about Jesus, such as John 3:16.
- Practice looking them up and explaining them.

PRAY

Thank God for speaking to us and to others through the Bible.

MEMORIZE

[Paul] used the Scriptures to reason with the people. Acts 17:2

WHAT'S THE POINT?

Stephen found the Bible to be powerful. God works through the Bible to teach people about his Son, Jesus. *BA*

NOVEMBER 28
Isn't It in the Past?

"What's that?" Abigail asked when a large envelope fell from her friend Jacqueline's backpack as she tried to stuff her homework in.

"Oh, my grandma sends me Bible stories every month. This month, she's starting to send stories about the Old Testament prophets."

Abigail looked confused. "Who?" she said, moving down the hall on her crutches.

"They were people God talked to, and then they told the people what God said."

"Well, wouldn't that be all in the past then?" asked Abigail. "Why would you want to know about them today?"

READ
2 Peter 3:1-2. All of Scripture gives us God's words. Some of the prophets warned people that God was angry with them. Some talked about how God loves us and wants us to turn to him for help and wisdom. They spoke about Jesus hundreds of years before he was born.

THINK
- How would the words of Jesus help us with right thinking?
- How would the Old Testament prophets help us with right thinking?
- Imagine an ending for this story, showing how the verses can make a difference for Jacqueline and Abigail. Then read the possible ending at the back of the book.

DO
- Look at the index of Scripture readings in this book for devotionals you have already read from the prophets: Isaiah, Jeremiah, Daniel, Micah, Zephaniah. Review them.
- Pick one thing you learned from the prophets. Tell your family how it will help you this week.

PRAY
Thank God that he continues to speak to us through all the books of the Bible.

MEMORIZE
Remember what the holy prophets said long ago and what our Lord and Savior commanded through your apostles. 2 Peter 3:2

WHAT'S THE POINT?
All of Scripture together contains God's words. God speaks to us through the prophets just as he speaks to us through Jesus. *SP*

NOVEMBER 29
Jesus Didn't Stay Little

Blake dragged the giant wooden cutout of Joseph across the front lawn. His big sister, Eva, was carrying baby Jesus.

"Can I help?" Their teenage neighbor, Yvonne, ran toward them, pulling on mittens. The kids steadied the figure of baby Jesus while Mr. Sheehan pounded stakes into the ground.

"Jesus didn't stay little," Yvonne commented, looking at the figure. "He grew up. And someday he's coming back to earth. I just saw a movie about it. It was scary."

Blake pushed up his glasses. "Jesus coming back is scary?"

"Not for people who know Jesus," Mr. Sheehan assured Blake. "The Bible doesn't tell us a lot about what it will be like. Mainly it tells us to be ready."

Blake picked up the figure of Mary. "How can we be ready?" he asked.

READ

Revelation 22:7. Jesus is talking in this verse. "Soon" to him may be a long time to us—or it may be tomorrow! He tells us one way to be ready.

THINK

- How would obeying the Bible help us be ready for Jesus' return?
- What else can you think of that would help us be ready for Jesus' return?
- Finish the story, showing how the verse can tell Blake how to be ready for Jesus' return. Then read the possible ending at the back of the book.

DO

Spend some time with Jesus. Tell him which of his commands are easy for you and which are hard. Talk to him about how you feel about obeying and disobeying. Ask for his help to obey.

PRAY

Thank Jesus that he is coming back. Ask him to help you obey the Bible while you wait.

MEMORIZE

Look, I am coming soon! Blessed are those who obey the words of prophecy written in this book. Revelation 22:7

WHAT'S THE POINT?

Blake and Eva learned that it's important to prepare now for Jesus' coming by knowing him as their Savior and obeying him. *BA*

NOVEMBER 30
Ice Fishing

Matt raced to the window for the tenth time. "Are you sure he's coming? Are you sure?"

"Your Uncle Fritz is good at keeping promises," Mom replied. "He said he'd take you ice fishing, and that's exactly what I expect him to do." Before long they heard a car coming up the driveway, honking. "Uncle Fritz!" Matt yelled. "You came!"

"I promised, didn't I?" Uncle Fritz said, giving Matt a bear hug.

In a few hours Matt was shoveling snow from the lake ice and helping Uncle Fritz drill a hole. They baited their hooks and dropped them into the hole. "Put a blanket over your head and look down the hole," suggested Uncle Fritz. Matt did—and saw fish investigating their bait.

"That is so cool!" he exclaimed as he sat back up. "I can't believe I'm here. I was so worried you wouldn't keep your promise!"

"I try to be good about keeping promises," Uncle Fritz said. "But I have to admit there's only one person who always keeps his promises."

READ
Luke 4:16-21. Jesus used Scripture to show the people that God had kept his promise of sending a Savior—Jesus himself.

THINK
- Why do you think Jesus read the Old Testament promises about himself instead of just saying, "God sent me"?
- How did Jesus keep the different promises in the Scripture he read?
- Finish the story, showing how the verses could help Matt have confidence in God's promises. Then read the possible ending at the back of the book.

DO
- What other promises do you find in the Bible?
- Decide which of these promises will encourage you the most with a situation that has bothered you. Design a bumper sticker of that promise.

PRAY
Thank God for being a promise-keeping God.

MEMORIZE
The Spirit of the LORD is upon me, for he has anointed me to bring Good News to the poor.
Luke 4:18

WHAT'S THE POINT?
The Bible contains many promises from God, and he keeps every one of them. *BA*

DECEMBER I
Family Traditions

Lynn leaned toward Amala. "These coconut cookies are really good!" she said, taking another.

"They're left over from our Diwali holiday," Amala said. "We always eat them for Diwali."

"My mom always makes fudge for Christmas," Lynn said. "And gingerbread men. We don't celebrate Diwali. I'm a Christian."

"Well, of course you are!" Amala shrugged. "It's part of your family, your country."

Lynn was startled. She'd never thought of it that way. Did she believe in Jesus only because her parents did?

READ
Revelation 3:19-20. Jesus wants to be in our lives, to know us personally.

THINK
- Jesus is not talking about an actual door or real eating. What do you think he really means?
- What choices does the person behind the door have? What does opening the door involve? (See verse 19.)
- Finish the story, showing how these verses could help Lynn make what she's learning about God more personal. Then read the possible ending at the back of the book.

DO
- With a partner, act out three kinds of knocks and what the person would say: police at the door looking for a criminal, someone selling magazines, a friend coming to visit. What do you think Jesus' knock would be like? What would he say?
- Write out Revelation 3:20, putting in your name as the person behind the door. Talk with someone about whether you've opened your life's door to Jesus.

PRAY
Thank God that he wants to enter your life.

MEMORIZE
Look! I stand at the door and knock. If you hear my voice and open the door, I will come in, and we will share a meal together as friends. Revelation 3:20

WHAT'S THE POINT?
Lynn wondered if she was a Christian just because her family was. She remembered that she needed to invite Jesus into her life personally by asking him to forgive her sins. *SG*

DECEMBER 2
Angels and Ornaments

"Sky, come here!" Skylar's friend Miranda waved at her from a shelf of glass figurines in the gift shop. Skylar picked up the Christmas ornament she planned to buy and walked over.

"Look at this angel! Isn't she beautiful?" Miranda pointed to a small lacy figure with wings, all glass with gold trim. "I'm going to buy her! I collect angels, you know. They help me think about my guardian angel. You have a guardian angel, don't you?"

Skylar wasn't sure what to say, but Miranda kept talking. She leaned close to Skylar. "Sometimes I pray to my angel," she said. "I mean, why not?"

Skylar looked down at the object in her hand: an ornament showing the baby Jesus in a manger. What should she say?

READ
Hebrews 1:1-6, 14. These verses say that Jesus is equal to God and greater than angels.

THINK
- Find things in the verses that Jesus does but angels don't do.
- What can you find in the verses about how angels compare with Jesus?
- Finish the story, showing how the verses could affect Skylar's decision about what to tell Miranda. Then read the possible ending at the back of the book.

DO
- Many people, TV shows, and movies talk more about angels than about God. Discuss some reasons why this might be.
- With your family, choose a way to worship Jesus as God's Son right now, just as the angels do.

PRAY
Thank God for speaking to us through his amazing Son, Jesus, and for angels, his servants.

MEMORIZE
The Son is far greater than the angels, just as the name God gave him is greater than their names. Hebrews 1:4

WHAT'S THE POINT?
Skylar helped her friend see how much greater Jesus is than the angels. He deserves our praise, just as the angels praise him. *SG*

DECEMBER 3
Follow the Shepherds

Tim tugged on his shepherd costume. Mrs. Donovan tied cloth around the towel on his head. It itched, and Tim scratched. *Stupid shepherd,* he thought. *I thought I was old enough this year to be Joseph. That's the important role.*

Mrs. Donovan got the kids into their places for the dress rehearsal for the Christmas pageant. "Show feelings," she said. "Look amazed. You're seeing a wonderful thing—the birth of the Savior of the world." But when she cued the shepherds, Tim couldn't make himself look excited. The other shepherds weren't doing any better.

Mrs. Donovan said, "Cut!" She came over to the shepherds. "Guys!" she said. "Do you know how important a role the real shepherds had on that first Christmas night?"

READ
Luke 2:1-20. The shepherds were ordinary people, but they were the first people God chose to tell about the birth of his Son.

THINK
- In the story, find the important things that the shepherds did.
- Why do you think the shepherds spread the word about the baby?
- Finish the story, showing how Tim's attitude and feelings could be changed by reading these verses. Then read the possible ending at the back of the book.

DO
- God has chosen you, too, to know about Jesus' birth! Choose a way to spread the good news: set up or make a manger scene for your room so you can tell friends about it when they come over; tell someone something you know about Jesus; make Christmas cards that have to do with the real meaning of Christmas; or think of another idea.

PRAY
Be like the shepherds and praise God for sending baby Jesus.

MEMORIZE
The shepherds told everyone what had happened and what the angel had said to them about this child. All who heard the shepherds' story were astonished. Luke 2:17-18

WHAT'S THE POINT?
Tim could see how important a role the shepherds had in telling others about Jesus and praising God. We can do the same today. *BA*

DECEMBER 4
The Journey of the Wise Men

Tam sat forward in her seat at the planetarium and stared at the big machine that was projecting a sky full of stars onto the curved ceiling. Her twin brothers whispered and pointed as the stars rotated overhead until the sky looked like it would have looked about the time Jesus was born.

Tam and her family were in the city watching a sky show about the star of Bethlehem. "What could the star have been that shone over the place Jesus was born?" the narrator asked. "Could it have been a comet? A gathering of planets?" Tam watched as the sky show told about each possibility.

Afterward her family ordered food from the snack bar. "I don't think the star was a comet or a planet," Tam said. "I think God created a special star just for Jesus."

"Whatever it was," said Dad, "the wise men were able to follow it to Bethlehem."

Mom said, "We don't think too often about how much time and money the wise men must have spent to make that trip to find baby Jesus." She paused. "I wonder how much effort we make to find Jesus in our Christmas celebrations these days."

READ
Matthew 2:1-8. The wise men traveled a long way to see the promised King of kings.

THINK
- Why do you think the wise men made such an effort to find baby Jesus?
- What parts of your family's Christmas celebrations focus on Jesus?
- Finish the story, showing how the verses could affect Tam's family. Then read the possible ending at the back of the book.

DO
- With your family, plan a way to make Jesus a bigger part of your Christmas celebrations this year.

PRAY
Thank God for leading the wise men—and you—to Jesus at Christmastime.

MEMORIZE
Where is the newborn king of the Jews? We saw his star as it rose, and we have come to worship him. Matthew 2:2

WHAT'S THE POINT?
The wise men made a big effort to find baby Jesus. Tam's family wanted to make an effort to focus more on Jesus during the Christmas season. *BA*

DECEMBER 5
Gifts of the Wise Men

Jayden put his finger on the shiny red ribbon to hold it while his mom tied a bow. Another gift for his cousins was finally wrapped. He put a toy truck onto a length of wrapping paper, measured how much he needed, and cut off a strip. "I sure have a ton of cousins," he said. "We're never going to get done."

"Come on, stick with it!" Mom said. "We need to get these presents boxed up and in the mail tomorrow."

Jayden tried to hold the wrapping paper in place while he taped. "I need three hands," he said. "Who ever thought of giving gifts at Christmas in the first place anyway? Isn't Christmas about baby Jesus?"

READ
Matthew 2:9-12. The wise men brought gifts to baby Jesus.

THINK
- From the verses, what can you tell about why the wise men gave Jesus gifts?
- Why did baby Jesus deserve their worship?
- Imagine an ending for this story, showing how Jayden could find the answer about gift-giving in today's verses. Then read the possible ending at the back of the book.

DO
- Choose something to give to Jesus for Christmas instead of just getting all the presents yourself: play with a younger brother or sister without complaining; buy a present for a needy child; decide to have devotions with Jesus regularly; invite a friend to church; decide to obey Jesus by obeying a parent or teacher; or come up with another idea.
- Write your choice on a piece of paper. Put it in a gift bag. Make out a gift tag from you to Jesus. Put the gift under your tree. Open it with your other gifts as a reminder to do what you thought of.

PRAY
Ask Jesus to help you do the thing you thought of for him.

MEMORIZE
They entered the house and saw the child with his mother, Mary, and they bowed down and worshiped him. Then they opened their treasure chests and gave him gifts of gold, frankincense, and myrrh. Matthew 2:11

WHAT'S THE POINT?
Jayden had a good idea: to follow the example of the wise men and give gifts to Jesus. *BA*

DECEMBER 6
Just Ordinary

"We can use lots of help for our nursing home Christmas program and party. Who wants to volunteer?" asked Bobbi, the Pioneer Clubs leader. Some kids waved their arms wildly. A girl volunteered to play a piano solo. A boy said he could juggle. Another girl knew how to make balloon animals.

"Great!" Bobbi said. "Who'd like to sing some of our club songs?" More kids raised their hands.

Morgan fidgeted. She was no star. She couldn't do anything special in a show. But she really liked older people—they reminded her of her grandmother. She raised her hand.

"Morgan, do you want to do something in the program?" Bobbi asked. Everyone looked at Morgan.

READ
Mark 1:16-20. Jesus didn't stay a baby. He grew up and began his ministry. He called ordinary people—fishermen—to be his followers (disciples).

THINK
- Why might Jesus have chosen these four men? What might he have been looking for in them besides money or power?
- How did God use Jesus' disciples to help Jesus and other people?
- Finish the story, showing how Morgan could find an encouraging idea from the passage. Then read the possible ending at the back of the book.

DO
- With family members, take turns talking about each other's strengths. Include qualities (kindness, patience) as well as skills and talents (good at reading, a talent for math).
- Talk about ordinary things you could do for Jesus this week. Choose one you will try.

PRAY
Thank God that he loves ordinary people and uses them in his work.

MEMORIZE
Jesus called out to them, "Come, follow me, and I will show you how to fish for people!"
Mark 1:17

WHAT'S THE POINT?
Morgan felt she couldn't help in the nursing home program because she didn't have a talent. She remembered that God uses ordinary people, and he could use her to simply be a friend. *SG*

DECEMBER 7
Questions

On the way to school, Nathanael and his friend Preston saw a police car in front of a house. An older woman was sobbing to a police officer, "Someone stole my baby Jesus!" An empty manger sat in the yard, next to plastic figures of Mary and Joseph.

Once they were out of earshot, Preston started to laugh. "That's really funny! Stealing baby Jesus! Why put a baby out in your front yard anyway?"

Nate didn't know what to say. He went into his house, feeling upset. It *was* weird to think about Jesus as a baby. Nate's baby brother couldn't do anything. He was helpless. *Why did Jesus have to get born as a baby?* he wondered.

As Nate walked toward his room, his dad called, "Is something wrong?"

READ
John 1:43-49. Nathanael in the Bible was full of questions about Jesus.

THINK
- How did Philip answer Nathanael's question? How can you "come and see" Jesus today?
- Did Philip or Jesus seem upset by Nathanael's questions? Explain.
- Make up an ending for the story, showing how these verses could help Nate feel comfortable with having questions. Then read the possible ending at the back of the book.

DO
- Write some things you wonder about God or Jesus.
- Write who you will ask your questions to.

PRAY
Ask God your questions. He cares about what bothers you! Ask for his help to find answers.

MEMORIZE
Nathanael exclaimed, "Rabbi, you are the Son of God—the King of Israel!" John 1:49

WHAT'S THE POINT?
Nate learned that Jesus welcomes our questions. We can find someone we trust to ask about what we don't understand. *BA*

DECEMBER 8
Sticky Job

Jorge chewed the last bite of his pizza. He was not thrilled to be stuck here baby-sitting while his mom and aunt were next door. His two-year-old cousin, Javier, was also eating pizza—though more seemed to be outside him than inside. Sauce covered his hands and cheeks. The toddler grinned at him.

"Javi, you are a mess!" Jorge said irritably. He got up to find a paper towel. Then the phone rang. He took a message.

When Jorge looked back at the table, Javier was gone! He heard the TV in the other room—and found the toddler pushing the buttons with sticky hands. Pizza sauce was everywhere.

"What's the matter with you?" Jorge yelled. "You'll wreck the TV!" He pulled Javi roughly back to the kitchen and plunked him in a chair.

Javi started to cry, but Jorge didn't care. He wet a paper towel at the sink.

READ
Mark 10:13-16. Jesus loved the little children.

THINK
- The disciples tried to keep the children away from Jesus. What reasons might they have had?
- Think of some words to show how Jesus treated the children.
- Finish the story, showing how Jorge could follow Jesus' example. Then read the possible ending at the back of the book.

DO
- Is it easy or hard for you to be with younger children? Ask family members what helps them to be kind and loving to little kids.
- Spend time with a little kid this week, showing care as Jesus would. If you don't know a little kid, treat a big kid kindly. Jesus loves big kids, too!

PRAY
Ask God to give you patience and love when dealing with younger children.

MEMORIZE
Let the children come to me. Don't stop them! For the Kingdom of God belongs to those who are like these children. Mark 10:14

WHAT'S THE POINT?
Jorge felt angry when his cousin made a mess, but he realized he could love Javier as Jesus would. *SG*

DECEMBER 9
Petting a Llama

Isaac looked forward to this event every December. The church set up a "living nativity" outdoors with wooden benches, straw, and a manger. Church members posed as Mary, Joseph, shepherds, and wise men—with a real baby as Jesus. The display also featured live animals—sheep, a cow or donkey, and sometimes a llama or camel! Lots of visitors came.

Isaac was petting the donkey when he spotted Devin at the edge of the parking lot. He was sitting on his bike looking at the manger. Isaac was surprised that he'd be interested. Devin was known for using bad language, and he thought it was fun to beat someone up.

Isaac's friend Keith was staring at Devin. "What is *he* doing here?" Keith asked loudly.

READ
Mark 2:13-14. Jesus invites someone else to be his helper (disciple).

THINK
- Tax collectors were known for being greedy, dishonest, and unpopular. What kinds of kids or grown-ups are known for bad behavior today?
- Why do you think Jesus asked this tax collector to be his follower anyway?
- Finish the story, showing how Isaac could follow Jesus' example. Then read the possible ending at the back of the book.

DO
- Think of someone you know who seems far from God. Draw a face to show how you feel about this person. Draw a face to show how God feels about them.
- You might be the one to show God's love to this person. Choose a way to reach out: smile and say hi; invite him or her to join a game; share cookies from your lunch; invite him or her to a special club or church event; or something else.

PRAY
Ask for the ability to care about people who seem far from God.

MEMORIZE
"Follow me and be my disciple," Jesus said to him. So Levi got up and followed him.
Mark 2:14

WHAT'S THE POINT?
Isaac remembered God's love for all people and welcomed Devin. *SG*

DECEMBER 10
She's a Cool Kid

As Robin rounded the corner by her school, the last kids were streaming from the playground into the building to start the day. She walked faster. Only one other girl was still outside now, an older girl, one of the cool kids. Robin was too shy to talk to her.

As the older girl started up the steps, her foot slipped. She landed on her knee on the concrete and fell. Robin saw her start to cry, holding her knee.

Robin hesitated. *Should I help? Should I get a teacher? But she's one of the most popular kids in school. Isn't she too cool to need my help?*

Confused, Robin walked by the girl and went inside.

READ
Matthew 14:13-14. Jesus felt concern and love for the people following him. *Compassion* means feeling sorry about someone else's problem and wanting to help.

THINK
- Imagine you're Jesus in the boat, and you see the crowd ahead on the shore. What choices do you have?
- Why did Jesus help the people?
- Finish the story, showing how Robin could find an example in these verses. Then read the possible ending at the back of the book.

DO
- Rate how often you *feel* compassion (L=a lot, S=sometimes, R=rarely). Now rate how often you take time to *help*.
- Make a mini poster with the title "Compassion." Write or draw ways you will try to show compassion this week.

PRAY
Ask God to help you be willing to care for others.

MEMORIZE
Jesus saw the huge crowd as he stepped from the boat, and he had compassion on them and healed their sick. Matthew 14:14

WHAT'S THE POINT?
Robin almost didn't help even though she cared about the girl. Thinking about Jesus changed her mind. *BA*

DECEMBER 11
Green Beans and Spaghetti

"Green beans here, spaghetti there," Asher muttered to himself as he ran around the church gym, sorting donations. Every December, needy families came for a free dinner and program about Jesus. Everyone received a bag of food and gifts to take home. Asher always worked at the big event. His mom was the director.

"Can you bring that in for me, Asher? It's heavy!" Mrs. Prachet pointed to a case of canned pineapple by the door. "I'm worried. More and more people keep signing up! I don't know how we'll get enough food and gifts for them all."

Asher frowned as he carried the heavy box. How much could one kid do? This was a big problem!

READ
John 6:1-14. Jesus fed a huge crowd in an amazing way.

THINK
- How much difference do you think the boy thought he could make?
- What does this story show about Jesus' power? What does it show about his love?
- Finish the story, showing how Asher could find encouragement in this passage. Then read the possible ending at the back of the book.

DO
- Talk to a parent or church leader about how you can get involved in something God is doing. You can make a difference! Ideas: food or toy drive, missions project, nursing home visit, or sponsoring a needy child.

PRAY
Ask God to give you a willing spirit and a creative mind when it comes to helping others.

MEMORIZE
Jesus took the loaves, gave thanks to God, and distributed them to the people. Afterward he did the same with the fish. And they all ate as much as they wanted. John 6:11

WHAT'S THE POINT?
Asher wasn't sure a kid could make a difference. But he got involved in what God was doing, and God worked through him. *SG*

DECEMBER 12
Wind Storm

Tanner huddled in the van with his two friends, staring out at the campground in amazement. The van swayed in the wind. Rain slashed against the windows so hard that they could barely see. A falling branch hit the roof with a *thunk*.

Tanner's dad opened the door and jumped inside. "Wow, that storm came on fast!" he gasped. "The wind is really strong! If you guys are okay here, I'll stay in the camper with the other kids."

The boys nodded, and he darted out again. A few minutes later, they heard a large crack and crash in the distance.

"That's a tree falling!" one boy gasped. "What if one falls on us?"

"Don't say that—it's bad luck!" said the other.

Fear squeezed Tanner. He had to do something.

READ
Matthew 14:22-33. Jesus shows his power over a storm.

THINK
- Jesus caught up with his disciples by walking on water. What do you think he wanted to show them by doing that?
- What would you want to imitate about Peter? What *wouldn't* you want to imitate about Peter?
- Finish the story, showing how Tanner could learn something from the passage. Then read the possible ending at the back of the book.

DO
- With your family, discuss how often you pray during storms, earthquakes, or other natural events. What happens when you pray?
- Draw something to stand for a type of storm or something else you're afraid of. Draw a big cross over it to show that Jesus is stronger than that scary thing. Thank Jesus for his power.

PRAY
Ask Jesus to help you trust his power and love when you're scared of storms or other dangers.

MEMORIZE
When they climbed back into the boat, the wind stopped. Then the disciples worshiped him. "You really are the Son of God!" they exclaimed. Matthew 14:32-33

WHAT'S THE POINT?
Tanner felt afraid in the storm. But when he remembered Jesus' power, he was able to pray and comfort others. When we're afraid, we can imitate Peter's trust in Jesus and readiness to ask Jesus for help. *SG*

DECEMBER 13
Learning English

"Class, this is Melaine," Ms. Monroe said, putting her arm around a thin girl in a flowered dress. "She's just arrived from Congo in Africa, and she doesn't speak English. I know you'll all welcome her. Carly, I'm having Melaine sit by you."

Carly smiled, and Melaine smiled back, her dark eyes sparkling. The kids soon discovered they could communicate by acting out or pointing. A special tutor came to help Melaine, who learned more English every day.

Once Carly invited Melaine over after school to play. "Mom," she said later, "let's invite Melaine to church too!"

Her mom frowned. "It might be hard for her to understand. I wish someone knew her language."

Carly went to her room, discouraged. *Oh well, Melaine is learning English fast. Maybe we can just wait.*

READ
Mark 7:31-37. Jesus meets the deaf man who could hardly speak.

THINK
- Imagine the deaf man's friends bringing him to Jesus. How might they have explained things to the man? How might he have felt?
- What can you tell about how the man and the others felt about Jesus for reaching out?
- Make up an ending for the story, showing how the verses could encourage Carly. Then read the possible ending at the back of the book.

DO
- With your family, list types of people at school, home, or church who might have trouble understanding what you are saying.
- Plan a way to help others understand (such as learning some words in sign language or another language).

PRAY
Ask God to help you reach out to those who have trouble understanding.

MEMORIZE
Everything he does is wonderful. He even makes the deaf to hear and gives speech to those who cannot speak. Mark 7:37

WHAT'S THE POINT?
Carly followed Jesus' example of reaching out to someone who had trouble speaking and understanding. *SG*

DECEMBER 14
Christmas Angel

Kaylee frowned at the mirror. "Mom, the sleeves are still too long!" she grumbled, tugging at the white cloth of her robe.

"What about the wings?" her mom asked patiently.

Kaylee squinted at the shimmering fabric stretched across a wire frame. "They're okay, I guess," she muttered.

Her mom bit her lip. "Why don't you go work on your lines while I adjust the sleeves?" she suggested.

Kaylee slipped out of the costume, hurried to her room, and picked up the script. She wanted her lines in the Christmas play to be just right. She would look at the shepherds and say, "Fear not, for I bring you—"

"Kaylee?" her mother called down the hall.

"Now what!" Kaylee snapped.

READ

Luke 10:38-42. Jesus visited the home of Mary and Martha, who responded to him in different ways.

THINK

- What do you think Martha was doing?
- Why do you think Jesus said that Mary made a better choice? Didn't the chores need to be done?
- Finish the story, showing how Kaylee could learn something from Jesus' teaching in the passage. Then read the possible ending at the back of the book.

DO

- Draw a clock with numbers. Write some things on it that keep you busy during the day.
- Choose some of these ways that you will be more like Mary. Add them to the clock: pray; read my Bible; sing a praise song to Jesus; listen in Sunday school; listen in church; or another idea.

PRAY

Ask God to remind you that loving him is most important.

MEMORIZE

My dear Martha, you are worried and upset over all these details! There is only one thing worth being concerned about. Mary has discovered it, and it will not be taken away from her. Luke 10:41-42

WHAT'S THE POINT?

Kaylee focused on her part in the play and got crabby. Then she realized that her relationships and the play's message were more important, and she changed her attitude. *SG*

DECEMBER 15
Grandpa's in Heaven

Daisy barely heard the phone ring as she combed her hair for school. But soon her mother appeared at the doorway. Her eyes were moist.

"That was Grandma," she explained. "Grandpa died this morning."

Daisy froze. Grandpa had been very sick, but it was hard to believe he was gone—gone forever! She felt as if she'd been punched in the stomach.

"If you don't want to go to school until later, that's all right," her mom continued.

"No, I'm fine," Daisy muttered. She slipped her jacket on, picked up her backpack, and walked through the snow to the school bus stop. *I'm a Christian, and I know Grandpa's in heaven now. I'll see him again someday, so I shouldn't be sad.*

Her friend Catherine was waiting. "What's the matter?" she asked.

"I just found out my grandpa died," Daisy said, "but that's okay."

Catherine stared. "It's okay? Are you crazy?"

READ
John 11:5-6, 11-13, 32-44. Jesus was very upset at his friend Lazarus's death. He cried at Lazarus's tomb.

THINK
- Why do you think Jesus cried, even though he knew he would bring Lazarus back to life?
- How might knowing verse 35 help you when you feel sad?
- Finish the story, showing how Daisy could learn from Jesus' example in the passage. Then read the possible ending at the back of the book.

DO
- Tell your family what helps you most when you feel sad or hurt. What could they do for you? Hug you? Let you cry? Pray with you?
- The next time you're sad, think of Jesus crying with you. Think how much he loves you—just as he loved Lazarus.

PRAY
Thank God that he loves you and cares about your hurts and sadness.

MEMORIZE
Jesus wept. The people who were standing nearby said, "See how much he loved him!" John 11:35-36

WHAT'S THE POINT?
Daisy thought she shouldn't be sad about her grandpa's death. Then she remembered that Jesus wept. *SG*

DECEMBER 16
Just a Nice Guy?

"Touchdown!" the TV announcer shouted as the university fans screamed wildly. Dillon and his friend Kurt jumped up from Dillon's couch and slapped hands.

"I'd love to be at a game in that stadium," Dillon said.

"My uncle's a big shot at the university," Kurt said. "He could get us tickets. Wanna go next Saturday?"

Dillon's mom overheard. "Remember the annual church carol sing is this Saturday, Dillon," she said.

When she'd left, Kurt rolled his eyes. "Church? Does that mean you believe in Jesus?"

"Well, yeah," said Dillon.

"My uncle at the university says there *is* no God. Jesus was just a nice guy, that's all." Dillon scowled. "Jesus *is* God—the Bible says so."

"What*ever*. Just chill, okay?" Kurt said. "Let's go play basketball."

READ
John 10:24-33. In these verses, Jesus was talking to the religious leaders who didn't believe in him.

THINK
- Who did Jesus claim to be? What did he claim to do for his followers?
- What did Jesus risk by telling people he was God?
- Imagine an ending for this story, showing how Dillon could learn from the passage. Then read the possible ending at the back of the book.

DO
- With your family, set up a pretend courtroom with a judge and jury. Pretend to be a detective giving evidence. Tell what proves Jesus is God.
- Tell someone what difference it makes to you that Jesus is God.

PRAY
Tell Jesus one reason you are glad he is God.

MEMORIZE
The Father and I are one. John 10:30

WHAT'S THE POINT?
Dillon realized it was worth it to stand up for the fact that Jesus is God. *SG*

DECEMBER 17
In the Tree House

After church, Angelo felt bored. It felt like a long wait before the neighborhood sledding party that night. And what if it started raining and melted the snow? The forecast said the rain could start in the evening.

"I'm going outside, Mom!" Angelo climbed up to the tree house and sat staring at the clouds. *Please make the rain wait, God.*

He leaned back with his hands behind his head. He'd already studied for his math test. *I hope I remember everything.* Then he thought of his friend Mac. *I wonder if he's still going to be mad at me when I see him at school.*

Angelo pulled his knit cap over his face and chewed on it, lost in thought. *I could talk to you about this stuff, couldn't I, Jesus?* he realized.

READ
Mark 1:35. Jesus took time to pray.

THINK
- Jesus was God's Son, but he was also human. Why might he want to talk to God?
- What might be good about being alone to pray?
- Finish the story, showing how the verse could make a difference for Angelo. Then read the possible ending at the back of the book.

DO
- Think of people you talk to often. List the kinds of things you talk about.
- Find a place to talk with God alone. Look at your list. Talk to God about some of the same things you talk about to your friends. He's your most special friend, and he loves you!

PRAY
Ask God to help you talk to him more often.

MEMORIZE
Before daybreak the next morning, Jesus got up and went out to an isolated place to pray.
Mark 1:35

WHAT'S THE POINT?
Angelo learned that even Jesus needed time alone with God. Angelo found out that God wants to hear anything that's on our minds. *BA*

DECEMBER 18
Danger in the Street

"All done with your bath, Corky!" Denzel gave the towel a final rub across his dog's wet fur. Then he pulled out a dog biscuit. "Good boy!" Corky's rough tongue slurped the treat out of Denzel's hand. Then the dog bounded happily across the yard.

Denzel emptied the pan of soapy water onto the driveway. Then he grabbed an old tennis ball. "Here, boy! Running will dry you off!" He threw the ball high into the air. Corky watched carefully and then caught it after the first bounce. He ran over to Denzel and dropped it into his hand.

Denzel reared back and threw again. This time the ball headed for the street. Just as Corky raced after it, a car came around the curve.

READ
John 10:1-5, 11-15. Jesus cares for us lovingly, as a good shepherd takes care of sheep.

THINK
- List some things that a good shepherd does for the sheep.
- What are things Jesus does for us?
- Finish the story, showing how Denzel could connect his experiences with these verses. Then read the possible ending at the back of the book.

DO
- Help take good care of an animal this week (or tell how you would do it). Tell someone how this compares to Jesus caring for you.
- Talk to God about a way you're glad he takes care of you. Thank him for his care.

PRAY
Thank Jesus for loving you and giving his life for you.

MEMORIZE
I am the good shepherd. The good shepherd sacrifices his life for the sheep. John 10:11

WHAT'S THE POINT?
Denzel saw his dog in danger and tried to save him. Jesus, the Good Shepherd, loves us even more. *SG*

DECEMBER 19
Cookie Thief

"What are you doing, Ashton?" his mom called from the living room.

"Nothing!" Ashton replied. He stuck six cookies in his pocket, quietly closed the kitchen cupboard, and headed to his room. There he munched the cookies and carefully hid the crumbs in a tissue.

Ashton knew he ate too much junk food. He was getting heavy like his dad. He tried to eat less, but it was hard! Besides, it wasn't fair. His best friend ate anything he wanted and stayed skinny.

What's the use? a voice inside seemed to say. *You'll always be fat, so you might as well give up.*

"Ashton, want a snack?" his dad called from the kitchen.

READ
Mark 10:46-52. The blind man could have gotten discouraged and given up, but he kept calling for Jesus.

THINK
- Pretend you're there with Bartimaeus. Why did he keep shouting even louder for Jesus when everyone told him to be quiet?
- What happened when he stuck with it instead of giving up?
- Finish the story, showing how Ashton could learn from this passage. Then read the possible ending at the back of the book.

DO
- Think about a bad habit or sin you're battling. Are you tempted to give up? Write the name of someone you could ask for help.
- Ask someone to pray with you. Mark a calendar to remind yourself to pray about your problem every day this week.

PRAY
Ask God for strength and help in battling your problem.

MEMORIZE
I will keep on hoping for your help; I will praise you more and more. Psalm 71:14

WHAT'S THE POINT?
Ashton felt like giving up on his problem. The story of the blind man who kept calling out to Jesus helped him decide to keep trying. *SG*

DECEMBER 20
Frozen Waterfall

Angela gazed up at the tall pines as her Pioneer Clubs group followed the park ranger down the trail. A light snow was falling. A stream bubbled beside the path, with ice at the edges. "Peaceful, isn't it?" the ranger said. Angela nodded.

When they rounded the next bend, Angela stopped in her tracks. A frozen waterfall gleamed in the sunlight. Hundreds of bluish-white icicles looked like frosting on a cake. She heard water running underneath the ice. Angela stared, awestruck.

As the other kids exclaimed over the waterfall, the ranger smiled. "Isn't nature beautiful?" he said. "Nature is my church, my way to God."

Angela wrinkled her brow. *That's not right,* she thought. "Do you want to hear my way to God?" she asked.

READ
John 14:6. Jesus says he is the only way to God.

THINK
- How do we come to God "through" Jesus?
- Do you think most people today agree with this verse? Why or why not?
- Make up an ending for the story, showing how the verse can help Angela find the right words to say. Then read the possible ending at the back of the book.

DO
- Role-play answering someone who says there are many ways to know God.
- Ask a grown-up to show you what a one-way street sign looks like. Make one to hang in your room, pointing up as if to God.
- If you have not asked Jesus to forgive you for the wrong things you do and asked him to be your Savior, find a Christian adult to talk to about it. If you have, practice explaining how you would tell someone that Jesus is the only way to God.

PRAY
Thank God that he provided the way to know him through Jesus.

MEMORIZE
I am the way, the truth, and the life. No one can come to the Father except through me.
John 14:6

WHAT'S THE POINT?
Angela knew that nature wouldn't get the ranger to God. We need to rely on Jesus, who died and came back to life to make the way to God for us. *BA*

DECEMBER 21
She Looks like a Chipmunk

Jenny peered up at the bulletin board and then down at the printed sheet in her hand. The display of class baby pictures had been up all week—without name labels. Now this sheet gave the answers. It was fun to see how everyone had looked as a baby.

Then she heard Mira's voice. "No wonder I didn't recognize Jenny!" she whispered loudly. "When she was little, she didn't have those huge front teeth. Now she looks like a chipmunk!" Another girl giggled.

Jenny's eyes filled with angry tears. *I know I need braces—but that's mean!* she thought. Just then the bell rang. As the rest of the class filed out, Jenny stayed by the board. She reached for her cell phone and started a text message.

"I hate Mira," she typed.

READ
Luke 23:18-25, 32-34. Even with all the wonderful things Jesus did for the people, the religious leaders hated him. Finally they got him sentenced to death on a cross.

THINK
- What wrong things did the people do, think, and feel about Jesus?
- Jesus prayed that God would forgive them. Why would he pray that after what they had done to him?
- Finish the story, showing how Jenny could follow the example of Jesus in these verses. Then read the possible ending at the back of the book.

DO
- Think of someone who's wronged you. Have you considered forgiving the person? Why or why not?
- Find or draw pictures of people to pray for—including someone who's wronged you. Ask God to help you forgive.

PRAY
Share your hurts with God and ask for help in forgiving.

MEMORIZE
Father, forgive them, for they don't know what they are doing. Luke 23:34

WHAT'S THE POINT?
After Mira's mean comment, Jenny wanted to lash back. When she remembered that Jesus forgave his enemies, she was willing to take a first step toward forgiving. *SG*

DECEMBER 22
Snowball Fight

"Ow!" A snowball hit Mckenna on the cheek, hard. Her eyes blurred with anger, and without stopping to think, she hauled off and punched the thrower. When she looked down, her mitten was stained with blood from the other girl's nose.

Her neighbor Carrie ran over and glared at Mckenna. "What's your problem? This was just a snowball fight!" She grabbed the injured girl's arm and pulled her away. "We don't want to be around this crazy maniac! Come on, let's go to my house."

After they left, Mckenna stood there, dazed. She'd done it again! She'd lived in this neighborhood only one week, and she'd already lost her temper. *What's the use?* she thought. *I keep messing up. No one likes me. Maybe I should run away.*

READ
Isaiah 53:5-6. This passage tells about a Savior, Jesus, who took the punishment we deserve.

THINK
- According to the verses, how many people in the world are perfect? Explain. Are you perfect?
- Why do you think Jesus suffered so much for us?
- Imagine an ending for this story, showing how Mckenna could be helped by this passage. Then read the possible ending at the back of the book.

DO
- Get out crayons or markers and choose the colors that represent disappointment or anger to you.
- On a piece of paper, write, "Jesus loves me and forgives me even though I . . ." Underneath, list bad things that you've done. Thank Jesus for his love, and then tear the paper into tiny pieces. If you are his child, he takes your sins away.

PRAY
Thank God for sending Jesus to take your punishment. Ask him to help you remember his love and forgiveness when you sin.

MEMORIZE
He was pierced for our rebellion, crushed for our sins. He was beaten so we could be whole. He was whipped so we could be healed. Isaiah 53:5

WHAT'S THE POINT?
Mckenna felt like giving up on herself until she remembered Jesus' love and forgiveness. Jesus doesn't give up on us. *SG*

DECEMBER 23
Lost in the City

Micah, his parents, and his big brother, Rob, were in the city seeing the Christmas lights. Streets glittered with white lights, silver decorations, and fabulous displays. Micah was overwhelmed at the crowds. He wondered how God could keep track of so many people. He was admiring a huge model train layout when he realized the rest of his family was gone.

"Dad!" he yelled, but his voice sounded small in the noisy crowd. *God, help me!* he prayed.

It felt like forever before he heard, "Micah! Where are you?" It was his dad!

"By the toy store!" Micah yelled back.

When his dad reached him, they hugged. "It sure was good to hear you calling my name!" Micah exclaimed.

READ

John 20:11-18. The most exciting part of Jesus' story is that God brought him back to life. When Mary went to the tomb she was in despair. But Jesus called her name.

THINK

- ▶ Why was Mary upset when she went to the tomb?
- ▶ What changed when Jesus called her name? How did she feel then?
- ▶ Finish the story, showing how Micah could find encouragement in these verses. Then read the possible ending at the back of the book.

DO

- ▸ Is it easy or hard to believe that Jesus knows *you* personally and loves you? Explain.
- ▸ Make and decorate a name sign for your room. Remember that Jesus knows your name and loves you!

PRAY

Praise God for creating billions of people—and caring for each of you as though you were the only one.

MEMORIZE

I have called you by name; you are mine. Isaiah 43:1

WHAT'S THE POINT?

Micah realized that even though Jesus made billions of people, he knows each of us by name. *SG*

DECEMBER 24
Eyewitness Report

Michaela stood under the basket on the playground. Her friend Jessie stood at the free throw line. Jessie dribbled the ball twice and shot. The ball bounced off the rim, and Michaela rebounded it.

Jessie dribbled a few more times. "That movie we watched about world religions today was interesting, wasn't it?" She shot and missed again. "Jesus and Buddha and Muhammad all sound like good people. I don't know about Jesus coming back to life after dying, though, like the Christians say. That's hard to believe!"

Michaela was startled. She'd always believed Jesus came back to life.

"Your turn!" Jessie said. Michaela stepped to the free throw line, still thinking.

READ
Luke 24:36-43. After Jesus died on the cross, something amazing happened to Jesus' disciples.

THINK
- What proofs did Jesus give that he was really alive again?
- Imagine you're a disciple. How do you think you were feeling at the beginning of this story? How might you feel differently by verse 43? Why?
- Finish the story, showing how the verses could help Michaela think of something to tell Jessie. Then read the possible ending at the back of the book.

DO
- Later in the disciples' lives, they preached about Jesus bravely and risked prison and death. Most were killed for their beliefs. Do their actions seem to show that Jesus' resurrection (coming back to life) was real? Explain.
- With your family, set up a "courtroom" with a witness stand, judge, and jury. Take turns being the witnesses and giving "evidence" that proves Jesus came back to life. Use things you've learned in these devotionals or other things you know.

PRAY
Ask God for confidence in believing Jesus came back to life—for you!

MEMORIZE
Look at my hands. Look at my feet. You can see that it's really me. Touch me and make sure that I am not a ghost, because ghosts don't have bodies, as you see that I do. Luke 24:39

WHAT'S THE POINT?
Michaela's friend had trouble believing that Jesus came back to life. Michaela remembered the disciples' eyewitness report. *SG*

DECEMBER 25
Human like Us

The Christmas presents were unwrapped, and Derek felt stuffed after a huge ham dinner. First he figured out how to work his new camera. Then he played with his one-year-old brother, Keshawn. Derek showed Keshawn how to hammer plastic nails into his new toy workbench. "Hammer," he said. "Hammer."

"Ham!" said Keshawn.

Before long, Dad lit a candle and called everyone for family devotions. "Today we celebrate Jesus becoming human like us!" he said. He read Hebrews 2:14-15. "Since *we* are human, Jesus became human," Dad explained. "He was all human and all God at the same time."

"Why did he have to become human just because we are?" Derek wanted to know.

READ
Hebrews 2:14-15. Jesus became a human being in order to save us.

THINK
- Why did Jesus become human?
- Why don't we have to be afraid of death when we believe in Jesus?
- Finish the story, showing how the verses could provide an answer for Derek. Then read the possible ending at the back of the book.

DO
- Here's a prayer to pray if you want Jesus to come into your life and give you life forever: *Dear Jesus, thank you for being born as a baby for me. Thank you for dying for me. Please forgive my sins. Please give me a fresh start and life forever someday with you. Thank you! Amen.*
- Ask permission to hold a candle. Tell Jesus how you feel about his becoming human for you.

PRAY
Thank Jesus for becoming human to save us from our sins.

MEMORIZE
Because God's children are human beings—made of flesh and blood—the Son also became flesh and blood. Hebrews 2:14

WHAT'S THE POINT?
Jesus became human so that he could die and come back to life for us. He promises us life forever when we believe in him. *BA*

DECEMBER 26
Winter Stars

The night was crisp and cold. Dad led the way to the frozen pond out back. Avery and her younger brother, Charlie, played hockey while Mom and Dad skated. Then they all played crack the whip.

Avery looked up at the sky glowing with stars. She lay down in a snowbank and stared. Mom joined her.

"The Milky Way's so bright," Avery said. "There's Cassiopeia!" She pointed at a constellation.

"There's Taurus the Bull," said Mom, pointing at another group of stars.

"What if the stars got all scrambled around tomorrow night?" Avery said. "Like scrambled eggs. We wouldn't be able to find any of the same constellations. We'd have to make up new ones."

"That's a fun idea," Mom said. "But it's not going to happen."

"Who says?" asked Avery.

READ
Colossians 1:16-17. Jesus existed before Creation. He was with God, and he is God.

THINK
- What was Jesus doing during the Creation?
- What do you think it means that Jesus holds things together now? What and who does he hold together?
- Make up an ending for the story, showing how the verses could give Avery confidence in the patterns of God's creation. Then read the possible ending at the back of the book.

DO
- Find a windup toy and make it go. How is this like what Jesus did with creation (including us)? How is it different?
- Look out your window at the weather, plants, and animals. Thank Jesus for continuing to take care of his world—and you.

PRAY
Praise Jesus that he didn't leave his creation alone but still takes care of us.

MEMORIZE
He existed before anything else, and he holds all creation together. Colossians 1:17

WHAT'S THE POINT?
The Bible says Jesus made everything and still takes care of everything he made. *BA*

DECEMBER 27
Over and Over

Ashlyn huddled with the other kids in the cool night air and gazed at the campfire crackling at the bottom of the hill.

"If you'd like to ask Jesus to forgive your sins and come into your life, you can do it right now," a retreat leader was saying. Some of the kids were standing up and walking to the other leaders below.

Ashlyn squirmed uncomfortably. She'd gone forward during a retreat last year to ask Jesus to save her. But she wondered if that prayer had worked. She was still having problems getting along with her sister.

The girl next to Ashlyn stood and started walking down the hill.

READ
Romans 10:13. Jesus is the one who saves us.

THINK
- What does it mean to call on the name of the Lord?
- What does it mean to be saved?
- Finish the story, showing how Ashlyn could depend on what Jesus has done rather than on what she's done. Then read the possible ending at the back of the book.

DO
- With your family, create a TV commercial. Compare something that needs to be done over and over (brushing teeth, washing dishes, making the bed) with asking Jesus to come into your life.
- If you've thought you need to ask Jesus to save you over and over, ask him to help you trust his promise to save you the first time. Talk to a Christian adult you trust too.

PRAY
Thank God for promising to save you when you ask.

MEMORIZE
Everyone who calls on the name of the LORD will be saved. Romans 10:13

WHAT'S THE POINT?
When Ashlyn wondered if she needed to be saved again, her club leader showed her she could trust Jesus to save her the first time. *SG*

DECEMBER 28
Come On, Live a Little

Brendan rode his bike down the country road with Clark. The cool breeze rustled through the orange groves and felt good on his face.

"Let's go into town," Brendan suggested. "I have to get a present for my mom's birthday, and then we could get ice cream."

"I don't have any money," Clark objected. "I was thinking we could get some oranges from the Witte place."

"I thought you didn't have any money."

Clark turned with a grin. "Who said anything about *buying* the oranges? Come on!"

Instead, Brendan slammed on the brakes. Clark whirled his bike around, irritated. "What's so bad about grabbing a few oranges? Come on, live a little!"

READ
1 John 5:11-12. God gives us new life because Jesus died for us on the cross and came back to life.

THINK
- When does life forever start for people who have asked Jesus to be their Savior? Explain.
- How do you feel about the idea of a new life starting *now*?
- Imagine an ending for this story, showing how the verses could help Brendan stick up for what's right. Then read the possible ending at the back of the book.

DO
- Imagine that God wrapped his gift to you (verse 11) and attached a tag. What might the tag say about what the gift is and when to open it?
- Wrap a small gift box. Attach a tag with your name. Write, "Life forever from God! Open right away!" Display the box.

PRAY
Ask God to help you enjoy his special gift of life to you *now*.

MEMORIZE
This is what God has testified: He has given us eternal life, and this life is in his Son.
1 John 5:11

WHAT'S THE POINT?
Clark wanted to steal just for the thrill, but Brendan realized that enjoying life in Jesus was better. *SG*

DECEMBER 29
The Missing Sled

Edward and his friend Tiffany raced each other down the neighborhood hill on their new blue sleds. "That's really funny—both of you getting the exact same sleds for Christmas," Smitty said, looking on. "How are you going to tell them apart?"

"I guess we can mark them or something," Edward said.

"I'm getting cold," Tiffany said. "Want to come to my house for hot chocolate?" The boys agreed. They left the sleds and waded through the deep snow to the row of nearby houses.

But when they went back, there was only one blue sled; one must have been stolen. Edward knew the sled that was left was Tiffany's because he'd left his by the tree. As Tiffany ran to catch up, he wondered if he could say it was his anyway.

READ
Hebrews 4:14-16. Jesus became human like us, and he faced the same kinds of temptations.

THINK
- If you realize Jesus was tempted like you are, how might that help you when you are tempted?
- According to the verses, how will God respond when we ask for help with a temptation? How does that make you feel?
- Make up an ending for the story, showing how Edward could depend on the teaching of the verses. Then read the possible ending at the back of the book.

DO
- Role-play seeing Jesus in person and asking for help with a temptation. What might Jesus say? What might his face look like?
- Write down a temptation you face. Write a note to Jesus, asking for help with it.

PRAY
Thank Jesus that you can go to him boldly and receive kindness when you need help with a temptation.

MEMORIZE
Let us come boldly to the throne of our gracious God. There we will receive his mercy, and we will find grace to help us when we need it most. Hebrews 4:16

WHAT'S THE POINT?
Edward faced a big temptation. Jesus was ready and willing to help him because he knows what it's like to be tempted. *BA*

DECEMBER 30
Many Voices

Time for refreshments! Kelsey left the church auditorium with her friend Gianna and headed for the fellowship hall. All around the room kids and grown-ups were finding friends and talking happily after the "Night before New Year's Eve" service. Near the wall, some girls huddled together, talking rapidly in Spanish.

"I think that's rude, talking so we can't understand!" Gianna grumbled. "Why don't they learn English?"

"They *are* learning," Kelsey said. She knew one of the girls, Valeria, from her school. "But it takes a long time."

Gianna scowled. "Well, they only seem to talk to each other. Come on, let's get a cookie." She grabbed Kelsey's arm. Kelsey looked over at Valeria and hesitated.

READ
Revelation 7:9-10. In John's vision of heaven and the future, he saw people from many nations.

THINK
- Picture these verses in your mind. How are the people in the crowd *alike*? How are they *different*?
- Imagine the sound of verse 10. In your opinion, was this praise to Jesus spoken in many languages or just one? Explain.
- Finish the story, showing how Kelsey could be influenced by these verses. Then read the possible ending at the back of the book.

DO
- Discuss how you think Jesus feels about people from other cultures and languages. How can you tell?
- Learn more about the language, culture, or food of someone you know in order to celebrate that Jesus values all people.

PRAY
Ask God to help you value people of other cultures as he does.

MEMORIZE
I saw a vast crowd, too great to count, from every nation and tribe and people and language, standing in front of the throne and before the Lamb. Revelation 7:9

WHAT'S THE POINT?
Kelsey's friend wanted to stay away from Valeria, but Kelsey remembered that Jesus loves people from all countries. *SG*

DECEMBER 31
New Year's Eve

"Isaiah, would you make popcorn?" his mom called.

"Sure!" Isaiah replied. He left his cousins with the video games and headed to the kitchen. Isaiah liked New Year's Eve. First his family always took time to remember the events of the past year. Then his goofy Uncle Rick and his family came over. They played games until midnight, when everyone yelled and blew party horns.

When Isaiah got to the kitchen, he was surprised to find Uncle Rick sitting by himself. "Sorry I'm not in a party mood," he told Isaiah. "I'm not looking forward to the new year."

Isaiah knew there were wars and hungry people around the world. And lots of people had money troubles. Maybe his uncle was right.

READ
Revelation 21:5-7. The writer, John, saw a vision of the future: Jesus sitting on a throne and telling what heaven will be like.

THINK
- Alpha and Omega are *A* and *Z*. These verses mean that Jesus always has existed and always will exist. How does that make you feel?
- What hope for the future do you see in verse 7?
- Finish the story, showing how Isaiah could help his uncle by using this passage. Then read the possible ending at the back of the book.

DO
- Play a ball-toss game with your family. Throw a ball to someone. Each catcher says one thing that excites him or her about next year and one thing that worries him or her. What difference does Jesus make in these excitements and worries?
- Write down some of your own excitements and worries about next year. At the bottom, write, "Jesus is with me!" Seal your paper in an envelope to open *next* December 31.

PRAY
Thank Jesus that he is the Beginning and the End, and that he has good plans for your future.

MEMORIZE
It is finished! I am the Alpha and the Omega—the Beginning and the End. Revelation 21:6

WHAT'S THE POINT?
Isaiah's uncle was discouraged about the future, but Isaiah shared a verse about hope in Jesus. *SG*

POSSIBLE ENDINGS

JANUARY 1
Before Mrs. Martinez saw his hand, Sam lowered it. Taking some deep breaths, Sam tried to pull his thoughts together. *It would be wrong to lie about being sick*, he decided. With his heart beating fast, Sam silently prayed, *God, please help me give my speech and not be so nervous*. Another student gave his speech, and then it was Sam's turn. When he stood up to walk to the front, Sam felt calmer, and as he began to speak, his voice was strong and clear.

JANUARY 2
The next day, Haley found that her classmate Chantel would be missing gym too. Chantel had broken her leg and had to use crutches. Haley didn't know Chantel very well since she usually played with other girls at recess. But after the first week sitting in the library together, Haley realized that Chantel didn't know Jesus as her Savior.

"Mom, God made something good happen from missing soccer," Haley said thoughtfully when she got home. "I was able to talk to Chantel about Jesus today! Do you think I can ask her to go to church with us sometime?"

Haley's mom smiled. "Of course you can ask her," she replied.

JANUARY 3
Lindy sniffled. "Daddy told me the Bible says to help others," she whined.

Brooke started to roll her eyes. Then she looked at her sister's trembling lip. She bent down and started to help Lindy put things away.

Lindy sniffled again. "I thought it was all my fault."

"Well, I decided to do what the Bible says."

Lindy smiled. "Thanks, Brooke," she said.

JANUARY 4
As Emma lay in bed, ideas swirled in her head. Finally, the right idea came to her! She and her mom could put food and items the family might need in a bag. They could give it to the man the next time they passed the corner. Emma relaxed and smiled. She would ask her mom about it first thing in the morning.

JANUARY 5
When Cole got home, he thought about his great play and the team's victory. Deep down he knew God had given him the ability to play well and the strength to keep going in those extra innings. After his dad tucked him in, they prayed together, and Cole thanked God for the talent he had been given and the victory.

JANUARY 6
Audrey found her jewelry box and lifted the lid. She noticed her grandma's earrings nestled in the bottom. They were the only pair her grandma had ever worn. Audrey remembered how beautiful Grandma had always looked and how content she had always seemed with just one pair. "God meets my needs," Grandma always used to say.

Audrey counted all her other earrings. Then she put on Grandma's earrings. She decided she didn't need to go shopping after all.

JANUARY 7
Lauren went to the piano and played some of her favorite pieces. Next, she picked up her violin and played her most recent recital piece. Lauren realized she couldn't make

a decision on her own. So she went to her room and quietly closed the door. She sat on her bed and bowed her head. Lauren prayed that God would help her know which instrument she should continue playing. When she opened her eyes, she didn't have an answer. "I'll trust you to give me an answer, though, God," she said.

JANUARY 8

Carter didn't even consider that suggestion. "I could get in trouble if I did that. Plus, stealing is wrong," he told Brad.

After Carter hung up, he sat for a long time tossing and catching his baseball with one hand. "Why is God letting this happen to me? God says he has plans for me that are good, but how can missing baseball camp be good?"

He really wanted to trust God, but it was hard. Carter decided to talk to his Sunday school teacher about it.

JANUARY 9

"Work while we talk!" called Dad. Grace jumped up and helped him carry in a long box. "The Bible talks about heaven," he said. "It says heaven is big, with lots of room."

"Like our new house," said Grace, setting down her end of the box.

"I'd say much, much bigger," Mom said. "Jesus said he was going to prepare a place for us in heaven."

"This is a great home," Dad said. "But we know we'll have an even better home someday in heaven with Jesus. We can trust him for our future."

JANUARY 10

Jacob sat in Sunday school and rolled his eyes. The lesson was about Jesus as a kid. But as the teacher read from the Bible, part of the passage stood out to Jacob. He had never thought about Jesus actually growing in wisdom.

Didn't Jesus always know everything? How could Jesus be learning from the church leaders? Jacob wondered.

This was a new idea for Jacob. He raised his hand to ask the teacher about it.

JANUARY 11

Connor knelt down that night and prayed that God would forgive him. The next morning, he felt a little better, but he still wasn't sure.

At breakfast Connor asked his mom, "Are you sure God will keep his promises?"

"Absolutely," said Mom. "Human beings sometimes break their word, but God never does. He will keep his promises to you."

Connor smiled. "That's a big relief," he said. And his cereal tasted even better than he remembered.

JANUARY 12

Noah put his towel over his head. Kelly sank back in her chair. They watched as Bonnie waded by herself in the shallow end. "She does look bored," Kelly noticed. "I feel guilty for lying," Noah said.

They watched awhile longer. "I would play with her if we played on the noodles instead of doing Marco Polo," Kelly finally said.

"All right, let's do it!" Noah got up and jumped into the pool.

JANUARY 13

Manuel walked up to the teacher. "I forgot my project. Can I turn it in tomorrow with no change to my grade?"

"No, I'm afraid that wasn't the deal," Mrs. Jimenez said.

"But I was so helpful today!"

"Is that why you were helpful, because you wanted me to excuse your lateness?" Manuel nodded, embarrassed.

"I'm glad for your help," said Mrs. Jimenez slowly. "But it's too bad that you did it for the wrong reasons."

"I'm sorry," said Manuel. He silently asked God to forgive his wrong motives.

JANUARY 14

Adam's dad thumbed through his Bible. He pointed to Psalm 47. Adam read it. "The Bible tells us to sing praise to God and be joyful, and that's just what we're doing," Adam's dad whispered. "Listen to the words of the songs."

Adam listened. "Praise his name!" he heard. "Glory to our God!"

We are praising God, he thought. He hummed along to the next song until he caught on to the melody, and then he sang loudly. *I liked my old church, but I think I'm going to like this church too.*

JANUARY 15

Sophia said, "Well, I was just thinking that *God* knows how many stars there are."

"You really believe in God?" Paige asked.

"Yeah!" Sophia said. "I believe that the huge number of stars shows how huge and powerful God is. The Bible says he even knows them by name."

"I dunno," Paige said.

Sophia nodded. "Think it over," she suggested.

JANUARY 16

Taylor sat motionless for several moments. She could hear her heart thumping in her ears. Lightning bugs flickered outside the windows. Then the idea came like a flash. "Mom, we should pray and ask God for help!" she exclaimed.

Her mom looked at her in surprise. "You're right! I can't call anyone on my cell, and there's no help around. Let's pray for God to bring us help."

JANUARY 17

Cooper moped all day. That evening he sat on the couch next to his dad, who was watching the evening news. "Today's thunderstorms have been welcomed by farmers all around the county," the weather reporter was saying. "We've been praying for rain so our crops wouldn't die," said a farmer who was being interviewed.

Cooper thought about his prayers and the farmer's prayers. "What does God do when different people pray for different things?" he asked his dad.

"God has a hard job, doesn't he?" his dad said, giving Cooper's shoulders a squeeze. "We may not always understand how God answers our prayers, but we can always trust him to be perfect and fair."

JANUARY 18

Erika opened her journal where she kept track of important events in her life. Before writing, Erika flipped back and reread the entry about her grandpa's death. Erika had written, "I'm worried about Grandma. What will she do without Grandpa?" But Grandma had trusted God to help her, and she was making it. *Maybe God will help me through this*, Erika thought. *Maybe I can trust him too. I'll call Aunt Holly. She'll talk to me.*

JANUARY 19

Peter explained, "You're dirty with sin—the wrong things we all do. But Jesus loves you so much that he offers to make you clean. If you accept his help, Jesus gives his forgiveness, which is like soap to clean you of sin. Then you are adopted by God. He lives with you and helps you every day."

Christopher looked interested. "I've got questions," he said. Peter opened his front door. "Let's get a snack and talk."

JANUARY 20

Jared flopped onto his bed and thought rude thoughts. Then he heard a knock and grumbled, "Come in!"

Nate opened the door and said to Jared, "You know, the Bible says that fools don't discipline themselves."

Jared threw a pillow at him. "Thanks a lot."

Nate threw the pillow back. "Do you want help figuring out a savings plan?"

Well, I do trust what God says, Jared thought. *I guess I can give discipline another try.* He told Nate how much he had and how much he could earn at different chores.

"If you keep feeding Tigger and pulling weeds, then add in your allowance, you can have a skateboard in three weeks," Nate concluded. He held up his hand for a high five.

JANUARY 21

Bailey ran to her room. She grabbed her stuffed porpoise, Splash, and opened her closet. Moving the hangers aside, Bailey curled up on the floor. This was her cozy spot, where she went when she wanted to be by herself. Tears came, and she held onto Splash. "God, it's me. I need to talk to you," Bailey prayed. Then she told God all about her feelings.

JANUARY 22

At first Susan looked away, but every time she looked toward the edge of the playground, she noticed how lonely Nia looked. Susan thought back to what her teacher had asked her to do. When her turn ended, Susan ran over to Nia. "Would you like me to show you how to jump?" she asked. Susan liked the way Nia's smile lit up her face.

JANUARY 23

The next day at Pioneer Clubs, the Bible Exploration was about God's love. Alejandra's leader read Exodus 34:6. "Since God doesn't get angry with us easily," she said, "we can be more patient with ourselves."

Alejandra thought about that as she took out her bead kit again. How could she keep from getting mad at herself again? *God loves me even when I make mistakes,* she told herself several times. Then she had another idea.

"Mom, will you help me learn how to make the bracelet?" she asked.

"Sounds like fun," said Mom.

JANUARY 24

Over lunch, Lexi's dad asked, "What Bible lesson did you learn in Sunday school today?" Lexi thought for a moment and then stopped chewing. She knew she'd behaved like the foolish man. After lunch, she called Abby and said she was sorry. "I wanted to play video games," Lexi said. "Could you come over here and we could do that?"

"I'm not so sure I want to play with you now," Abby said. "You lied to me."

Lexi hung up and thought of the foolish man's house. "Jesus," she prayed, "I want to be like the wise man. Help me figure out how to make things right with Abby."

JANUARY 25

Nathan sat on his bedroom floor feeling miserable. He wished he had never cheated. He wanted to talk to someone, so he began to pray, "Dear Jesus, I know cheating is wrong. Please forgive me for cheating on my science tests!" When he was finished, it was like a weight had dropped off his back. Nathan decided he should tell Mrs. Chung what he had done.

JANUARY 26

After church, Kristin took out her Bible to look for the passage the teacher had been reading. She found Romans 8:38-39 and carefully reread it. *Yes, it says* nothing *can separate us from God's love,* she realized. Kristin hugged herself happily. *You would hug me, too, wouldn't you, God?* she silently prayed. *Please forgive me for getting back at Will. Help me ask Dad what I can do different. And thanks for loving me no matter what! Amen.*

JANUARY 27

Madison walked over and sat down. Hannah gave her a smile and said, "Hi! This is going to be fun. We get to answer all these questions together."

Madison looked at the list of questions and told herself she didn't care about Hannah. But as Hannah answered the questions, Madison realized they had many of the same likes and dislikes. And Hannah was funny too. By the end of their time together, Madison had made a new friend.

JANUARY 28

Tyrese silently prayed, *God, I need your power—please!* He took a deep breath and told Patrick, "That sounds really fun, but I'm not allowed to go on the Internet without my mom or dad."

Patrick pleaded, "Oh, come on. I can show it to you really fast!"

Tyrese stood up. "No, let's go ride bikes."

JANUARY 29

"What did you do at Joseph's?" Dad asked that night.

Liam felt butterflies in his stomach. "Played video games," he said.

"I'm glad we can trust you not to play violent ones," said Dad.

The butterflies flapped harder. Liam confessed to his dad what he had done. Dad looked serious. "I know those games seem harmless, but they affect our attitudes and our thoughts. When we play violent video games, we're thinking about things that don't please God, like hurting people and doing bad things. God wants us to be holy and pure in our thoughts." Dad said, "Do you think you would play violent games again if you had the chance?"

Liam thought it through. "No, Dad. You can trust me now."

JANUARY 30

Brandon hit a long drive and Milo ran to get it. Brandon had a minute to think. *What do you want me to do, God?* he asked. He realized he could keep the card and know he'd broken God's rules or give the card back.

When Milo was getting his coat, Brandon stuck the card back in Milo's pack. *Thanks, God, for telling me the right thing to do,* he prayed.

JANUARY 31

Olivia took a deep breath, threw off the covers, and ran for the light switch. When the light came on, she relaxed. She went to her shelf and took down her Bible.

What were those verses Mom said? Oh, Psalm 121:3-4. She turned to the verses and read. *Not slumbering means not sleeping,* she thought. *Mom's right! I never have to worry that God's not here.*

She turned off the light, jumped back in bed, and began to pray.

FEBRUARY 1

At their next break, Malik and John went back to the snack counter. "Another cola?" the girl behind the counter asked.

Malik thought for a minute. "No, I'll have water instead. It's better for me."

"You're right," said the girl. "Caffeine makes your heart race."

Malik unscrewed the cap and took a long gulp. *Not bad,* he thought.

FEBRUARY 2

Matthew didn't want to lose video game privileges, so he got ready. At the gym, the instructor was talking about why exercise is good for you. "It strengthens muscles all over your body. It improves your heart health and your coordination. It lowers your body fat."

As Matthew worked on dribbling exercises, he prayed, *God, you made my muscles. I guess my body does belong to you. Help me give it a good workout.*

FEBRUARY 3

Justin said a fast prayer. "Why don't we race back to Ben's house and get a drink there?"

"Oh, I just remembered we've got ice cream, too!" Ben added. "Let's go!" The boys turned around and raced each other back down the path.

FEBRUARY 4

"Let's give your worries to God," said Grandma. She asked God to help Steven talk to his teacher and not worry, whatever the outcome. "It's good to take responsibility for our mistakes," she said. "You can do that. I have confidence in you."

As he lay in bed that night, Steven repeated Grandma's words. "Dear Lord, thank you for caring for me even when I mess up," he prayed. "I give my worries to you."

FEBRUARY 5

Angel answered, "God!"

A bushy-tailed fox trotted across the field in the distance.

"Cool," Angel breathed.

"God gives life to the fox and meets its needs," Aunt Yolanda commented.

"I guess that means we're alive because of God too."

Aunt Yolanda hugged her. "I'm glad you're here, Angel," she said. "I think God is happy that you enjoy all the things in nature that he made. God enjoys us a lot more. People are his favorite creation!"

FEBRUARY 6

"Standing up for yourself is not causing trouble," Mom said.

"But what can I do?"

"You could pretend she said something nice. Call me a loser and I'll show you."

Samantha gave a half smile. "You're a loser," she said.

"Why, thank you!" Mom said. "What a kind thing to say." Samantha laughed.

"Or you could ask questions to help her start thinking," Mom said. "Like, 'If I'm a loser, why would you want to be seen talking to me?'"

Samantha nodded.

"If it doesn't help," Mom said, "tell me and we'll decide who to talk to."

FEBRUARY 7

Grandma said, "I always wished I could sing the way you do, Kylie. You've been given a special gift by God."

"But Grandma, you're so good at painting," Kylie responded. "I've always wished I could be an artist like you."

"Each of us is created different by God," Grandma said. "If all of us were artists, we wouldn't have music and singers. Even though I wish I had a voice like yours, I'm glad I can paint."

Kylie thought about Grandma's words. A while later, Kylie asked, "Grandma and Grandpa, what song would you like me to sing?"

FEBRUARY 8

The new kid, Cassidy, pointed at Payton. "Doesn't she get to play? I had a friend at my old school who used a wheelchair, and she always pitched."

Lillian and Anna stared at her and then at Payton. "Not a bad idea," Anna finally said. "Payton, can you pitch for us?"

Payton's face lit up. "Yeah, cool!" The girls took their places, and Payton rolled the first ball. When it was her team's turn to kick, Anna kicked the ball and Payton wheeled to first base.

FEBRUARY 9

Beth took her bowl home and showed her mom. "I like the way you molded the fun rim and the stripes," her mom said. "That reminds me of how I have seen God molding you. He is helping you become an intelligent and considerate young woman. I like watching him at work in your life."

Beth was proud that her mom liked her work. She felt even better that she liked the way God made her.

FEBRUARY 10

Logan thought. "The Bible is like a light for us," he said. "It shows us the way to live. And God's love *warms* me. Get it? *Warms* me, like the sun?"

"Good one!" said Dad. "I can think of more good things from God—you, Mom, your sister, and pepperoni pizza," Dad teased.

"Da-ad," Logan said. He moved from side to side and watched his shadow change.

"It's a good thing God doesn't change," Logan said. "We can count on him."

FEBRUARY 11

When Natalie's dad picked her up, he said, "I got you a special gift for Valentine's Day." He handed Natalie a beautiful silver locket. Inside was a picture of her and her dad. "Natalie, I love you forever," he said.

She threw her arms around him. "I thought maybe you had too many other people to pay attention to me," she sniffled.

"No, sweetie, never," he said, holding her close. "Think of how much God loves you even with all the other kids in the world. I can love you, too, no matter how many people I have in my life. God and I want to be close to you."

FEBRUARY 12

Just then, Sarah's mother walked in. "Honey, what happened?"

"I knocked the box on the floor," Sarah said.

Mom picked up the X-ray–like picture. "Oh, Sarah, you found your ultrasound. It's the very first picture ever taken of you!" her mom said. "Before you were born, we could see you forming inside of me. Look, you're sucking your thumb."

The image no longer looked like a blur. Suddenly Sarah could see her arms and legs and tiny feet. "Sarah," her mom continued, "this picture shows us how God was knitting you together inside of me. I'm sorry we don't have more pictures of you. After you were born, your dad and I just got so busy we stopped taking pictures. But this is the most precious picture to us. Look how perfectly God created you!"

Sarah's mom gave her a big hug. "I love you, Sarah, and God loves you."

FEBRUARY 13

Kyle looked across the field to the other team and sized up the players. They didn't seem as big as he had made them out to be in his mind. He prayed, "Lord, I'm glad you love me. Please help me get over being scared. Help me think what to do." Then Kyle started to remember how fast he could run. *Maybe I can outrun them instead of worrying about getting tackled,* Kyle thought.

He turned to Andrew and said, "We're faster and smarter with our plays. We don't need to be afraid of them."

Andrew smiled. "Yeah, you're right. If we play our best, we can stand up to any team in our league."

FEBRUARY 14

"It means we do bad things," Madeline explained. "Sin is wrong things we do, like lying and being mean."

"That's a dumb thing to put on a card about love," said Jade.

"No, 'cause God loves us sooooo much even though we're sinners. We couldn't get into heaven because we are sinners, so God sent Jesus to be born on earth. That's what we celebrate at Christmas. We can't live a perfect life, so he did it for us. Then he died to take our punishment in our place."

"That's sad," Jade said.

"No, 'cause Jesus came back to life again. If we believe in him and ask him to forgive us, he will come into our lives and make us part of God's family."

FEBRUARY 15

"My parents say we need to give some of what we earn too," said Jeremy. "My church is collecting money for a family that had a fire. It's good to help them."

Cody thought that over. "Why don't we sell lemonade again next Saturday? If we keep doing this every Saturday, we'll have a lot of money to give *and* to get cards with by the end of summer."

FEBRUARY 16

Jenna knelt by her bed. "Dear God," she prayed, "help me concentrate on pleasing you." Then she was quiet, letting Jesus bring things to her mind. *My messy room,* she thought. *I'll clean it up like Mom asked me to yesterday.* So she did.

The next day, she noticed a box on the front porch. "To Jenna, from a Secret Friend," it said. Inside were several outfits, exactly her size. "Thank you, Jesus!" she said out loud.

FEBRUARY 17

Lucy couldn't stand waiting any longer. She began digging in the dirt to find worms. Just then a bird swooped overhead and landed in the nest. Lucy watched Mama Bird dangling worms, busily feeding her hungry babies. *The worms are the perfect size for the babies' little beaks,* she noticed. *God made the birds so perfectly.* Lucy started to grin in delight. *God takes care of me much, much more!* she told herself.

FEBRUARY 18

Alondra could tell that Maya was enjoying being line leader. She realized she was feeling jealous. She repeated Miss Gutierrez's words silently to herself: "You do a great job highlighting the date for us each day and recording the weather." Miss Gutierrez's praise felt good. Alondra repeated her Bible verse for the week about having a peaceful heart.

"I'll have a turn to be line leader too," she reminded herself.

When Maya saw Alondra get in line, she smiled at her and said, "Okay, let's go to art."

FEBRUARY 19

As Cameron limped home, trying to keep from stepping on his heel, he realized that someone might step on the glass again when walking through the woods where he had thrown it. "Oops, sorry, God," he said. Cameron limped over to the spot, searched around, found the jagged piece of glass, and carried it up to the cabin where his family was staying.

FEBRUARY 20

Jackson's heart beat fast in the darkness. He realized his thoughts were beginning to run away from him, causing him to be more afraid. Just then, the nurse walked back in. She brought him a cup of cold water and rearranged his pillow to make him more comfortable.

"Thank you," Jackson said.

"I know this is hard," the nurse said, "but God is with you. He will never leave you alone, even when you feel all alone."

Jackson closed his eyes, feeling comforted and not so afraid.

FEBRUARY 21

Rodney was sure a bear would find its way into their tent—even though the club leaders said there were no bears in the park. When he realized he was letting his imagination get away from him, Rodney remembered a Bible verse about God watching over him. He repeated it to himself several times. Gradually, his heart stopped beating so fast and he drifted off to sleep.

FEBRUARY 22

As Tony hurried to the bus stop, he stopped suddenly. *God, you saw me even though no one else did, didn't you?* he prayed. It was too late to do anything about the garbage bags and recycling bin, but he thought of Mrs. Yoshida's newspaper sitting on the end of the driveway. Tony ran back, picked up the paper, and placed it on Mrs. Yoshida's porch. *You saw me do that, too, didn't you, God? I'll get the garbage next week.*

FEBRUARY 23

Jeremiah's dad knocked on his son's bedroom door. "Jer, we'll all get through this, and we'll be better because of what God will teach us through it. Can I come in?"

"I don't think God cares about us," said Jeremiah.

"God's love for us is ginormous," Dad said. "Our family's problems didn't catch God by surprise. He knew about them before we were even born. He planned how he would work with you and me and Mom and Jamie even through this bad time." Dad rubbed his back. "The Bible says God thinks about you all the time, Jer. God knows every detail of our situation, and he will help us get through it."

FEBRUARY 24

James's dad sat on the bed beside him and put his arm around him. "Buddy, I know this is really hard on you. But wherever we go together, our whole family's love goes with you. It doesn't matter whether we live in Minnesota or Manitoba."

"I know, Dad, but I just wish we could live in one place forever."

"Son, I know this doesn't help you right now, but God promises that we will live in his house forever. Someday, we'll get to stay put. But for now, let's remember that God is good wherever we go."

FEBRUARY 25

"You didn't surprise God," said Mom. "Guess why! He designed you. Isn't it amazing how God made you a blend of me and your dad? It's like he mixed two colors of paint together and came up with you! You are God's wonderful work."

"I am his wonderful work," Allison repeated happily.

FEBRUARY 26

Truman laughed loudly at his favorite cartoon. But then a little "voice" inside started reminding him of what his mother said: "No television until the bathroom is done."

But it's my favorite show, Truman argued. *And I'm still eating breakfast.* But the little "voice" wouldn't stop. Truman felt guilty. He punched "off" on the remote. He was scrubbing the tub when his mom got home.

"You're not very far along," she said.

"I turned on the TV," he mumbled. "But then I felt guilty and turned it off."

His mom nodded. "That was your conscience talking to you. God can talk to us through our conscience. I'm glad you paid attention."

"Me, too," said Truman.

FEBRUARY 27

After a while, the coach came and sat next to Jessica. "When I was in high school, I thought I was a better football player than anyone else," he said. "I needed to learn that my teammates were important too." He gave her a high five and left.

Five minutes later, Alyssa scored her first goal. Surprised, Jessica started cheering from the bench. The more she cheered, the more she wanted to cheer. Alyssa beamed. She played her hardest during the entire game.

FEBRUARY 28

Coach Mike called Diego up next. Putting his hand on Diego's shoulder, he said, "Diego was one of our most improved players this season. I'm proud of all he accomplished."

Coach Mike placed a trophy in Diego's hands. Diego felt happy. After the party, he said shyly to Coach Mike, "I didn't feel like I did very good. I don't feel like I do very good in school or church either."

"I think you're a great kid," said Coach Mike. "I know someone else who thinks you're great, and it doesn't depend on what you do or don't do."

"Who?" said Diego. Coach Mike pointed up.

Diego grinned. "I know—it's God!"

MARCH 1

This isn't fair, Lily thought. *This is my time alone.* But then she thought of how boring it was to swim while Aunt Stephanie read by the pool. And Uncle Scott wouldn't pretend the woods were full of wild animals like her brother and sister would. Her favorite video game was no fun to play alone, and she missed giggling with her sister and brother during cartoons.

"Yeah, I guess it will be okay if they come," Lily told her mom. "We'll have fun together."

MARCH 2

Lamar took a deep breath and got to work. He threw the basketballs that wouldn't hold air in the garbage. The leather baseball glove from his grandpa went in his memory drawer. The sight of his first bike made him think. "Dad, the kid next door just turned four. Could he use a bike?" They wheeled it next door and rang the neighbor's doorbell.

MARCH 3

Francesca had an idea. "We'll make our favorite snacks." Esteban and Carmela cheered and raced to the kitchen. "But then we'll trade snacks with each other. And we'll give each other two compliments before we eat."

They pouted. "How come?"

"Because we're a family, and Jesus wants us to show our love to each other."

MARCH 4

Rebecca stared at the eggs and imagined baby chicks coming out of their shells. Then she imagined Jesus leaving the tomb. "I never connected Easter eggs with new life before." She sat up straight. "No wonder you tell us the story every year—because you want us to think about it and learn what it means."

"That's right." Mom smiled. "Now let's dye those eggs."

MARCH 5

Chase moped in the backseat. "I don't want my birthday celebration to change."

Grandpa handed Chase a stack of past birthday pictures. "What changes the most in these?"

"I do."

Grandpa nodded. "On your birthday, we celebrate how you've grown and changed."

Thad had changed too, Chase thought. At first, he just slept and ate. Now he wanted Chase to play and read with him. That was something to celebrate.

"Let's pray for you," Grandma said. Chase felt glad Jesus cared about his feelings.

"Do you think you can pick out a present for Thad?" asked Grandma.

Chase thought it over. "Okay, I think I can."

MARCH 6

Mariah heard a knock. Mrs. Jones came in carrying a box. "Some friends dropped this off. There's more food than I can use." She unpacked cereal, canned goods, and muffin mixes.

After her neighbor left, Mariah set the pudding back in the refrigerator. She wanted Mrs. Jones to have it tonight.

MARCH 7

"Why do you think that?" Mamá asked. Miguel repeated what he'd overheard.

"You wasted the day worrying." She touched his cheek. "Papá and I have been praying every day. Papá called his boss and asked for work to do at home. People from church are helping too." She kissed him and left.

Miguel's stomach quit hurting as he grabbed a book to read.

MARCH 8

Rachel remembered when she'd been Molly's age. An older neighbor girl had teased Rachel until she cried. "Don't upset her," another girl said. That girl played a board game with Rachel. From then on, Rachel called the girl her "bestest" friend.

Rachel looked at Melanie, then said to Molly, "Yes, you can be Princess Rachel, and you can play with us."

MARCH 9

Shanise found Dad. "Would you teach me the hobo story so I know it by heart?"

"Sure," her dad answered. "But why?"

"'Cause someday, when my kids complain about supper, the story will help them thank God for what they have."

MARCH 10

Sophie knelt to pet her dog. Muffy had been a birthday gift a few years ago. The puppy took lots of work, but she was the best gift Sophie had ever received.

Muffy nudged at Sophie's hand. She smiled. The same love she felt when Brian curled his tiny hand around her fingers washed over her. *You know, I really do love Brian, God,* she prayed. *Maybe you could help me look for ways that he's a gift.*

MARCH 11

Julian paused. "My Sunday school teacher said it's good to stop and think about what God has done for us."

Barrett said, "So you think God helped you find your glasses? *I* told you about them."

"Well, I think God sent you to tell me because I needed to know."

Barrett struck a cocky pose. "I'm an answer to prayer!"

"Yeah, and that also means God cares about me," Julian said.

"Remember that the next time you lose your glasses," Barrett said.

MARCH 12

Caroline imagined one of her brothers racing into the kitchen and running into the handle. She dried her hands, grabbed a pot holder, and pushed the handle out of the way. *I'm glad I did that, God,* she prayed.

MARCH 13

No big deal, Ryan thought as he climbed. *The refrigerator doesn't have a battery so the open door won't make it quit working.* He stopped. He felt a little guilty. *Maybe God is nudging me,* he thought. *It will waste energy, and maybe food will spoil. I'd better double-check.* Ryan scrambled down the ladder.

MARCH 14

The angry words stuck in Bianca's throat. Dominic wasn't usually a blabbermouth, and she didn't like to fight with him. Instead, she asked a question. "Do you know how Chad found out about me and the play?"

"Sure," he said. "He was in the hall when you talked to your teacher. Now he wants to try out too."

MARCH 15

Shao blushed. Why had he been ashamed of his family? His mother knew so much about China. She could speak two languages. And he liked his grandmother's exciting stories about being a Christian in China when the government was trying to stamp out religion.

"Maybe you and Grandmother can tell us about life in the old village when you come again," Shao said after club. "You can translate for Grandmother."

MARCH 16

Sabrina hesitated at first, but then she called her mom. Mom came over and sat on the floor with Sabrina. "Isn't it amazing how God made these tiny kittens?" Mom said in awe.

Sabrina thought Mom looked more relaxed. Sabrina felt more cheerful too. "I'm sorry I yelled at you, Mom," she said.

"Oh, sweetie, I'm sorry I didn't listen to your side," Mom said. "We need some more fun things in our life so that we can feel better. How would you like to have one of these kittens for your very own?"

Sabrina shrieked. "I think that's a yes," said Uncle Harlan.

MARCH 17

"Hmm," Zoe said. "Peace of mind sounds like it must be peace in your thoughts."

Phoebe added, "So if Dad's thinking about us, he can have peace if he knows *we* know how to escape and stay safe."

"Dad's been a fireman for a long time," Zoe said. "He's seen some bad fires. Remember when he told us about the kids who helped get their family out of their burning house?"

Phoebe nodded. "He said without a plan, that family would have died. No wonder he wants us to be prepared."

Zoe stood. "It's your turn to pry off the screen, Phoebe. Are you ready?"

MARCH 18

"Would you pray with me while we wait?" Craig asked Chris.

After they prayed, Craig felt comforted. Soon a car entered the parking lot. Craig's mom opened the door and waved. "Sorry I'm late. A truck spilled a load of pipes and blocked the road. What a mess! And my cell phone died so I couldn't call. Were you worried?"

Craig nodded. "But God helped me stomp the worries out."

MARCH 19

"Do you still want my help?" Bethany asked. Her brother and sister nodded. "Okay, you each have one minute to tell why I should pick your game. And you have to listen to each other without interrupting."

When they finished, Bethany suggested, "You could play Brodie's game for a half hour and then play Brianna's. We can keep track with a timer. Does that sound fair?"

"Yeah," Brianna agreed. "Come on, Brodie, let's play."

MARCH 20

Max sat on the porch later that day, playing with the flashlight. He remembered how he and his sister begged his mother to take them camping every summer before she married Tom. But she didn't like packing and hauling all the gear. But with Tom there, they could finally go camping. *Thank you for the gift of my family, Lord, and thank you that we can go camping,* Max prayed. He went to find Mom and Tom.

"Thanks for the presents," he said. "Camping will be cool."

MARCH 21

Mason ran outside and climbed the monkey bars. He thought about a Bible story he'd read to Aidan. When people crowded around Jesus, he listened and healed them. Then Mason thought of a Bible verse that told how much Jesus loves us.

Mason hung upside down from the monkey bars. Being alone calmed him down. Hey! That might make loving his brother easier. He jumped down and ran inside. "Dad," he asked, "if I play with Aidan some every day, can I have some time alone too?"

MARCH 22

Ashley scuffed her toe on the floor. "I'm kind of scared of all the old people," she admitted.

"Oh," Dad said. "Why don't we talk about it when we leave? I don't want you to be scared. Let's pray about it too."

Ashley felt some relief. She thought of Dad's stories about how Gram cared for her as a fussy baby. And until Gram broke her hip, she came over whenever Ashley was sick. Now Ashley only visited Gram once a week, when Dad made her.

"Okay," said Ashley. "I'm going with you."

MARCH 23

Deondre spoke up. "I heard you talking about money," he said. "I wish I was old enough to get a job too."

His dad knelt down. "I was just thinking out loud. You're a big help. Things would be much worse if you complained and refused to do your chores. Do you believe that?" Deondre nodded. "Another way you can help is to pray for us. We always want to go to God with our problems. Will you help us by praying?"

Deondre nodded again.

"Thank you. That's important," Dad said. "Now hustle back to bed. We've got lots to do tomorrow."

MARCH 24

"I'll be right back." Daniela dashed to the bedroom. She rubbed out the chalk line and returned to the kitchen.

"What was that about?" Mamá gave Daniela a tamale.

"Something I needed to do."

After they prayed, Daniela took a bite. "Hey, Mariana, how about we clean our room tonight? I'll try not to boss you around."

MARCH 25

Kevin was speechless. Landon was right. Whenever he made fun of him, Landon gave him a compliment. Usually, it took all the fun out of calling Landon names.

"Okay." He leaned toward Landon. "If you help me think of what to say, I'll try it."

MARCH 26

Serena felt more and more guilty as she watched her show. She thought about what her mom and dad had told her about her conscience helping her know right from wrong. *I think my conscience is telling me what to do,* she thought.

Serena took a deep breath, reached for the remote, and turned off the TV. "Mom, my room might look clean, but I didn't do what you asked. Will you give me another chance to do the right thing?"

MARCH 27

Bryce wondered if honoring his parents had more to do with how he acted day after day than with buying presents. When was the last time he'd obeyed without a reminder or a quarrel? *But God,* he prayed as he walked home from Pioneer Clubs. *I don't want to turn off the video game.* He waited and listened to see if Jesus would give him an idea. Then he thought, *Maybe I can get a time tracker to help me keep track of how much time is left. Jesus, please help me not to argue anymore.*

MARCH 28

"Being a parent is hard work. Sometimes I goof." Dad tousled Eric's hair. "I know it didn't feel good to hear what I said. I told God I'm sorry. Now I'm telling you. Can you forgive me?"

Eric didn't want to forgive his dad. Dad should have listened instead of yelling. But then Eric remembered all his bike accidents. Every other time, his dad had repaired the bike and then gone over the safety rules again.

"Yeah." Eric hugged his dad. "I forgive you."

MARCH 29

Trudi stared at her cousin, but saw herself as a four-year-old with her face smeared with lipstick. When her mother found her, she got the camera and took a picture before she moved her makeup to a high shelf. Her mom said, "I drew on my little brother with *my* mom's lipstick when I was little. Mom and Jesus forgave me, so I can forgive you."

Trudi gave Ava a hug. "I know you're sorry. Let's get you cleaned up."

MARCH 30

That night as Lucas lay in bed, he remembered the times he'd lied to Mom or Dad or called Kallie names. He got up and called Grandpa. "I want a new life with Jesus," Lucas said.

"I'll pray, and you can repeat after me." And Grandpa and Lucas prayed: "Dear Jesus, I'm sorry for the wrong things I've done. Thank you for dying in my place. Please forgive me. Please give me a new life with you. Amen."

MARCH 31

Cheyenne bent over the plants and saw a yellow blossom nestled between the green leaves. There was another, and another. "Jake," she called. "Look!"

Her brother ran to her. "Wow, they're blooming!"

Cheyenne touched a blossom. "I think Jesus is trying to teach us something about paying attention to Gramps."

"Ya think?" Jake grinned. "Let's keep working in the garden. I can't wait to taste a fresh tomato."

APRIL 1

When Keisha stopped crying, she remembered how Grandma always said, "Don't worry. Be thankful and pray." Keisha closed her eyes. "God, I'm really worried about Grandma. Please heal her and bring her home soon. Please give me your peace so I don't worry."

She stopped and opened her eyes. What could she thank God for? She closed her eyes again. "Thank you that Mom has a job. Thank you for my bird, JoJo." When she opened her eyes, Keisha felt better. She realized Grandma had been right.

APRIL 2

Rosa laughed. "No, that's a crazy idea."

Her club leader explained, "Just as an athlete can't win a race without practicing, we can't have much of a relationship with Jesus if we never spend time talking with him or reading his words in the Bible."

Rosa understood. "Sometimes swim practice is hard, but I stick with it. I see that I need to stick to my regular time with Jesus too."

Her leader gave her a playful, gentle punch on the shoulder. "Life with Jesus is way better than any trophy you'll ever win."

APRIL 3

The next morning was Saturday. Damon watched cartoons until it was time to run errands with his parents. Before leaving, he saw his Bible again. On the cover was this year's Sunday school challenge: "Love the LORD your God with all your heart, all your soul, and all your mind" (Matthew 22:37).

Damon remembered his Sunday school teacher saying, "The best way to show you love God is to spend time with him every day reading his Word, the Bible, and praying." Damon grabbed his Bible and ran to ask his mom if the errands could wait. "I need to read this before we go," he explained. "In fact, I'm going to read it every day."

APRIL 4

"Milk helps babies' bones get strong. It gives their brains energy to develop," Mom said. "The Bible helps you learn to know God better. It helps you learn to please him. It helps you know more and more how much he loves you."

Isabelle smiled a baby smile at Spencer. "She looks happy now," Spencer said.

"Eating and growing strong make babies happy," Mom said.

Spencer considered that. "I want to be a strong Christian. I'll go pick a Bible story to read now," he said.

APRIL 5

Mom sat on the bed by Irena. "Sometimes we need to be brave and strong. We can be brave and strong because God is with us. The Bible says God will go ahead of us to show us the way."

Irena sniffled. "How can God be with us *and* ahead of us?"

Her mom smiled. "Because he's God. I'll pray with you as you talk to God."

Irena bowed her head and prayed, "Dear God, I'm really scared to go to camp alone. Please be with me and give me the courage I need. Amen." She looked up and said, "I don't feel brave yet, but I'll trust God to give me courage tomorrow."

APRIL 6

Nyla started listing good things she did in hopes of getting to heaven.

Dawna took a deep breath. "Actually," she said, "did you know that the Bible says we can never be good enough on our own? The Bible says heaven is a free gift from God when we believe in his Son, Jesus."

"I have never heard that," said Nyla. "What do you mean?"

APRIL 7

Dylan said, "All the guys at school do it."

"I know," Homero said. "It's not right. Seems like you need to decide if you're going to follow God and do what he says or follow other people."

Dylan thought about that all day. At bedtime he prayed, "This is going to be hard, Jesus, but I want to do what's right."

APRIL 8

"Go away!" Riley yelled.

"Hey, I'm sorry I got mad about you using my bow. Will you forgive me?" Chip asked through the closed door.

After a few moments, Riley peeked out. "I always let you play with my stuff. Why are you so picky about me using your stuff?"

"I don't know. But I don't want you to be mad, so I've changed my mind. You can play with my bow and arrows anytime you want," Chip replied.

"Thanks!" Riley said with a smile.

APRIL 9

Niko grabbed a pencil and was about to mark off that he had read a few more hours. Then he stopped. *No, that wouldn't be right,* he thought as he threw his reading log aside. *But if I don't, I'll never get that mini-golf coupon!*

Niko picked up the log again to mark it, but he couldn't bring himself to lie. He put the log down and found a book. *I'll just start reading again. If I read every day, maybe I'll still get that coupon,* he decided.

APRIL 10

Javon sat up in his seat. "You know," he said, "my teacher did say that we might have more than one career in our lives. Maybe I could be a computer programmer for a while and then become a chef."

Javon's dad smiled. "Son, you have a lot of options," he said.

"I know," he replied, "but I'm not sure what God wants me to be. I guess I'll have to wait and see."

APRIL 11

Shelby's dad answered, "Yes, I know God cares. If you ask him to give you good dreams, I am confident he will listen to you. He doesn't always answer just the way we expect, but we can always trust what he does." Shelby agreed and they prayed.

The next morning Shelby awoke before her dad came into her room. She ran downstairs and exclaimed, "Dad, I didn't have any bad dreams last night!" Shelby's dad smiled and said, "There you go—God said yes to your prayer!"

APRIL 12

When Zack and his family arrived home, his mom brought in the mail. "Zack, there's a letter for you," she called.

Zack opened it. "It's from the children's choir I tried out for last fall." Zack scanned the letter. "Mom! There's an opening now and they want me to join!" he shouted.

"Great!" his mom replied. "Looks as though God is working things out after all."

"Could be. . . . Seems like baseball wasn't his plan for me, but maybe choir is," Zack decided.

APRIL 13

"All those things are important," Christy's guy said. Just then another player came by and high-fived him. When he turned back to the reporter, he grinned. "Really," he said, "the one I have to give credit to is God. God gave me great abilities. I'm playing for him first of all." He pointed up.

The reporter nodded, and Christy and Mark looked at each other. "Cool!" they said.

APRIL 14

Amy's mom continued, "Instead of just getting more all the time, let's give something away. The kids at the homeless shelter may not have any toys of their own."

When they got home, Amy went to her room and looked at her overflowing shelves and closet. Mom followed her. "Birthdays are for *getting*," Amy said.

"As you get older, you'll realize that you can *get* by *giving*."

"Get what?"

"Pleasure from making someone happy," said Mom. "Imagine all the laughter and fun you can provide for the kids at the shelter."

Amy looked at her black-and-white stuffed penguin stacked on top of a family of bears with their own clothes. "Will you help me decide what to give?"

"Absolutely," said her mom.

APRIL 15

"Please, Jesus, help me tell someone," Andrea prayed. She picked up the phone again and called her friend Amelia. After telling about her camp activities, Andrea said, "I met the most awesome person you could ever meet!" She told Amelia about her experience with Jesus. Amelia was curious and wanted to know more later.

When Andrea hung up, she still wanted to talk about Jesus. She went outside to play and saw her neighbor riding a scooter. "Hi, Alejandro!" Andrea called, and she ran over to tell Alejandro about her new relationship with Jesus.

APRIL 16

Brett tossed his game aside and picked up his Bible. Since he didn't have much time, he opened it, closed his eyes, and pointed to a verse. The verse read, "You must not have any other god but me."

That's easy. I obey that! Brett thought. He said a quick prayer while he brushed his teeth.

"What verse did you read?" Mom asked. Brett told her.

"That means not letting anything become more important to us than God is," Mom said.

Brett stopped. *Like video games,* he thought.

APRIL 17

That night Troy went to Ethan's room. "You've been pretty mean to me lately when Mom and Dad aren't around." He pointed out the things Ethan had done. "Those things hurt. I feel bad because you're my big brother and I want to get along. I want you to stop."

"You're too sensitive," Ethan said. "Go to sleep."

In his own room, Troy talked to Jesus. Then he decided to go tell his parents what was going on.

APRIL 18

For a moment, Allie considered joining them. She was excited they wanted to include her. But then she remembered her memory verse about being kind. She decided whispering about someone wasn't kind. "I better not. Mrs. Phillips said to stay in our place in line," Allie responded.

APRIL 19

Cassandra was tired of waiting. "But complaining won't help," she said to her friend César. "It would just make Mom and Dad and me feel worse."

"But you can pray," said César.

"True," Cassandra said.

A few weeks later, a surprise came in the mail. It was a letter explaining that the adoption process was now complete and they would have their baby soon. Cassandra was thrilled! Her time of waiting would be over, and she would have her baby sister.

APRIL 20

José didn't know who to listen to. As he tried to decide, his friends were coming up with all kinds of ways he could spend the money. Daniel finally said, "Let's take it back. I'll walk back with you, if you want."

José really wanted to keep the money, but deep down he knew Daniel was right. "You're right. Let's go," José said.

APRIL 21

Marissa was still talking to her new friends when Elizabeth and her family came out to the parking lot. Elizabeth looked sad, and Marissa wished she'd acted differently. "Elizabeth, come here a minute," she called. Marissa introduced her to the other girls.

"So what's MissionsFest?" the other girl asked again. Marissa took a deep breath and told her.

APRIL 22

Laura needed a tissue. She quietly tiptoed by her sister's bed. A voice said, "You're still awake too?" It was Dana.

"Yeah, I'm so worried about Mom."

"Me, too. Let's pray."

"We've done that a gazillion times," Laura protested.

"Come on, Laura." Dana grabbed her hands. "Jesus says never give up praying. Nothing is impossible for him. Remember—he came back to life when he was dead! He loves us, and he wants to hear from us."

"Okay," said Laura. Together they sat on Dana's bed and prayed for their mom.

APRIL 23

"A life jacket saves you from drowning," Mr. O'Connor said. "Jesus is called our Savior because he saves us from the punishment of death that we deserve for the wrong things we do. Who can name some wrong things we do?"

"Lying, disobeying," said Elijah.

"Being mean, playing favorites," said Jada.

"Even sins that seem small deserve death and separation from God," said Mr. O'Connor. "But Jesus loves us so much that he died on the cross in our place. If we believe he is God's Son and ask him to forgive us, he will forgive us and take the punishment for us."

"I get it!" Elijah said. "That's how we get life forever in heaven with him."

APRIL 24

Thomas's cue came, and he walked onstage with the rest of the children's choir. They nervously got into place, the lights came back up like an explosion, and "Jesus" was alive again! "He's alive, he's alive, he's alive, and I'm forgiven," sang Thomas with the others. The bell choir chimed in, and Thomas thought he would burst from excitement. The congregation rang bells and sang with the children's choir. Over and over they sang, "He's alive!"

APRIL 25

"I haven't been paying attention, either," said Wes. Both boys sat down on a rock to figure out their next step. "Maybe we should pray," Wes suggested.

Grady agreed. They closed their eyes and asked God to show them what to do. When they opened them, they felt better.

"Let's keep going," Grady said. As they continued down the path, they heard someone behind them. It was their parents. "What are you doing here?" exclaimed Grady.

His dad explained, "We've been following you just in case you had trouble and needed someone to show you the way."

APRIL 26

"Dad, will you pray for us?" Katrina asked.

"Sure," her dad said. They closed their eyes, and he prayed, "Dear God, we hear the thunder and see the lightning. We ask for your shield of protection now. Please keep us safe during this storm and give us peace that you are with us. Amen."

The lightning flashed bright and the thunder boomed, but Katrina didn't jump. A small seed of trust in God was growing inside her.

APRIL 27

Vanessa said, "There are so many to choose from. Do you want to hear about a blind man being healed, five thousand people being fed from just five loaves of bread and two fish, or a guy whose ten brothers sold him into slavery and he ends up becoming the second most important man in Egypt?"

"They all sound cool! Read them all!" Asha responded.

APRIL 28

Surprised, Leah sat back in her seat. Immediately she thought about her plan for taking revenge on Calista and all the mean things she wanted to happen to her. *Wow! I'm really glad no one can see what I'm thinking!* Leah thought to herself.

Then Leah remembered that God could see her thoughts. She knew God wouldn't be pleased. *I'm sorry, God,* she whispered. *Help me think of a better way to deal with this.*

APRIL 29

Instead of yelling, Kwan remembered that ever since he had asked Jesus to come into his life, he had been trying to not be mean when he got mad. He felt another surge of anger when he realized that he couldn't fix the airplane. Just then Min peeked in the door of his room. "I'm sorry about the airplane. It was an accident. I'll pay for it," she apologized.

"Go away," he grumbled. "I'm really mad right now, but I'm trying to forgive you." Kwan took a deep breath. He hadn't yelled. He quickly prayed that God would help him forgive his sister.

APRIL 30

In the car on the way home, Mei described the missions project to her parents. "There's no way I'll be able to go. I'll never get everything done before Saturday afternoon!" Mei exclaimed.

Her mom thought for a moment and then said, "We'll help you do your chores in the morning so you can serve in the afternoon."

Mei couldn't believe it. "Really? Thank you! If I work hard and complete the book report this week, then Saturday morning I can practice my violin before I go to the soccer game. I'll be finished by lunchtime and can help out with the missions project."

MAY 1

Desiree felt her excitement about picking a souvenir disappear. In fact, she felt nervous and a little sick to her stomach. *That woman didn't care that I saw what she did because I'm just a kid,* thought Desiree.

She hurried to her mom and whispered what she'd seen. Her mom rushed to the front of the store and pointed out the woman to the salesperson. When Mom came back, she put an arm around Desiree's shoulders. "That woman did something very wrong," she said. "The store owner wouldn't have gotten the money he deserved. I'm proud of you for speaking up, Desiree."

MAY 2

Kirstin prayed, "Jesus, I really want that scooter. But I really want to help the kids too. What can I do?" She waited to see if Jesus would give her an idea. And he did. She would give two weeks' worth of her scooter savings and wait two more weeks to buy it.

"Good plan," she whispered to Jesus.

MAY 3

Rudy was feeling well enough to see the last fifteen minutes of the assembly. Sammy even saved him a seat.

"The next time someone dares me, I'm going to listen to you!" Rudy said. "Just say, 'mac and cheese,' and I'll remember!"

MAY 4

Griffin remembered that God wants us to treat others with kindness. "If you put the hot dog on the stick this way, it won't fall off," Griffin said, demonstrating his technique to Ricky. Griffin even got a bun ready for him. Ricky didn't poke him once during the cookout.

MAY 5

"This isn't a fun game," blurted out Nina. "It hurts people's feelings."

"Play or go sit downstairs all by yourself," Cynthia said. Nobody defended Nina, so she went downstairs. She curled up on the couch with Kara's dog, Taco, and started to pray. *At least I'm not going to do something that you'd be unhappy about, God.*

Soon Kara came looking for her. "The game is pretty bad," she said. "I left. I'm glad you left first. I wouldn't have had the guts to otherwise. Let's find something to play together."

MAY 6

By the time Caleb found Diesel, he was so mad that he wanted to yell. But when Diesel wagged his tail and looked up with his big brown eyes, Caleb realized yelling wouldn't make things better. *I'm the one who left the action figure out,* he realized. *And Diesel won't understand if I yell at him now. He'll just feel bad and won't know why.*

He took a deep breath and rubbed his dog's head instead, which made Diesel's tail wag faster.

MAY 7

When Ramón got home from school the next day, he was amazed to see walls everywhere. "Why did they wait so long?" Ramón asked his dad at dinner.

"The builder knew how important the foundation is in a home," explained his dad. "It needed time to get solid. A solid foundation prevents the walls from caving in.

"It's the same for us as Christians; God and his Word are a firm foundation for us to build our lives on. He gives us salvation, wisdom, and knowledge. We need to love and obey him."

MAY 8

"If I get on my tiptoes, I can see over the top of the hay," Lewis said out loud. Sure enough, now he could see the right path. He followed it and found Amber and the other club members. "There's only one way to get through the maze," he said to them.

"You just made a smart comment about Jesus," his club leader, Mrs. Gonzalez, said. "I did?"

"There's only one way to get through the maze of life and get to heaven. It's by trusting Jesus to save us from our sins—the wrong things we do."

Lewis nudged Amber. "Mrs. Gonzalez says I'm smart."

She nudged him back. "My turn in the maze!"

MAY 9

Finally Jen couldn't stand it anymore. "Mom, do you love Jonah more than me?"

"Of course not, honey," her mother explained. "I've noticed how hard you've worked this week. I love you for that, but not *because* of that. My love couldn't be any bigger for you, no matter what you do. God's love for you is that way too. You already have all of God's love, no matter what you do or don't do." Her mom gave her a big hug, and Jen breathed a happy sigh of relief.

MAY 10

Quinn's mom read, "For my birthday I'd like a new stove and a job for my dad. Our stove doesn't work anymore."

Quinn picked up his long, colorful wish list and looked at it again. "My list is all about me and lots of stuff," he realized out loud. "I'm not supposed to ask for any presents?"

"No, buddy, it's okay for you to want presents. We have money to get you presents," Mom said. "But what's more important is who you are inside. Are you greedy, or are you caring and sharing?"

"I think I'll start a new list," Quinn said.

MAY 11

Gabe went back to his position and the game continued. He felt bad. He didn't normally call friends mean names. What had happened? He was acting like Kirby.

Then he remembered his Bible memory verse, "Be kind to each other." He doubted that Kirby tried to live by that rule; probably trash-talking sports players didn't either. Gabe apologized to his teammate for calling him a name.

MAY 12

Their mother had Rocío sit on one end of the couch and Miguelito on the other. She listened to both sides of the story.

"Did Miguelito wreck your drawing on purpose?" she asked.

"No," Rocío admitted.

"Did shoving him make things better?"

Rocío felt stubborn. "It helped my mood," she said.

"If you had wanted to be a peacemaker, what could you have done?" said Mamá.

Rocío didn't want to answer. Miguelito spoke up. "I could have stopped following Rocío," he said. "Rocío could have forgiven me."

Rocío looked at him in surprise. "You mean you're sorry you messed up my picture?"

"Yeah," he said.

Rocío felt relieved. "I forgive you," she said. "I'm sorry I pushed you."

MAY 13

Dr. Lambert handed Caitlyn a colorful chart filled with boxes.

"Put this up in your bathroom. Each time you brush, check off a box," Dr. Lambert said. "Patients who bring me a chart with nearly all the boxes filled out get a coupon for the skating rink down the street."

"Awesome!" Caitlyn said.

Then Dr. Lambert explained more about why teeth are so important and how to take care of them properly.

MAY 14

Zander suddenly remembered what he'd learned in Sunday school. His teacher said, "Instead of worrying, pray." Maybe he'd give it a try. Quickly he asked God to help him not be so nervous. He felt a little better. Three spelling words later, he said another short prayer. By the time he got to the last word, he felt a lot less tense and knew that he'd done his best.

MAY 15

Theresa turned one more page and then closed the comic book. But even then, she could still see one of the scary pictures in her mind.

"Mom always tells me to stay away from scary things on TV or I'll have nightmares. I think she'd say that applies to comic books too," Theresa said.

"Well, let's do something else then," Corinne said. "I think they're too scary too."

MAY 16

Later that afternoon, Mr. Barnes discussed the social studies projects that the students had handed in.

"I wanted to point out a project that caught my eye," he said. "It really explains the chapter we've been working on." Shelley was sure Mr. Barnes was going to pick up Amanda's. But he chose Shelley's instead.

"Good job, Shelley. You must have worked hard. It really explains what we've been studying." Shelley grinned from ear to ear because she *had* worked hard on it.

MAY 17

When Mom heard Mariel's response, she looked at Mariel in surprise. "Lying is lying," Mom reminded her. "Telling the truth one minute and a lie the next makes it hard for others to trust you."

Mariel had never thought about how trust related to lying. As she lay in bed, she realized that her occasional lies shaped what her mother thought of her. "I feel sad, God," she prayed. "Please help me to tell the truth from now on."

MAY 18

"We've talked about how God says stealing is wrong," Luke's mom said. "Could you have come to me and asked for more chores to earn money faster?"

"I don't want to work all the time," Luke muttered.

"God gives us a choice between working and stealing," Mom said. "Which side do you think God is on?"

"Working," Luke admitted.

"How do your dad and I know we can trust you now? We will talk about consequences tonight."

Luke argued with his conscience that night. Finally he took out his bank and counted out the amount of money he had stolen. "Here's your money back, Mom," he said. "I'm sorry, and I've asked God to forgive me."

"Thank you, Son," Mom said. "There will still be consequences, but I'm proud of you."

MAY 19

As he swung so high that the swing jumped, Benjamin yelled, "Awright!" On the way down, he caught sight of Gordy's sad face. Suddenly he remembered how bad he felt when he didn't get a turn. *Are you reminding me, God?* he wondered.

Still, he didn't want to give up his turn. *God, help me want to be kind,* Benjamin prayed. By the time he slowed to a stop, he felt a little better about sharing. It was hard, but it felt good to see Gordy's smile.

MAY 20

Just before he opened his mouth, Marcus remembered that "shut up" wasn't something he was allowed to say at home. Those words showed a lack of respect toward another person. He took a deep breath.

"I don't have a problem," Marcus said, as he walked away. For once, Ross didn't seem to know what to say.

MAY 21

"I understand why you feel like you do, Vince," said his father. "But when Jakob says he didn't do something on purpose, have you found that he's usually lying?"

"No," Vince admitted.

"Then I wonder if you would want to give him something unexpected—kindness and forgiveness."

"He doesn't deserve it," said Vince.

"None of us deserves it, which makes what Jesus did for us on the cross even more amazing," said his father. "God has shown us great mercy so we can show mercy. What's more important in God's eyes: your chair or your relationship with your brother?"

MAY 22

"I'm happy I get to work in this school—even when the job is smelly," Mr. Cricket said with a smile. "It's how God uses me." He told Josh that a long time ago he had an accident. He wasn't sure he'd be able to work again. "Once I was better, being able to work was more important than the job itself."

MAY 23

When Lina got home, her mother saw her tears and asked what was wrong. Lina told her the whole story. "It's okay to pour out your feelings to me," Mom said. "We don't have to be afraid of feelings, and we don't have to act on them in mean ways."

"I want to do something to leave Sydney and Becky out so they know how it feels," Lina said.

"Your plan might make *you* feel better," her mother cautioned. "But like your grandmother used to say to me, 'Two wrongs don't make a right.' What if I help you plan an ice cream party? You can invite Sydney and Becky and all the other girls in the neighborhood over for ice cream so everyone can get better acquainted."

MAY 24

"Your enjoyment of Meatball is a picture of God's enjoyment of you," Dad said. "On the other hand, your sister feels close to God when she takes her Bible and a flashlight into the closet and spends time alone with him there."

"I do feel close to God, but can I know that's for real? Is he really with me?" Jonathan asked.

His dad ruffled his hair. "The Bible says that God always meets us when we make the effort to spend time with him."

When Dad left, Jonathan lay back in bed. "God, I'm glad you like to be with me even more than I like to be with Meatball," he prayed. Meatball licked his hand.

MAY 25

Tristan decided he'd better not run. "You're damaging someone's property. That's against the law," the police officer said. "You need to tell me the name of that boy who ran."

Feeling miserable, Tristan did. The police officer visited each of their homes. The boys had to agree to work around the house and yard of the garage's owner to pay him for the cost of repainting.

"I think I'll stick with keeping the law and not breaking it from now on," said Tristan.

MAY 26

Toby did come back on Saturday with his parents. Together they assembled boxes for the shoppers to use and also helped carry full boxes to waiting cars.

"These people are really happy to get toys for their children and clothes they need," Toby said to his mother. "I'm glad I got to help out more than just one day." He felt good inside at the end of the day.

MAY 27

Jocelyn saw the taxi out of the corner of her eye and heard people scream. She ran as hard as she could to get out of the way. The taxi swerved just in time to miss her. Her father rushed across the road and scooped her up in a big hug. She trembled in his arms.

"The next time I say 'wait,' obey me," her father said sternly, as he continued to squeeze her tightly.

"I promise I will," Jocelyn said, hugging her father back.

MAY 28

"Let's ask Mom for some help," Lori suggested.

"Maybe that's a good idea," said Harrison. He was getting hungry. He had to admit he hadn't taken the time to read the recipe very carefully.

"I'm glad you want to do things on your own," their mom said. "But as you're learning, it's always a good idea to ask for help."

A few minutes later their mom was able to fix the mess. Soon the kitchen was filled with a wonderful smell.

MAY 29

"Roberto, what are you doing?" asked Mamá. He looked up and knew he'd been caught.

"Well, Guillermo won't let me in," he said. "It's not fair!"

His mother invited him to sit down on the porch beside her. "People will hurt our feelings from time to time," she said. "What we do in response is what matters to God." She encouraged Roberto to talk with her first rather than let his anger control his actions.

MAY 30

"That's right, Jack," Mrs. Camp said. "That was one of our memory verses from a few weeks ago."

Jack looked surprised. "But that's not the whole verse, not word for word," he reminded Mrs. Camp.

"I know, Jack, but you remembered the most important parts of the verse, and now it's in your mind," said Mrs. Camp. "Someday you'll remember the whole thing just fine."

MAY 31

"We did it!" shouted Jesse. Helping out was a lot more fun than he had expected. When everyone finished their jobs, they got together and cheered and gave high fives. It felt like a party. Then the director told them how many families would be helped because of the day's work.

Working with a friend and hearing about the families they helped made Jesse feel good inside. "Hey, Jimmy, let's come back next month," he suggested.

JUNE 1

Dennis reluctantly went to the foot washing. He sat in the circle waiting to see who would wash his feet. Wow! It was Joaquin, the quarterback on the high school football team. Joaquin was someone he admired and wanted to be like someday. *Why would Joaquin do something like wash someone's feet?* Dennis thought Joaquin was too special to wash feet.

Joaquin patted Dennis on the shoulder and said, "Thanks for letting me wash your feet." That *was* a cool thing. *Washing someone's feet is a way to show someone you care about the person,* Dennis thought. *Maybe I should wash someone else's feet now.* Dennis went over to the table and picked up a basin of water and a washcloth.

He was glad he had gone to the foot washing.

JUNE 2

Bridget did talk to God about it. She told him that she didn't really want to pray in front of her class. She said, "Please, God, if I have to do it, help me pray without getting all jittery inside. Give me the words to say."

After she prayed, Bridget felt better. She now felt sure she would not be standing before the other kids alone. She had a source of strength—the greatest in the universe, God. He would help her remember she was talking with him and not feel nervous about which words to say.

JUNE 3

Dustin finished the test and waited for the recess bell. But as he was getting ready to tell his friends about Anne, he remembered how embarrassed he had been when his dad was out of work. He couldn't go bowling or to the swimming pool with the other kids. He knew he couldn't draw the other kids' attention to Anne's dirty, ragged clothes. But how could he help Anne avoid the embarrassment of everyone knowing about her tattered clothes?

He went to the front of the room where his teacher, Mr. Boyd, was working at the desk. Dustin gave him a note that said, "I'd like to give Anne some of my big sister's clothes. Do you think it would be okay to give them to the social worker for her?" Mr. Boyd promised to talk to the school social worker after class.

Dustin was pretty sure he could bring in a bag of hand-me-down clothes the next day without Anne knowing where it came from. Dustin looked forward to seeing if Anne would come to school in clean clothes soon! Dustin had shown compassion for someone who was in need.

JUNE 4

Kendra took a deep breath and told them how Jesus had healed Grammy. "I believe Jesus is God's Son and he can do anything. He died on the cross for us because he loves us."

"If he's dead, how could he do anything for anyone?" asked Kathryn.

"Jesus came back to life! That's what Easter is all about. You could come with me to Pioneer Clubs to find out more about him."

Later that night Kathryn told Kendra that she might like to come to Pioneer Clubs with her.

JUNE 5

As Nolan was about to convince Vito, he suddenly thought, *Am I talking Vito into doing something he shouldn't?* Nolan hurried to talk to his mom. "Mom, I want to watch Action Rangers, but Vito's mom doesn't let him watch that show. Would it be wrong for him to watch it, since you let me watch it?"

Nolan's mom put down the paper she was holding. "Do you think if Vito's mom were here she would say it's all right for him to watch it?" Nolan shook his head. "Well, then you need to decide if it's pleasing to God to talk Vito into doing something his mom wouldn't want him to do."

Nolan thought about it and ran to find Vito. "Vito! Let's play basketball outside instead." Vito smiled and nodded.

JUNE 6

Dawson remembered a verse about telling others about Jesus. *If Mrs. Patel could tell about Ganesh, I can tell about Jesus,* he thought. *You promise to be with me, right, Jesus?* he prayed.

Then he said, "I believe there is only one God. He sent Jesus to earth to die for us and come back to life so that we could have new life."

"Jesus didn't really exist—his life is just a story," said Tanner.

"Jesus is real, and he's the one I pray to," Dawson said. "Can I tell you why?"

"Umm, sure," Tanner said.

Thanks, Jesus, Dawson prayed.

JUNE 7

At first Callie wouldn't say much. Shari asked Callie where she lived. Callie said nervously, "Umm, my dad is gone, and my mom doesn't have a job. We mostly stay in shelters. Sometimes we sleep in our car."

Shari remembered when her parents worried about paying the bills. But she also remembered them praying. God finally answered their prayers by giving her dad a new job.

She decided to encourage Callie by telling her about God and what he had done for her family.

JUNE 8

The church phone rang several times. Finally the pastor answered. When he heard about Tammy's problem, he said, "I'll wait for you to get here so you can look for it."

While he waited, he searched everywhere he thought Tammy might have been. He met Tammy and her mom at the door with the cross in his hand.

Whew! Tammy breathed a sigh of relief. "Thank you, pastor!" she said. She was pleased that he had cared enough to search for what she had lost. She was also thankful that God had used the pastor to help her.

JUNE 9

Tori knew that if Jesus said something in the Bible, it must be true. The next day Tori saw Clarice at recess. She hadn't played with Clarice since the last time she'd asked for her horse back. *Please, God, help me show love to Clarice,* Tori prayed.

At that moment one of the girls Clarice was playing tag with tagged Clarice too hard. Clarice fell in the mud. "Hey! You pushed me!" she yelled.

"You're just clumsy!" the other girl said. As they argued, another girl started to splash more mud on Clarice.

"Here, let me help you up," Tori said. "I'll walk you to the bathroom to get cleaned up."

"Thanks," Clarice said. "I didn't think you'd help me."

"Well, I still need my horse back, but we're still friends, right?"

Clarice nodded.

JUNE 10

The Sunday school class read Revelation 21:1-5. They decided to make a list of things about heaven that would help Anya. Mrs. Larsen suggested they make a card to send to Anya. Monica said, "Let's list the things in verse 4 on the card."

Each kid in the class wrote one thing on the card that he or she had learned from the verses in Revelation.

JUNE 11

Christine was gloomy as she watched Gina practice at rehearsals. Even so, she still helped organize and complete the scenery in time for the play.

On opening night, parents and friends filled the auditorium. Christine was surprised at how well Gina played her role. When the play was over, there was another surprise for Christine. Many people congratulated her on the beautiful painting she had done for the scenery.

Christine felt her anger draining away because of the compliments. Later she found Gina and told her, "Good job! You played your part really well."

Gina congratulated her on the scenery. "I wish I could draw as well as you can," she said.

JUNE 12

Kirk could not get the kids in Haiti off his mind. As he ate his sandwich at lunch, he wondered what *they* were eating for lunch. He looked around the kitchen and thought, *Maybe they don't even have a kitchen.*

He didn't want to think about those Haitian kids anymore, so he went to his bedroom to play. There on his table he saw all the structures he had built. It reminded him of his family who had given gifts to him at Christmas and on birthdays. *They probably don't get birthday gifts, either,* he thought.

Kirk opened his dresser drawer and pulled out the five-dollar bill. *Maybe I could give some of my money to help the kids in Haiti,* he thought. He began to wonder if there was anything else he could share.

JUNE 13

Bella sat in church with her arms crossed and a frown on her face. People around her were singing praises to God. She felt as though she must be the only grumpy person there. Then she spotted a family who had lost a son in an accident, a woman whose husband had cancer, and a boy with a cast on his arm.

Why are they worshiping? she wondered. *Maybe they know something I don't.* She began to sing the songs, joining with the others in thanking God.

When Bella left church, she felt better. Her problems hadn't changed. But she knew God would help her have joy whether she was grumpy or glad.

JUNE 14

Shane's thoughts about Sean began to bother him. He didn't want to ignore his only brother. Shane decided that maybe he could be more patient.

The next day, Shane asked if he could hold his brother. Shane's mom showed him gentle ways to hold Sean.

"I'm glad you want to hold the baby," his mom said. "Maybe you can be my helper with Sean."

Shane smiled as he realized this might be a good way to spend time with Sean *and* his mom.

JUNE 15

It was cool for Campbell to think of himself as God's child. But why wasn't that like being a foster child? God wasn't his biological parent, was he? His parents loved him and took care of him. He knew he belonged to them. They were his mom and dad.

He and his dad talked about what it meant to be God's child. "Well, Campbell," his dad said, "when we believe that Jesus is God's Son, ask forgiveness for the wrong things we do, and ask him to come into our lives—then the Bible says God accepts us as his own children! We belong to him. That's forever! No one is going to take us back or love us more than God."

"Does God love me more than you do?" Campbell asked.

"I know it's difficult to understand, but yes, he does," Campbell's dad said.

JUNE 16

Just then the youth pastor showed up and put a hand on Lars's shoulder. "Hey, guys, guess what? Remember when Lars fell off his bike and was in the hospital? I visited him there. We talked about Jesus, and Lars accepted Jesus as his Lord and Savior!"

"Pastor Noel says Jesus will help me learn about being a good friend," Lars said.

Marcy shrugged. "Okay, you can play with us." She handed Lars a beanbag.

JUNE 17

"I got it," Kip exclaimed. He figured out that the leaders in charge of the early church had too much to do, so they divided the work among other people. Then they could concentrate on preaching. Because of that, God's message spread and more people became Christians.

"Today the guys divided up the work," he told his mom. "We helped Andy do his chores, and we all got to play ball."

"'Division leads to multiplication' is an idea that can work in many situations," said his mom.

JUNE 18

"Change doesn't usually happen all at once," Leon's dad said. "When we become God's children, that doesn't mean we'll never sin again."

"Really?" said Leon.

"We have to keep asking God to forgive us and change us, and he will more and more as we keep following him. God promises to give us the Holy Spirit to help us learn to do the things we should. We also need to ask others to forgive us."

Leon nodded. "Yeah, Marie needs to ask me to forgive her." Mr. Montaigne cleared his throat. "Oh yeah," said Leon. "I guess I need to ask her to forgive me too."

Leon's dad smiled. "Looks like the Holy Spirit is already having an effect on you. I don't think I've ever heard you say that before!"

JUNE 19

Dad stirred his coffee. "God answered your prayers today, Carson."

"Huh?" said Carson.

"Haven't you been praying for a sunny day?"

"Oh yeah. So why can't I enjoy it?"

Dad put pepper on his eggs. "You can. It's God's good gift to you. First we're going to church, which is God's good gift to us too."

"Why is it a good gift?" Carson was still sulking.

"Let's brainstorm," said Mom. "I like singing praise songs to Jesus."

"I like learning more about God, because I love him," Dad said.

"I get snack time," said four-year-old Benji. Everyone laughed.

"I like seeing my Christian friends," Carson realized. "I don't have Christian friends at school."

"Good one," said Dad.

When Carson's family got home from church, they went to the beach. They all built a sand sculpture dog and doghouse that were the best ever.

JUNE 20

Uncle Bob took Elise into the farmhouse and opened a Bible to Matthew 25:31-40. "Jesus is talking about people who know him and people who don't know him," Uncle Bob explained. "You've invited Jesus into your life. So you're a sheep."

"But I do bad things," said Elise.

"Yes, we all do. But the Holy Spirit is teaching you to do good things. You helped Aunt Linda when she was sick, you fed the hungry animals, and you helped your little sister crawl over the fence."

Elise reread the verses. "That was like helping Jesus then, right?"

"Yes, it was." Uncle Bob gave her a hug. "Jesus loves a certain one of his sheep named Elise."

Elise rolled her eyes. "Cheesy," she said, but she was smiling.

JUNE 21

Austin's mom said, "Where did our bodies get the ability to heal?"

"Oh!" Austin said. "God made them that way."

"Right!" said Austin's dad. "It's an everyday miracle that we might sometimes overlook. When we celebrate what God has done, we remember how awesome and special he is, and we give him praise for the little and big things he does."

Austin's mom lit the candles on the giant cookie. "Thank you, God," Austin said as he blew them out.

JUNE 22

Barnaby finally talked the kids into playing in the parking lot, not the grass. When Mr. Snead came out again, he walked onto the parking lot and said, "Hey, thanks for staying off the grass to play. I could really use your help next Saturday. If anyone can come, I'll treat him to ice cream afterward."

All the tag players showed up on Saturday and helped Mr. Snead. They saw how hard he worked. They discovered he was not such a grouchy old grouch after all. And the ice cream was delicious!

JUNE 23

In church the next Sunday the pastor began speaking about the early church. "The believers even sold what they owned and shared the money with each other," he said.

Colin slouched in his seat. He wasn't going to listen. Then he remembered himself saying, "It's not fair!" *Maybe it would be fairer to at least listen and think about giving,* he thought. Finally he sat up and tuned back in.

JUNE 24

Renee and Stacy took their bowl of popcorn back to Renee's room. "I guess my mom makes a difference for me in ways that seem unamazing. She's always there for me. She listens. She does what she says she'll do." Renee crunched a handful of popcorn.

Stacy said, "My Sunday school teacher is like that. She's patient. She never gets tired of teaching about Jesus."

"Maybe God can use the little things we can do too," Renee said. "Maybe we can be God stars, not pop stars."

JUNE 25

"Miss Hicks, we both need the red pipe cleaner for our design," explained Hayden. "I got it first," he added, hoping that would resolve the situation. He saw Miss Hicks close her eyes for a moment.

"I have the perfect solution," said Miss Hicks. She pulled out a pair of scissors and cut the pipe cleaner in half. "Now you can both finish your designs with a little bit of red."

JUNE 26

The next week in Sunday school, Akira brought up the question. "Let's name some types of people in our church," said Mrs. Allen. She and the kids named the ministers, the secretary, choir members, teachers, babies in the nursery, greeters, and kids who learned in Sunday school.

Mrs. Allen said, "The Bible helps us understand that we're all important by using the word picture of all of us as body parts that make up a body."

"My science teacher said it didn't matter if it was a knee or a knuckle, all our body parts are important," Akira said.

"Just like the church," said Mrs. Allen. "It doesn't matter if you're the janitor or preacher or a kid in Sunday school. We are all important when it comes to making the church work."

"I get it," said Akira.

JUNE 27

God heard Sergio's prayer. But he answered it a different way. Sergio remembered the camp counselor saying, "Every time the path forks, go right." It didn't take long for him to find his way back to camp.

When he got there, the other campers were praying. "Please help us find Sergio, Jesus!" Wow! They were praying for him. He shouted, "Here I am."

Suddenly he was surrounded by campers and counselors who were grinning and giving him high fives. Sergio said, "Thanks for praying. God helped me find the way."

JUNE 28

"Jesus came to earth to die in our place, to pay the penalty for the wrong things we've done," Shreya said. Finn's mouth dropped open in surprise.

Shreya continued, "If we believe Jesus is God's Son, we can ask him to forgive us, and he will. Then we become God's children."

After class, Finn said hi to Shreya. "I became a Christian when I was six," he said.

"I became a Christian when I was seven, in India, before we came here. There are quite a few Christians in India."

"So if we're both God's children," Finn said, "that makes you like my sister, even though we're from different countries."

Shreya grinned. "Okay, brother!" she said.

JUNE 29

Twenty days were finally over. Chelsea's parents named the baby Faith. When Chelsea saw her, Faith had a head covered with blonde fuzz. Her eyes were blue, but they were shaped differently than other babies'. Something was different. Chelsea's mother explained. "Faith has Down syndrome. She will learn things more slowly than other kids. We'll have to give her lots of extra help."

When Chelsea finally got to hold her baby sister, she whispered, "You are beautiful." She promised to love Faith just as God did—no matter what.

JUNE 30

The pastor had invited people from other countries, such as Japan, China, Germany, Russia, and Mexico, to church. They each got up and said John 3:16 in their own language. When Francisco heard it in his language, he smiled.

Then the church lights were turned off. There was a loud roar. Flames of fire shot out of a huge candle. The people from other countries stood together and loudly said John 3:16 again in their own languages, all at once. "For God loved the world so much that he gave his one and only Son."

Francisco whispered to his mom, "Just like Pentecost." He decided God speaks to all people in their own languages because he wants them to know him and believe in him.

JULY 1

Vivian remembered her mom's answer last night after Vivian had asked her mom why she took a blind neighbor shopping each week. "God gave me two good eyes," her mom said, "so I can help her."

Vivian looked at her strong legs and thought of Livvy. "I have two good legs," Vivian told her teacher, "so I can help her."

JULY 2

After the parade, Dixon's family made a plan. When they got home, Dad and Mom got out envelopes and cards. "Thank you," Dixon and Kenton wrote on the cards, "for risking your life for our country."

JULY 3

Darrell thought about how lonely he'd been last year, when he first came here. Nobody invited him to play soccer all summer. Only when school started and he scored a goal in gym class did they finally include him. Until then, he was miserable.

"Hey, Carlo!" He ran after the new kid. "Want to play?"

JULY 4

Ivy frowned. "I don't know if you'll be able to say that to me again," she said. Then she confessed what she'd done. "I'm sorry. I won't do that again. I guess you don't want me to have the pop, either."

"Apology accepted." Walt's face was serious. "And you can still help."

"Why?"

"Because you confessed. But you'll have to empty your pockets before you leave, at least until I'm sure I can trust you again. Is it a deal?"

"Deal," Ivy said, and they shook hands.

JULY 5

"I have an idea," Louis finally said. "Instead of getting angry, what if I pretend that it's a joke and laugh?"

Dante looked confused. "You mean if he calls you 'Looueee!' in that weird voice, you'll just smile and wave?"

"Right!" said Louis. "And if he trips me, I'll laugh and tell him it was funny. I bet he won't know what to do! But one thing's for sure, at least I won't be fighting him!"

"Okay, I guess it's worth a try," said Dante.

JULY 6

Feeling frustrated and angry, Pamela turned to Sadie and yelled, "Look what you've done! You haven't even said you're sorry. I wish you weren't in club!" Suddenly the entire room was quiet.

Sadie stood in shocked silence with tears in her eyes. "Pioneer Clubs is the only place I thought I had friends," she said. "No one is nice to me at school. I'm sorry about your project."

Pamela felt bad and wished she'd been more patient. "I'm sorry too, Sadie. I shouldn't have gotten so angry. And you do have friends! Look around you!" Sadie looked around at the other concerned faces and nodded.

JULY 7

Ty wanted to go out for ice cream, not serve at the shelter. But then he thought of how quickly Lance had finished his leftover sandwich. Were the people in line that hungry too?

He reached for the apron. "I'll give it a try," he said.

JULY 8

Nadia stared at the dishwater. Trusting Maggie was like trusting God. He did what was best for everyone, not just what Nadia wanted. Besides, did she want fat horses and dirty dishes?

Nadia picked up the dishcloth. "Yeah, I'll trust you."

JULY 9

Martin and Darcy studied the child's picture in the ad. Martin thought of his family's huge piles of vegetables. "Darcy, what if we use some of our vegetable money to sponsor one of these kids? We'll have plenty."

Darcy smiled. "I was ready to ask you the same thing. Let's do it!"

JULY 10

Pete hadn't thought of forgiveness that way before. "So if we're friends again, I don't have to let Dewayne have whatever he wants until I trust him?"

Mom nodded. "You can tell him how to earn your trust back. That's what friends do."

"In that case," Pete said, "I need to make a phone call."

JULY 11

Juliana had an idea. "Would you give me a list of the treats you can eat so I can bring healthy stuff to the sleepovers too? If I eat what you do, maybe you won't be quite so tempted. And what if we pray together before each sleepover too?"

Karina grinned and hugged her friend. "You're the best friend in the world. It'll be lots easier with your help."

"And God's," said Juliana.

JULY 12

Simon remembered the money he'd saved from his allowance and doing chores. He wanted to spend it on other things, but he wanted to help the orphans too. *Maybe,* Simon thought, *God could be using me as a way of providing for their needs!*

Simon raised his hand again. "How can someone make a donation for these kids?" he asked.

JULY 13

After church the next Sunday, Adele told her mom about the great lesson her Sunday school teacher, Mr. Ross, had led.

Mom said, "He spends Saturday afternoons at church preparing your lessons."

Adele was surprised. "Why?" she asked.

"Because he knows the best leaders are people who serve others."

Adele thought about the student council service projects. *I'd like to be a leader,* she thought. *I'll volunteer for picking up litter.*

JULY 14

Wendell thought of the way the other team had passed the ball. It would be cool to learn those moves and to teach them about basketball.

"Can we stop for the other guys on the way?" Wendell asked.

"The more the merrier," Mom replied. "Let's go."

JULY 15

Uncle Sal said, "People like *that*? Don't you mean people who are sinners, people who need Jesus?"

"Yeah, but doesn't your church have any sinners?"

Uncle Sal laughed. "Of course, we're all sinners, Whitney. But some people need us to go to them and show them what Jesus' love is all about. That's all."

"I get it!" Whitney smiled. "Can I come too?"

"No, I don't think your mom can spare you. But you can pray for me, okay?"

JULY 16

Mateo wondered why Mr. Ho didn't take his newspapers in. Then he thought if Mr. Ho was in pain, maybe he couldn't manage the stairs. *Should I bring him his papers, Jesus?* Mateo asked. *What if he calls the police?*

Then Mateo thought of asking first. "Can I bring you your newspapers?" he called.

At first the old man was quiet. Then he nodded. "Thank you, Son," he said with a sigh.

JULY 17

Roxy imagined Mrs. Hoover in the hospital and Mr. Hoover sitting beside her bed. Were they scared? lonely? "How long does mowing their yard take?" Roxy asked.

Dad studied the lawn. "About an hour and a half, I think."

"If we got up early and did it together on Saturday mornings, could we go to the pool in the afternoons?"

Dad smiled. "We can be Good Samaritans together," he said.

JULY 18

Jeff licked at his melting ice cream. "I'd want them to play with me anyway and help me learn their language."

"I wonder how *you* could do that," Mom said.

"I could show him something and say the word. Or say a word like *run* and act it out." Jeff grinned. "Can I practice on you two?"

"Go for it," Dad said.

Jeff held up his cone. "Ice cream," he said.

JULY 19

Maci's words reminded Iris of something Jesus said. He told his disciples he would lay down his life for them. His words described Maci a whole lot more than Tina.

Iris punched a number into the phone. "Maci," she said, "your secrets are safe with me."

JULY 20

After practice, Julio played computer games with Petey, the kid next door who was in a wheelchair. Petey always asked Julio a ton of questions about his team and coach. "I wish I could play," said Petey.

Julio suddenly realized that he knew a way to help: the Challenger League. Maybe it would be cool to be a Buddy after all. He told Petey about it. "That would be awesome to get to play baseball!" Petey said. "Would you really do that? We could be a great team."

JULY 21

Perry put on his glove. "Uncle Paul, you pitch and I'll catch. That's how Grandpa and I used to do it."

Meredith held out the bat to Mom. "This is a great way to remember Grandpa, Mom. Do you want to go first?"

Mom wiped her eyes and reached for the bat.

JULY 22

Nora knew she should choose to do homework, fix supper with Josie, and *then* play on the computer. *But that's not what I do*, she told herself. *If I want more freedom, I have to ask God to help me change.*

JULY 23
Howie thought about other changes in Trent. He didn't talk back like he used to. And at night, Trent played with their little sister so Mom could take a walk. *If God is changing Trent, then he can change me too,* Howie realized.

"What is the fruit of the Spirit?" he asked. "Maybe I need it too."

JULY 24
Grant wanted to throw the ball on the ground and stomp away. But reluctantly he admitted to himself, *Coach is right.* He'd been a hotshot, choosing to make himself look good instead of working for the team.

Grant looked up. "You're right, Coach. What should I do to be a better team player?"

JULY 25
The woman looked so eager. Her expression reminded Celia of her grandpa's face when he took her to the Vietnam War Museum and told her about being a soldier. She'd learned a lot about Grandpa that day, and she felt closer to him.

She tucked the MP3 player in her backpack. "Sure! I'd like that."

JULY 26
Christian realized that his mom wouldn't trust him to babysit again if he let Jayla get away with misbehaving. "Jayla," he said, "I'm sorry I yelled. But Mom doesn't want us going to the park by ourselves. It isn't safe."

JULY 27
Tanya mentioned her thought to Marlee.

"I think it's pretty cool that she would have the guts to praise Jesus in front of everyone," Marlee said. "Think how many people are listening on TV and radio and the Internet and hearing about Jesus."

Tanya remembered something her grandma had said. "Jesus left his throne and came to earth. When he won the fight against sin, his Father gave him the highest throne. That's why I praise him every day."

Tanya looked at Marlee. "In our next awards ceremony, maybe I'll thank Jesus too."

JULY 28
Chloe remembered Dad saying, "You have a way with words." And her grandma had said, "Your letters cheer me up." Chloe realized that being jealous of Theo took away from being grateful for her own talent.

Chloe began to smile. "I'm glad my card cheered you up," she said.

JULY 29
Nash pictured the day his dad took off *his* training wheels. "You help me remove them," Dad had said. "Then you can put them back on anytime you want." Knowing he could put the wheels back on had given him courage to take the risk.

He gave his brother the wrench. "Let me show you how to take them off."

JULY 30
Suddenly both girls saw their Sunday school teacher run over to them and gently pull Tessa out of the sandbox. "Girls! That's no way to treat each other. Don't you know that how we treat each other shows how much we love God?"

Rosalind instantly felt terrible. She hadn't exactly acted loving toward Tessa lately.

"Rosalind, I'm sorry for dumping you off the swing. That wasn't nice," Tessa said.

"Tessa, I was mean too. Sorry! Look at you! You're really dirty!" She started brushing Tessa off.

"Thanks," said Tessa.

JULY 31

Chandler started to feel bad. He'd acted as though he didn't love Winnie because she'd changed. But God loved him, no matter what he did, and even sent Jesus to die for him.

Chandler went downstairs and gave Winnie a bear hug. "I'm glad you're home. I missed you."

AUGUST 1

Tamika crossed her arms and said nothing. Megan ran down the hall, and the front door slammed behind her. After a minute, Tamika went out to the driveway. She picked up a blue piece of chalk.

It would be more fun to draw with someone else, she admitted to herself. She thought of Megan's words. *Am I really bossy, like she says? Maybe I can do better with her next time.* She quickly asked God for help and started toward Megan's house.

AUGUST 2

Moshe knew God would want him to stick up for Archie. "Sorry, Denny," he began, "but I'll only play if Archie plays too."

Denny looked startled. He pushed up his glasses and then shrugged. "All right, I'll take you both."

Moshe gave Archie a thumbs-up sign. Archie grinned and ran onto the field. *Maybe this game will turn out all right after all,* Moshe thought happily.

AUGUST 3

It doesn't matter what the other kids do, Keenan realized. *I belong to Jesus, and Jesus wants us to help people who need it.* He crossed the lunchroom and picked up the chips. "Here," he said, placing the bag back on the tray.

The boy smiled. "Th-thanks! M-my name is C-Curtis. I just m-moved here."

"I'm Keenan. Um, do you like baseball?"

Curtis nodded, and the boys talked briefly about favorite teams. When Curtis's assistant returned, Keenan went back to his friends.

"Let's sit at Curtis's table with him tomorrow," he suggested. "He's a nice guy."

AUGUST 4

Annika's probably right, Noelle thought. Soon she had black hair instead of blonde. But when she shampooed, the dye didn't come out completely. She washed again, but her hair stayed a muddy green.

When her big sister came back to pick her up the next morning, Noelle walked out sheepishly. "Don't say anything," she muttered. "I've learned my lesson! Don't believe everything your friends say or everything you read on a package!"

Her sister laughed. "I could have told you that! Let's go home."

AUGUST 5

Later Sunisa got a call. "Can I come over tomorrow?" Diana asked. "Mom'll drive me. I've got a surprise!" The next afternoon, Sunisa ran out her door when she heard the car. "Sunisa, I'd like you to meet my mom and my grandma!" Diana said. Everyone nodded and smiled. "And here's the surprise—Skipper came to visit!" Diana pulled the cage out and waved good-bye as her mom drove away. She handed a gift bag to Sunisa.

Sunisa looked inside, puzzled. "Peanut butter? Uh, thanks!"

"We can't play at my apartment," Diana explained, "so I wanted to say thanks for having me here."

"No problem! I like having you come," Sunisa replied. The girls carried the cage and present inside.

AUGUST 6

"I don't think God wants you and Davon and Miss Constance to give up, LaToya," her mom said. "Let's think of something to give you all a little reminder of God's love."

"I've got an idea!" LaToya said. The next morning she carried a box to the lot. "I brought a surprise to cheer everyone up," she announced. "Juice boxes!"

The box was soon empty. Not long after that, the broken bottles were cleaned up and the sweeping began.

"You're full of ideas, LaToya!" said Miss Constance. "What colors do you think we should paint here?"

AUGUST 7

Corey knew he had lied to Hughie and was thinking about disobeying his parents. *Maybe I could invite Hughie. . . .* Soon the two were on the muddy bank together, watching minnows. Then Corey started across the river, stepping carefully from rock to rock. Suddenly his shoe slipped, and he fell. Pain shot through his ankle.

Hughie splashed out to him. "Are you okay?"

Corey grabbed Hughie's hand and got up on his good leg. "It hurts really bad. I'll have to hop back. Can you help me? I'm glad you were here!"

AUGUST 8

Elena said a quick prayer and then looked at her friend again. Kinzie had stopped wrecking the castle, but she was still banging the bucket on the sand.

Elena approached her. "Kinzie, what's wrong?"

Kinzie gestured with the bucket toward their mothers. "I know what they're talking about! Mom and Dad can't afford to send me to my Christian school anymore. I'm going to have to give up all my friends and all the great teachers."

"Wow!" Elena felt bad. "I'd be upset too! What are you going to do?"

"I'll have to make all new friends," Kinzie said. "I'm scared. Thanks for listening."

"Sure," Elena replied.

AUGUST 9

"Is Conrad scared of the dark?" someone asked.

Fernando was tempted to tell, but he didn't give in. "He didn't look scared. He must have had another reason to go. Hey, let's ask my mom to make popcorn!"

In the morning, Conrad was outside the tent. "I'm back!" He sounded uncertain.

Fernando crawled sleepily over to the tent flap. "Well, you didn't miss too much. Mostly you missed these guys *snoring*!"

"What? *You* were the worst, Fernando!" said another boy. *Thwap!* One pillow hit Fernando. Soon more were flying. Conrad was in the middle, laughing.

AUGUST 10

Deena, you're so stupid, always goofing around! Mallory fumed inside. But she knew those words would hurt. *God, help me,* she prayed.

She looked at Deena's face. Her friend was clearly sorry. Mallory felt calmer now. "Everybody makes mistakes," she said. "Mom, is there a way to fix these?"

"I have vanilla frosting," her mom said. "Would you like to see if that helps?"

"Yes!" both girls agreed.

AUGUST 11

Rory took a deep breath. "My mom wouldn't know the difference, but I would. I'd rather tell the truth."

Jordan shrugged. "It's your life! I'd better be going. Thanks for lunch!"

Rory sent Timmy to another room and started cleaning up the mess. *I guess I learned something by having Jordan over,* he thought as he worked. *I can still do stuff with him, but I won't ask him for advice!*

AUGUST 12

Tabitha had heard Bible verses warning about gossip. "I don't want to call anyone names. Let's just play our game and have fun now, okay?"

Later, Tabitha walked over to Belinda's.

"I'm glad to see you!" Belinda smiled. "We just got back from vacation. Want to play a board game?"

"But I thought you didn't want to play board games anymore."

"Well, maybe not every day, but I like them," Belinda said.

After the game, Tabitha decided, "Well, I'm not going to believe everything someone says about someone else. I'm going to talk directly *to* the people. That's a lot better!"

AUGUST 13

Reed had been excited about watching the planes. *But if I were Marshall, I'd like some company,* he realized. He explained his idea to his dad.

"I'm proud of you," his dad said. "You're thinking of others the way God wants us to. We can see the planes another time."

Soon Reed was at Marshall's door. Inside, Marshall lay on the couch with his leg propped up, looking pale. He looked startled to see Reed.

"I brought some video games—that is, if your hands still work," Reed joked.

Marshall grinned. "Are you kidding? I could beat you with *one* hand!"

AUGUST 14

After the ride, Eleanor headed for the shelter. Their club leader, Vickie, looked angry.

"Sit down, everyone," she said firmly. "If you brought a phone, lay it on the table." Phones clattered down. "Someone told me that there have been some mean texts this morning. That is *not* pleasing to God! He doesn't want any of us to put someone else down." No one said anything.

"I want you each to send a message to someone else here, apologizing for taking part in this mess," Vickie said. "After that, *no more* texting except for emergencies!"

Eleanor prayed silently and then started a message to Shauna, apologizing for her comments. She sure hoped the afternoon at the park would be more fun than the morning.

AUGUST 15

Flynn took a deep breath and asked God to help him get Doug and Renaldo calmed down. "Look, you guys are friends, but you have different opinions about this, right?"

"Yeah!" the boys yelled.

"Well, is it really worth arguing about?" he asked. "Can't you just let it go?"

Doug crossed his arms. Renaldo looked down at the ground.

"I'd rather *enjoy* the zoo with my friends," Flynn continued. There was a short silence.

"Okay, we'll just have different opinions," Doug said. Renaldo nodded.

Flynn grinned. "I'm glad that's settled. I was ready to put you two in a cage!"

"Oh yeah? Let's get him!" Doug and Renaldo started making monkey noises. Then they chased Flynn. All three of them laughed.

AUGUST 16

Brock was pretty sure what Jesus would want him to do. "I'm going to help Damien. We'll be there soon!" He turned his bike around.

Back in the garden, Damien was surprised and pleased to see him. "Okay, let's do this! You get the tomatoes. Make sure they're ripe. I'll pick beans." He put the bag around Brock's neck. Brock examined a tomato and tugged.

Damien ran down the row and then turned back. "And thanks a lot! This is great."

AUGUST 17

I hope he breaks his board! Philip fumed. But a few days later he started feeling bad. *It's true that Maury sneaked around me, but Jesus wouldn't want me to hate him.*

At the skate park, Maury stopped riding and clutched the new board when Philip approached. "I wish you'd treated me the way you would have liked to be treated," Philip said, nodding toward the skateboard. "But I forgive you anyway."

Maury looked surprised. He shrugged and started riding again. Philip turned away. He'd done the right thing. The next move would be up to Maury.

AUGUST 18

Hilary knew God would want her to help her friend. "Wait! Don't sit!" Hilary darted between Debbie and the curb. "It doesn't matter how fast we go. We just have to finish— for the shelter!"

"I don't know," Debbie hesitated.

"You can do it!" Hilary urged. "We've only got a third of the way to go. That's like walking from school to the bakery!"

"Well, maybe," Debbie said. The girls starting walking.

AUGUST 19

Walker threw down his bike and ran to Silas. He pulled some tissues out of his pocket. "Here, push down where it's bleeding!" he said. "I'll get help."

Soon Silas's mother was checking the leg. "We'd better go to the hospital; that may need stitches!"

Walker helped Silas to the car, and mother and son drove off.

It all happened so fast, Walker thought as he went back to his bike. He was glad that he'd remembered that verse about enemies. Maybe the next time they met, Silas would treat him better.

AUGUST 20

Mitch remembered a Bible verse about not bragging. "I mean, I'm the funniest one with red hair and glasses!" he finished. His friends smiled and rolled their eyes. Ms. Huffman started to read her list and called Mitch's name for the musical. Mitch felt crushed.

Ms. Huffman handed out scripts for the kids in the musical. "I think you'll be perfect for this role, Mitch," she noted. "There's a lot of clowning around, and you're a pretty funny guy." Mitch smiled. Maybe this would work out after all.

AUGUST 21

I know, God, Gayle sighed a prayer. *Jodie's not really a monster. I still want her as a friend.* She decided to get to the heart of the matter. "Jodie, you've been mean to me lately, and that hurts. I'd like to know why."

Jodie's expression softened, but all she did was shrug. Finally Gayle walked on ahead. A few days later, Jodie caught up with her at recess.

"Why aren't you hanging around with the new kid?" Gayle asked grouchily.

Jodie looked embarrassed. "Gayle, I did a dumb thing. I wanted to be friends with her because she's so popular."

"But couldn't you still be friends with me too?"

"That's what I finally figured out. I'm really sorry. Do you still want me as a friend?"

"Yeah, of course," Gayle said. "Do you want to come to my house after school?"

AUGUST 22

At the park, Joel and his friends hurried off the bus. He heard Mischa call, "Wait, Joel!" from behind him, but he didn't stop. Later during the game, he looked over and saw Mischa sitting by himself. Joel felt bad, especially when Mischa glanced at him with a hurt look on his face. Joel knew his behavior didn't please God. He quickly asked God for forgiveness and decided he would make it up to Mischa by sitting with him on the way home.

But later when Joel tried to sit with Mischa, Mischa got up and moved to another seat. Joel realized it might take time to repair their friendship.

AUGUST 23

"That's okay. I'll take three," said Lisa. She looped the strap from one pail around her neck and picked up two others.

Yay! I lucked out, April thought happily. "Well, okay, if you're sure," she said out loud. The girls started back down the path. Lisa was walking slowly and the pails looked hard to carry. April felt a little guilty. *What should I do, Jesus?* she asked silently. Then she had an idea.

"Stop!" she called out. "It's my turn to carry the extra pail. We'll take turns."

Lisa gave her a big smile. "Thanks, April," she said.

AUGUST 24

Graham remembered hearing a Bible verse about welcoming others. "Come play with us!" he said, motioning with his hands. The boy trotted over. Graham dribbled and took a shot that bounced off the backboard. He rebounded and passed to the boy. "You try."

The boy dribbled awkwardly, but his shot went in!

Graham grinned. He looked at Winston. "I vote to let him play." Winston shrugged in agreement. "My name's *Graham*," he went on, pointing to himself. Then he pointed to the boy. "What's your name?"

The boy pointed to himself. "Temo."

Graham introduced the other guys. "Okay, let's play!" he said.

AUGUST 25

Deonte's mom flopped down on the couch. "Another load done!" she sighed. In the kitchen, Deonte and Maxwell pulled out ham, cheese, and lettuce.

"Where's the mustard?" Maxwell said. He turned to call out to Deonte's mom and then poked Deonte. "I think your mom's asleep."

Deonte peeked into the living room. His mom's head was back on the couch and she was snoring softly. "I guess she really is tired!" Deonte whispered. A Bible verse about serving others came to mind.

When Deonte's mom woke up, the boys were eating sandwiches—and they had made one for her too. There were even flowers from the garden in a glass of water on the table.

"Surprise!" Deonte exclaimed. His mom grinned. Deonte thought of Jesus grinning at him too. *Serving others can be fun,* he decided.

AUGUST 26

The woman was watching her. *Jesus, help me think,* Talia prayed. She carried the lip gloss to the cashier. "Hi, I'm Talia," she said. "I just met your niece. She told me about your store."

The woman frowned. "I don't have a niece," she replied. "Did you want to buy that?"

"Sure." Talia pulled money out of her pocket. *Whew, that was close!* Gwen and the other girls had left, but it didn't matter. Talia knew now that she couldn't trust them.

AUGUST 27
"Just get out of here!" Drew didn't feel like listening to anything Alan might say. Finally Alan trudged upstairs and left.

Soon Drew's dad came down and examined the damage. "I tried to catch the drums when they fell over, but I couldn't," he said.

Drew gulped. "You mean Alan didn't break them?"

"No, didn't he tell you?" Mr. Hawthorne asked.

Drew felt terrible. He had a big apology to make.

AUGUST 28
Kay saw her mom looking at her closely, and she suddenly understood. "I get it," she said. "We talked about it in Pioneer Clubs. Jesus doesn't want us to play favorites because of someone's stuff."

Her mom smiled. "So what are you going to do?"

Kay thought awhile and then came back to her mom. "Can I invite both of them over here?" Kay asked. "We'll find something to do that's fun."

AUGUST 29
Then Juliet heard from the tryouts: "Allelu, alleluia." Someone else was singing that praise chorus! It seemed like a reminder from God. So Juliet kept her mouth shut as the others bad-mouthed the judge.

Later she told her dad about it. "I'm proud of you for not joining in," he said. "Do you feel good about your decision?"

"Not really," Juliet said. "I'm totally disappointed, and it's all the judge's fault."

"You could look at it that way," said Dad. "Or maybe you could think that the judge might have written something insightful on the paper that could help you next time."

When Juliet read the paper before bed, she decided the judge *did* have some remarks that could help her. "Thank you, Jesus," she prayed.

AUGUST 30
Splash! The canoe tipped, and both boys tumbled into the shallow water. "Look what you did, you klutz!" Eli sputtered. They dragged themselves and the canoe to shore and sat, panting and arguing. The camp counselor walked over.

"Do I have to split you guys up?" he asked, raising his eyebrows.

They looked at the counselor and then at each other. *I don't really want that,* Rafael realized. *We're buddies.*

"No, we want to be together," Eli finally said.

"Even good friends can find it hard to work together sometimes," said the counselor. "How about if I give you some tips?"

AUGUST 31
Matthias looked out the window again at the smoke. Chaz's house was out there somewhere—what was left of it. He remembered the pastor talking about sharing cheerfully with guests. *I've still got a house and food to eat, so I can share,* he thought. He looked down at Chaz. "The Choco Crunchers are gone, but let's see if we have any Marshmallow Munchies."

"Yummy!" Chaz said.

SEPTEMBER 1
The boys peered into the murky depths of the creek. "I can't see any fish. It's getting too dark," Emilio said. "Let's go home."

Timothy nodded. "You know, I was just thinking, what if God had never created the sun?" he said.

"What made you think of that?" said Emilio.

"Because you can't do a lot in the dark, and I am sooo glad we don't have to."

"Yeah, me too!" said Emilio. "But I know one thing we can still do in the dark—race! See you at the house!" he shouted over his shoulder.

SEPTEMBER 2

Heidi's grandmother said, "God planned for seeds to always grow into their own kind of plant. That way, farmers and gardeners like us can always know what kinds of plants we'll get from our seeds."

Devlyn giggled. "It would be a mess if maple tree seeds grew carrots."

"Or if dill seeds grew roses!" Heidi said.

"There's a lot more to gardening than I thought," Devlyn commented.

Grandma dug a hole in the dirt with her finger and dropped in some seeds. "I'm happy to help you learn," she said, "because learning about gardens helps you understand how special God's creation really is."

SEPTEMBER 3

Leo's dad reminded them where they'd seen the sun set and pointed them a quarter turn to the right. "This is north. Look up. Once you've seen the Big Dipper, you can find the other constellations—even with the extra stars."

Sawyer pointed out the Little Dipper. "Can we really know the time of year by what constellations are overhead in the evening?"

Leo's mom answered, "Yes! Cool, huh?"

"I see the man in the moon!" Leo said.

"I think God is amazing," said Sawyer.

SEPTEMBER 4

Mercer looked at Jordi. He shrugged. Mercer said hesitantly to Marilyn, "We believe God made the birds."

"He gave them their instincts," Jordi added. "It's really fun today to see all the different kinds of birds he made."

"Well," said Marilyn, "we can agree to disagree. But I'm glad you kids know what you believe. That's a good thing."

SEPTEMBER 5

Sebastian thought some more and started modeling. Soon he had a figure wearing a cap.

"What's that?" Paulo asked.

"It's a baseball cap. I'm going to add a bat and glove, because I'm playing in the park league this year."

"I'm making a keyboard because I like music."

When they were done, their mom came back and studied the images. "Your clay images don't look like you, but they show some qualities of you. How does that help you understand how we're each made in God's image?"

"I get it," Paulo said. "We don't look like God, but we have some of his qualities."

SEPTEMBER 6

"Mom! Can you heat up a pizza for us?" Ariana asked.

"Sure, but that's a big pizza. You girls can't eat that whole pizza for lunch."

"Don't worry, Mom. We're going to share it. Aren't we, Meg?" Meg nodded.

Later, as they stood outside the tree house, Ariana said loudly, "Yum! I can't wait to eat this *pizza!*"

"Yeah, I know what you mean. I love *pepperoni pizza!*" Meg replied, just as loudly. The boys poked their heads out of the tree house doorway.

"Can we have some for lunch?" Kaden asked.

Meg and Ariana looked at each other. "Well, I don't know, seeing as we're so useless. We couldn't possibly be counted on to give you something as yummy as pizza." The other boys whispered something to Kaden.

"Maybe you're not as useless as I thought." The girls just rolled their eyes at Kaden. "Okay, I'm sorry. You're very useful. You can play in the tree house too!"

"Great! Come down and have some pizza!" Ariana invited them.

SEPTEMBER 7

"I can name a *lot* of animals!" said Jasper. "How long have you got?"

Ron laughed. "I thought you'd say something like that. How do you remember all the names, anyway?"

Jasper said, "I guess I remember how they look first, then the name and where they live."

"Remember what we learned in Pioneer Clubs?" Ron asked. "I think it's cool that the first thing the man gets to do, right after God creates him, is name all the animals."

"Yeah, but I bet he got tired! That's a lot of animals to name!" Jasper said.

SEPTEMBER 8

Dad nodded. "The Bible says that God's love for us is as high as the skies are above the earth. That doesn't change when we do something wrong. When we tell God we're sorry, the Bible says he takes our sins as far away from us as the east is from the west."

"That's pretty far," Joshua said, feeling a little hopeful.

"God doesn't want us to call ourselves names or feel like we're rotten," Dad said. "He just wants us to be sorry for what we did and be willing to change. Would you like to pray right now and hold on to God's promises to love and forgive you?"

Joshua finally smiled. "Yeah," he said.

SEPTEMBER 9

It seemed like forever before the radio announcement finally came: "The tornado warning is over." Christina and Gareth ran up the stairs. The neighbors were outside, so they ran out too.

"The tornado fizzled out," Mr. Alvarez said. "Praise the Lord. It didn't cause any damage—just dumped a lot of rain." Gareth felt his muscles start to relax. He grinned as Mrs. Alvarez held up her hand for a high five.

"When Noah and his family came out of the boat, they worshiped God," Mrs. Alvarez said. "Let's do that." She grabbed Gareth's and Christina's hands and squeezed. "Dear Lord," she prayed, "thank you for keeping us safe, and our neighbors, too."

SEPTEMBER 10

"What do you mean?" Verity asked.

Julia turned the water back on the flowers. "Rainbows are signs of a promise," she said. "After the Flood, God told Noah he promised all living creatures that another flood would never destroy the earth."

"God promised?" Verity asked.

"Yeah," said Julia. "He always keeps his promises—unlike me!" She turned the water on Verity, and the girls ran screaming around the yard.

SEPTEMBER 11

As the boys approached the house, the back door suddenly swung open, and Rich's Saint Bernard, Goliath, ran toward them. "Look out, Rich!" called Zachary as the dog jumped up and knocked Rich over. Rich laughed as he struggled to push the big dog off of him.

"Why can't Goliath be a little more afraid of us like those deer back there?" Rich said. "I have slobber all over me. Yuck!" Just then Rich's mom came out on the back porch and told them lunch was ready.

As they ate their sandwiches Rich asked his mom, "Mom, how come the animals are so afraid of us? I just don't get it."

"Well, honey, God caused them to be that way. Did you know that in the book of Genesis, it tells us that God gave us authority over all the creatures? But that also means we have a responsibility to treat them with care and respect." Just then Goliath started sniffing near Rich's plate. Before Rich could stop him, Goliath grabbed what was left of his sandwich and gulped it down.

"I wish God would tell Goliath to treat *me* with respect!" Rich sighed.

SEPTEMBER 12

"I didn't even get to say good-bye to her." Terrence blinked back tears. "She wasn't supposed to die."

"Terrence," Trevor began, then paused. He tried again. "You know, Biscuit had a happy life with your family, even if it was short."

"I know." Terrence didn't say anything for a bit. "I'm really glad God gave us Biscuit, and I'm glad she wasn't sick for long."

"Do you think you'll get another dog?" Trevor asked.

"Dad wants to go look at puppies this weekend. He says plenty of dogs need homes, and God will show us the right one." Terrence smiled, if crookedly. "Biscuit will always be special, but . . . I guess I'll love a new dog, too."

SEPTEMBER 13

"What if he's just too busy with everything else?" Khalil answered.

William's dad came over with graham crackers and chocolate bars for the boys to make their s'mores. "Hey, you two! I heard what you were talking about. Did you know that the writer of Psalm 8 in the Bible wondered the same thing? In fact he actually wrote, 'What are mere mortals that you should think about them?'"

"Really?" Khalil asked.

"Did the writer ever come up with any answers?" William asked.

"Yup—and that's the really interesting part. God made us a little lower than himself, and the psalm says he crowned us with honor and glory. Then he gave us charge over all his creation," William's dad said.

"God must love us a lot to do that!" William exclaimed.

"Yes, in fact I'd say that his love for us is higher than any of those stars you were looking at. So does anyone want to roast some more marshmallows, fellows?"

"Oh yeah!" both boys answered in unison.

SEPTEMBER 14

Kaya thought for a bit. "That we're going to get wet if we stay out here much longer!"

Dad grinned. "Does it say anything to you about God?"

"The storm clouds tell me that God is big and powerful," Kaya said.

"The sunset tells me that God loves lots of colors and beauty," Leslie added.

"I see God's power every time I look at the sky," Dad said. "Quick, here comes the rain!"

SEPTEMBER 15

"Dad explained it to me," Domingo said. "Tides happen because the moon and sun pull on the oceans. A beach has small or big tides depending on the shape of the coast."

"But twenty feet?" asked Ray in disbelief.

"Or even more. Between Maine and Nova Scotia, the water funnels from a wide mouth into a very narrow part of the bay."

Ray said, "I think God has as much imagination as power!"

"And I'm really glad that an all-powerful God loves us too. That's why I can trust that he'll help and protect us," said Domingo.

SEPTEMBER 16

Courtney's mom helped the girls make a comfortable "nest" for the bird in an old shoe box stuffed with cotton.

"What do birds eat?" Brynn asked.

"I don't know. Worms, bugs, and seeds, I think. Yuck!" Courtney answered.

"Should we pray to God and ask him to heal the bird? The Bible says that he knows every bird on the mountains. I'm sure he cares about what happens to this little bird," Brynn said.

"Okay, that's a good idea. This bird needs all the help he can get—especially from God." Courtney added. Both girls bowed their heads and prayed for God to help the bird's wing to heal so it could fly again.

SEPTEMBER 17

Clay's mother explained from the front seat. "Meteor showers happen when a comet has passed along Earth's orbit and left bits of rock and ice behind. Big comets leave lots of debris behind, so every year when the Earth gets to that section of its orbit, we get a meteor shower."

"With all that debris floating around in space, it's amazing that more of it doesn't hit the Earth," said Terry.

"That's a good point," said Clay's father, who was driving. "Remember what you learned in club about God's power? Well, God has the power to create other planets, stars, and outer space, but he also has the power to protect us."

"I guess he does that because the Bible says he cares for us too. Right, Dad?" said Clay.

"Right, Son. He takes care of us because he loves us."

SEPTEMBER 18

"Why does nature scare you?" asked Katelyn.

"Because forest fires, lightning, earthquakes, and big storms are so out-of-control and powerful."

"But God can control all of it with the same power he used to create everything," said Katelyn. "He has the power to protect us too. Remember? God rules!"

SEPTEMBER 19

The next week when Morgan came over to Hakim's house to go to Pioneer Clubs, Morgan said, "Thanks for the Bible. I looked up the verses on the bookmark."

"Really?" said Hakim surprised. "You read them on your own?"

"Why not? I can read, you know!" Morgan gave Hakim a funny look.

"Yeah, but I just thought that you needed me there to explain."

"Not really, but I do have a few questions. Maybe we can talk about them in the car on the way to Pioneer Clubs," Morgan said.

"Cool!" said Hakim.

SEPTEMBER 20

Marianne leaned down and grabbed a handful of mulch. "My grandfather tells me that gardening brings us closer to God."

Cami looked from the vegetable garden to the roses, the herbs, and the corn stalks. "I guess creating all this does make you feel like God."

"That's not what he means!" Marianne searched for the right words. "He says we plant the seeds and water them, but God sends the sun and helps them grow. It's like working together with God."

SEPTEMBER 21

"Actually, a humpback glided up right beside us. It made our sailboat look pretty small. I think it was wondering if we were some kind of whale."

Anthony asked, "What did you like the most?"

"How *big* and deep the ocean is," Kai said. "I also kept wondering what fish and other creatures were swimming underneath our boat. What if there'd been a shark underneath us? We wouldn't even know it!"

"Did you know that the Bible mentions all the sea creatures God created? How about that big fish that swallowed Jonah?" Anthony reminded Kai.

"Well, I'm glad I wasn't thinking of *that* Bible story when we were out there sailing! Then I really would have been scared!" Kai laughed.

SEPTEMBER 22

"Hearing birds sing is better than hearing the whine of mosquitoes!" Karen replied.

Savannah laughed. "Yeah, except I like the buzz of cicadas better. And the chirp of crickets reminds me of camping out in the summer."

"What about the leaves rustling? It sounds like they're whispering," said Karen.

"My family read a psalm during our devotions last night that you're beginning to sound like," said Savannah. "It was all about how nature praises God. I don't get how things in nature praise God. They don't have voices!"

"I think it means that all the things we're seeing in nature show how God deserves to be praised," said Karen.

"Okay. But I'm not praising God for the mosquitoes!" said Savannah.

SEPTEMBER 23

"Hey, Sun Hee! Nicole! You girls ready to go? We've got a long drive before we stop for lunch," Nicole's dad called. "Sun Hee, are you okay?" he called again.

"I guess," Sun Hee sighed.

Nicole's dad walked over to the two girls. "Sun Hee's just feeling sad and worried about life, Dad." Nicole shrugged.

"I'm sorry, Sun Hee. Did you see those eagles?"

Sun Hee nodded.

"When you see an eagle, remember to trust God with your worries. He gave us a verse in the Bible that says, 'Those who trust in the LORD will find new strength. They will soar high on wings like eagles.' Let's get back to the car, and I'll teach you the verse."

Sun Hee smiled.

SEPTEMBER 24

"What does the Bible say about mist?" Bradley asked his dad.

"Well, in the book of Isaiah it says that God scatters your sins 'like the morning mist.' And you can see from the lake that the morning mist is quickly scattering, isn't it?" said Bradley's dad.

"If God forgives my sins as quickly as this mist is evaporating, then that's awesome!" Samuel replied.

SEPTEMBER 25

Later that afternoon, Lizzie and her mom went to the salon. As the hairdresser put an apron around Lizzie, she asked about her hair. "Oh, cut it any way you want. My face is big and round, and nothing will look good on me anyway," she grumbled.

"Lizzie! How can you say that?" her mom said. "You have beautiful, shiny dark hair and big, blue eyes. Having a rounder face is just as pretty as having a narrow one. God planned what you would look like, and he doesn't make mistakes."

Lizzie looked in the mirror. *Well, I do have nice eyes,* she thought. *And I like my nose.*

Maybe I'd look good if my hair was short with layers. "Well, I guess God did know what he was doing. He did give me a nice nose." Lizzie smiled at her reflection.

"And a nice smile," said the hairdresser.

SEPTEMBER 26

Karl answered, "That's easy! The container with the good soil has the most sprouts. There are a few in with the weeds, but none in the other two."

The teacher smiled. "That's right! The seeds we planted represent God's truth for knowing Jesus as our Savior. The seeds scattered in the container with no soil stand for people who don't believe. The seeds planted in the rocks stand for people who believe at first but later ignore the truth. The seeds planted in the weeds represent people who believe but let life's problems get in the way of following Jesus."

"I get it!" interrupted Casey. "The seeds planted in good soil are people who believe and follow Jesus and learn to obey him."

SEPTEMBER 27

"But what about nature?" Tara asked. "Look at the stars, or all the creatures and insects— there are so many! I don't need to have an image in front of me because there's proof of all Jesus has done around me."

"Yeah, and did you know that space goes on for millions and millions of miles? Just think of all the stars and planets we haven't even found yet!" Hope exclaimed.

"But mostly I know Jesus is real because I feel him with me." Tara pointed to her heart. "Since I asked him to be my Savior, I can feel him helping me to remember to do what's right and making me glad."

SEPTEMBER 28

Grayson pulled Vic toward the door. "Come *on*! I'll tell you while we go out." The boys pounded down the stairs. "The invisible guy knocked something over, for one thing," Grayson said as he slid open the back door. "And he couldn't open doors—like this— when anyone was looking, or they'd get suspicious."

"I get it," Vic said. "He affects the world around him, so people can figure out he's there if they pay attention."

"Yeah. It's like our memory verse, Romans 1:20. We can know about God even though we can't see him because we see what he created and we know how he's affected our lives."

SEPTEMBER 29

"I don't have to earn extra credit for heaven," Cara said. "I know I'm already going to heaven."

Thanne stopped and looked at her. "Right. Because you're a good person too." She started raking leaves again.

"No, that's not why," Cara responded. "You don't get to heaven by being good. You get to heaven because of God's gift to us when we believe in Jesus and turn our lives over to him. That's how."

"I've never heard that before," Thanne said.

"Let's finish up this raking, and then I'll explain everything," Cara smiled.

SEPTEMBER 30

"My cousins live up in the mountains of Arizona, and they sometimes get snow showers even in August," said Alexander. "But I think freak weather like that would be weird here. I like to count on fall being fall."

"What if a hurricane comes instead, or a bunch of tornadoes?" asked Jerome.

"Umm, we don't live near an ocean, so there can't be hurricanes. And you need to chill out and stop worrying. You do know that God controls everything, don't you? That includes the weather," Alexander said, shaking his head.

"How can you be sure about that?" Jerome asked, giving Alexander a funny look.

"Because the Bible says so! In Psalms it says God is in charge of the rains, wind, and lightning. And, just so you know, God sent the first rainbow as a promise to Noah that he wouldn't flood the earth again. So there's no chance of *that* happening, either!"

OCTOBER 1

Alexis clung to the wall. *God, help!* She remembered the instructor's words: "There's nothing to fear if you follow the directions." *I did follow them!* Alexis thought.

She took a deep breath and let go. In an instant, the belay system caught her with a gentle bounce. The counselor let the rope out, and Alexis felt as though she was floating to the ground.

Now I see how following rules can keep me from being afraid, she thought. *God knew that all along!*

OCTOBER 2

Helena remembered Joshua marching around Jericho seven times—and how God made the walls fall. She decided to knock on the door of 3F one more time. There was still no answer. Helena sighed and put down a flyer and muffin. She was partway to 3G when she heard a door creak. A small woman was peeking out from 3F.

"Hi!" Helena said, surprised.

The woman didn't smile, but she waved. Then the door closed again.

Helena went on to 3G feeling happy. *Thanks for opening her door, God!*

OCTOBER 3

It was tempting to tell his dad the yard was clean. But Seth had learned something from the Bible stories he'd heard: doing the right thing may be hard.

"Sorry, Dad," he admitted. "I didn't want to pick up after Rusty, so I've been putting it off. I'll do it now."

His dad sighed. "Thanks for telling the truth. Call me when the yard's ready. I'll go work on the grill."

Seth got to work. A few hours later, as he dived for the volleyball, he was glad he'd cleaned up the yard. *Obeying was worth it,* he thought.

OCTOBER 4

What was wrong with Uncle Pedro? Suddenly Eliana realized she'd forgotten something very important: saying thank you!

She put the dollhouse down and gave her uncle a big hug. "Thank you *so* much!" she said. "This is the best dollhouse ever!"

Her uncle grinned. "It feels good to be thanked," he said. "There's someone else we need to thank. Remember how sick I was for a while? God helped me get well just in time for me to make your little house."

Eliana grinned too. "Thank you, God!" she said.

OCTOBER 5

Alvaro felt like he was going to explode. He punched his pillow. "I'm mad, God!" he said. He started telling God all his mad thoughts and feelings. *Like water pouring out of a fire hose,* he thought. Then he felt sad about being left out, so he told God that too.

After a while he cooled down a bit. *I guess I wasn't very nice to Mom,* he realized. He went downstairs. "Sorry I was rude, Mom," he muttered.

"You're forgiven," Mrs. Bentsen said. "But I'm not the only one you can talk to about things. You can talk to God, too." She handed him a cookie.

"Thanks, Mom," he said. "I already did."

OCTOBER 6

Cassie's mom didn't say anything. Cassie knew she had to admit the truth. "I was too slow about helping with the dishes, wasn't I?"

Her mom nodded. "If you're *too* slow to obey, it's just like disobeying."

Cassie stood up. "I'm sorry. Can I go to Crystal's after I put away the dishes?"

"What do you think?" her mom asked.

"Well," Cassie thought a bit. "Maybe I could do a second chore and then go to Crystal's—to show I learned a lesson."

Her mom hesitated.

"And I'll do it *right away*," Cassie added.

"Sounds good!" Her mom smiled.

OCTOBER 7

Gideon knew God wants us to trust him in *all* areas. "Praying about it isn't so weird," he said. He pointed at the trees and sky. "God made everything, right? So he knows about everything. And we learned at church that he cares about us."

Scott frowned. "If I pray about football, what will God do? Drop a letter from the sky?"

Gideon laughed. "No! Maybe he'd give you a new idea or help you think of someone else to talk to."

Scott shrugged. "I'll see. Let's get back to practicing, okay?"

"Sounds good," Gideon agreed.

OCTOBER 8

At first D.J. felt like yelling at Hailey. But she looked so ridiculous that he couldn't help laughing.

"This stuff is itchy!" Hailey pulled the straw from her sleeves. "I came out to help."

"Hey, thanks!" D.J. handed her the hose and reached for a broom. "You rinse, and I'll scrub." He thought he remembered a Bible verse about cheerfulness bringing good health. *Thanks, God, for a sister who helps me feel better.*

OCTOBER 9

"Danielle, this is Mrs. Hutton, down the street," said the elderly voice on the phone. "I need my leaves raked, and I can see you're a hard worker. I'd like to hire you!"

Soon Danielle came back outside. "I've got a job!" she announced. "Mrs. Hutton's going to pay me a lot!"

Her mom beamed. "Your actions tell others a lot about you, just as the Bible says. You never know who might be watching!"

OCTOBER 10

Levi felt very alone. Then he remembered the story of Daniel, who was far from home but still obeyed God. He opened the motel room door.

"Coach," he said bravely, "they're playing Blood Weapons, and I was wondering if there was something else I could do."

"Good for you, Levi," the coach said. "I have an idea." He leaned into the room. "Who wants to go swimming?"

Lots of boys shouted yes. The coach and Levi smiled at each other.

OCTOBER 11

Sierra wanted to say, "You're the weirdo," or "I'm not churchy!" But she knew many believers had stood up to worse things than name-calling—like the three young men facing the huge fiery furnace.

She tried to calm down. "I *want* to go to church because I believe in Jesus," she whispered to Gabrielle. "What do you believe in?"

414

Gabrielle squirmed a little. "I don't know," she finally muttered.

"Who can come on Thursdays?" the coach was asking. Sierra raised her hand. She hoped Gabrielle would think about what she'd said.

OCTOBER 12

Gretchen's mother took some books and put them in the backpack. "Try lifting this," she said.

Gretchen held it. "It's heavy!" she said.

"Would you rather carry it alone or have help?" her mom continued.

Gretchen sighed. "I get it! I should let other people help me with my reading."

"And Jesus, too!" her mom added. "Jesus said to come to him when we're weary. He wants to take a load off your mind. Let's pray about it."

Gretchen bowed her head. She was glad to have her mom's help—and God's.

OCTOBER 13

The others might not even know I'm gone! "Help!" Ahmed yelled. "Help!" But the woods around him were completely silent.

It felt like forever before he heard voices: "Ahmed! Where are you?"

"Down here!" he yelled.

Soon Ned and Colleen slid down the slope. "Are you okay?"

"I hurt my knee," Ahmed explained. "I'm sorry I left you guys!"

As the club leaders helped Ahmed up, Ned asked, "Do you remember Jesus' story about a shepherd who left ninety-nine sheep to find *one* that wandered off?"

"I think so," Ahmed said.

"We'll read about it later," Ned said. "I think we'll all understand it better!"

OCTOBER 14

"Sin isn't just a list of bad things," Mrs. Durant explained. "It's having a selfish attitude. Jesus told one man that he loved his money too much. The man had a sin attitude that said his things were more important than God or other people."

Jasmine was surprised. She'd always thought she was good. She'd never thought that sin could be an attitude.

She looked at her bucket of shells. She had plenty! Maybe she'd give one to Magda after all. She had some thinking to do.

OCTOBER 15

Sara pulled a brownie from the edge of the stack and popped it into her mouth. Other brownies started to fall. "Oh no!" Sara quickly tried to make the platter look nice again.

Just then her mother and little sister Marjorie arrived. "What happened?" Mom said.

"I—I ate one, and then . . ." Her voice trailed off.

Her mom looked sad. "Sara, I want to be able to trust you, even about little things."

Sara felt bad to see her mother unhappy. "I'm sorry," she said—and she really was. *God, please help me to do better next time, even when it's just a little thing.*

OCTOBER 16

As Toshiko held the candy bar, another thought came to her. *The Bible says that stealing is wrong—even stealing little things.*

"Time to go, Toshiko!" her dad said.

Toshiko quickly put the candy bar back and followed her dad to the car. *I was just tempted to steal!* she realized. *Then I remembered what the Bible says. The Holy Spirit must have been helping me.*

Outside the store, she saw more pirates and ghosts. She smiled. *Costumes are fun, but the Holy Spirit is real!*

OCTOBER 17

Breanna said, "We aren't being mean—we're doing what's best for Cocoa! If we let her out, she could run into the street and get hit by a car."

Suzi nodded. "I guess you're right. My neighbor's dog got hit by a car."

Breanna walked across the grass to the shoe. "We love Cocoa. With the fence, she can have fun in the backyard *safely*." She handed the shoe to Suzi. "Now you throw it!"

Suzi threw, and Cocoa ran. It reminded Breanna of something her parents had said: God made rules for our good, because he loves us.

OCTOBER 18

Tommy knew God wanted him to obey authorities—for his own good. "It's safer to cross at the corner!"

Just then they heard screeching brakes and crunching metal behind them. They turned to see the policeman dash into the street, where a bike lay in front of a car. He shouted into the police radio, calling an ambulance.

Nathaniel looked pale. "It's Zach!"

"He's lucky the policeman was there," Tommy pointed out. "That cop's not a jerk. He's trying to help." After the ambulance left with Zach, they rode slowly to the corner.

OCTOBER 19

As they planned mean things to say, Destiny suddenly had one of those flashes where she pictured herself in someone else's shoes. *How would I feel if I was Claudia?* she thought. But then again, she really, really wanted to do prank phone calls. She'd never done them before.

But she kept picturing how she'd feel if the mean things were said to her. *What should I do, God?* she asked. Then she remembered that her mom had said to call for a ride.

"Ginger, let me use your phone first," Destiny said. "I need to go home."

"Why?" Ginger snapped. "You just got here!"

"I know." Destiny stood up. "I just need to go."

OCTOBER 20

At home, Darius told his mom why Mr. Murphy said he was proud of Darius.

"I agree," said Mom. "God is working in you to help you want to do unselfish things. I think you pleased God very much by volunteering. I'm proud of you too!"

"Can God help me stop wasting time and get the shields done?"

"Of course. Let's pray about it." Darius nodded, and they bowed their heads. When they finished, he reached for a piece of paper. He had a good idea for one of the shields.

OCTOBER 21

Lola reluctantly decided not to sneak out. She went back to her dad. "You just don't understand!"

"How can you say I don't understand?" her father teased. "I loved makeup when I was your age!"

"Very funny!" Lola looked at him sourly.

"I'm kidding," he went on, "but I do understand. When I was ten, I wanted a great baseball glove. But it cost too much. I almost decided to steal it from the store."

Lola looked at him. "What happened?"

"I went to the store over and over, thinking about it," her dad said. "Then I asked God to help my attitude. Jesus was tempted just as we are—not about makeup or ball gloves, but maybe other things."

Lola had never thought of Jesus wanting things he couldn't have. She knew she needed help with her feelings. Maybe she could try praying.

OCTOBER 22

Malcolm saw a poster about a Christian athlete. "My friend would miss out on seeing some Christians who are pretty cool!"

"That's right," the pastor agreed. "Special speakers can tell us amazing things God has done. Ordinary people in church help us too, as examples of living for Jesus every day."

Malcolm noticed a big painting of Jesus in the clouds. "My friend would miss out on learning about heaven."

The pastor nodded. "It's exciting to hear God's plans for us now *and* in the future."

Malcolm's parents came by, and he waved good-bye to the pastor. "Thanks!" He planned to hang on to his faith. He also had some ideas for Ramiro.

OCTOBER 23

Alicia pressed further. "Are you sure you don't want to come in and talk? Your friends here could pray for you!"

"All right," Mackenzie said reluctantly. The game was over, and soon Alicia called everyone together for a prayer circle as usual. When Mackenzie managed to talk about her dad, she found out that someone else's dad had also been laid off. Her friends and club leaders prayed for both families.

"You were right," Mackenzie told her mom on the way home. "I'm glad we came."

OCTOBER 24

Wyatt wondered about what the woman had said. He knew a verse: *Faith . . . gives us assurance about things we cannot see.* He remembered that his pastor had said you don't have to know *everything* in order to have faith.

Wyatt decided to keep talking. "I don't understand how planes fly, but I know they do!" he told the woman. "And I don't understand everything about God, but I believe in him."

She looked startled. "Thank you for sharing your thoughts," she finally said. Then they both looked out the plane window.

OCTOBER 25

Ian knew he should think about what really happened. "I guess it wasn't just about the cat," he admitted.

"Yeah, I wanted the cat because I was in a bad mood," Linnea explained.

"I was jealous 'cause I can't have the shoes I want," Ian said.

"What could you do with your feelings instead of fighting?" Mom asked.

"Talk to you," Linnea said after thinking it over. "Figure out what to do about what's really wrong."

Ian heaved a sigh. "You always say that if I'm thinking something that's not true, I can change it to something that *is* true. Like I was thinking you don't care about me, but you do."

"Good ideas!" Mom said. "Now you guys go apologize to Misty!"

OCTOBER 26

"You can't always *see* a fake," Mr. Myers said, "but there are other clues. For example, a fake medicine wouldn't work. Now, tell me how you might detect a fake Christian."

Dallas paused. "Maybe they *say* they love God, but they don't *act* like it."

"That's right," his dad agreed. "People who really love God will want to please God. They'll never be perfect, but they'll try."

They parked by the bank and walked in. "How do they find fake bills?" Dallas wondered.

"Under a special ultraviolet light," his dad replied.

"Cool!" Dallas didn't know if their twenty-dollar bill was real. But he planned to show that he really loved God.

OCTOBER 27

"What is Brody right about?" Peyton asked angrily.

"He said you're not Mr. Perfect," Lydia explained. "You don't break doors. But you haven't been very nice to Brody."

"That's easy for you to say—you're not sharing your room!" Peyton growled.

Lydia kept going. "*Perfect* isn't just keeping out of trouble, you know," she said. "It's being loving and patient."

"Maybe I could *try* to be nicer," Peyton admitted. Then he saw Brody in the hall. *How long has he been listening?*

OCTOBER 28

"Brody, Jesus can help anyone!" Mrs. Howard said. "You need a new life. That's the only way we get out of being stuck in sin."

Brody looked doubtful. "I'm not sure I deserve anything like that."

Mrs. Howard smiled. "You don't have to *deserve* it—it's a gift!"

"Thanks, but I don't think so," Brody said, getting up to leave.

Peyton grabbed an apple and went up to his room. *I don't think Brody deserves another chance. Why are my parents being so nice to this kid? Can't they see he'll never change?*

OCTOBER 29

Lydia looked thoughtful. "I don't know about Peyton. I've never asked him."

Inside the house, Peyton was listening. *It's none of your business!* he thought angrily. *I don't need any help!*

Brody turned to Lydia. "I'd like to have Jesus give *me* a new life."

Lydia's eyes widened. "That would be great! Let's find Mom or Dad."

Peyton hid around a corner as they came in. *Brody's probably faking this,* he grumbled. *Even if he isn't, I don't think anything will change.*

OCTOBER 30

"I don't think you understand, Brody," Mr. Howard said. "Have you ever lost something and found it again?"

"My dog ran away once and then came home."

"How did you feel?" Mr. Howard asked.

Brody smiled. "Great! I was really glad he was back!"

Mr. Hanson smiled too. "That's why we're having a party, Brody," he explained. "God knows you're not perfect. He's just glad to have you back again!"

Peyton was thinking. *Am I far away from God?*

OCTOBER 31

"Dad, I've never asked Jesus to give me new life," Peyton said. "I didn't think I needed it."

"What changed?" Mr. Howard asked.

"When Brody came, I started to see that I'm not always a very nice person inside."

"God loves you just as much as he loves Brody," his dad said. "Let's talk to God right now!"

Peyton prayed with his father. He asked Jesus to forgive his sins and to give him a new life. When the others came back from the river, Mr. Howard shared Peyton's good news.

"Can we have a new-life party for Peyton?" Brody asked.

"We have a great picnic lunch here," Mrs. Howard offered, "and the Bible says the *trees* sing and rejoice because God forgives us."

Peyton grinned and picked up a hot dog.

NOVEMBER 1

Raul thought about the Bible being an "old church book." "No, it's not," he said. "God inspired all the stuff in the Bible. It's good for teaching us what God wants us to know." He noticed

Gregory didn't tell him to stop, so he kept going. "The verse I was going to tell you says not to let people look down on you because you're young, but be an example for them."

Gregory's eyes widened. "Really? The Bible stands up for people who are young?"

"Yeah."

Gregory sat up straight. "Maybe I could start a petition and get lots of kids' signatures. Then I could take it to the principal. Dude! I bet it would work! Thanks to you and your Bible thing."

"Bible verse," Raul corrected with a grin.

NOVEMBER 2

Piper knew Jesus was with her. "Yes, I believe the Bible has God's words in it, and he says it's true."

Some of the girls looked surprised. But Gabrielle grinned and said, "Me, too!"

After everyone went to sleep, Piper lay awake in her sleeping bag singing "Give Thanks with a Grateful Heart" silently to Jesus. *Thank you for giving me courage,* she prayed.

NOVEMBER 3

"We need to look for a Web site that knows about rattlesnakes and has good reasons to tell the truth," Paul said.

"You've figured out a good rule for your research," said Mr. Kim. "It's important to know if a source is trustworthy. How do we know if we can trust the Bible?"

"The Bible was written by God, right?" Paul asked, typing on the keyboard.

"Yes, God told the writers what to write," Dad said.

"And God hammered the Ten Commandments out of stone himself," Shawn added.

"Hey, I found a national park service Web site," Paul said. "Snakes don't chase you at all."

"Good!" said Shawn, with relief.

NOVEMBER 4

Brent put his head on the dog. The rest of the family gathered around and read the first two commandments. "What do you think these mean?" asked Dad.

"Not to worship someone like Buddha, I guess," said Claire.

Their mother said, "An idol is anything you make more important than God."

Dad said, "It reminds me of something you guys were doing a few minutes ago."

Brent scratched Mo's ears and thought. "You mean watching TV instead of having devotions?"

"Yes," Dad said. "We can record favorite shows to watch later. But as a family we want to put time with Jesus first."

NOVEMBER 5

"Quit saying what?" Henry asked.

"You're not supposed to misuse God's name!" Andre exclaimed, frustrated. "It says so in the Bible."

"Who cares?" Henry said, poking his toad.

"I care! And God cares," Andre said. "How would you like it if I yelled, 'Oh my Henry,' all the time as a swear word?"

Henry looked embarrassed. "I don't do it all the time," he said.

"You do it a lot!" Andre replied.

Suddenly Henry's toad turned and leaped across the finish line.

"Oh m—" Henry began and then broke off suddenly. "Score!" he yelled instead.

NOVEMBER 6

Dad gave a half smile. "I know it feels hard," he said. "We can see if there's another league you can be in."

"But my friends are in the park district league." Rosita rolled the ball around on the picnic table.

"Sometimes we have tough choices to make," Dad said. "Church is most important for us on Sundays because we worship God, he teaches us, and we're keeping his commandment to meet with other believers. God wants us to set apart the Sabbath for him."

Rosita said nothing. Dad snagged the ball from her. "What if we ask your uncle and cousins if they'd like to have a family soccer game Sunday afternoons?"

Rosita perked up. Uncle Oscar was a funny guy. "That would be fun," she said.

NOVEMBER 7

Penny and her mom sat in the emergency room waiting for the results of the X rays. Penny's eyes were turning black and blue. "You look like a raccoon," Mom said, with a bit of a smile.

"I'm sorry about the hay bale," Penny said. "I guess you knew this could happen."

They looked up as a nurse approached. "No concussion and no broken bones," she said. "You'll be black and blue for a week or so, but then you'll be as good as new."

Mom gave Penny a hug. "Let's go home," she said.

NOVEMBER 8

Judah quickly counted out four dollars and put the box back. The next day he excitedly bought the comic book with his buddies. "Where'd you get the money?" Pablo asked.

"I raided my brother's bank." Judah laughed. Pablo laughed too.

But Victor frowned. "Isn't that stealing?"

Judah couldn't get Victor's question out of his mind all day. It nagged at him in math, in science, and in PE. By the time the bell rang to go home, he couldn't stand it any longer. He ran back to the library. The book lady was packing up. He handed her the comic book.

"I need to return this," he said. "Here's the receipt."

NOVEMBER 9

Camilla's jaw dropped open. "I did not!" she said. "She's lying!"

"Camilla, you're grounded this weekend," said Mom.

The weekend seemed to last forever. Camilla tried to get Mom to believe her. Finally she went to her room and started planning what she could tell Mom about Clara.

After a while her mom knocked. "I overheard Clara on the phone telling her friend what really happened. I'm sorry I didn't believe you. Parents have a tough job figuring out who to believe sometimes."

"You need to believe me," said Camilla grumpily.

"But sometimes you lie about Clara too. That's why God tells us not to lie about each other. Lies cause a lot of hurt. And they keep people from believing you when you're telling the truth." Mom patted her knee. "Think it over." She left the room.

Camilla knew Mom was right. She couldn't change Clara, but she could change herself. *Jesus, help me stop lying about Clara,* she prayed.

NOVEMBER 10

Dave counted on his fingers. "Lissa broke three of the Ten Commandments," he said, "and you pointed it out to her: don't covet, don't steal, don't lie about someone."

"What's 'don't covet'?" asked Kristi.

"When you really, really want something that belongs to someone else."

"Lissa wanted the MP3 player so bad she was willing to steal it," said Kristi.

The bus lurched around a corner. "I'm sorry she's mad at you," said Dave. "But you did the right thing."

NOVEMBER 11

Later that afternoon, Maria's teacher told them what happened. "Someone brought peanut butter," he said. "A kid with peanut allergies used the same knife after her. He had to go to the emergency room."

"Is he okay?" asked Maria.

"Yes," Mr. Rowe said. "But it's a good reminder to us that we can be pleased we have rules. School rules are for our good, and so are God's rules."

NOVEMBER 12

Braeden said, "Well, I've kind of been reading the Bible more since I went to vacation Bible school with my cousins last summer. It says stealing is wrong."

Alec looked away, focusing on the Ferris wheel going round and round.

Braeden said, "I'll meet you inside if you're going to sneak in. I'm buying a ticket."

Alec looked back at him. "Okay, fine. I will too."

NOVEMBER 13

"I didn't splash her!" Latham protested. "The waterfall splashed her."

"Not good enough!" Dad said. "You disobeyed your mom."

Mom looked Latham in the eye. "It's not enough to be able to say a verse about obeying your parents, you need to follow through with it too."

NOVEMBER 14

Jennifer grinned. "You know me pretty well, but it's more than just winning a prize each week."

"Which you do—"

"Most weeks, yes." Jennifer flipped through the cards. "But I've also found that the verses I learn pop into my head at times when they fit. Like yesterday. Emory called me a name, and I wanted to get back at him. But this verse about doing good for our enemies popped into my head." She showed Michelle a card. "The verses help me make the right decisions by reminding me what God says."

NOVEMBER 15

Grandma was thrilled. "You found our family Bible," she exclaimed. "See, there's a list of all our family members clear back to 1845."

"That's awesome," breathed Maddie, reading the old-fashioned names.

"We pick out a life Bible verse for each child when they're born," Grandma said.

"Why?" asked Clinton.

"People in our family have always believed that the Bible's words are more precious than gold. They guide us in our lives. I think of my life verse often when I have a decision to make."

"Can we have life verses?" Clinton asked.

"Why don't you ask your mom and dad to help you choose," Grandma suggested. "Then we can add your names and life verses to the family Bible."

Maddie hugged the Bible. "This was a good treasure to find," she said.

NOVEMBER 16

Lindsey said, "The Holy Spirit is God's Spirit."

"Yes," said Gracia's mom. "He's God's gift to us when we accept Jesus as our Savior. The Holy Spirit helps us understand the Bible and remember what we've read. He helps us live for Jesus."

Gracia bit into a cookie and licked melted chocolate chips off her fingers. "So we look like the same person, like the old house looks the same—"

"But we have God's Spirit living in us and helping us," finished Lindsey.

"Let's go meet the new people," Gracia suggested.

NOVEMBER 17

"The Bible tells us that studying it gives us wisdom," Victoria's mom said. "The Bible guides us. God wants us to love it and think about it often. It's the way he talks to us."

Victoria had an idea. She ran to her room and came back with her old Bible. "You can have my old Bible, Ramona. Maybe we could use my daily devotional book together."

Ramona was paging through the book. "I think I might like that," she said.

NOVEMBER 18

"Kendall said you took her sidewalk chalk without asking," Dad commented.

"I gave it back!" Owen protested.

"She bought it with her own money, and you used up a couple of the colors. That's like stealing from her."

"I didn't think of it that way," Owen said, feeling tense.

"That's why God tells parents to teach kids about his commands in the Bible," Dad said. "He had to make us parents good for something."

Owen looked quickly at Dad's face and saw he was teasing. Owen relaxed. "Should I ask Kendall if she wants me to pay her back?"

"I think that's a good idea," Dad said.

NOVEMBER 19

After dinner, Jay asked Reilly, "Do you want to hear about Jesus' miracles?"

"Okay," Reilly said. So Mom got out a Bible storybook, and the boys sprawled out on the couch to listen. Mom read the story of Jesus healing the blind man. Then she read about Jesus bringing the dead girl back to life.

"Jesus saved my grandpa's life when he had a heart attack," Jay said. "The doctors said it was a miracle."

"That's pretty cool," Reilly said finally. "Maybe I could believe that Jesus is God. Maybe I could start praying for him to bring my dad home."

"I'll pray too," Jay promised.

NOVEMBER 20

"Okay everyone, I'm going to start class by reading a psalm from the Old Testament," their Sunday school teacher said. Alison glanced over at Tricia, who had a startled look on her face.

"I thought you said the Old Testament wasn't important anymore," whispered Alison.

Tricia quickly raised her hand. As the teacher nodded to her, Tricia asked, "I thought we didn't need to read the Old Testament since we have the New Testament."

Their teacher smiled. "The Bible tells us to read the words of Jesus and his apostles, as well as the Old Testament. All of the Bible teaches us about God."

NOVEMBER 21

Alexandra thought it over. "Memorize it?" she guessed.

"Good idea," said Mom, chopping up a green pepper. "I was thinking of a verse that says to keep God's Word near us all the time and commit ourselves to it."

Alexandra spread sauce on the crust. "We're supposed to carry our Bible around all the time?"

"No," her mom said. "But we can memorize it like you said, or just think about it often and talk about it with others. We can do that right now. What do you like about the verse in the lighthouse picture?"

NOVEMBER 22

"What do name-calling and talking out of turn have to do with God's commands?" Mr. Collins asked at last. Gage looked at Mr. Collins and shrugged.

"Jesus said, 'Do to others what you want them to do to you,'" Mr. Collins commented. "Does that give you a clue?"

"If I don't want people to call me names, I shouldn't call them any?"

"And if we don't want people interrupting us, we shouldn't interrupt. Gage, sometimes we get what we give," Mr. Collins said. "If you give respect, people are more likely to give it to you. Do you understand any better now?"

Gage thought about it and then smiled. "I think so," he said.

NOVEMBER 23

After about fifteen minutes, Luz handed her dad a Bible and pointed to a verse. "Here it is, Dad. God does say that he removes our sins as far away as the east is from the west. That's a long way."

"Good for you, Luz. How did you check that out?"

"I looked up 'east' in the concordance in the back of the Bible," Luz said smugly.

Dad read the verse out loud. "This will really help me feel forgiven," he said. "I'm glad you looked in the Bible."

NOVEMBER 24

Christa gulped. "I'm really, really sorry, Mom. I threw a shoe."

"You threw a shoe?" Mom echoed. "I'm not even going to ask. We'll talk about it after Jacki goes home. Get this cleaned up."

Jacki whispered, "Why didn't you say Caden did it?"

Christa sighed. "I just learned a Bible verse in Pioneer Clubs." She said Psalm 119:105. "It means the Bible helps us know what to do." She shrugged. "And I know the Bible says to tell the truth."

Jacki giggled. "I bet it also says not to throw shoes at your brother."

NOVEMBER 25

Later that night, Tori went over her weekly memory verses for Sunday school. "The word of God is alive and powerful. It is sharper than the sharpest two-edged sword." Suddenly the beginning of the second verse began to bug her: "Nothing in all creation is hidden from God." Tori suddenly felt uneasy. *Uh oh, this verse says God knows everything. What if God knows I took the extra change and lied to my mom?* As if reading her thoughts, Tori's mom walked into her room.

"Tori, it's time for bed. You need to get enough sleep for school. Tori?" Her mom looked concerned. "Are you okay, honey? You don't look well."

Tori cleared her throat. "Mom, I took the change from the lunch money to buy candy and lied to you about it. I'm really sorry—and I'm going to tell God I'm sorry too."

NOVEMBER 26

Katherine handed the cashier her lunch ticket and started toward Sofia's table. A memory verse she'd learned popped into her head: "Gossip separates the best of friends." *God,* she prayed, *that's you telling me what to do, isn't it?*

Sofia waved at Katherine. Katherine waved back but pointed to her regular group of friends at another table. Then Katherine went to sit with them instead. She noticed Sofia scowl and whisper to the girl next to her.

I guess she's talking about me now, God, Katherine prayed. *But I'm still glad I followed you.*

NOVEMBER 27

Stephen's grandma got up and went to the bookshelf. "There are verses in the Bible that could help you," she said, bringing back a Bible. "The apostle Paul used the Bible when he wanted to tell people about Jesus." She and Stephen looked up some verses to use.

The next day Stephen ran in the door excitedly. "Grandma!" he called. "I showed Oscar a couple of verses. He wants to come to Bible club with me tomorrow night!"

NOVEMBER 28

"Let's read this month's story and see," Jacqueline said.

The girls sat on Jacqueline's bed. They opened Gran's package and a Bible. "The verses are Habakkuk 3:17-19," said Abigail. They took turns reading. "'Even though . . . the fields lie empty and barren; even though the flocks die in the fields, and the cattle barns are empty, yet I will rejoice in the LORD!'" read Abigail.

"'The Sovereign LORD is my strength,'" read Jacqueline. "Abigail, why are you crying?"

Abigail sniffled. "Well, you know my mom's so sick, and now I broke my leg. Everything seems like it's going wrong. But Habakkuk said he would still trust God. I want to too."

"I guess the prophets do still help us today," said Jacqueline.

NOVEMBER 29

"Knowing Jesus as your Savior is the first thing," Eva said.

"Also, Jesus said that to be ready, we need to obey his Word," Dad said.

"No one knows when he's coming!" Yvonne exclaimed. "Any day, BAM!"

Dad grinned. "Good point! That's why it's important to obey Jesus all the time."

Blake stood Joseph up. "Like having my room clean all the time because I never know when a friend will come over?"

"Right!" Dad said. "Why don't you hammer this time, Blake?"

"Yes!" Blake said.

NOVEMBER 30

Matt said, "The only perfect promise keeper is God, right?"

"Right!" said Uncle Fritz. "I was just reading some verses about how the Old Testament promised us a Savior. Then Jesus came to earth to fulfill those promises. What else does the Bible promise us?"

Matt adjusted his pole and thought. "That God loves us. God is always with us."

"I'm glad we have a promise-keeping God," Uncle Fritz said. "Hey! There goes your bobber. You got one!"

DECEMBER I

As Lynn loaded the dishwasher that night, she sensed God wanting to talk to her. *God, she prayed, is being a Christian something that just happens to you, like being born in this country or having a certain skin color?*

She'd been told at church that you must choose to follow Jesus. He stands at the door of each person's life and knocks. It's up to each person to open the door and let Jesus in.

Have I ever done that? Lynn wondered. She didn't know for sure, but she planned to talk to her mom about it that night. Then maybe she could explain it to Amala, too.

DECEMBER 2

Skylar remembered learning about Jesus and angels at church. She looked at her manger ornament and then back at Miranda. "Jesus is God's Son. He's greater than angels. He's God. The Bible says we're supposed to pray to God, not angels."

Miranda looked thoughtful. "What about guardian angels?"

"Angels are God's servants," Skylar explained. "Some of them guard us. Maybe we could learn more about them from the Bible sometime."

"That would be great!" Miranda said. She picked up the glass angel, and the girls headed to the checkout together.

DECEMBER 3

"Just imagine," said Mrs. Donovan. "You're not kings or world leaders or important preachers. You take care of animals on a hillside. But God chose you to send a whole army of angels to. You're the first ones to hear about baby Jesus. You're important!"

Tim scratched again. Mrs. Donovan went on. "And after you see the baby, you're the ones who take the good news to everyone around. You're God's messengers! You praise God and give glory to him."

Tim stood up a little straighter. He nudged his fellow shepherds. "We can do it!" he urged them.

DECEMBER 4

One of the twins blew bubbles in his drink. "Christmas is mostly about presents, I think," he said.

"How could we change that?" Tam's mom asked.

"Rudolph the Red-Nosed Reindeer" blared from the speakers overhead. "We could play some carols about Jesus," Tam said. "Like when we're wrapping presents." She munched on her pizza and thought some more. "At Pioneer Clubs they were talking about kids who don't get any presents. Could we buy something for them?"

"That would be a great way to show Jesus' love," said Dad. "I'll look into it tomorrow."

DECEMBER 5

"I can give you a hint," Mom said. She sorted through the stack of last year's Christmas cards they were using to make gift tags. She held up one that showed three wise men.

"Oh," Jayden said. "The wise men brought gifts for baby Jesus." He stuck a bow on a present for another cousin. "Shouldn't we give gifts to Jesus then?"

"We give to Jesus by giving presents—and love and kindness—to others," his mom explained. "All of the giving of this season is about following the examples of giving in the Christmas story: God gave his Son, and the wise men gave their best to worship him."

DECEMBER 6

Why did I raise my hand? Morgan wondered. Then she remembered that God uses regular people, too. "I don't want to be in the show," she explained. "Could I just sit and talk to people?"

Bobbi smiled. "That's a great idea. Most of these folks would appreciate your friendship more than any program."

The group started talking about board games to bring. Morgan was glad to know she could help after all.

DECEMBER 7

Nate told Dad about Preston laughing. "Wouldn't it have been better for Jesus to come to earth as God?"

Dad sat on the bed. "Even as a baby, Jesus was God," he explained. "But he was also human at the same time."

"I don't get it," Nate said.

"Jesus coming as a baby is one of God's great gifts to us. Jesus had to grow up just like we do and go through the same struggles as us," said Dad. "I'm glad you're asking questions. Jesus welcomes our honest questions."

"None of the people in the Bible ever had questions," Nate said.

"Not true," Dad said and suddenly grinned. "I'm thinking of one of Jesus' first followers who asked questions before he would believe Jesus was God. Guess his name."

"I don't know," said Nate.

Dad laughed. "Nathanael, just like you!" he said.

Nate grinned.

DECEMBER 8

Jorge approached Javier, ready to give him a rough scrubbing. The toddler looked up with sad, teary eyes. Jorge remembered a sermon about Jesus welcoming little children. Jesus saw their love and trust, the pastor had said.

Javi trusts me, Jorge realized. *I shouldn't be mean to him.*

"Sorry I yelled at you, Javi," he said, dabbing gently at the little boy's face. "I was mad about the mess, but I still love you!"

He gave Javi a hug, and Javi wrapped his little arms around Jorge's neck. Now Jorge had pizza sauce on his shirt. *Oh well, just a little more cleanup!* he thought.

DECEMBER 9

Jesus loves all kinds of people, and so should I, Isaac thought. He crossed the parking lot. "Hi, Devin," he said nervously.

"Hi," Devin muttered, looking down.

"I like this because of the animals," Isaac continued. "Want to see the llama?"

"A llama?" Devin looked up, surprised.

"Yeah, really!" Isaac said. The two started toward the displays. "We've got the animals because Jesus was born in a stable."

"I thought Jesus was just a swear word," said Devin.

Isaac felt shocked. "No," he finally said. "I'll tell you the real story."

DECEMBER 10

As she started up the inside stairs, Robin stopped. She felt sorry for the girl and hated to leave her. *Jesus wants me to care about others. That girl is hurt, and maybe I can help, even if she is older and cooler.*

She walked back outside. "What can I do?" Robin asked. "Can you walk?" The girl sniffled. "I don't think I can get up the stairs. I'm so embarrassed. Can you get the nurse without anyone else knowing?"

"No problem," said Robin. The nurse headed outside right away. "I'm glad you were kind enough to help," she called over her shoulder.

Robin slowly walked back to her classroom. *I didn't know cool kids got embarrassed,* she thought. *I'm glad I was kind too.*

DECEMBER 11

Then Asher had an idea. "Can I use the phone, Mom?" he asked. He called his friends Kenya and Gus. That night the three kids made flyers on the computer, telling about the event and asking for donations.

The next day they met in the middle of town. "Let's pray first," said Asher. They prayed and then walked around to businesses. Most shop owners let them post flyers in the windows. The grocery store owner said he would put flyers in people's bags.

The next day the grocery store owner showed up with a van full of supplies. "How could I not help once I found out about your event?" he said. "I can tell God is at work here, and your son is right in the middle of it!"

"Thank you, Jesus!" said Mrs. Prachet.

DECEMBER 12

"There isn't any such thing as luck. I think we should pray," Tanner said over the howling wind. To his surprise, his friends nodded.

"Dear Jesus, you made the world," he began. "Please keep us safe—and the other people in the campground too. Amen."

No one said anything, but Tanner felt better just thinking about Jesus' power. When the storm finally let up, the boys peeked out. Huge branches lay all over the ground. But no one had been hurt!

"Thanks for praying," one of Tanner's friends said.

DECEMBER 13

Carly thought some more. *I want Melaine to hear about Jesus—soon!* She went back to her mom, who smiled. "If you really want to do this, I've got some ideas."

At school the next day, Carly asked about Melaine's country. Carly's parents looked on the Internet for others who spoke Melaine's language. At church, the missions chairman got Melaine a special Bible.

A few weeks later, Melaine came with her whole family to Carly's church! When Carly saw them smiling and listening, she knew her efforts were worth it.

DECEMBER 14

Kaylee was stomping down the hall when she realized how ridiculous she must look. *I'm trying on an angel costume, but I'm not acting much like an angel.* She quickly prayed for help.

"I'm sorry, Mom," she said. "You're working hard on this costume, and I'm not being very nice. I've been thinking about my own part instead of what's really important—Jesus!"

"Apology accepted!" Her mom smiled. "I can make this costume look good. But your attitude matters more—and it's better already!"

DECEMBER 15

Daisy looked at her friend's shocked face. Then something popped into her head: Jesus wept when Lazarus died. He felt the hurt and sadness.

Daisy felt tears start. "Well, dying is good for Grandpa—he's in heaven," she told Catherine, "but I'm going to miss him!" Daisy started to cry. Catherine gave her a big hug.

I guess it's okay to believe in heaven and still feel sad about death like Jesus did, Daisy realized.

DECEMBER 16

After Kurt left, Dillon flopped down beside his mom in the office. "Mom? Kurt made fun of me when I said Jesus is God."

Mom put her papers aside. "Maybe Kurt will think it over anyway. Do you know that when Jesus claimed to be God, the religious leaders did more than make fun of him—they threatened to kill him by throwing stones at him?"

Dillon said, "I didn't know that."

"If you get teased for believing Jesus is God, remember that Jesus suffered many times more. I'm proud of you for sticking up for what you believe—and so is Jesus."

DECEMBER 17

So Angelo prayed about everything on his mind. He liked thinking about just Jesus and him, alone in the tree house. When he got so cold he felt half frozen, he went back inside.

After dinner the neighborhood gathered at the hill. A crackling bonfire made the snow twinkle and glow. Angelo yelled as he shot down the hill. When he crashed into his big sister, they both lay in the snow laughing. *This is the best,* Angelo thought.

For family devotions before bed, Dad read Mark 1:35. "Even Jesus needed time alone to pray," he said.

Angelo perked up. "That's what I did today!" he said. "In the tree house. It was nice—peaceful." *You kept the rain away, didn't you?* he prayed silently. *I think you're going to help me with my test and with Mac, too.*

DECEMBER 18

"Corky, stop!" Denzel yelled and waved. Corky turned to look. The driver hit the brakes.

"Here, boy!" Denzel called Corky over, and the car drove on. Denzel hugged his dog tightly, but he soon wriggled free. *He doesn't know what a close call that was,* Denzel thought.

Then Denzel remembered some verses he'd heard. A good shepherd loves his sheep and does everything to protect them. Jesus said, "I am the good shepherd."

Denzel looked at Corky again. He knew what it felt like to love his dog. "Jesus loves me even more," he said.

DECEMBER 19

Ashton walked to the kitchen. He felt tired of trying to change. Then he remembered the story of the blind man. He kept calling out and didn't give up till Jesus came.

Ashton's mom and dad had the cookies on the table. "I just sneaked some cookies in my room," Ashton admitted. His parents looked surprised. "I know I shouldn't do stuff like that, but I keep messing up!"

"We're glad you told us," his dad said finally.

"Some problems are hard to solve," his mom added. "Maybe we can all work on this. How about some frozen grapes, you two?"

"Great! I love frozen grapes!" Ashton replied.

DECEMBER 20

The ranger looked amused. "Sure," he said.

"My way to God is Jesus," she said. "He's the one who created that." She pointed to the waterfall.

"Well, there are many ways to God," the ranger remarked.

Angela shook her head. "Jesus said he is the Way, the Truth, and the Life. He said no one comes to the Father—that's God—except through him."

The ranger cleared his throat. "Well, that's nice," he said. Arturo came over with a question, so the ranger excused himself. Angela sat on a rock, smiling. *I stood up for you, Jesus,* she prayed happily. *I'm glad you're my way to God.*

DECEMBER 21

Jenny paused before sending the message. Her eyes wandered to Mira's baby picture. *God, you created Mira,* she prayed. *You don't want me to hate her. But that was so mean! Please help me forgive like Jesus would.*

Jenny wasn't quite ready to forgive yet. But there was something she could do right now. She bent over her phone and canceled the text message. Then she went out to recess.

DECEMBER 22

Carrie's words echoed in Mckenna's head. *No one wants me around.* She looked at her mitten. Suddenly the blood reminded her of something.

"Jesus wants me," she said softly. "He died for me. I can't give up."

She asked Jesus to forgive her. Then she started toward Carrie's house. *I'll say I'm sorry and offer to make it up to that girl. Maybe they'll give me another chance.*

DECEMBER 23

Later, at the restaurant, Dad said, "Micah said something cool after I found him. He said, 'It sure was good to hear you calling my name.' It reminded me of when Jesus called Mary's name at the tomb. Suddenly she knew him—and knew that he knew her by name. What would it have been like to be standing at the tomb and hear Jesus call, 'Micah!' or 'Rob!'"

Micah imagined it and felt warm and fuzzy. "Jesus does know our names, right? The Bible says."

"Yes, he definitely does," said Mom.

DECEMBER 24

Michaela bounced the ball. *God, help me think of something to tell Jessie.* Then she had an idea. "Jessie, do you think I'm a good free shooter?" Michaela's ball swished through the net.

"Definitely!" Jessie nodded.

"How do you know?" Michaela dribbled and shot again. Swish.

"Because I've seen you!" Jessie replied.

Michaela held the ball. "Jesus' disciples said they saw him alive. Then they risked death to preach about it. Would you die for a lie?"

"No," Jessie admitted.

"So that's pretty good proof that the disciples told the truth!" Michaela shot the ball again. She was glad Jesus had helped her think of something to say.

DECEMBER 25

Mom said, "I'm thinking of a comparison. Did you involve Keshawn in talking about your new camera?"

Derek laughed. "No."

"You played with his toys. You taught him words. You got down on his level."

"He couldn't come up to my level," Derek said.

"And we could never get up to God's level," said Mom. "So he came down to ours. Jesus became human so he could die in our place and free us from death. When he died and came back to life, he defeated Satan and death."

Derek looked at the baby Jesus in the manger under their tree. "I never knew Christmas meant all of that," he said. *Thanks, Jesus,* he prayed.

DECEMBER 26

Dad and Charlie skated over. Dad stopped in a spray of ice and lay down beside Avery. "What are you talking about?" he asked.

Avery told him.

"Oh, I know the answer," Dad said mysteriously. "Can you guess?"

"I think it probably has to do with Jesus creating the stars," Avery said.

"Right!" said Mom. "The Bible says Jesus holds together everything he created. That's why the constellations don't go flying apart."

Avery tilted her head back, taking in the endless night sky. "I think that's why we don't go flying apart either," she said.

Charlie snickered. Mom rubbed Avery's shoulder. "I think you're right!" she said.

DECEMBER 27

Abruptly, Ashlyn hurried down and found one of the club leaders. "I've done this before," she said. "I just don't know if it worked."

"I'm not sure what you mean by 'if it worked,'" the leader said kindly. "You don't get saved from sin by going forward or saying a prayer. Salvation is not up to you—it's up to Jesus. He paid for your sins. Your prayer shows you're accepting what he's done." The leader opened up a Bible.

"'Everyone who calls on the name of the LORD will be saved,'" Ashlyn read.

"If you keep saying the same prayer over and over, it's as if you're not trusting Jesus' promise to save you," the leader said.

"I do trust him," Ashlyn murmured. She didn't have to do this over and over! She looked at the flickering fire and thanked God quietly.

DECEMBER 28

Brendan took in Clark's words. Come on, live a little! He remembered a Bible verse: "Whoever has the Son has life."

"Look, Clark," he said, "stealing is wrong. And I don't need to do crazy stuff to feel alive! I have something better." He got back on his bike. "I'm going into town for ice cream."

Clark was still standing there as Brendan rode away. Brendan didn't know what Clark would do next, but he hoped he'd follow him into town after all.

DECEMBER 29

Edward picked up the sled just as Tiffany came up. "Where's mine?" she said.

I really want a sled! She'll never know, Edward argued with himself. *But God will know. Jesus, help me do the right thing.*

"This is yours, Tiff," he said reluctantly. "Someone must have taken mine."

When he got home, he told his mom what happened. "I'm unhappy that you left the sled," Mom said, "but I'm proud of you for telling the truth. Do you know why Jesus can help us resist temptation? Because he was tempted in every way, just like us."

"Because he was human too?" Edward asked.

"Yes," said Mom. "Because he became human for us."

DECEMBER 30

Kelsey knew Jesus loved all the people of the world. She'd read that in heaven, people from every country and every language will sing praises to Jesus.

"I'm sure it's just easier to talk in the language you already know," she told Gianna. "You can get a cookie. I'm going to say hi."

As Kelsey approached, Valeria looked up and smiled. Maybe if they spent more time together, that would help Valeria's English. And maybe Kelsey could learn a little Spanish, too.

DECEMBER 31

Isaiah wondered how to cheer up his uncle. "Uncle Rick, didn't Jesus say that he is the Beginning and the End?"

"Yes," his uncle answered. "Why?"

"You don't like beginning a new year," Isaiah explained. "But maybe if you think about Jesus always being there, you'll feel better."

Uncle Rick gave Isaiah a bear hug. "That is a great thing to think about. And you are a great nephew!"

"Thanks! Now I'd better make popcorn!" Isaiah grinned.

INDEX OF MEMORY VERSES

Proverbs 15:1 *March 14*
Proverbs 15:18 *July 5*
Proverbs 15:30 *October 8*
Proverbs 16:28 *August 12*
Proverbs 17:6 *March 15*
Proverbs 17:17 *August 13*
Proverbs 17:22 *March 16*
Proverbs 18:24 *August 2*
Proverbs 19:11 *July 6*
Proverbs 19:17 *August 3*
Proverbs 19:20 *May 28*
Proverbs 20:11 *October 9*
Proverbs 22:9 *June 3*
Proverbs 23:19 *May 3*
Proverbs 25:21 *May 4*
Proverbs 26:20 *August 14*
Proverbs 28:13 *July 4*
Proverbs 29:11 *May 29*
Proverbs 29:17 *March 17*
Ecclesiastes 3:1 *March 5*
Ecclesiastes 4:9 *March 1*
Ecclesiastes 4:12 *August 7*
Isaiah 33:6 *May 7*
Isaiah 40:31 *September 23*
Isaiah 41:10 *January 18*
Isaiah 43:1 *December 23*
Isaiah 44:22 *September 24*
Isaiah 44:23 *October 31*
Isaiah 45:12 *September 25*
Isaiah 48:17 *October 17*
Isaiah 53:5 *December 22*
Isaiah 55:11 *September 19*
Isaiah 58:9 *March 7*
Isaiah 64:8 *February 9*
Isaiah 66:13 *March 18*
Jeremiah 29:11 *January 8*
Jeremiah 31:3 *February 11*
Daniel 2:23 *October 10*
Daniel 3:17 *October 11*
Micah 6:8 *April 9*
Zephaniah 3:17 *February 28*
Matthew 2:2 *December 4*
Matthew 2:11 *December 5*
Matthew 4:4 *November 14*
Matthew 5:7 *May 21*
Matthew 5:9 *March 19*
Matthew 5:16 *May 5*
Matthew 6:9-10 *July 8*
Matthew 6:11 *July 9*
Matthew 6:12 *July 10*
Matthew 6:13 *July 11*
Matthew 6:20 *May 6*
Matthew 6:33 *February 16*
Matthew 7:11 *March 20*
Matthew 7:12 *August 16*
Matthew 7:24 *January 24*
Matthew 10:31 *February 17*
Matthew 11:28-29 *October 12*
Matthew 13:23 *September 26*
Matthew 14:14 *December 10*
Matthew 14:32-33 *December 12*
Matthew 18:14 *October 13*

Matthew 18:15 *April 17*
Matthew 18:21-22 *August 17*
Matthew 22:37 *April 3*
Matthew 25:21 *July 26*
Matthew 25:40 *June 20*
Matthew 28:5-6 *April 24*
Matthew 28:19 *June 6*
Mark 1:17 *December 6*
Mark 1:35 *December 17*
Mark 1:41-42 *July 14*
Mark 2:14 *December 9*
Mark 7:37 *December 13*
Mark 10:14 *December 8*
Mark 10:25 *October 14*
Mark 10:45 *July 13*
Luke 2:17-18 *December 3*
Luke 2:52 *January 10*
Luke 4:18 *November 30*
Luke 5:32 *July 15*
Luke 6:27-28 *August 19*
Luke 6:36 *June 9*
Luke 8:39 *June 7*
Luke 10:27 *July 16*
Luke 10:36-37 *July 17*
Luke 10:41-42 *December 14*
Luke 12:15 *May 10*
Luke 12:31 *April 30*
Luke 14:11 *August 20*
Luke 15:10 *October 30*
Luke 16:10 *October 15*
Luke 16:13 *February 15*
Luke 17:3 *August 21*
Luke 18:1 *April 22*
Luke 19:10 *August 22*
Luke 23:34 *December 21*
Luke 24:39 *December 24*
John 1:49 *December 7*
John 3:16 *April 23*
John 6:11 *December 11*
John 10:11 *December 18*
John 10:30 *December 16*
John 11:35-36 *December 15*
John 13:14-15 *June 1*
John 13:34 *March 21*
John 13:35 *July 18*
John 14:1 *February 13*
John 14:2 *January 9*
John 14:6 *December 20*
John 14:16 *October 16*
John 14:26 *November 16*
John 15:10 *February 26*
John 15:12 *August 23*
John 15:13 *July 19*
John 20:31 *November 19*
Acts 1:8 *April 15*
Acts 2:4 *June 30*
Acts 2:38 *June 18*
Acts 2:42 *June 12*
Acts 3:6 *July 20*
Acts 4:12 *May 8*
Acts 4:32 *June 23*
Acts 9:36 *June 24*

Acts 10:34 *January 22*
Acts 12:5 *June 27*
Acts 14:17 *September 27*
Acts 17:2 *November 27*
Acts 17:11 *November 23*
Acts 17:24 *February 5*
Romans 1:16 *April 21*
Romans 1:20 *September 28*
Romans 3:23 *October 27*
Romans 5:8 *February 14*
Romans 6:16 *April 29*
Romans 6:23 *October 28*
Romans 8:28 *April 12*
Romans 8:38 *January 26*
Romans 10:13 *December 27*
Romans 12:2 *May 11*
Romans 12:3 *February 27*
Romans 12:6 *June 11*
Romans 12:13 *August 5*
Romans 12:18 *May 12*
Romans 13:1 *October 18*
Romans 15:7 *August 24*
1 Corinthians 3:16 *February 1*
1 Corinthians 6:20 *February 2*
1 Corinthians 9:25 *April 2*
1 Corinthians 10:13 *October 19*
1 Corinthians 10:31 *April 13*
1 Corinthians 10:32 *June 5*
1 Corinthians 12:7 *February 7*
1 Corinthians 12:27 *June 26*
1 Corinthians 13:7 *March 22*
1 Corinthians 13:7 *July 21*
2 Corinthians 1:4 *August 8*
2 Corinthians 5:17 *June 16*
2 Corinthians 9:7 *May 2*
2 Corinthians 12:9 *January 2*
Galatians 3:28 *June 28*
Galatians 4:5 *January 19*
Galatians 5:13 *July 22*
Galatians 5:22-23 *July 23*
Galatians 6:2 *March 23*
Galatians 6:4 *May 16*
Galatians 6:9 *August 18*
Galatians 6:10 *June 22*
Ephesians 2:8-9 *April 6*
Ephesians 2:10 *September 29*
Ephesians 3:17-18 *May 9*
Ephesians 4:2 *March 24*
Ephesians 4:16 *June 17*
Ephesians 4:25 *May 17*
Ephesians 4:26 *October 25*
Ephesians 4:28 *May 18*
Ephesians 4:29 *March 25*
Ephesians 5:2 *January 4*
Ephesians 6:1 *March 26*
Ephesians 6:2 *March 27*
Ephesians 6:4 *March 28*
Ephesians 6:10 *January 28*
Philippians 2:3 *August 1*
Philippians 2:4 *July 25*
Philippians 2:5 *August 25*
Philippians 2:9 *July 27*

Philippians 2:13 *October 20*
Philippians 4:6 *April 1*
Philippians 4:8 *May 15*
Philippians 4:19 *March 6*
Colossians 1:10 *January 3*
Colossians 1:17 *December 26*
Colossians 3:8 *May 20*
Colossians 3:12 *June 14*
Colossians 3:13 *March 29*
Colossians 3:16 *November 20*
Colossians 3:20 *May 27*
Colossians 3:23 *May 22*
1 Thessalonians 5:15 *May 23*
1 Thessalonians 5:21-22 *August 26*
2 Thessalonians 3:13 *October 2*
1 Timothy 6:17 *July 12*
1 Timothy 6:18 *April 14*
2 Timothy 3:15 *March 30*
2 Timothy 3:16 *November 1*
Hebrews 1:4 *December 2*
Hebrews 2:14 *December 25*
Hebrews 2:18 *October 21*
Hebrews 4:12 *November 25*
Hebrews 4:16 *December 29*
Hebrews 6:12 *October 22*
Hebrews 6:15 *April 19*
Hebrews 10:25 *October 23*
Hebrews 11:1 *October 24*
Hebrews 12:11 *March 31*
Hebrews 13:1 *March 3*
Hebrews 13:5 *January 6*
Hebrews 13:16 *May 31*
James 1:5 *January 7*
James 1:17 *February 10*
James 1:19 *August 27*
James 1:22 *November 13*
James 2:1 *August 28*
James 3:10 *August 29*
James 3:18 *August 15*
James 4:8 *May 24*
1 Peter 2:2 *April 4*
1 Peter 2:13-14 *May 25*
1 Peter 3:9 *August 30*
1 Peter 3:15 *June 4*
1 Peter 4:9 *August 31*
1 Peter 4:10 *July 28*
1 Peter 5:7 *February 4*
2 Peter 3:2 *November 28*
1 John 1:9 *October 29*
1 John 2:5-6 *October 26*
1 John 3:1 *June 15*
1 John 3:17-18 *May 26*
1 John 3:23 *July 29*
1 John 4:11 *July 31*
1 John 4:19 *July 30*
1 John 5:11 *December 28*
Revelation 3:20 *December 1*
Revelation 7:9 *December 30*
Revelation 21:4 *June 10*
Revelation 21:6 *December 31*
Revelation 22:7 *November 29*

INDEX OF SCRIPTURE READINGS

Ready for more?
The NLT Kids Bible
is the perfect Bible
for kids like you!

It makes reading the Bible easy.

This new Bible has several special features
that break down ideas—and help you
understand the Bible better!

The NLT Kids Bible is just the right fit for you.

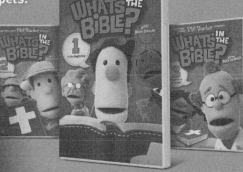

K-3 Kawai
UST-9 Kawai
Yam G-7